Strategic Social Media

Strategic Social Media

From Marketing to Social Change

Second Edition

L. Meghan Mahoney and Tang Tang

WILEY Blackwell

Library of Congress Cataloging-in-Publication Data Applied for:

Paperback ISBN: 9781119890362

Cover Design: Wiley
Cover Image: © Yuichiro Chino/Getty Images

Set in 10/13pt Minion by Straive, Pondicherry, India

SKY10067856_022124

Contents

Introduction

There are over 60,000 books available on Amazon Marketplace that include the phrase "social media" in the title. Most of these offer guidance on how to maximize the new technology toward a desired outcome. The inherit definition of social media is grounded in its ability to support interactive dialogue across various media platforms (Baruah, 2012). However, most social media references measure success by its ability to maximize profit or attract a viral number of followers. As social media scholars we wonder, if the entire premise of social media is the ability to hold a conversation online, would not a successful social media endeavor be to successfully engage the intended users through interactive dialogue rather than top-down diffusion? Thus, the idea for *Strategic Social Media: From Marketing to Social Change* was born.

Since the publication of the first edition of this book in 2016, many of our predictions about the digital world we live in have come to fruition, specifically, a call for greater privacy and security measures, enhanced visual communication, and the spread of social e-commerce through mobile technology. However, the first edition was written when 10,000 followers on Instagram made someone an influencer. The sheer magnitude of today's omnichannel marketing environment would have been dizzying to imagine, not to mention social advancements of artificial intelligence and Internet of Things. Today, for better or worse, social media is easily embedded into everything we do.

The authors of this book have now been teaching college-level social media courses for over a decade. Today's college students enter our classroom with digital skills that surpass our own. We understand that students no longer need a step-by-step "how to" manual in social media marketing practices. Just imagine if a decade ago, our students spend thousands of dollars to learn "how to" Vine. Instead, today's students need theoretical explanations for the role social media plays in facilitating behavior change in users that will prove useful throughout their digital lifetime. It is important to create a reference that covers the many opportunities that social media affords users in breaking down barriers with institutions of power, achieving greater transparency, and encouraging dialogue to mobilize users. Our hope is that this book provides a balance between best social media marketing practices and the application of traditional communication, behavior change, and marketing theories.

Social media can inspire human behavior change, whether that behavior change is intended to inspire marketing decisions or social change. We believe it is important to provide social media strategies that readers can apply to any past, present, or future social media platform. The intersection of theory, practice, and mindfulness will help practitioners make better decisions regarding brand objectives and the world they impact, as well as make them more valuable than a professional who is only familiar with social media tools and marketing business models.

This book is divided into five distinct sections: (i) social media landscape; (ii) social media users and messages; (iii) social media business models and marketing strategies; (iv) social responsibility and cause marketing; and (v) the future of social media. Each chapter has been updated using examples from today's digital social media landscape. Additionally, international modern case studies have been added to illustrate key concepts in each chapter.

We begin by exploring the role of social media in today's convergence culture by asking questions such as: What is the current social media landscape? How are individuals and organizations utilizing new media tools? The section introduces three primary functions of social media – diffusing information, providing a sense of community for users, and mobilizing users into action. These functions will build the foundation for all social media strategies outlined in later sections of the book.

The second section of the book focuses on constructing social media messages that reach intended users and ignite dialogue and behavior change. It examines how social media alter the way we view media users. Rather than viewing social media users as a passive entities who only consume online messages, we favor theoretical assumptions about how users participate and negotiate in the information-exchange process while recognizing the structural constraints brought by new technologies such as artificial intelligence and machine learning. By transforming social media messages from modes of information diffusion toward more interactive communication for mobilization, we can establish a sense of community among users. We conclude this section with a new chapter on utilizing social media for personal branding efforts before we dive into discussing how to use social media for businesses. We believe that it's difficult to create an authentic message for a company's brand if one is unable to create an authentic, aware personal brand.

Third, the book examines various social media business models and marketing strategies. Classic marketing literature has focused on how to best compete with similar products.

This book explains the importance of collaborating and communicating with your competitors to promote mutual gain. It also offers insights on mobile marketing and e-commence. The section concludes by introducing various ways that best evaluate and monitor social media marketing efforts.

Next, this book explains why marketing for social good is more important than ever. By examining case studies in public health, civic engagement, and cause marketing, we identify the potential of social media to make a positive difference in the world. Social media users demand increased transparency with how products are manufactured, sold, and reviewed by other consumers. By taking control over social media narratives, practitioners are able to increase their return on investment, while also promoting social good.

Finally, this book explores the future of social media landscape. The section explains how to integrate traditional media with new and argues for a general framework for social media scholarship. The book concludes by offering insights on how Internet of Things, artificial intelligence, and other new technologies could impact future social media practices.

In writing this book, we were fortunate to receive enormous help and support from family, friends, and colleagues. We are particularly grateful to our families, who have been a tremendous support since the first day of this project. We would especially like to thank Wiley-Blackwell and its editors for their constant support and guidance; the faculty members and graduate assistants at Kent State University and West Chester University who have helped us along the way. Our gratefulness is extended to the anonymous reviewers who read the manuscript in various stages of development. There is no doubt that the book becomes a stronger effort through the implementation of their comments. Finally, to our kids, who have grown in wonderful and magnificent ways – Beatrice, Spencer, Greta Mahoney, and Maxx Yang – thanks for motivating and enriching us every day.

Ultimately, the goal of this book is to share with our readers – students, social media practitioners, and current/future generation of social media users – the power and positive possibilities that social media holds in influencing personal relationships and social change. While it would prove impossible to predict all of the new media changes that we will see in our lifetime, we hope this book can shed light on the future of social media landscape – a world where marketing and social change will no longer exist in mutually exclusive entities. We hope that *Strategic Social Media: From Marketing to Social Change* continues to serve as a valuable resource for anyone interested in successfully persuading people through social media messages.

Reference

Baruah, T.D. (2012) Effectiveness of social media as a tool of communication and its potential for technology enabled connections: a micro-level study. *International Journal of Scientific and Research Publications*, 2(5), 1–10.

Part I

Convergent Social Media

1

The Foundational Principles of Behavior Change

Learning Objectives

After reading this chapter, you should be able to:

1 Explain the potential of social media to transform traditional audiences into more participatory, globalized, and civically engaged users through information interaction and dissemination.
2 Distinguish assumptions about media users between linear mass communication models and social media transactional processes.
3 Understand the role of behavior change theory in the social marketing process.

Introduction

Generation Z, individuals born between 1997 and 2012, grew up with social media and constant Internet access, with the average getting a personal smartphone by the age of 12. While previous generations' use and interaction with digital technologies earned criticism for their lack of interest in reading print books, erosion of basic grammar skills, lack of memory recall ability, and a fascination with distributing mundane status updates through social networking sites (Bauerlein, 2009; Palfrey & Gasser, 2010), Generation Z is believed

Strategic Social Media: From Marketing to Social Change, Second Edition. L. Meghan Mahoney and Tang Tang.
© 2024 John Wiley & Sons, Inc. Published 2024 by John Wiley & Sons, Inc.

as the most ethnically diverse generation with promising commitment to diversity and inclusion initiatives (Meola, 2022).

The initial purpose of this book, *Strategic social media: From marketing to social change*, was to explore the ways in which technology inspires behavior change, leading toward greater opportunities for businesses and positive social changes. Since the publication of the first edition of this book in 2016, much has changed about the digital world we live in. Today's media environment is more mobile, visual, and personalized. We saw digital tools such as enhanced visual communication, digital experience sharing, omnichannel marketing, Internet of Things (IoT), artificial intelligence, mass personalization, and social e-commerce change how and why average social media users and marketing professionals use digital technologies. Despite advances in technology and the many emerging new social media platforms, the guiding communication theories and strategies that inspire behavior change in social media users remain timeless. Practitioners who enter the field with the foundational knowledge of behavior change theories can adapt media strategy to meet technological advancements throughout their career. Whether your behavior change messages are intended to inspire business decisions or positive societal changes, you will be able to inspire any generation using the behavioral change communication theories offered throughout this text. Thus, the second edition of this text includes many updated case studies and technological trends, while highlighting the large scope of applications of the core strategic social media theories in various fields.

Individuals today have more frequent interaction with information about a wider range of issues, making them more engaged with events happening around the world. Many express concerns about the potential negative influence social media have on our youngest generations. However, after over two decades of social media adoption, it is clear that social media technologies are not a fad. The commitment toward inclusion and diversity of future generations could inspire positive behavior change through social media use.

The definition of what new media includes is perpetually changing. To say that one generation's media use is better than another is ill-informed. Most often, individuals fear the unfamiliar and unknown when it comes to technology. Today, an average Internet user worldwide spends 147 minutes per day on social media platforms (Statista, 2022). It is only natural to question what type of influence media has on everyday lives. However, this reflection must consider the complicated process of igniting behavior change through media content.

Years of communication research have taught us that the cause-and-effect process is not as simple as previously thought. Media is often identified as the cause for negative behavior, whether it is making us more violent, obese, or over-sexualized members of society. However, the process of behavior change is far more complicated than what a direct media effects model suggests. It is easier to blankly assume that because person A consumed media B that they were led toward behavior C. These types of causal relationships seem justified, especially when the media message in question is something unfamiliar or scary. However, this type of assumption is sometimes referred to as "hypodermic-needle theory" (Scheufele & Tewksbury, 2007) and is an outdated notion of how media directly influences behavior through a linear cause-and-effect process. A strong understanding of behavior change research outlined in this chapter will help illustrate this process.

Social media is defined as a group of Internet-based applications built on the ideological and technological foundations of Web 2.0 that allow the creation and exchange of user-generated content (Kaplan & Haenlein, 2010). Social media platforms are used by one-in-three people in the world and more than two-thirds of all Internet users (Ortiz-Ospina, 2019). It is a primary tool for users to gain access to information, social connection, and entertainment. Thus, it is logical to turn to social media when attempting to inspire behavior change. The user-generated profile feature of social media is the closest connection many media producers will ever have to the individual personality of a consumer. Social media does not fundamentally change the ways in which media users make decisions about their everyday actions, but instead simply maximizes the opportunity for marketers to reach and interact with consumers. This book investigates how individuals turn to social media as a space to create and recreate personal and perceived identities, which in turn helps social media marketers understand how social media tools are used by their consumers to inspire behavior change through engaging content.

Many alternative social media references provide readers specific "how-to" guides about social media uses. For example, they share information about how TikTok videos are structurally different than Instagram stories. However, the authors of this book believe that it is more useful for marketers to have a strong understanding of how social media inspires human behavior change than it is to inform about platform-specific tools. Rather than constantly looking ahead at what is new or trendy in social media, it is more strategic and pragmatic to learn about how humans make decisions based on their own life experiences, including media content consumption. Marketers can then use this knowledge to develop social media strategies on any social media platform of their choice and adapt to the next trending platform.

Through a solid understanding of foundational communication theories, one will be able to apply the tools of behavior change to any past, present, or future social media platform. It is better to understand the link between media and behavior change than it is to know the technological differences between platform interfaces. By the end of this book, it should be clear that regardless of your goal as a social media strategist, whether it is for social media marketing, personal social media use, or creating large-scale social change campaigns, the process through which media users are inspired toward permanent behavior change is the same.

Thus, the authors believe that the most effective marketers blend traditional communication theories and social media strategies to help individuals meet their goals via technologies. This chapter aims to discuss how social media has been able to push individuals toward more participatory, globalized, and civically engaged users by changing the ways in which users gather and disseminate information (Jenkins, 2006; Levine, 2007; Scheufele, 2002). While this chapter provides a substantial overview of communication theories, future chapters will help guide readers toward developing specific social media strategies, and thus illustrating the promising opportunities brought by social media.

Bridging Communication Theories and Social Media Practices

This chapter provides a basic communication theoretical framework for individuals looking to advance their career through the effective creation and dissemination of social media messages. One basic definition states that communication is "who says what to whom and with what effect" (Lasswell, 1948). This definition of communication intrinsically links the construct to persuasion. Whether it be the source of the message (who), the content of the message (what), or consumer characteristics (whom), the process of communication is all about behavior change (Griffin, 2011). Understanding human behavior is one of the most crucial things that social media specialists need to learn before developing successful social media marketing campaigns.

Because this book is vested in constructing effective social media messages, it will mostly examine the communication process through the mass communication paradigm. Traditional models of mass communication were long thought of as a *"one-to-many" model*, where one message was crafted to appeal to as many people as possible and broadcast through a mass medium to reach a large audience. Here, mass media audiences were seen as homogeneous, individually anonymous, and geographically dispersed. With a simple click of a button, an advertisement could be distributed to the masses in print, over the radio, or on television. Mass media disseminates a single message multiple times in a more efficient manner than any other type of communication (Dominick, 2008). However, just like the other types of communication, scholars and communication specialists have learned that this top-down linear model that posits one individual as a sender of a communication message and another as a receiver was not an accurate portrayal of the user experience.

Media users are not made up of a single homogeneous mass. They include many individuals that come to the media experiences with unique personalities, motivations, experiences, and goals. Users are most engaged with media that account for these unique qualities of their life experiences. It is important for communication strategists to take a more nuanced perspective to the role that media users play in the mass communication reception process.

Persuasive communication models integrate the interaction between senders and receivers of messages. These range from linear models of communication, where information is transferred from the sender to the receiver in a step-by-step process, to a more transactional process where the information exchange is fluid and takes participation from both sides. It is important to understand the differences between these models in order to most effectively persuade people toward desired behavior change outcomes via social media messages.

Linear Communication Models to Transactional Processes

Theoretically, our understanding of communication models has gone through great transformations over the past 100 years. This chapter suggests that these transformations and trends are a guide for emerging communication contexts, specifically those in the digital and

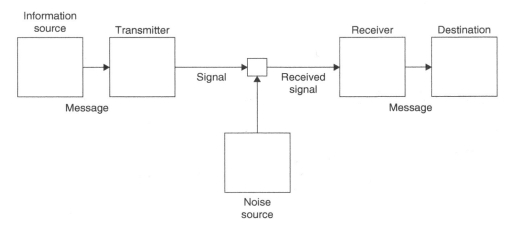

Figure 1.1   Shannon–Weaver model of communication. Source: Shannon (1948). Reproduced with permission of *The Bell System Technical Journal*.

social age. The 1947 *Shannon–Weaver model of communication* (Figure 1.1) is used as the foundation for much of our knowledge of communication today. It highlights many important takeaways for effective communication. The model identifies eight key elements for information transfer: source, encoder, message, channel, decoder, receiver, noise, and feedback.

In this model, shared meaning is imperative for effective communication. Most importantly, it provides an explanation for miscommunication. The receiver of a message could walk away without the intended message, not only due to external noise but also due to the encoding and decoding process. This applies to social media conversations as well.

For example, your friend may comment on your Instagram post. She knows that Instagram is a public space where others can also see the message. She then uses personal jokes and acronyms in her message, rather than being more forthcoming, because she wishes to be discreet about the meaning of her message. The message is so secretive that even you, the intended receiver, do not understand the meaning of the message or why it was sent. In this example, there was no external noise to cause the miscommunication; the technology worked appropriately and there was no language barrier between the sender and receiver. However, the encoding and decoding process did not align, thus resulting in miscommunication. This is one of the first models of communication that included an explanation for why miscommunication occurs even without external noise.

Regardless of the foundational importance of the Shannon–Weaver model of communication, researchers came to realize that the process of communication is much more transactional in nature than what the Shannon–Weaver model illustrates. Rather than communicating through a linear process, which posits one individual as a sender of a communication message and another as a receiver, a *transactional model of communication* (Figure 1.2) accounts for all participants as senders/receivers in a simultaneous and fluid exchange.

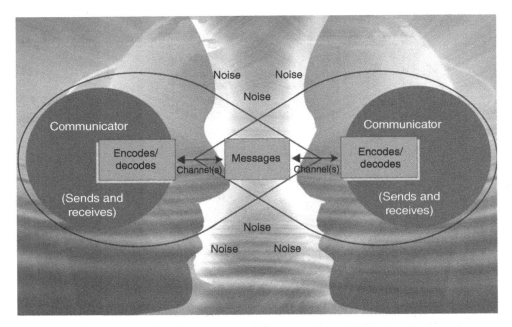

Figure 1.2   Transactional model of communication. Source: Adapted from https://www.natcom.
org/about-nca/what-communication.

The quality of this exchange depends on the ability and willingness of communicators to gather necessary information and disseminate in an appropriate manner for the target user. While one individual is speaking, the other communicator is providing simultaneous feedback through nonverbal cues, relational history, and the setting of the conversation. People constantly shape their communication patterns based on real-time events in the communication environment.

While the linear model of communication gives limited power to the receiver of the message, the transactional model equalizes their role, as communication can only take place when the two meet on an agreed-upon meaning. In the earlier example, the subtle Instagram message causes miscommunication between the sender and receiver of the message. However, you don't just examine one Instagram post as a singular communication process. You consider the relational history with the person who constructs the message, the time of day that the message was posted, and the technology through which the message was constructed. Maybe see that the message was posted through your friend's new iPhone and assume that the autocorrect spelling function of the new technology made the message unreadable. Each of these pieces of information influences how you interpret the message and is just as vital to the communication process as your friend's intended meaning.

Regardless of the communication process, whether it be communication between two friends, a public address in front of hundreds, or a 280-character tweet, the better message can account for this gathering and dissemination process, the more effective the message becomes. Through this transactional lens, a more inclusive view of mass communication studies emerges. This leads us to our first action plan for social media strategists. Each chapter will include a similar action plan to help you apply concepts to real-life marketing strategies.

Transactional Communication Action Plan

There are three steps toward maximizing communication between the sender and receiver of social media messages.

1 Be certain that you are not just creating social media messages based on your own goals and objectives.
2 Determine who your target users are, the technologies that they utilize, and their own needs and gratifications.
3 Identify any barriers to an effective communication process, such as competence, access, or complicated relational history.

Your friend's decision to write a subtle message on your Instagram was based on her own predetermined objectives. Despite her Instagram account being a more public forum, she still chose the medium to disseminate a private message. Rather than considering the message target, technology options, and the audience decoding process, your friend only considered ways in which the message could be altered for her own purposes. Instead, she should have chosen a more appropriate medium where the message could have been more forthcoming and easier to interpret, such as a private mobile messaging application, like Snapchat or even Instagram Direct Messaging.

Now that you understand the differences between linear and transactional models of communication, we must take a deeper look at the ways in which the human decision-making processes influence marketing. Social media technologies have made it more important than ever to understand how individuals make sense of media messages. This information exchange navigates the items we purchase, the groups we join, and the recommendations we share with friends. Human behavior change is an essential area of study for anyone who is interested in marketing.

Marketing and Behavior Change Theory

The American Marketing Association (2023) defines *marketing* as the activity, set of institutions, and processes for creating, communicating, delivering, and exchanging offerings that have value for customers, clients, partners, and society at large. The definition is intrinsically linked with marketing research, which helps connect customers to the market through monitoring and evaluation efforts. Ultimately, marketing practitioners are responsible for designing and implementing a strategic plan to reach specific objectives. Marketing, advertising, public relations, and branding all fall under the broader umbrella of strategic communication. In today's ever-changing digital landscape, strategic communication vision is a critical component to any organization's success (Tariq, 2021).

Behavior change communication is an evidence- and research-based process of using communication to promote certain predetermined behaviors through an appropriate mix of interpersonal, group, and mass media channels (Manoff Group, 2012). Traditionally, behavior change theories have been utilized to develop public health interventions. The hope is that through strategic mass media dissemination, pro-social messages prompt human behavior change so that individuals may engage in more positive and healthier lifestyles. These messages are important to the safety and well-being of mass media users. Mass media provides the most efficient and cost-effective means for message dissemination. However, the approach does not always prove the most persuasive. Often, these mass media messages compete against hundreds of years of cultural rituals and practices that prove antagonistic to their health goals. While inciting this type of permanent behavior change in lifestyle can prove very difficult to achieve, this area of research has made great strides in our understanding of how to best influence human behavior change through mass media messages.

It was not until the early 1970s that marketers began using human behavior change theories to explore how to influence consumer behavior through mass media messages. Before this time, the focus was on the product and brand itself. Very little research went into the preference and lifestyle of target consumers. *Social marketing* emerged as a systematic way to design, implement, and control programs that are calculated to influence the acceptability of social ideas, including product planning, pricing, communication, distribution, and marketing (Kotler & Zaltman, 1971). Here, marketers began to see that it was much more effective to sell an idea and lifestyle, rather than a product.

Since the inception of social marketing, several alternative frameworks have been offered. Researchers have explored the possibilities for persuasion through target consumers, a change in mind-set process, and a more planning-centered approach (Thackeray & Neiger, 2000). Each of these approaches offers unique challenges and benefits for using mass media to influence human purchasing behavior. However, they all consider the transactional role that media users play in the communication process. Rather than focusing solely on the product or the media message, marketers have begun to realize the potential of considering consumer lifestyle and preferences as a central ingredient to behavior change.

Social marketing and behavior change theory are complementary approaches for understanding how consumers make purchasing decisions (Thackeray & Neiger, 2000). The best approach to marketing is a hybrid process. Strong media messages can influence human behavior, but only if they speak to the goals and experiences of their users. Consumers have their own preferences and life experiences, and the more that they identify with media messages, the stronger that the message will speak to them. Though mass media can reach a large number of consumers, people do not like being seen as a member of a mass homogeneous crowd. The efficient and cost-effective nature of disseminating messages through mass media was making the content less individualized, thus proving less persuasive. Social media has made it easier than ever for marketers to integrate the mass and individuality of these two approaches.

It is the role of marketers to ensure that consumer behavior is positively reinforced at every point of engagement. As the marketplace grows with new products, brands, and services, it is essential to the survival of businesses to have a steady core of loyal customers. In fact, the industry named this cognitive procedure *shaping*, where the product is seen as a positive or negative reinforcer to the consumer purchasing behavior (Rothschild & Gaidis, 1981). It is the goal of marketing to ensure that purchasing is positively reinforced at every stage, including in retail stores, as well as its consumption at home.

Shaping procedures are used so that consumer purchasing trials become more than a random process. Rather than ensuring that customers choose your product or service when faced with endless options available in a global marketplace, marketers hope to shape consumers so that there is no question as to which product they purchase in the future. This helps marketers rely on a sale before consumers even walk into a store. Consumption is much more than a one-time transaction. Shaping leads to long-term patterns of consumer behavior.

For many years, it was difficult to track longitudinal patterns of consumer behaviors and consumption. Traditional marketing research, such as surveys and focus groups, was unable to capture user data over time. However, advances in technologies, such as customer loyalty reward cards, credit card history and scanner data, have made long-term tracking easier. While these technologies provide effective ways to understand the history of products customers purchased, this book argues that social media technology is the most effective tool for marketers to use when interested in shaping consumer behavior.

The use of social media for transactional communication with consumers is critical to any marketing practitioner. Today, 71% of online users turn to social media when making purchasing decisions (Barysevich, 2020). Research has found that social media increases brand recognition and customer loyalty, generates greater exposure for business, increases user traffic, improves search ratings, reduces marketing expenses, results in new business partnerships, and yields a higher conversation rate (DeMers, 2014; Stelzner, 2011). Rather than secretly tracking purchasing behavior with technology, social media allows marketers to engage directly with consumers through an open transactional process. This is especially useful as customer concerns for privacy and data security increase.

Companies are now able to utilize numerous platforms to engage customers, including company websites, blogs, discussion forums, emails, YouTube, Instagram, Facebook, X (formerly Twitter), TikTok, mobile messages, and affiliated pins on Pinterest. While it is important for marketers to reach out to their customers offline, it is equally important for sales and customers to be able to communicate with one another via social media

(Mangold & Faulds, 2009). This develops a strong community among members, a concept discussed in detail in Chapter 3. Social media provides an ideal way to communicate with customers without disrupting their everyday rituals.

Once transactional communication is in progress, and consumers are shaped by positive social media reinforcement, they are more likely to return for repeat business. The positive reinforcement no longer just comes in the form of purchasing or product experience. Social media allows marketers the ability to check-in, monitor, and listen to customers at every step of the consumption process, including the period of time before they even make a purchase and long after they bring the product home. Social media can prompt consumers to think about a product or brand when they otherwise would not.

For example, as a consumer, you may put great thoughts into purchasing a new pair of athletic shoes. There are a lot of competing brands to choose from. You may examine consumer blogs or reviews to determine which pair best suits your particular lifestyle. Maybe you will use the shoes primarily for walking daily. Social media helps guide your decision based on your unique preferences and price point, and personalize the consumption process to suit your individual needs.

Once the purchase is made and you wear the shoes a few times, you are likely not to think about them very often. This is what consumers want in a product. If the shoes are meeting the purchase goals, they become a part of your daily routine and habit. The only time you are likely to consider the shoe purchase again is if something goes wrong and the experience is negatively reinforced, such as the sole wearing thin and the shoe hurting your foot.

This is an unfortunate challenge faced by marketers in the consumption process. How can repeat brand loyalty be encouraged when customers only buy new products because their previous purchase no longer meets their needs? Social media allows the opportunity for marketers to build a relationship with consumers during this critical period when the product is working well. Marketing practitioners can ask customers to share pictures of their purchase, provide information about local hiking trails, or offer exclusive promotions for being such a good customer. Each of these positive interactions helps reinforce or shape the way consumers feel about their purchase. In fact, it makes it easier for transactional dialogue at every point along the consumption process: before, during, and after the sale. This way, consumers are thinking about your brand when their experiences are positive.

Humans have always exhibited markedly habitual behavior regarding their purchasing decisions. We tend to buy the same brand of products, eat similar types of food, and go to the same stores when shopping. This proves even more true in today's digital world, where shopping applications keep track of previous purchases and save our bank account information. Consumers even spend a similar amount of time and money in stores each visit. Knowledge of these patterns of human behavior can prove very lucrative for marketers. This information is missed when marketers only focus on media messages and products. Social media provides new opportunities to get to know your consumers on a much more intimate level.

Generally, *consumer habits* are a form of automaticity that is guided by past experiences (Wood & Neal, 2009). This is why shaping is so essential to repeat business. Repetition is central to all facets of human life, including our daily media consumption. Humans tend to have a limited *media repertoire*, or the entirety of media channels that a person regularly uses (Hasebrink & Domeyer, 2012). Though a larger supply of media content from multiple media sources exists, your consumers tend to only use a very limited number of media sources in their everyday lives. The notion that digital users have the totality of information in the world at their fingertips is true. However, they tend to only visit their favorite websites on a routine basis. This helps to organize all the information, but also drastically decreases the amount and type of content received.

Repetition is also an important facet of consumer purchasing. It helps ease the uncertainty of such a saturated marketplace. In fact, the more bogged down individuals feel by time pressures, distraction, and self-control depletion, the more heavily they rely on routines (Hasebrink & Domeyer, 2012). Often, these are the very same negative moods and attitudes that guide media-seeking behavior. If you are feeling stressed out or bogged down at work, you may be more likely to come home and watch hours of television to relax. Repetition and routine help ease stress in our everyday lives.

As such, breaking consumer habits is difficult. Creating new routines requires a more mindful decision by the user, especially when it requires a new digital search or the effort of entering your bank account information again to create a new account. Why bother when you already have the information stored somewhere else? Communication theory tells us that it can be very difficult to change the daily routines of individuals. The theory of *cognitive dissonance* helps explain the discomfort that individuals experience when they are confronted by new information that is contradictory to their current beliefs, attitudes, and ideas (Festinger, 1962). Humans do not like their daily repertoires disrupted.

When met with media messages that are not consistent with current practices, people use communication to make things more consistent and reduce dissonance. Humans strive for internal consistency. Dissonance reduction is achieved in one of four ways: (1) change the behavior or cognition; (2) justify the behavior by changing the conflicting cognition; (3) justify the behavior or cognition by adding new cognitions; or (4) deny any information that conflicts with existing beliefs.

Let's assume that you read a media message that states how a new brand of athletic shoes recently introduced to the market is better than the one that you just purchased. You have already invested substantial time researching social media prior to your purchase to determine which brand would be best for your lifestyle. However, this new information is not consistent with your purchasing decision.

There are many ways that you may try to reduce the dissonance brought by this new media message. You may decide that you will no longer purchase the brand of shoes that you just bought, justify all the money that you saved by buying a pair of lesser quality shoes, or decide that the new shoes are probably not better at all, and simply a new fad that will go away. All these are ways that you would make things more consistent with your previous behavior.

The cognitive dissonance process often leads individuals avoiding or ignoring situations and information that are likely to increase dissonance. This helps explain why consumers ignore so much of traditional media marketing. In addition, because of a limited media repertoire, it is likely that consumers never actually receive these media messages unless they are shared on the platforms that have already been visited as part of their daily routine. This is especially true now that media users can fast-forward or skip commercials/advertisements altogether.

Social media provides a space where marketers and consumers coexist. It allows marketers to focus their attention on customers who are already interested in their brand and would be more impacted by media messages that are consistent with their current cognitions.

Based on this understanding of human behavior, marketers need to consider behavior change theory when developing a social media marketing strategy. This book will help practitioners understand how to best research media users to craft social media messages, choose an appropriate social media platform, and monitor the resulting information exchange. Moreover, it encourages the social media strategy to fit within a larger marketing campaign to reach product goals. These social media strategies will help transform customers into lifelong brand advocates.

While most of the book focuses on crafting social media messages for marketing purposes, Part IV explains why it is a smart idea to use social media to market for social good. This is consistent with the roots of behavior change theories. A more socially conscious brand strategy can prove mutually beneficial for businesses, consumers, and the globalized world alike. Given the more civically minded nature of Gen Z, these positive social efforts should be important to all organizations looking to thrive in future media landscapes. Now that we understand the benefits of using behavior change theory in marketing strategies, let's examine a case study that promotes transactional communication and creates a culture of belonging.

Case Study: Starbucks #whatsyourname Campaign

The Starbucks mission statement is to "inspire and nurture the human spirit – one person, one cup and one neighborhood at a time," which is consistent with the commitment to diversity and inclusion initiatives of Generation Z by creating a culture of belonging where everyone is welcome (Starbucks, 2020). While this mission statement does not directly speak to the sale of coffee that the brand is best known for, it does speak to the "third place" experience that consumers often experience in store. Coffee shops are often cited as a third-place destination, as they exist outside an individual's home and workspace, and host regular, voluntary, informal gathering of people who enjoy one another's company (Rosenbaum *et al.*, 2007). Drinking coffee from the same place, during the same time each week can create a ritualistic consumption experience referenced above. Undoubtably, Starbucks marketers understand the value of focusing on creating a warm and inclusive space for this routine.

One ritual of the Starbucks third space experience is the process of placing an order. Starbucks personalizes this experience by utilizing unique jargon from other American baristas. Patrons specify whether they would like a tall, grande, or venti size, rather than small, medium, and large (Owens, 2023). Consumers are also encouraged to select unique ingredients to make up their drink order, including the type of milk, syrup, topping, and level of caffeine. Once an order is placed, the Starbucks barista asks the customer's name, writes it on the cup, and calls it out when the drink is ready. This personalized experience not only ensures that the correct drink order ends up in the hands of the appropriate recipient but also personalizes the experience between the barista and the customer. Over time, baristas often get to know a customer's drink based on the routine customer experience of always going to the same place, with the same order, at the same time.

In 2020, this routine customer third place experience was the focus of a social media campaign. Starbucks UK launched a #whatsyourname campaign to help raise awareness and support gender-diverse youths (Figure 1.3). The campaign included traditional television commercial, as well as content on Instagram, X (formerly Twitter), and YouTube to promote dialogue. The social videos included portrayals of people who offered their new name in a public space for the first time during the

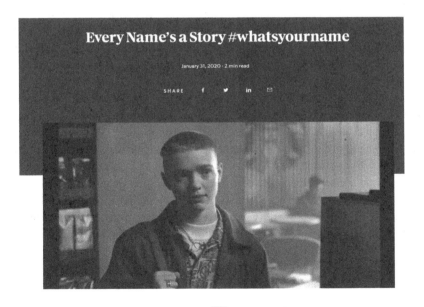

Starbucks welcomes you, whoever you are and whomever you want to be.

Figure 1.3   Starbucks Campaign Website. Source: Starbucks Corporation/https://stories. starbucks.com/emea/stories/2020/whatsyourname/last accessed 26 September, 2023.

Starbucks ordering process. They found Starbucks to be a safe and accepting environment for a significant moment of their transitioning process, as they are recognized for who they want to be (Starbucks, 2020). The social media campaign received Channel 4's Diversity in Advertising Award for addressing the transgender community's lack of representation in UK advertising.

The Starbucks UK #whatsyourname campaign successfully utilized social media to communicate with customers about the unique and personalized experience they can expect when they engage the brand. The campaign communicated with customers on an individual level in a way that was consistent with their brand mission, reduced dissonance, and captured loyalty of a key demographic. Here, you see how mass television broadcast, in-person consumer purchases, and social media can all work positively together.

The #whatsyourname campaign encourages transactional communication by consistently communicating with, and responding to, customer comments on their social media platforms. They regularly prompt customers to participate with user-generated content by inviting consumers to share their personal story on Instagram, X (formerly Twitter), and YouTube. This communication with individuals that consumers already know and trust builds brand loyalty. Rather than just creating media messages based on the goals and objectives of selling coffee, the company has directed attention toward the challenges and initiatives that are consistent with the values of their consumer demographic. Direct communication creates meaningful and personalized transactional communication that leads to brand loyalty (Shandrow, 2013). The socially conscious nature of the #whatsyourname campaign makes people feel good about changing their purchasing habits.

Here you see how social media provides an opportunity for businesses to reach out to potential and current customers through multiple channels to promote engaging transactional dialogue. Social media is used to prompt users to share their positive experiences with others, not simply as a place to complain or share negative experiences with a brand. Not only does this become a part of their new schemata of interpretation, but it also allows new customers to hear about the product through an already trusted source, rather than through a business's self-promotion. This is just one example of how social media can be used to build a positive consumer and community experience. Each chapter of this book will explore additional case studies where social media helped in reaching these goals.

Discussion questions

1   What personalized elements of the #whatsyourname social media campaign help target individual customers, rather than a homogenous mass audience? What challenges would Starbucks have faced through a similar campaign in a more traditional media environment?

2   Think about a social media campaign you like. Has the campaign spoke to the "third place" experience? How did the campaign create a culture of belonging where you feel you're welcome?

3   If you oversaw your company/organization/club's social media efforts, how would you use social media to promote transactional communication with your consumers?

Summary

There is much to learn about how we utilize new media to make decisions in our daily lives. Throughout this chapter, we have discussed the complexities of this process and identified the role that media users play. Most importantly, we have learned how mass communication is no longer viewed as a vehicle for "one-to-many" messages. Selective targeted messages are most effective in establishing behavior change no matter which type of communication specialty you are interested in engaging. This shift from viewing a mass audience to targeting individuals is essential to successful social media marketing.

Because of social media, media users now see themselves as content generators, rather than passive receivers of media texts. Businesses need to personalize content and allow room for participation. People are no longer shocked when a website addresses them by their first name, and it will not be long, if we have not reached the point already, where this level of individuality and customization is expected. Social media makes it easier than ever to encourage this type of transactional communication. It is an efficient and cost-effective way to reach your business objectives, as well as the goals of your customers.

Social media has brought forth new opportunities for information gathering, dissemination, and socialization. However, these new technologies have not completely altered our purposes for doing so. The tools for behavior change are the same, and once you understand the theoretical underpinnings, you will be better equipped to create and disseminate efficient and effective messages for your social media campaigns. This chapter has presented the first rule of an effective social media marketing strategy: stop thinking about communication in a linear fashion. Ask questions about the interests of target consumers, rather than wondering how to get media messages to reach the largest number of people possible.

This book is interested in guiding strategy for producers of social media messages that inspire behavior change in people. A strong practitioner is the one who can apply technological competence and critical thinking skills to a long-term strategic plan. Using behavior change theory, marketers can create media messages that meet the goals and experiences of their consumers. Through a mindful strategy, consumer behavior can be positively reinforced at every point of engagement. This will reduce dissonance in the behavior change process and result in more loyal and long-term brand advocates. These customers will then influence their own social network to continue increasing your return on investment.

This chapter has laid the foundation for how communication theories approached behavior change. Hopefully, a stronger understanding of the complexities of the relationship between media content and subsequent behavior change has been gained. The following chapters will examine historical shifts in behavior change literature and the opportunities and challenges of information diffusion, community building, and mobilization. These three constructs will become the core of your social media strategy and will set you apart from other social media experts in the field.

Key Takeaways

1 Communication theories help teach social media specialists how to gather necessary information, package it for specific target consumers, and disseminate it through an appropriate medium.
2 Our understanding of the communication process has shifted from a linear model toward a more transactional process that accounts for all participants as senders/receivers in a simultaneous and fluid exchange. Determine who the target consumers of the message are, the technology that they utilize, and their specific needs and gratifications.
3 Marketers are turning toward behavior change theory to better understand the lifestyle and experiences of consumers. This focus on consumer behavior helps transform customers into lifetime brand advocates.
4 Social media should be used to engage in dialogue to help build relationships with customers. This positive reinforcement will keep them coming back.
5 Humans markedly exhibit habitual behaviors. A strong understanding of these routines will help practitioners better construct social media marketing messages that appeal to consumer lifestyle.

References

American Marketing Association (2023) Available at http://www.ama.org.

Barysevich, A. (2020) Search engine watch. Available at https://www.searchenginewatch.com/2020/11/20/how-social-media-influence-71-consumer-buying-decisions (accessed November 18, 2023).

Bauerlein, M. (2009) *The Dumbest Generation: How the Digital Age Stupefies Young Americans and Jeopardizes Our Future (Or, Don't Trust Anyone Under 30).* New York: Tarcher/Penguin.

DeMers, J. (2014) The top 10 benefits of social media marketing. *Forbes.* Available at http://www.forbes.com/sites/jaysondemers/2014/08/11/the-top-10-benefits-of-social-media-marketing (accessed November 18, 2023).

Dominick, J. (2008) *The Dynamics of Mass Communication: Media in the Digital Age.* New York: McGraw Hill.

Festinger, L. (1962) *A Theory of Cognitive Dissonance.* Stanford, CA: Stanford University Press.

Griffin, E. (2011) *Communication: A First Look at Communication Theory.* New York: McGraw Hill.

Hasebrink, U. & Domeyer, H. (2012) Media repertoires as patterns of behavior and as meaningful practices: a multimethod approach to media use in converging media environments. *Participations: Journal of Audience and Reception Studies*, 9(2), 757–779.

Jenkins, H. (2006) *Convergence Culture: Where Old and New Media Collide.* New York: New York University Press.

Kaplan, A.M. & Haenlein, M. (2010) Users of the world, unite! The challenges and opportunities of social media. *Business Horizons*, 53(1), 59–68.

Kotler, P. & Zaltman, G. (1971) Social marketing: an approach to planned social change. *Journal of Marketing*, 35, 3–12.

Lasswell, H.D. (1948) *The Structure and Function of Communication in Society.* New York: Harper & Bros.

Levine, P. (2007) *The Future of Democracy: Developing the Next Generation of American Citizens.* Lebanon, NH: University Press of New England.

Mangold, W. & Faulds, D. (2009) Social media: the new hybrid element of the promotion mix. *Business Horizons*, 52(4), 357–365.

Manoff Group (2012) Defining social and behavior change communication (SBCC) and other essential health communication terms. Available at http://manoffgroup.com/documents/DefiningSBCC.pdf.

Meola, A. (2022) Generation Z. news. *Insider Intelligence.* Available at www.insiderintelligence.com/insights/generation-z-facts.

Ortiz-Ospina, E. (2019) The rise of social media. Available at https://ourworldindata.org/rise-of-social-media.

Owens, E. (2023) The real reason why Starbucks uses tall, Grande, and venti. *Travel & Leisure.* Available at https://www.travelandleisure.com/food-drink/starbucks-cup-sizes (accessed November 18, 2023).

Palfrey, J. & Gasser, U. (2010) *Born Digital: Understanding the First Generation of Digital Natives.* New York: Basic Books.

Rosenbaum, M.S., Ward, J., Walker, B.A. & Ostrom, A.L. (2007) A cup of coffee with a dash of love: an investigation of commercial social support and third-place attachment. *Journal of Service Research*, 10(1), 43–59.

Rothschild, M. & Gaidis, W. (1981) Behavioral learning theory: its relevance to marketing and promotions. *Journal of Marketing*, 45, 70–78.

Scheufele, D.A. (2002) Differential gains from mass media and their implications for participatory behavior. *Communication Research*, 29(1), 45–64.

Scheufele, D.A. & Tewksbury, D. (2007) Framing, agenda setting, and priming: the evolution of three media effects models. *Journal of Communication*, 57, 9–20.

Shandrow, K. (2013) 3 Innovative ways startups are driving results over social media. Available at http://www.entrepreneur.com/article/227399.

Shannon, C.E. (1948) A mathematical theory of communication. *The Bell System Technical Journal*, 27, 379–423.

Starbucks (2020) Every name's a story: #whatsyourname. Available at https://stories.starbucks.com/emea/stories/2020/whatsyourname/ (accessed November 18, 2023).

Statista (2022) Daily time spent on social networking by Internet users worldwide from 2012 to 2022. Available at www.statista.com/statistics/433871/daily-social-media-usage-worldwide (accessed November 18, 2023).

Stelzner, M. (2011) Social media marketing industry report: how marketers are using social media to grow their businesses. Available at http://www.socialmedia.examiner.com/SocialMediaMarketingReport2011.pdf.

Tariq, H. (2021) Own an essential business. *Forbes.* Available at www.forbes.com/sites/forbescommunicationscouncil/2021/06/22/five-components-of-a-successful-strategic-communications-plan/?sh=5051dd765813 (accessed November 18, 2023).

Thackeray, R. & Neiger, B.L. (2000) Establishing a relationship between behavior change theory and social marketing: implications for health education. *Journal of Health Education*, 31(6), 331–335.

Wood, W. & Neal, D.T. (2009) The habitual consumer. *Journal of Consumer Psychology*, 19(4), 579–592.

2

Information Diffusion

Learning Objectives

After reading this chapter, you should be able to:
1   Explain Rogers' diffusion of innovations theory and be able to determine the opportunities and challenges of social media message diffusion.
2   Distinguish the differences between Web 1.0 and Web 2.0 technology structure.
3   Analyze the construct of transparency and understand how to utilize it to maintain control of your social media messages.

Introduction

Chapter 1 explored how our conceptualization of the communication process has shifted from a linear model toward a more transactional process and examined basic assumptions regarding the role media users play in the sense-making process. This chapter introduces the basic structures and content of social media technologies. These structures have gone through a similar trend, where media consumers have been transformed from passive entities that simply consume online messages (Web 1.0) into active users (Web 2.0) that participate, negotiate, and generate content in the information-exchange process.

Strategic Social Media: From Marketing to Social Change, Second Edition. L. Meghan Mahoney and Tang Tang.
© 2024 John Wiley & Sons, Inc. Published 2024 by John Wiley & Sons, Inc.

There is little that marketers can control over personal preferences, life experience, personalities, and internal or external noise. We do not know how individuals will negotiate and make sense of media texts. However, what we can do is to gain a better sense of how to maximize messages for persuasion. The next three chapters lay the foundation for all social media strategies by focusing on three historical shifts in behavior change literature: diffusion (Chapter 2), community (Chapter 3), and mobilization (Chapter 4). These three chapters lay the theoretical groundwork for social media strategy. Each chapter will discuss the significance and takeaways of utilizing these strategies in social media marketing to prompt human behavior change and reach organizational goals.

There are many opportunities and challenges for using diffusion, community, or mobilization strategies in social media messages. In general, an inverse relationship exists between user participation and message control. Therefore, it is important to make informed decisions about when to use more top-down approaches for tight control over media messages, and when more participatory approaches are necessary for mobilization. To begin, let's focus on Rogers' diffusion of innovation, a foundational linear theory for utilizing mass media for behavior change.

Diffusing Your Message

Marketers and communication specialists have long been interested in how and why new ideas spread through cultures. Have you ever wondered why some trends become popular, while other ideas never take off? It is challenging to predict just how your consumers will respond to a message, especially when messages are distributed through a mediated channel, rather than through face-to-face communication. When creating a social media message, whether it be to promote a new product purchase or invite friends to a party, you are hoping that they receive the message and follow through with a desired behavior change. While the process seems simple enough, there are many things that could go wrong throughout the process. How do you ensure that the message actually reaches the target consumer? How do you make the content of the information appropriate and understandable for all users? What can you do to ensure that the content is enticing enough to prompt behavior change?

Everett Rogers (1962) explored this process in his book, *Diffusion of Innovations*. Diffusion of innovations (also referred to as *diffusion of innovations theory* and/or *diffusion*) explains how new ideas spread through media outlets over time among members of a targeted community (Haider & Kreps, 2004). Researchers identified five stages of diffusion of innovations to explain the process: (1) awareness, (2) interest, (3) evaluation, (4) trial, and (5) adoption. This process highlights how important the basic assumptions, preferences, and life experiences of consumers are to the effectiveness of media messages. If adoption is successful, individuals will follow through with the new desired behavior change (Haider & Kreps, 2004; Rogers, 1976). A strong understanding of this theory will help marketers, media organizations, political candidates, or even just everyday citizens better understand the diffusion, adoption, or rejection of new ideas.

Let's use the launch of the first Apple Watch in 2015 as an example. How does a brand's new innovative technology, different from any other smart watch on the market, become a universally known and trusted product? Through Rogers' diffusion of innovations process:

Step 1 Users need to become aware of the Apple Watch existence. Generally, this is achieved through traditional means of advertising, "show and tell" displays, or word-of-mouth approaches. Apple is famous for their product launch events where they introduce new and updated technology to the public.

Step 2 Users would have to believe that the media message is intended for them and that its content would benefit their everyday life. Prior to Apple Watch, most fitness bands had useful individualized smart metric capabilities. For Apple Watch to transcend this step, it must offer something unique from alternative smart watch products.

Step 3 Users complete an evaluation of the product. Evaluation can come in many forms, such as buying the product and evaluating whether they are satisfied with the purchase. However, with a high-ticket technology item like an Apple Watch, this is unlikely. More realistically, users would want to do some research on their own. They may search customer reviews online, visit their local Apple store to play with the interface, or ask a friend if they could borrow theirs to see if the technology meets expectations.

Step 4 The trial stage of the diffusion process is the most critical and time-consuming step. During this period, users may consider themselves as current satisfied customers of Apple Watch, but may still be open to alternative products, or disengage if there is social backlash. No one wants to use a previously popular technology that has become so unpopular that their friends are going to tease them for it (think of outdated social networking sites here, such as Friendster or Myspace).

Step 5 Finally, a point of saturation is reached where users adopt the brand, in this case the Apple brand. Users may switch their personal computer to an iMac, or invest in a new secondary device, such as an iPhone or the newest model of Apple ear buds. Through the diffusion process, users have transformed into loyal brand advocates. In this final stage, it is the user (consumer) that becomes the disseminator of the brand message to their personal social network.

While this theory does a nice job of explaining the diffusion process, criticisms of this dominant media-centric approach exist (Melkote & Steeves, 2001). Many believe that the diffusion structure allows little room for user feedback and participation. However, we know from Chapter 1 that media users are participatory in the information-exchange process. Diffusion of innovations theory demonstrates how unlikely it is for individuals to complete all five stages of the adoption process. They could fall off the process at any point. Only a small percentage of your target consumers will actually reach the adoption phase. Therefore, social media practitioners must learn as much as they can about their consumers to ensure whether people desire the information that they are hoping to disseminate.

Despite the low likelihood that consumers will reach all five stages of the diffusion process, most advertisers and corporations continue to use linear top-down approaches to reach consumers, such as tweeting messages like "We're having a sale. Buy now!" This could be because these types of messages often prove the most efficient and cost-effective method to reach a large number of consumers, especially through traditional mass media like radio or television commercials. The way to reach many people with a single message often referred to as *"push and pray" marketing* (Stratten, 2012).

"Push and pray" marketing indicates that traditional media campaigns distribute their messages to as many people as possible to create awareness-only campaigns. Message producers can only hope that message receivers follow the remainder of the behavior change process. Most often, these producers never receive any feedback from their consumers and are unaware whether consumers follow through with the desired behavior change (i.e., purchasing behavior).

While the "push and pray" strategy helps to increase awareness, the importance of interpersonal communication in the decision-making process cannot be overemphasized. A friend's recommendation earns much more than a celebrity endorsement in a TV commercial. This has always been a struggle that mass media campaigns must overcome: how can they compete with an interpersonal network of community and friends? Not only do satisfied customers have strong brand loyalty, but they also bring in their own personal network of friends. This is why a community-centric technique is so critical to a successful behavior change campaign (the community-centric approach will be discussed in Chapter 3). Nonetheless, today, the interactive nature of social media allows new opportunities for diffusion-centric campaigns. It is easier than ever before for friends to share recommendations through mediated channels. Therefore, let's take a more detailed look at the structural shift in technology use from Web 1.0 to Web 2.0.

Web 1.0 to Web 2.0 Technology Structure

Technology structure plays a critical role in how we respond, interact with, and create media content. Once you understand opportunities and challenges between various technology structures, more can be done to manipulate social media messages for behavior change. How does social media differ from traditional mass media, or even alternative new media platforms? You often hear the term "social media" interwoven between buzzwords such as "user-generated content," "online interactivity," and "Web 2.0." Each of these points to the structures and opportunities of social media, but none explicitly explain its definition.

Social media

Chapter 1 explained how social media includes any Internet-based applications that build on the ideological and technological foundations of Web 2.0 and allow the creation and exchange of user-generated content (Kaplan & Haenlein, 2010). *User-generated content* includes everything from blogs, collaborative projects such as Wikipedia, social networking sites such as Instagram, content communities such as YouTube, and virtual game worlds such as World of Warcraft. While social media is an umbrella term that includes all forms of online user exchange, participation, and dialogue, user-generated content is a more specific type of social media that allows people to work together to create online content.

Some main characteristics of social media include an online space where users can create, share, and evaluate content for the purpose of social interaction through technology (Lietsala & Sirkkunen, 2008). These spaces are personalized and hold individual URLs that link to external networks. Often these spaces serve as ever-changing communities, where members post messages free of charge through a tagging system. In addition, there are many functions of social media, including improving identity, conversations, sharing, presence, relationships, reputations, and groups (Kietzmann *et al.*, 2011). Marketers who are interested in developing a social media strategy must first understand these various functions and structures and seek for the appropriate balance between each in achieving their marketing goals.

Mass media

Mass media is defined as a group of technologies that allows one-to-many communication through mediated channels (Pearce, 2009). In the context of mass media communication, the audience is seen as large, anonymous, and homogeneous, making it an ideal form for information diffusion. If you are interested in broadcasting a message to thousands of users, why not turn to a mass medium such as radio or television? Even as the Internet became a commercial service in the 1990s, most content only addressed audiences in a top-down manner with little interactive features for feedback. If you wished to seek out additional information about a company, you could go to the company's index page and read whatever content they had created. A typical user's role was primarily that of a passive receiver of information, where they could access information, but not change or respond. However, users were still able to negotiate and make sense of the message according to their own life experience, preferences, and personality, even within the traditional mass media environments, which is why the concept of a "passive audience" was never really true.

The World Wide Web was initially created as a platform to facilitate information exchange between users (Kaplan & Haenlein, 2010). Mangold and Faulds (2009) explained how the first purpose of Internet communication is consistent with traditional mass media tools – to communicate to a large audience. In the early 1990s, most online content resembled traditional published mass media material, where users accessed content created by a relatively small number of publishers who had control over the content. A decade later,

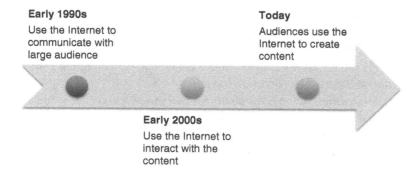

Figure 2.1   Timeline interactive progression.

in the early 2000s, as participatory technology became more readily available, users began interacting with the content, rather than just consuming the content. Today, we are well into an era of content creation among users. The role of social media (i.e., users communicating with one another) brings many opportunities for information distribution (Agichtein *et al.*, 2008). This timeline of interactivity progression from the 1990s to the present is the shift from Web 1.0 to Web 2.0 (Figure 2.1).

Shift to Web 2.0

Web 1.0 is identified as the era where the Internet was used as a one-to-many model (Cormode & Krishnamurthy, 2008). Though the Internet was always designed for users to participate with messages, the tools to do so were not always available to media users. In its initial inception, Internet content tended to mirror traditional mass media structures, where individuals used websites to gain information, not interact with the content. It was not until advancements in interactivity and participation that social media emerged. *Web 2.0* allows any participant to be a content creator and is exemplified by a large number of niche groups who exchange, tag, comment, and link content. These advancements in technology allowed users to share stories, recommendations, and communicate directly with a product source.

Indeed, Web 2.0 extends beyond just providing users with the ability for feedback. Wirtz *et al.* (2010) proposed four fundamental constructs to the Web 2.0 phenomenon. Each of these constructs allows for increased participation among users:

- social networking;
- interaction orientation;
- personalization/customization; and
- user-added possibilities.

Social networking is the ability for users to find and keep in contact with a personal community, including interpersonal contacts or interest-based networks. Users share thoughts, pictures, and events. *Interaction orientation* identifies the interactivity nature of Web 2.0. Users can provide feedback and engage with content according to the structure that producers allow. This is one step beyond the individual negotiation and sense-making process, as users can physically alter the media content. So you do not like what you read on Wikipedia? Web 2.0 allows you to change it.

Personalization/customization is the ability for users to pick and choose the content that is of most interest to them. Users can block information, set up personal toolbars and bookmarks, and deny Facebook friends they do not wish to communicate with. All these are ways in which users are taking control of their own Web 2.0 experience. Users demand these features in almost everything that they access online now, including customized content on news networks, Amazon, and ESPN (Krishnamurthy, Wills, & Zhang, 2001). Finally, *user-added possibilities* transform users into producers of online content. Media users are no longer just seeking information/content, but are creating it through Wikis, blogs, video, and photo-sharing sites. All these features were not possible in a Web 1.0 environment and maximize behavior change potential in media users.

This shift from Web 1.0 to Web 2.0 not only allows users more control over their online experience but it also influences the type of content available. O'Reilly (2007) explains how this user-controlled space allows for collective intelligence, where the blogosphere represents the voice Internet users used to only hear in their heads. For the first time in history, media users can decide what is important, thus turning the concept of a traditional mass media gatekeeper upside down. Today's social media users have unlimited opportunities to receive, create, or ignore online content and are proving more empowered and motivated than ever before (Boulos & Wheeler, 2007; Buenting, 2006; Dijck, 2009). This undoubtedly changes historical notions of who and what deserve media and marketers' attention and which groups are left muted.

There are certainly many opportunities for today's media users to participate. In fact, it would seem unusual, and perhaps even frustrating, for new media content not to have participatory features for feedback, comment, or interactivity. Marketers who create mass media campaigns used to struggle between the ability to reach large numbers of individuals and create personalized messages that invite individualized consumer participation and dialogue. Today, social media resolves this conflict between user participation and message control. There are times when limiting the amount of participation users have may be appropriate to retain control over the message. In this case, it becomes a choice for marketers to utilize a diffusion approach to behavior change.

For example, the Center for Disease Control and Prevention may choose to limit the amount of participation users have on their official social media channels. Their brand is to disseminate messages that protect the public's health. Since their message content is science based and data driven, the goal is not to invite alternative narratives or viewpoints. Additionally, the target audience includes every American; therefore, it is much broader in scope than the average niche social media site. Although participation is a great tool for user engagement, the Center for Disease Control and Prevention must find alternative social media strategies for prompting behavior change in its users. If the content of your message is critical, it may be wiser to go the route of message diffusion.

Every organization should have a space online that diffuses information about the product. Generally, this is the home index page of your organization's website, a place for users to go if they would like to gain more knowledge about your product. Almost every social media and marketing messages should link users back to this page. Without this "home base," users may begin to distrust your brand. It is critical for every online agency to have a clear transparency strategy and control plan for their brand. As such, diffusion is usually the first strategy practitioners focus on when launching a brand. Once you have clear information about your product or service, you can start utilizing more participatory tools. Web 2.0 allows the opportunity for increased participation. It is up to the producer of the message to determine when it is best to increase participatory options and when it is best to keep strong control over content.

Transparency, Control, and Public Relations

In today's fast-paced lifestyle, there is no shortage of home delivery meal kit options promising to take the guess and prep work out of mealtime. One company, Blue Apron, advertises as a more sustainable way to cook and cut down on food waste (Blue Apron, 2022). Part of their marketing effort is to release a yearly Better Living Roadmap, which reports on the environmental, social, and governance efforts of the company. While one may expect the company to market its achievements and sustainable improvements, Blue Apron was recognized for its transparency in sharing both positive and negative sustainability efforts.

The Blue Apron website is forthcoming about the ingredients in its products. Beyond what was regulated and required by the government, it has also published personal profiles on suppliers, videos on how ingredients are made, and updates on sustainability practices (Sprout Social, 2018). Most notable, the company shares sustainable shortcomings and ways that they aim to improve their efforts. Transparency is more than just sharing ingredient information with consumers. It can be admitting mistakes, providing honest reviews of products, sharing diversity demographics of employees, or taking political stances on social issues. This transparent communication strategy bolsters ethos with consumers and acts as an important differentiator between Blue Apron and its competitors. Increasing transparency is a vital tool for engaging consumers while utilizing a diffusion social media strategy. Additionally, transparency allows Blue Apron to be more in control of how this disclosure reaches its consumers.

Create additional transparency

One of the foundational communication theories, the *theory of social penetration*, explains the relationship between self-disclosure and trust. Researchers demonstrate how the development of relational closeness ranges from individuals with whom we feel a superficial bond to those with whom we feel a more intimate connection. One of the most significant indicators of relational closeness is self-disclosure. The more willing one party is to open up and disclose personal and private information, the closer the receiving party feels towards their relationship. For people to trust and connect, both parties must be willing to engage in a level of transparent disclosure (Altman & Taylor, 1973; West, 2009).

Not only is self-disclosure beneficial for interpersonal relationships, but this increased transparency is the expected norm for today's social media marketers. With so many conversations happening online, if a consumer seeks information that a marketer is not willing to disclose, he or she most likely will be able to find it from someplace else. You must take control and not let others write your own brand narrative.

Wright and Hinson (2008) point out how social media creates alternative information channels, making it difficult for organizations to manage and control information diffusion. The more marketers can control the transparency and accountability of their product, the more opportunities there will be for listening and true dialogue. *Transparency* implies openness, communication, and accountability (Phillips & Young, 2009), and the more you are willing to do this, the more your consumers will trust your products.

This idea of transparency is important for all aspects of a company, external and internal. In 2008, Apple came under fire for the working conditions of their manufacturing plant in China, Foxconn. The online public sphere erupted, linking the production of the iPhone with underpaid workers, extreme working hours, violent supervision, and worker suicides (Warren, 2012). Many Apple users were sharing petitions urging other people to boycott Apple within their online social networking circles. This outrage went viral in just a few days.

However, many of the claims presented in the investigative report of Foxconn proved exaggerated and false (Smith, 2012). Apple communication specialists found themselves in the middle of a public relations crisis, with little to do but push out traditional press releases stating that claims were untrue. Yet, users' curiosity in learning more information was not satisfied with the official press releases and found little to no information on Apple's website regarding the production process of the company's products. Therefore, they were relying on alternative media outlets to construct Apple's production narrative. The CEO of Apple, Tim Cook, seemed unable to answer many of the questions consumers were asking about the scandal.

Having little transparency into the production of Apple products was a mistake by the company. Consumers expect to be able to find out unlimited information regarding merchandise, and if Apple was not going to provide it, others could effectively push forth this narrative, no matter how exaggerated. Fortunately, Apple was able to turn this public relations crisis into a key case study of image rebranding through transparency.

Cook eventually called for a voluntary inspection of Foxconn factories by the Fair Labor Association. This vow to ensure safe business practices was critical, even though the initial story of wrongdoing was admittedly proven exaggerated. Moreover, Cook personally visited production factories and posted many of his thoughts, findings, and pictures from the trip on the Apple website (Apple Press Info, 2012). Now if you were to search the production of Apple products online, you would encounter a very different narrative. You would see pictures and reports detailing how Apple products are made in a safe and responsible environment. Increased transparency grants corporations the chance to tell their own story.

Apple was not the only company to face a public relations crisis regarding the production of their goods. Chinese social media called for a boycott of the Swedish clothing brand H&M after the company cut ties with a cotton supplier sourced from Xinjiang Uyghur Autonomous Region (Wu, 2021). H&M attributed the move to a human rights report that outlined evidence of forced labor practices, but the social media campaign called the report a defamatory political conspiracy. Hashtags were shared, translating as #IStandforXUARcotton, and the boycott resulted in multiple store closings around China. Had H&M considered increasing transparency of its product and not relying on external reports, they could have prevented the public relations crisis and had more control over its brand narrative.

Gen Z is more mindful of fair labor practices and sustainable brand efforts as we continue to grow as a globalized and connected marketplace. While it was once possible to remain ignorant on how consumption decisions impact the world we live in, social media magnifies the lives around us. Unfortunately, oftentimes this attention comes as the result of a tragedy.

In April 2013, over 1000 garment workers died and over 2500 were injured when the eight-story Rana Plaza factory building near Dhaka collapsed (BBC, 2013). This tragedy has been referred to "deaths by negligence" as the building had failed several safety regulations in prior inspections. Many social media boycotts emerged as news of the tragedy spread (Bennett, 2023). This boycott targeted companies such as The Gap, Wal-Mart, and other American retail stores that had not yet signed a labor-backed plan to improve factory safety, but instead work on their own alternative plans. In fact, The Gap was one of the leading entrepreneurs seeking global *corporate social responsibility* programs, where companies voluntarily incorporate a social good campaign into their business strategy. European companies such as Abercrombie & Fitch that had agreed to the labor-backed plan were not subject to the same public scrutiny after the tragedy, possibly due to the transparency of their production plan over others.

This case demonstrates how social media has become the leading platform for consumers to voice their frustrations and solutions to the products that they buy. Nine out of ten consumers report that they are willing to boycott socially irresponsible companies (Bennett, 2023), and many experts believe such tragedies could be avoided if the cost of garments increased by just 10 cents (Covert, 2013). The National Consumers League took this concept and created a Facebook campaign where users were able to pledge to companies that they would be willing to pay 10 cents more for socially responsible garments. Hopefully, as more individuals become aware of such irresponsible business practices, more policies, and regulations will be put in place that force companies to make more ethical and transparent decisions regarding the production of their products. It is important to consider a transparency action plan to maintain control over your brand narrative and prevent a public relations crisis.

Transparency Action Plan

There are three steps to create greater social accountability and transparency for your company.

1   Create additional transparency regarding the production, consumption, and profit of your product. Ensure that it is visible on the index page of your website.
2   Be transparent about the planned and perceived obsolescence (explained below) of your product.
3   Decide which other elements of brand transparency will lead to a stronger emotional connection with consumers.

Transparency of your product

Transparency extends beyond just the production of goods, but this is the critical first step when developing a diffusion plan. It is easy to be transparent about the everyday tasks within an organization such as the employees and wages but is more challenging when it comes to out-of-house stages, such as manufacturing, shipping, and environmental impact. Nonetheless, transparency should also include the mission statement, the consumption and the profit of your products, and long-term satisfaction and customer service.

Organizational *mission statements* come in many forms with various purposes. Swales and Rogers (1995) defined mission statements as "a management tool for projecting corporate integrity and instilling loyalty and normed behavior in the corporate workforce" (p. 228), but noted the complexities between genres. When crafting a mission statement, it is important to be succinct and consider your organizational goals and objectives. Mission statements should be between one and three sentences in length. Here you should be clear to your customers why you are in your line of business, what you can do for them, as well as how you differ from your competitors. It is critical to differentiate the mission statement from a company's branding efforts (discussed further in Chapter 3). Mission statements need to focus on ultimate transparency instead of getting too creative with messaging.

It is also important that your organization is forthcoming with the price of your product. Nothing is more frustrating than making your consumers take the time to visit your organization's website and not finding any information regarding how much a good or service costs. Consumers will assume that the price is too expensive to list or that it is negotiable. Even if these assumptions are true of your product, be forthright with consumers on why.

Be transparent. Tell your consumers directly that even though your product may cost more than competitors, it is worth the extra money, or why you encourage them to negotiate the price based on their personal needs. Don't leave your customers guessing.

The price of your product goes beyond just a monetary price tag. Whatever it is that you are selling to consumers (yourself to a potential employer, an invitation to a party, or a Facebook status to "like"), you need to be forthcoming about what the cost and benefits are if they follow through with your prompt. How much time are you asking for? Will you be willing to share any information provided? What future obligations are involved? This is the golden rule of communicating: Do unto others as you would have others do unto you. Not doing so will catch up with you eventually and will leave a lingering impression on how your consumers view you.

It is also important to consider the "price" of your product regarding the global environment. This is a great chance to showcase some of the socially responsible decisions that you made during the production stage of your goods to differentiate yourself from other competitors. Is the packaging of your product recyclable? Be sure to take extra steps to prompt users to do so. Does your organization sponsor charities or causes in the local community? Provide that information too. Tell consumers what social issues are important to you. Disclosing these individual preferences is meaningful to consumers and helps build rapport and trust. Customers prefer to see their hard-earned money go to responsible individuals, not a salesperson who is only interested in selling a product. Finally, in terms of creating transparency of your product, you want to provide information regarding the long-term satisfaction of your product. What lasting impact does your product have on the world?

Planned and perceived obsolescence

When creating a transparency action plan, you also want to consider the planned obsolescence and perceived obsolescence of your product. *Planned obsolescence* is the production of goods with uneconomically short useful lives that force customers to make repeat purchases (Bulow, 1986; Fitzpatrick, 2011). Selling a product that breaks too quickly will turn consumers away and prompt them to buy from someone else. Selling a product that never breaks means that the consumer will never have the need to return for business because their original product is still working. If your product obeys the concept of planned obsolescence, your customers will trust the product after it breaks and will pay additional money to fund a replacement.

The premise behind planned obsolescence is that most rational consumers are short-term oriented when it comes to purchases, meaning they pay for the present value of a service or product. Therefore, to maximize profit, some companies construct products to break after a period of use. The ethics of this type of business practice has been debated for years. This is another opportunity for complete transparency, especially if you have risen above some of your competitors. Also, encourage your customers to share their experiences with your product or service through social media.

Even though the desirability for a product is a little more difficult to measure and control, it is still an important factor to consider. Kaspar (2004) describes how *perceived obsolescence* is the limitation of products based on social appeal, rather than function. Even though a product may still function correctly as your customers intended with purchase, it is no longer fashionable or appropriate for modern society. This explains why some people upgrade to the newest model of phone or computer even though their previous model still works and serves its intended purpose. If customers are willing to invest in your product, especially if the investment proves substantial, the social desirability of your product may be something worth addressing. How invested is your company in customer loyalty and keeping up with modern updates?

Additional elements of brand transparency

In addition to fostering the transparency of your products and their planned and perceived obsolescence, it is important to consider the profit transparency of your brand. You may want to share information with your customers about the wages and benefits for your employees. This is the most overlooked stage of transparency, as many do not believe it is the business of everyday customers to know how much employees and CEOs make. However, one of the biggest fuels of the H&M scandal was the discrepancy between labor practices of product sourcing and the company's CEO. Companies should strive to empower all members of their organization to feel as though they are a meaningful part of the success. When the organization benefits, all employees should feel as though they benefit as well.

Customers want to know where their money goes, even once it is out of their hands. Let's refer to The Gap social media boycott as an example. Say that you work for The Gap. Your customers received a social media message that asked them to boycott The Gap because the company did not sign a labor-backed plan to improve factory safety for production employees. They then went online to The Gap's website to learn more about the production of your goods. On the website, your consumers learned more about your efforts to seek global corporate social responsibility programs on an individual level. Moreover, they also learned that the company that owns The Gap also owns the garment stores they trust such as Old Navy, Banana Republic, PiperLime, and Athleta. Transparency regarding the production of goods and ownership of businesses makes them trust the brand even more. Instead of boycotting The Gap, your consumers may decide to share this information with their social network and support you.

In 2023, the Anheuser-Busch leading beer brand Bud Light announced a partnership between the beer company and Dylan Mulvaney, a 26-year-old transgender influencer (Bloch, 2023). Mulvaney is a social media LGBTQ activist with over 10 million followers on TikTok. Many right-wing loyal fans of Bud Light were surprised by the partnership in an era where Republican state lawmakers propose controversial legislation that regulates young transgender rights and restricts drag shows (Holpuch, 2023). Social media erupted with many celebrities and companies showing support for the partnership, and others calling for a boycott by sharing videos of celebrities shooting or destroying cans of Bud Light. Today, consumers expect to know the social alignment of brands and political issues. Companies can use political transparency as a tool to attract new customers who value the company for taking a particular social stand.

Perhaps a more surprising political comment was made by Robert Unanue, the CEO of Latin food purveyor Goya. In 2020, Unanue praised then-President Trump for the White House Hispanic Prosperity Initiative, comparing him to his grandfather, a Spanish immigrant who founded the company (Reyes, 2020). The comment sparked a social media boycott from many of the brand's most valuable customers, citing a discrepancy between the Trump administration immigration policies and support of the loyal Latino community. The social media boycott, using the hashtag #Goyaway, encouraged consumers to purchase from a different brand. It is important to again note that there is nothing illegal or even unethical about the head of a company having political affiliations or religious beliefs. However, it was the lack of transparency and cognitive dissonance that consumers felt in both examples.

There are many companies that have utilized social media to provide transparency regarding their employees' wages and working conditions. Some simply disclose in job postings under the "human resource" tab on their home page. Others allow employees to blog about their experiences on the company's website. These extra efforts allow consumers to feel good about putting their money toward these organizations and the individual lives that they are helping by doing so.

Zappos.com has taken this transparency strategy one step further by allowing consumers to take a 60-minute tour through the Zappos headquarters in Las Vegas, Nevada to learn about the Zappos Family culture. During the tour, consumers experience "how a values-based organization uses strong culture to live out every day." They can also take a free (and funny) virtual tour through the Zappos website. When consumers order a pair of shoes from Zappos, they are introduced to an actual employee from Zappos, making it a more personal experience.

Finally, and perhaps most importantly, companies should be transparent about the societal benefits of their organization. This is, if nothing else, a smart branding and marketing strategy. While we will explore the marketing benefits and how to link these societal benefits to socially responsible business models in later chapters, it is important to note here that societal benefits should be as specific and tangible as possible. Use social media to provide pictures of the actual people, places, or initiatives that your customers are benefiting from your service. Do not just say that your product is "green"; demonstrate visually and specifically state what that means for your organization. If your product is linked to a cause or charity, be specific about the percentage of profits that are donated. This will increase sales, while keeping your organization out of trouble.

You should also consider including a blog in addition to a home index page for increased transparency. This blog should not necessarily be centered around the promotion and selling of your products, but instead be a place that your customers want to visit, even if they have no interest in purchasing your products. It is important to remember the value of forming relationships with individuals outside your niche users. Whole Foods, an American food supermarket specializing in natural and organic food, has a blog that shares healthy eating recipes; PetSmart, a retail of pet supplies, has a blog for pet safety; and Lowe's, a home improvement and appliance store, has a blog for "Do It Yourself" ideas. Each of these offers something for people who are not just looking to buy products.

It is also important to implement this strategy even, and perhaps especially, when the product you are promoting is yourself. For example, when Philippe Dubost, a web product manager from Paris, was looking for a job, he decided to develop a social online résumé that resembled the infrastructure of an Amazon product page (Phil Dub, 2014; see Figure 2.2). The résumé was traditional in many senses; it provided the usual professional content, including experience in the field, education, and recommendations (found under the "Product reviews" section of an Amazon page). However, Dubost was able to give employers a better sense of his own skills and characteristics by increasing the amount of transparency regarding many professional and personal elements in his life. Rather than simply stating that he is open to traveling for work, Dubost included a link to his personal travel blog, where employers were able to see pictures, read about travel experiences, and see a proficiency in multiple languages. He also provided snippets of private sphere information regarding personal hobbies by pairing his product with a favorite pair of running shoes. Interested companies can even add his résumé to their cart to see his price of hire. More information about how to integrate social media into personal branding will be discussed in Chapter 8.

Figure 2.2   Amazon résumé. Source: http://phildub.com. Reproduced with permission of Philipee Dubost.

Of course, these additional links all showcased Dubost in a positive manner – who would not want to be associated with marathon running? Technology allows an opportunity for job seekers to increase the amount of positive information employers can receive in an easy-to-navigate and interesting way. Be forthcoming with this information so that employers do not feel that they must search alternative platforms to find out more. By taking control of your own online content and being transparent with private information, you are providing your own narrative with the public information that you want to be included. The online Amazon-style résumé received over 1.3 million unique visitors from 219 countries and landed Dubost a job working with BirchBox in New York City.

In sum, increasing transparency is a necessary step in today's digital media landscape. Your consumers have unlimited access to information at their fingertips, and if you don't provide information regarding your product, someone else will. Moreover, increased transparency leads to a stronger connection with consumers. Transparency should be considered at every level, including production, consumption, and profit.

Case Study: Man Therapy

This chapter has discussed message diffusion, and how an increase in transparency, openness, communication, and accountability leads to greater trust and connection with users. If practitioners find themselves working for a brand or organization where social media messages must be top-down in nature, increasing transparency is a great tool for engaging their consumers. Diffusing social media messages can be the best strategy for marketing practitioners who primarily wish to stay in control over their brand narrative, especially when dealing with a serious or important topic. Though message diffusion does not have the greatest likelihood for behavior change, it is the safest option for critical message distribution.

Effective public health communication is imperative to encouraging positive and healthy behavior change among users. Often, medical physicians are trained to communicate in academic jargon, difficult for the everyday patient to understand. As such, communication specialists are hired to tweak messages to better suit their target audiences. Public health often requires top-down message diffusion, where a medical expert distributes messages about new behaviors that the target audience must understand and adopt. It is critical that the target audience follows the diffusion process to prompt permanent behavior change. The challenge is that top-down health messages are not always the most interesting or engaging to audiences. Here, the goal of social media communication is not promoting dialogue. Instead, the strategy is to diffuse messages to key at-risk demographics.

Man Therapy is a public health social media campaign that was created in conjunction with the Office of Suicide and Prevention at the Colorado Department of Public Health and Environment and the Carson J Spencer Foundation (Granz, 2022).

The online campaign is designed to prevent suicide among the highest risk male demographic, who often do not seek out mental health support. *Man Therapy* aims to break down barriers to help-seeking behavior by smashing the notion that men cannot talk about their feelings (Man Therapy, 2023). The public health website uses "bro humor" to address sensitive topics that men are not always comfortable communicating about with their close friends or family. Given this resistance to open dialogue, a more participatory social media campaign would not prove effective.

The campaign utilizes linear mass media content, such as videos and resourceful information to encourage struggling men to privately visit the platform (Figure 2.3). While most social media campaigns attempt to get users to talk and engage content via social media channels, *Man Therapy* understands the private, often stigmatization nature of mental health, especially for middle-aged men. Rather than creating a social media community for users to communicate with each other, all campaign content links users to an anonymous platform. The campaign is built around a fictional therapist, Dr. Rich Mahogany, and uses humor and practical advice for men to help combat depression. The website also presents helpful resources, testimonials, and tools to help manage depression, anxiety, and stress (Granz, 2022). *Man Therapy* makes mental health support a fun experience for users.

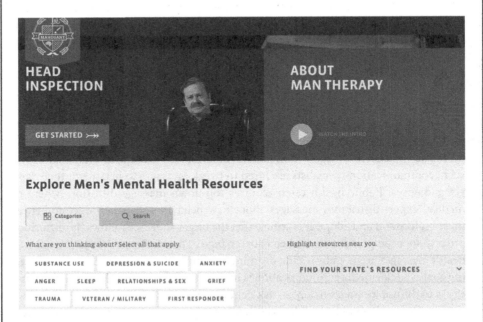

Figure 2.3   Man Therapy Website. Source: Grit Digital Health/www.mantherapy.org/last accessed 26 September, 2023.

The effectiveness of *Man Therapy* (2023) shows that the campaign helps reduce depression, suicide risk, and poor mental health in users. Additionally, it improves help-seeking behavior in working-aged men who may not be willing to share or join a mental health community in a more public online environment. By providing online testimonials of men who are willing to share their struggles, members can see that they are not alone and take steps toward getting the help that they need for positive change.

One big takeaway from the *Man Therapy* social media campaign is that you do not always need to use social media to promote public dialogue. Depending on your topic, traditional linear messaging may be more appropriate. To diffuse information that transcends the diffusion of innovation process, it is imperative that the messaging is culture specific so that users identify and follow through with the requested change. If *Man Therapy* did not use humor as the core of their campaign messaging, users would not have engaged the campaign so widely. A strong diffusion strategy requires a thorough consumer analysis and increased transparency of messages.

Discussion questions

1   One of the greatest advantages of utilizing a diffusion approach in your communication strategy is that you can maintain tight control over message content. Have you preferred a diffusion approach in your communication strategy? How were you able (or not able) to utilize Web 1.0 components to attract people to your messages?
2   Consider the number of diffusion-centric messages that you receive in a day, including billboard, radio, television, and online advertisements. Why are you more likely to share a humor based linear campaign (e.g., *Man Therapy*) with friends instead of a more serious informative campaign?
3   Based on what you know about the behavior change process, how could a strong consumer analysis entice long-term behavior change?

Summary

This chapter focuses on the structure and content of social media. Specifically, it has explored how media consumers have transformed from passive entities that consume online messages (Web 1.0) into active users (Web 2.0) that participate, negotiate, and generate content in an information-exchange process. Diffusion of innovations explains how a new idea can spread through media outlets over time among members of a targeted community via a process of awareness, interest, evaluation, trial, and adoption.

There are many challenges with a diffusion-centric approach to a successful social media marketing campaign and behavior change. We learned in this chapter that if just

Table 2.1   Diffusion: A single media message designed for homogeneous mass audience dissemination.

Pros	Cons
Efficient way to reach a mass audience	Not a personalized method of distribution
Cost-effective	Limited user participation
Disseminates large amount of product information in one place	Top-down content is less interesting to people
Allows tight control over media messages	Low likelihood of consumer adoption

one of the steps is not met, adoption becomes less likely. In general, an inverse relationship exists between user participation and message control. However, message diffusion does allow for tight control over media messages. If you are unsure of the public dialogue surrounding your product, or you are in a position where message dissemination is crucial (i.e., the White House), strict message diffusion may be a more appropriate option (Table 2.1).

Regardless of your product, you should always allow an online space where users can go to find out more information that is controlled by the message source. This "home base" is generally the index page on your company's website. In addition, alternative social media platforms need to be included to provide additional participatory features and to answer any transparency questions your consumers may have. Companies with limited transparency begin to lose control over their own narrative, and as more users participate, the message becomes more and more diluted. Transparency is necessary in today's social media landscape and should be considered at every level of your product process. If you choose not to make this transparent move, you are allowing others to control your brand narrative.

If you are willing to give up some of the control that strict message diffusion allows and encourage more participation from your users, you will begin to increase the chances for behavior change. However, this is a much riskier marketing strategy that requires a solid understanding of community building and identity development. Let's explore these participatory approaches more in Chapter 3.

Key Takeaways

1   Diffusion of innovations is a foundational model for behavior change, which allows tight control over media messages, providing consumers with increased information and disclosure about your product.
2   A diffusion strategy is ideal for practitioners who are introducing a new product, managing a public relations crisis, or disseminating a message with high importance.

3   Diffusion strategies should disclose information about all three stages of a product life cycle: production, consumption, and profit.

4   Your company's website should include a mission statement, the cost of the product, long-term satisfaction, customer service, the message source, wages and benefits for employees, planned and perceived obsolescence, and societal benefits.

5   Message transparency is important. Today's consumers are expecting more disclosure about the products and organizations than ever before. There is a strong correlation between self-disclosure and feelings of trust in a relationship. This trust will keep consumers coming back to the message source.

References

Agichtein, E., Castillo, C., Donato, D., Gionis, A. & Mishne, G. (2008) Finding high-quality content in social media. In: *Proceedings of the International Conference on Web Search and Web Data Mining*, pp. 183–194. New York: Association of Computing Machinery.

Altman, I. & Taylor, D. (1973) *Social Penetration: The Development of Interpersonal Relationships*. New York: Holt.

Apple Press Info (2012) Fair labor association begins inspections of Foxconn. Available at http://www.apple.com/pr/library/2012/02/13Fair-Labor-Association-Begins-Inspections-of-Foxconn.html (accessed November 18, 2023).

BBC (2013) Bangladesh factory collapse toll passes 1,000. Available at http://www.bbc.co.uk/news/world-asia-22476774 (accessed November 18, 2023).

Bennett, S. (2023) Corporate social responsibility. *WebinarCare*. Available at https://webinarcare.com/best-corporate-social-responsibility-software/corporate-social-responsibility-statistics/ (accessed November 18, 2023).

Bloch, E. (2023) Bud light's partnership with a transgender influencer has sparked a boycott. *Time Free Press*. Available at https://www.timesfreepress.com/news/2023/apr/14/bud-lights-partnership-tfp/.

Blue Apron (2022) Investors: Blue Apron. Available at https://investors.blueapron.com/ESG (accessed November 18, 2023).

Boulos, K. & Wheeler, S. (2007) The emerging Web 2.0 social software: an enabling suite of sociable technologies in health and healthcare education. *Health Information and Libraries Journal*, 24(1), 2–23.

Buenting, D. (2006) *Audience involvement with Yellow Card, an entertainment-education initiative promoting safe-sex behavior among African youth*. Dissertation, Regent University, Virginia Beach, USA.

Bulow, J. (1986) An economic theory of planned obsolescence. *Quarterly Journal of Economics*, 101(4), 729–749.

Cormode, G. & Krishnamurthy, B. (2008) Key differences between Web 1.0 and 2.0. *First Monday*, 13(6).

Covert, B. (2013) Bangladesh factory upgrades could cost consumers as little as 10 cents per garment. Available at http://thinkprogress.org/economy/2013/05/07/1972201/bangladesh-factory-upgrades-consumers (accessed November 18, 2023).

Dijck, J. (2009) Users like you?: Theorizing agency in user generated content. *Media, Culture and Society*, 31, 31–58.

Fitzpatrick, K. (2011) *Planned Obsolescence: Publishing, Technology, and the Future of the Academy*. New York: New York University Press.

Granz, K. (2022) A year of success with man therapy. Available at https://www.michigansthumb.com/aroundthethumb/article/A-year-of-success-with-Man-Therapy-16930341.php (accessed November 18, 2023).

Haider, M. & Kreps, G. (2004) Forty years of diffusion of innovations: utility and value in public health. *Journal of Health Communication*, 9, 3–11.

Holpuch, A. (2023) Behind the backlash against bud light's transgender influence. *New York Times*. Available at https://www.nytimes.com/2023/04/14/business/bud-light-boycott.html (accessed November 18, 2023).

Kaplan, A.M. & Haenlein, M. (2010) Users of the world, unite! The challenges and opportunities of social media. *Business Horizons*, 53(1), 59–68.

Kaspar, R. (2004) Technology and loneliness in old age. *Gerontechnology*, 3(1), 42–48.

Kietzmann, J., Hermkens, K., McCarthy, I. & Silvestre, B. (2011) Social media?: Get serious! Understanding the functional building blocks of social media. *Business Horizons*, 54(3), 241–251.

Krishnamurthy, B., Wills, C. & Zhang, Y. (2001) On the use and performance of content distribution networks. In: *Proceedings of the 1st ACM SIGCOMM Workshop on Internet Measurement*, pp. 169–182. New York: Association of Computing Machinery.

Lietsala, K. & Sirkkunen, E. (2008) Social media: introduction to the tools and processes of participatory economy. Available at http://tampub.uta.fi/bitstream/handle/10024/65560/978-951-44-7320-3.pdf?sequence=1firstmonday.org/htbin/cgiwrap/bin/ojs/index.php/fm/article/viewArticle/2138/1945 (accessed November 18, 2023).

Man Therapy (2023) About us. Available at https://man-therapy.org/about (accessed November 18, 2023).

Mangold, W.G. & Faulds, D.J. (2009) Social media: the new hybrid element of the promotion mix. *Business Horizons*, 52(4), 357–365.

Melkote, S.R. & Steeves, H.L. (2001) *Communication for Development in the Third World: Theory and Practice for Empowerment*. New Delhi: Sage Publications.

O'Reilly, T. (2007) What is Web 2.0: design patterns and business models for the next generation of software. *International Journal of Digital Economics*, 65, 17–37.

Pearce, K. (2009) Media and mass communication theories. In: S.W. Littlejohn & K.A. Foss (eds) *Encyclopedia of Communication Theory*, pp. 623–627. Thousand Oaks, CA: Sage Publications.

Phil Dub (2014) Philippe Dubost: Web product manager. Available at http://phildub.com/.

Phillips, D. & Young, P. (2009) *Online Public Relations: A Practical Guide to Developing an Online Strategy in the World of Social Media*. London: Kogan Page.

Reyes, R. (2020) Latinos boycotting Goya. *NBC News*. Available at https://www.nbcnews.com/news/latino/latinos-boycotting-goya-say-it-s-not-about-politics-it-n1234052 (accessed November 18, 2023).

Rogers, E. (1962) *Diffusion of Innovations*. New York: Free Press.

Rogers, E. (1976) Communication and development: the passing of the dominant paradigm. *Communication Research*, 3(2), 213–240.

Smith, C. (2012) "This American Life" retracts Mike Daisey story about Foxconn factory visit. Available at http://www.huffingtonpost.com/2012/03/16/this-american-life-mike-daisey-retraction-foxconn_n_1353933.html (accessed November 18, 2023).

Sprout Social (2018) Social media transparency. Available at https://sproutsocial.com/insights/data/social-media-transparency (accessed November 18, 2023).

Stratten, S. (2012) *UnMarketing: Stop Marketing. Start Engaging*. Hoboken, NJ: John Wiley & Sons, Inc.

Swales, J.M. & Rogers, P.S. (1995) Discourse and the projection of corporate culture: the mission statement. *Discourse and Society*, 6(2), 223–242.

Warren, C. (2012) Petitions demand Apple improve Foxconn conditions. Available at http://mashable.com/2012/01/31/apple-supplier-petitions (accessed November 18, 2023).

West, R. (2009) *Introducing Communication Theory: Analysis and Application*. New York: McGraw-Hill.

Wirtz, B., Schilke, O. & Ullrich, S. (2010) Strategic development of business models: implications of the Web 2.0 for creating value on the Internet. *Long Range Planning*, 43(2–3), 272–290.

Wright, D. & Hinson, M. (2008) How blogs and social media are changing public relations and the way it is practiced. *Public Relations Society of America*, 2(2), 1–21.

Wu, X. (2021) Chinese social media campaign leads to boycott of H&M and other brands over Xinjiang controversy. *Euro News*. Available at https://www.euronews.com/green/2021/03/26/chinese-social-media-campaign-leads-to-boycott-of-h-m-and-other-brands-over-xinjiang-contr (accessed November 18, 2023).

3

Establishing Community

Introduction

Chapter 2 focuses on the structure and content of social media technologies, and how media users have transformed online content from Web 1.0 messages into more interactive Web 2.0 messages. Despite the increased options for interactivity and participation, most behavior change strategies still prioritize diffusion approaches, where a single message is disseminated to a mass audience with limited opportunity for active participation. This approach proves best if your primary objective is maintaining tight control over your media message. However, a more effective and empowering approach to incite behavior change in media users is to build interest, collaboration, and dialogue through a community strategy.

This chapter explores the power of community persuasion and why individuals are so influenced by their own social networked community. Imagine a world where all mass

Strategic Social Media: From Marketing to Social Change, Second Edition. L. Meghan Mahoney and Tang Tang.
© 2024 John Wiley & Sons, Inc. Published 2024 by John Wiley & Sons, Inc.

media were social in nature. What if you turned on your television set, and your best friend was on the screen encouraging you to buy the same brand of yogurt that she eats every day? You trust her and value her opinion much more than a paid actor. For the first time in history, social media makes this type of personal network promotion possible.

Remember that social media is built around principles of interactivity, participation, creation, and exchange (Kaplan & Haenlein, 2010). These structural features are the reason that 81% of online adults utilize social networking sites (Pew Research, 2021). It is more exciting to receive media messages from those you know interpersonally and have already built a relationship with, than strangers who are trying to sell you products for profit. We tend to call the second type of messages spam.

Humans naturally seek community. Hopefully, you cherish those in your own social network and have filled it with individuals that you identify with and admire, as these are the people through which you are socially constructing your own world. This chapter explores how these same people are fueling your own consumption habits and behavioral decisions. More importantly, it explains how a marketing practitioner utilizes these social media communities to fulfill the needs and expectations of consumers.

Community Development Theory

Individuals are unable to escape the culture in which they live. You may be able to resist certain cultural rituals or expectations, but you are still very much influenced by the world and people around you. These cultural norms shape who we are and how we behave. Therefore, it is important for social media marketing practitioners to take great efforts in getting to know as much as possible about how their consumers live through a thorough audience analysis. An *audience analysis* helps practitioners identify pertinent elements regarding audience demographics and psychographics. A strong audience analysis is the greatest tool of effective strategic communication. Generally, audience research helps practitioners construct media messages that are appropriate and appealing to their target demographic. These culturally specific messages are an important part of the behavior change process.

Cultural theorists have long examined cultural insights to best identify how individuals make meaning out of situations, events, and relationships (Thompson *et al.*, 1990). This body of research demonstrates how individuals socially construct themselves through the world around them. Media is a large institution of power within the social system. Therefore, social media is a powerful vehicle for behavior change, provided producers understand the role of users.

Bandura's *social learning theory* helps explain the power media has in influencing our everyday behaviors. This theory views media users as self-developing, proactive, self-regulating, and self-reflecting. Though media does influence the way we behave, it is just one small piece of a much larger equation. Humans are not just reactive in nature (Bandura, 2004).

We are producers of social systems, rather than merely products. We comprehend and regulate our environment to make meanings regarding what we see (Bryant & Oliver, 2009). Through these experiences, we process symbols into cognitive models that serve as guides for judgment and action. How influential these experiences can be depending on personal determinants, behavioral determinants, and environmental determinants.

Social learning theory also suggests that humans learn through modeling the behaviors of others. We are very much influenced by the people in our daily lives. While media can present images and behaviors of characters to model, the real-life interpersonal relationships, and cultural norms around us provide much stronger models for how we act. It is much more persuasive to hear a recommendation from a friend than from a character on a television commercial. This is why the power of community is of such great importance to social media marketing practitioners.

Often, society loses sight of the complex sense-making process and credits media effects for poor decision making by others. Playing one violent video game will not prompt someone to act violently in real life, even if cable newscasters continually make this connection in their broadcast coverage. A person's social network and life experience play a stronger role in how they subsequently behave. However, this does not mean that as a practitioner you should not be concerned with consumer behavior change. It is just important to realize how difficult it is to influence behavior change through a single mass media message. This is why diffusion techniques so often fail to prompt change.

Organizations have always been concerned with ways to create the strongest media messages to spark behavior change. Social learning theory highlights the importance of identification in this decision-making process. People are more likely to model behavior if they identify with the person they are viewing, and if it results in valued outcomes (Bryant & Oliver, 2009). Individuals may not necessarily need to experience those same behaviors in order to make a change (Bandura, 2004). Instead, they see that someone with whom they identify enjoy success when behaving in a certain manner, and that experience becomes a part of their own cognitive process. Identification with media messages is a crucial step in the modeling process. It is essential for social media marketing practitioners to develop messages that are consistent with their target consumers' life experience.

The greatest advantage to social media marketing is that the characters portrayed on social networks are actually those within our interpersonal network. We already identify and relate with them. Social media allows you to see the behaviors of your social network in a new way. You can see your friends conduct product reviews on YouTube, brag about the large discount they received while shopping, or view photos of them at the new restaurant in town. You identify with these individuals and are prompted to engage in the same behaviors. This community dialogue promotes collective action that produces a change in behavior (Figueroa *et al.*, 2002).

Word-of-mouth marketing, where current satisfied customers recommend a service to other potential customers, has always proved a strong vehicle for sales/promotion. However, previous generations were bound by proximity to target consumers through this strategy.

Marketing practitioners could only rely on current satisfied customers to promote products to those who live in a reasonable distance from the marketplace. Today's social media landscape allows for a global marketplace where people can seek the products that best suit their needs, without the constraints of proxemics.

Community is a natural necessity for humans. It guides how we perceive our daily decision-making processes and ourselves. We grow looking to others as a model for our own behavior, and this continues as we grow. Your consumers are going to talk to each other about their experiences with your product no matter what. By promoting messages through a diffusion strategy only, you invite these conversations to happen behind a closed door. By promoting dialogue through public social media channels, you allow for increased positive word-of-mouth marketing. Additionally, you can manage and rectify any unpleasant experiences your customers may have. Diffusion strategies allow marketers to talk with a mass audience using a single media messaging platform. Community strategy allows media users to talk with each other through mediated channels.

There are many structural elements of social media that make community dialogue possible. A discussion forum is a great place for users to communicate with one another about shared goals. Other social media platforms also have their own dialogue features. One of the best places to encourage conversation is through the Instagram Stories feature. Here you can ask your consumers questions and easily poll their lifestyles and interests. Try not to use this space as a place to sell your product. Instead, keep the tone lighthearted and personal. Focus as much on your consumers as possible so that they feel as though it is their place to achieve community and engage with the person behind the brand.

There are four dimensions to establishing this sense of community with users: membership, shared emotional connection, influence, and needs fulfillment (McMillan & Chavis, 1986; see Figure 3.1). As a social media marketing/communication practitioner, it is imperative that you meet each of these dimensions for your consumers when trying to promote a space for community, as they allow individuals to share in an identity, the conditions and constraints of power, and a set of social representation, as well as allow participation from members (Campbell & Jovchelovitch, 2000).

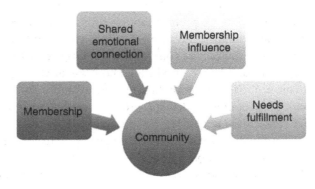

Figure 3.1   Community dimensions.

Individuals must feel as though they have done something to become a member of an organization before they feel they are a part of the community. Many organizations establish a sense of membership through frequent-buyer clubs or by sending people exclusive benefits. Traditional public relations professionals conduct audience analyses to determine which demographic, or niche, is most likely to buy their product, and then explore like-minded characteristics (age, gender, education level, and ethnicity) among these consumers to help make target decisions. While this is an effective way to target a group of consumers, with the new technologies, social media professionals can take the audience analysis one step further and target individuals.

As a marketer, you should try not to get too caught up in targeting consumers who are already likely to purchase your product or follow through with an intended behavior change. Instead, focus your energy on a secondary consumer, which does not yet know that they would benefit from your product or service. It is very likely that the individuals most inclined to seek out and buy your product will continue to do so. You want to capture the latent niche, or potential consumers. We will discuss this process further in Chapter 9.

The second critical step to establishing membership is building emotional connectedness between members. Think about the many groups and organizations that you belong to on your own social media. Chances are you have joined a community where you do not know anyone else in the group. Perhaps you only joined because a friend sent a request, and the cause was important to him or her. While there is no harm in joining, you may not feel emotionally vested in the purpose of the group or the people inside. Even though you are a member of the community, you do not identify yourself within it. Simply being a member of an organization does not make it feel like a community for users.

As you begin to target consumers online, be sure that you are not getting too obsessed with having high numbers of fans or followers. The goal of social media marketing is not to become the most popular kid on the social media playground. It is better to have fewer emotionally vested members than to have thousands of people who do not identify with your product. It is easy to gain members online. There are numerous sites you can go to, pay a sum of money, and they will increase your numbers depending on the amount of money paid. However, what does this really do for business or your organizational goals?

We learned in Chapter 2 about social penetration theory. One of the most significant indicators of relational closeness among humans is self-disclosure. The more willing one party is to be open and disclose personal private-sphere information, the closer the receiving party feels toward their relationship. Therefore, you must provide a space for dialogue that seems safe enough that community members feel emotionally safe to disclose. Being authentically passionate about your cause or mission is a great way to foster like-minded conversations.

Often media is seen as a *public sphere*, a place people gather to discuss "water cooler" issues of civic activity, such as news, politics, weather, and sports (Habermas, 1991). However, social media allows a chance for media content to center around *private sphere* issues, such as family, relationships, goals, values, and health. If a community member feels comfortable disclosing at this intimate level, members will be more likely to feel emotionally connected to the organization. There certainly is a complicated balance with the quantity of ideal social media disclosure. We all know someone in our social network who we feel discloses too much information. It can be unsafe to ask people to disclose personal information on a public forum. Thus, social media marketers need to find a balance between public and private sphere to create this emotional connectedness for their consumers.

A great way to establish this balance is to promote member influence within your organization. Make members feel as though their participation and contribution within your community matter. Ask them to share recipes, experiences, and pictures. Feature a fan of the week. Showcase a day in the life of a consumer or host an "Ask me anything" series. Let users know that you value their opinion and input. Put members at the front and center of your organization. Do not be afraid to ask for critical criticism and then embrace it.

One example of a company that rebranded itself through community influence is Weight Watchers. In 2018, after 55 years of weight loss marketing, the company Weight Watchers found themselves under scrutiny for dated calls for dieting, specifically for showing before- and after photographs in their social media posts. The company launched a marketing campaign to pivot the company from a dieting resource to a tool for managing overall health. They launched a new logo and tagline: "Wellness that works," or WW (Wischhover, 2018). By switching marketing efforts from diet management to more body positivity and wellness workshops for users, WW was able to respond to the body positivity movement and modernize their mission. This case demonstrates an important lesson for marketers: Use social media as a tool for listening and feedback.

The final stage in establishing community is needs fulfillment. Hopefully, you are confident that your product serves a purpose. This stage of community building should draw from your mission statement (see Chapter 2). Ask your consumers questions often so that you can hear how being a member of your community benefits them. Be sure to keep attention on your consumers, not your product, when communicating.

As discussed in Chapter 1, people prefer routine in their lives. It is incredibly difficult to prompt individuals to change their status quo, especially if the benefits of doing so are not presented clearly. Remember how the theory of cognitive dissonance demonstrates that humans seek consonance between their expectations and reality (Festinger, 1962). We become uncomfortable when our ideas, beliefs, values, or emotional reaction expectations are not met. If your customers receive information that is not consistent with their expectations, they will have a motivational drive to reduce dissonance by adding new cognitions or reducing importance of the dissonance element.

One of the founding goals of communication is to spark interpersonal dialogue that promotes cultural identity, trust, and commitment (Waisbord, 2001). Imagine how difficult these constructs are for an organization that consumers know is just trying to sell them a product. By relying on an individual's social network, you allow a sense of ownership to community members through the sharing and reconstructing of experiences. Rather than disseminating information from the top to the mass, communication becomes a process where everyone discusses possibilities together. This more human-centered approach believes that the role of media and technologies should be used to supplement rather than dominate interpersonal methods (Gray-Felder & Deane, 1999; Waisbord, 2001). Based on this understanding, an action plan for establishing community through social media is outlined below.

Sense of Community Action Plan

There are five steps toward maximizing a sense of community.

1 Establish criteria that individuals must meet to join your social network. Though you may lose some consumers, those that do commit will feel that their membership holds exclusivity.
2 Focus audience research on slightly less obvious secondary niche consumers. These consumers are likely not targeted by any of your competitors and could increase your return on investment.
3 Prompt dialogue between users as much as possible by asking questions. Try to center conversations on private-sphere issues, rather than public issues, when appropriate.
4 Identify key members of your community and promote them often through giveaways or feature stories.
5 Continuously monitor and evaluate how satisfied customers are with your product or service.

Community participation is empowering and allows individuals to reclaim their interests in the public sphere, reaffirms their identity in relation to other social groups, and allows for better decision-making (Campbell & Jovchelovitch, 2000). As you can imagine, individuals hate being told what to do, particularly if they feel as though they are being talked down to. Remember this when creating your social media messages. Value your users and promote community rather than top-down advertising. Perhaps most importantly, social capital values human diversity and uses participation and empowerment as formative goals of communication (Kretzmann & McKnight, 1993). Thus, once you reach a place where communication is exchanged naturally within a community, members begin to trust one another (Perkins & Long, 2002).

Behavior Change and the Power of Social Networks

Younger generations are often criticized for having too many social networks with too many online acquaintances. For example, Gen Z spends over four hours a day on social media. By comparison, only 18% of adults spend that much time online, demonstrating the generational divide when it comes to social media use (Roberts, 2023). In addition, Gen Z talks to the same friend throughout the day via text message, Snapchat, and Instagram messaging (Seemiller & Grace, 2019). This fragmentation of communication is very different from how individuals kept in touch in the past.

Putnam's (2001) book *Bowling Alone* criticizes young generations for having the lowest trends of civic engagement and social capital, citing new technologies as an eroder of social capital. It is filled with statistics showing decreased numbers of individuals marching on Washington, joining the army, and volunteering at local charity organizations. However, Gen Z should take issue with this claim. It is not as though younger consumers care less about the world they live in. Instead, their sense of community has simply shifted with the opportunities of new technology.

Today's social media users have access to more information, more people, and more cultures than any previous generation. Though they may not necessarily be volunteering at the local Red Cross, this does not mean that they are not engaged in the world. Consider your own passions and philanthropies. Maybe you are concerned with bringing clean water to developing countries (charitywater.org) or invested in the end of human trafficking (PEHT) around the world. Your sense of the world in which you live is much larger than your parents' and grandparents'. It is easy for you to find socially positive organizations that fit within your own schemata of experience today. These online causes may be far removed from your personal proxemic community, but it is still possible to feel strongly attached to the community goals and mission.

Community is no less important to Gen Z and Millennials than it was to any previous generation. Bandura (2002) explains how personal agency operates within a broad network of socio structural influences. We see and construct ourselves in relation to others. More importantly, our sense of mattering and importance also hinge on those we surround ourselves with. This has not changed. We need the community of others to understand our own selves. The ideals of our own culture help us see who we are and how we fit within it.

As consumers, we rely on others' opinions to make purchasing decisions for most of our transactions (Trusov *et al.*, 2009). Word-of-mouth marketing is 30 times stronger than traditional mass media marketing. There is no other marketing technique that provides returns this high. Word-of-mouth marketing proves influential when it comes to obtaining new customers. Regardless of what you are trying to promote online, you must be concerned with social network endorsements.

Search advertising brought in over $616 billion and is on track to surpass 1 trillion dollars by 2027 (Statista, 2023). Companies are competing to land the number one spot in search engines, particularly Google, as search is the most profitable advertising business. However, Stratten (2012) explains, through his hierarchy of buying, why this may not be the best business strategy. In order of importance, marketing strategies that bring the highest *return on investment* (ROI), or the benefit of an investment divided by the cost of the investment, include (Figure 3.2):

1   current satisfied customers;
2   referral from a trusted source;
3   current relationship but have yet to purchase;
4   recognized expert in the field;
5   search through ads; and
6   cold calls.

Figure 3.2 Hierarchy of buying. Source: Reproduced with permission of Scott Stratten.

Individuals make purchasing decisions based on their trusted personal network over experts in the field. Marketers spend millions of dollars on search engine optimization (SEO), celebrity endorsements, and traditional mass media advertising. However, marketing and communication theories demonstrate how few times these methods actually lead to human behavior change. We are much more influenced by our friends, family, and trusted social network. Diffusion techniques are not the strongest strategy for prompting permanent behavior change in media users. Let us use one of the standard lessons that a parent must teach their child as an example to illustrate how much more influential community messages are than diffusion.

Consider how you learned not to touch a hot stove when you were younger. Chances are it was done through a top-down diffusion fashion. Your guardian saw you approaching the hot stove, knew that it would hurt you, and relayed that information to you: "Don't touch that hot stove. It will hurt you." You did not need to experience this lesson on your own. Instead, it was diffused through a person you strongly identify with and trust and who holds great power over you. For many, this would be a persuasive enough message to follow through with the desired behavior change of not touching the hot stove. For others, their personality is such that it would just make them want to touch it more.

Now, let us imagine you are trying to convince an individual to make the switch from plastic to a reusable water bottle. You could just diffuse information about how bad plastic is for the environment. Maybe you could choose an influencer to diffuse the message that the individual already highly identifies with and trusts. However, most individuals have questions, or want to see more examples of how the new product would fit into their own everyday life.

Even if a trusted source of information diffuses a message in an authoritative top-down fashion, it may not be persuasive enough to promote behavior change in a community setting. If all your new friends that you strongly identify with, feel connected to, and are invested in emotionally, take turns touching a hot stove, you may be likely to touch it yourself, despite your guardian's previous warnings. We enjoy feeling as though we are part of a community and do not want to do anything to jeopardize this. Even though a very strong diffusion message from a trusted source was effective, a social community provides a stronger call to action.

The potential of community messages is great news for social media practitioners. Social media campaigns are cost effective and efficient. Regardless of your industry, it is not only important that users feel as though they play an important role in your community but that you also play an important role in theirs. One way you can do this is by increasing your authenticity and message branding.

Brand Authenticity

Chapter 2 discussed the importance of transparency when it comes to media messages. Transparency helps build trust and connection between the source and receiver of messages. However, while constructing these messages, it is important to consider the authenticity of your brand. Brand authenticity will help your consumers better understand who you are and what you are trying to market.

Authenticity is about being yourself and harnessing what you uniquely bring to the table. As Stratten and Stratten (2016) said, "If you're your authentic self, you have no competition." There are unlimited companies and products being sold online. Chances are, whatever it is you are trying to sell (your employment, a service, and merchandise) someone else is already selling it. However, there is something unique and special about your contribution to the field. When it comes to successful social media promotion in today's media environment, it is important to "niche down". Thus, focus on what you uniquely bring to the market.

Authenticity deals with a company's objective, ownership, consumer experiences, identity construction, and confirmation (Leigh *et al.*, 2006). It has many definitions in psychology, communication, and marketing literature. Every organization has a story to tell. Consider how your story reflects the values and personality that you are trying to relay to your consumers. You want your customers to feel a certain way about you whenever they read or see your media messages. These decisions should engineer how people think and feel about your brand whatever product you are selling (Holt, 2002). Once you have a sense of your organizational authenticity, you can begin your message branding strategy.

The American Marketing Association (AMA) defines *branding* as the name, term, design, symbol, or any other feature that identifies one seller's goods or service as distinct from those of other sellers. Think of authenticity as what makes your organization unique from other competitors and your brand as how you are going to demonstrate your uniqueness to consumers.

Consumers should be able to distinguish your products and services from other companies through six variables: physique, personality, culture, relationship, reflection, and self-image (Kapferer, 1997). If they are not able to do this, there is more work to be done on your branding strategy. Be sure to monitor and evaluate your brand often (Figure 3.3).

Integrity must be the pillar of your brand. Most often, if you are not honest with yourself, there will be a disconnect between your authenticity and the product or service that you offer. One great way to ensure the authenticity of your brand is through storytelling.

Storytelling has evolved as one of our most primary, powerful, and persuasive forms of communication (Ohler, 2008). Individuals have always told narratives based on the culture of folklore passed from generation to generation. Stories reflect the values and ideologies within society, and therefore become incredibly valuable to how we make everyday life decisions. Through the deepest roots of humanity, stories were told orally and passed down through generations of families. Today, media has allowed us to record these stories. Just because these stories are being told through a different medium, their value is not at all diminished; in fact, many would claim social media amplifies our desire to narrate our own stories.

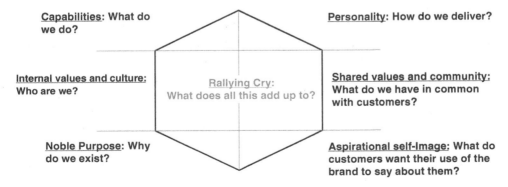

Capabilities: What do we do?

Personality: How do we deliver?

Internal values and culture: Who are we?

Rallying Cry: What does all this add up to?

Shared values and community: What do we have in common with customers?

Noble Purpose: Why do we exist?

Aspirational self-Image: What do customers want their use of the brand to say about them?

Figure 3.3   Brand identity framework. Source: Copyright © 2015 Brand Amplitude, LLC. All rights reserved. Adapted from J.-N. Kapferer, Brand identity prism. *The New Strategic Brand Management*, 2012, 156. Reproduced with permission of Carol Phillips.

Folklore is the art of storytelling within a culture. Through folklore, a similar lesson, theme, or structure pattern is resembled, recycled, and retaught, providing cultural continuity (Patterson, 2006). Folklore consolidates the interaction of literary and oral, professional and nonprofessional, formal and informal, constructed and improvised creativity (Degh, 1994). These media messages represent similar structure and content that provide guides for the way a culture behaves. The more you understand your target consumers' culture, the more you are able to tap into these patterns of behavior.

People learn through stories, so it only makes sense that you provide one for your company. Discuss who you are, what goals you have, and why they are important to you and your consumers. Many successful organizations have started with a story. For example, TOMS Shoes began when the owner traveled to Argentina in 2006 and witnessed the hardships of children without shoes. Ikea owner, Ingvar Kamprad, began selling matches from bulk to neighbors in Småland, Sweden. These stories stay with people and create a much longer-lasting emotional connection than would a bullet point list do. Determine your authenticity and then build a brand that helps tell your story. Finally, and most importantly, allow your consumers to share their experiences and narratives through social media.

Move beyond the constant top-down diffusion of your messages. Remember that your social media sites really should not focus on you or your product. Your diffusion site (likely your home website) is the space for these types of messages. Social media should be about community, dialogue, and participation. People do not want to be sold to all the time. Having a designated place where individuals can go to learn as much information about your product as possible allows you to use social media as a place to build relationships and have dialogue with customers. Social media sites should be filled with questions for users to answer. Most of these questions should have nothing to do with your product, but instead build your authenticity.

For example, if you work for a restaurant that only sells organic food, ask customers questions such as "Why is eating organic food important to you?" or "Share your favorite all-natural food recipe." Your role is not to be an expert, but to facilitate authentic dialogue and help create a space for community. By allowing your consumers to talk to each other, you are allowing the possibility for these cultural dialogue patterns to emerge naturally about a topic that is important to the brand and consumers alike.

Increasing participation and dialogue by users via social media requires you to give up some control over your messages. Your consumers will likely not say the exact things that you hope them to say. In fact, sometimes they will say things that you really wish they would not. As such, before opening your social media to increased dialogue, it is imperative that you have a strong diffusion strategy already in place. Have clear, transparent messages that answer any questions that users may have. Use diffusion to link people back to your website. Once strong consistent social channels are established, and you have acquired a loyal target following, it is time to begin your community strategy.

If your community strategy prompts a surplus of negative commentary, reflect on the product that you are providing, rather than shutting the dialogue down. Try your best not to edit or censor user dialogue unless it is obscene and/or disrespectful to other community members. The more you are able to facilitate the direction of conversation through prompts the better. Of course, the more natural the conversations that take place, the greater insights you have into how your target consumers think, act, and value. When used appropriately, social media is an inexpensive marketing research tool into the cultural norms and expectations of your consumers (we will discuss more about social media monitor and research in Chapter 12).

Case Study: KFC Secret Menu

As discussed, community is established through four dimensions: membership, shared emotional connection, influence, and needs fulfillment (McMillan & Chavis, 1986). Most marketers fall into the trap of using social media to increase the membership of their community. However, this is not a very effective strategy if the other three dimensions of community are absent. One of the most effective strategies for encouraging community among users is to observe what users are sharing and creating.

The TikTok food community often shares inspiration or creative ways to enhance their meals. One recent trend on the platform is for users to share menu hacks for other people to try at various chain restaurants (TikTok, 2023). Understanding the influence of exclusivity to membership, fast-food chain KFC jumped on this trend by partnering with TikTok food influencer @jen.heifer to promote secret menu items using the branded hashtag challenge #KFCSecretMenuHack (see Figure 3.4).

One goal of the KFC Secret Menu campaign is to encourage users to download the fast-food chain's mobile app. The company could have used social media to deliver diffusion messages to make users aware of the app and encourage them to take efforts

Figure 3.4 Screenshot of the KFC Secret Menu campaign mobile application.

to make the change. Often, fast-food chains bribe users with discounts or promotions to claim freebies by downloading their mobile apps. However, only 23% of users keep the app within the first three days after download (Caples, 2021). KFC decided to use a more community strategy via social media that hits on the dimensions of membership, shared emotional connection, influence, and needs fulfillment.

Based on the trending food hack social media phenomenon, KFC decided to hide their hack creations in a secret menu that can only be found within the KFC App and did not promote the new products through social media message diffusion. Instead, they waited for TikTok users to share the discovery that they found on their own, not something they were told to do in a top-down manner. This ownership of social content fuels more authentic marketing of the secret menu from users' own social network and algorithm. Additionally, every time the secret menu is updated, the conversation is reengaged without spending any advertising money (Caples, 2021). While most other businesses beg customers to download their mobile applications, KFC consumers are drawn to the app through a more organic and engaging message.

This secret menu campaign works for KFC, given the demographic of their target consumers. The company followed trends and social media behaviors that the target demographic naturally engages. While it is unlikely for someone outside of this demographic who may not follow TikTok to hear about the secret menu, the exclusivity of information is worthwhile to drive sales.

There are hundreds of popular fast-food chains across the world. It is important for KFC to find its authenticity to reach the niche of individuals who may become brand advocates for their products. KFC's authenticity boasts a rich, decades-long history of success and innovation (KFC, 2023). The KFC secret menu marketing campaign certainly aligns with their mission and engages with the young target demographic. Consumers can join the KFC community through app membership, sharing an emotional connection over the excitement of #foodhack TikTok trends, influencing the community by sharing content when new items are added, and fulfilling needs with new food trends.

Discussion questions

1 Reflect on ways that KFC was able to meet the four criteria of community (dimensions of membership) through their secret menu campaign. What is the authenticity of KFC and how does it differ from other fast-food brands?
2 Who do you feel are the target consumers of KFC? How does the secret menu campaign seek out their digital behaviors and trends?
3 What is your favorite brand (business/organization) on social media? How do they use social media to build brand authenticity?

Summary

It has always been difficult for marketers to promote community among consumers because there was no efficient or cost-effective technology for dialogue to take place. Marketing practitioners were only able to measure the success of their messages by sales or direct customer feedback. Social media has changed the exclusivity of mass media, and now individuals are able to communicate on an intimate level with organizations online.

Social learning theory shows us how individuals make decisions through modeling the behaviors of others. Mass media messages have always been a part of this process, but those messages included characters that were not a part of our own real-life social network. Social media has allowed this distinction to merge, as users are able to receive messages from individuals that they are already networked with on a personal level. These messages become a part of the cognitive process and help to construct reality.

Our sense of membership, shared emotional connection, influence, and needs fulfillment are all crucial factors to how influenced we are within a community. One of the most significant indicators of relational closeness within a community is self-disclosure. The more willing individuals are to open-up and discuss private-sphere issues, the more emotionally vested they, and the other members of the group, will feel.

The value of member participation and contribution cannot be understated. One must constantly seek feedback and critiques from community members so that they feel as though they are a critical part of its success. However, this requires organizations to give up some level of message control that strict diffusion allows. Social media marketing practitioners must be confident in the brand authenticity of their messages to engage on this level of participation.

One way to ensure success is to share your narrative. This narrative will allow your consumers to identify with your story and provide the chance for you to explain your authenticity, or niche within the market. This more human-centered approach supplements, rather than dominates, interpersonal networks. Be sure to consider how this story reflects the individuals and personality, or brand, of your product.

Research demonstrates the power of word-of-mouth marketing through current satisfied customers. Social networks are creating personal agency through sociostructural influences. Your consumers are more likely to make purchasing decisions based on their trusted personal network than they are through experts in the field or information that they seek through search engines.

The power of social network in our everyday decision making is huge. Social media allows marketers a space to harness this networked power and allows consumers the chance to talk to each other about their experiences. Do not waste your chance by only diffusing information in a top-down manner. Be confident enough in your product to lose a little control so that your community can become empowered and participatory (Table 3.1).

Table 3.1   Community: An online space where users engage in transactional dialogue about a shared topic or interest.

Pros	Cons
Out-of-the-box feedback	More niche consumers
Strong consumer identification with a brand	Requires careful monitoring and frequent feedback
Higher behavior change yield	Loses some control over messages

Social learning theory taught us how individuals make meanings and decisions regarding their lives based on what they see. These cognitive models serve as guides for judgment and action. Yes, media do present images, messages, and behaviors, but these experiences tend not to be as powerful vehicles for behavior change as actual real-life lived realities.

Consider the example above of the parent teaching a child not to touch a hot stove. While a person's individual community is a stronger form of persuasion than a top-down diffusion message, social learning theory taught us that the biggest driver of decision making is personal experience. That is why most people do not touch a hot stove more than once. Once you have experienced the painful feeling of getting burnt, it does not matter what information a person in power diffuses, or what your individual social network says. You make the decision based on your own schema of events. You touched the hot stove. You know what it felt like. You know that there is little, if any, reward in doing so. You are not going to do it again.

These types of experienced decisions are much more likely to be permanent models for behavior change and are one of the most difficult constructs to establish through social media. How do you get someone to have a real-life experience through a computer screen? This construct is also the furthest to the right on our social media continuum, meaning that it lends very little control of the media message to the producer. However, if you are successfully able to mobilize your media users, there is nothing more powerful for permanent behavior change. Let us now turn our attention to social media mobilization in Chapter 4.

Key Takeaways

1   When prompting behavior change through media, it is important that individuals identify with your messages. A comprehensive audience analysis can help ensure this.
2   Social media allows a unique opportunity for an individual's social network to share their product experiences with the public and with each other.
3   Community is a more participatory approach to marketing, and thus it is a more powerful tool than diffusion-centric approaches in behavior change. It includes four dimensions: membership, shared emotional connection, influence, and needs fulfillment.

4 Be confident in your product to lose a little message control and encourage more participatory and community-oriented social media marketing efforts.

5 Your social media sites should not focus on you or your product. Tell your brand story and invite your consumers to share their stories/experiences with your product.

References

Bandura, A. (2002) Social cognitive theory of mass communication. In: J. Bryant & D. Zillmann (eds) *Media Effects: Advances in Theory and Research*, pp. 121–153. Mahwah, NJ: Lawrence Erlbaum Associates.

Bandura, A. (2004) Health promotion by social cognitive means. *Health Education and Behavior*, 31, 143–164.

Bryant, J. & Oliver, M.B. (2009) *Media Effects: Advances in Theory and Research*. New York: Routledge.

Campbell, C. & Jovchelovitch, S. (2000) Health, community and development: towards a social psychology of participation. *Journal of Community and Applied Social Psychology*, 10(4), 255–270.

Caples (2021) KFC secret menu. Available at https://caples.org/2020-winners-results/?id=241&cat=Radical%20new%20strategy (accessed November 17, 2023).

Degh, L. (1994) *American Folklore and the Mass Media*. Bloomington, IN: Indiana University Press.

Festinger, L. (1962) *A Theory of Cognitive Dissonance*. Stanford, CA: Stanford University Press.

Figueroa, M., Kincaid, D., Rani, M. & Lewis, G. (2002) Communication for social change: an integrated model for measuring the process and its outcomes. New York: The Rockefeller Foundation. Available at http://www.communicationforsocialchange.org/pdf/socialchange.pdf (accessed November 17, 2023).

Gray-Felder, D. & Deane, J. (1999) Communication and social change: a position paper and conference report. New York: The Rockefeller Foundation. Available at http://www.communicationforsocialchange.org/publications-resources?itemid=14 (accessed November 17, 2023).

Habermas, J. (1991) *The Structural Transformation of the Public Sphere: An Inquiry into a Category of Bourgeois Society*. Cambridge, MA: MIT Press.

Holt, D.B. (2002) Why do brands cause trouble? A dialectical theory of consumer culture and branding. *Journal of Consumer Research*, 29(1), 70–90.

Kapferer, J.-N. (1997) *Strategic Brand Management*. London: Kogan Page.

Kaplan, A.M. & Haenlein, M. (2010) Users of the world, unite! The challenges and opportunities of social media. *Business Horizons*, 53(1), 59–68.

KFC (2023) About. Available at https://www.kfc.com/about (accessed November 17, 2023).

Kretzmann, J. & McKnight, J. (1993) *Building Communities from the Inside Out: A Path Toward Finding and Mobilizing a Community's Assets*. Chicago: ACTA Publications.

Leigh, T.W., Peters, C. & Shelton, J. (2006) The consumer quest for authenticity: the multiplicity of meanings within the MG subculture of consumption. *Journal of the Academy of Marketing Science*, 34(4), 481–493.

McMillan, D. & Chavis, D. (1986) Sense of community: a definition and theory. *Journal of Community Psychology*, 14, 6–23.

Ohler, J. (2008) *Digital Storytelling in the Classroom: New Media Pathways to Literacy, Learning and Creativity*. Thousand Oaks, CA: Corwin Press.

Patterson, B. (2006) Historical Viewpoint on Television, Folklore. Available at http://houstonianonline.com/2006/02/16/historical-viewpoint-on-television-folklore (accessed November 17, 2023).

Perkins, D. & Long, D. (2002) Neighborhood sense of community and social capital: a multi-level analysis. In: A. Fisher, C. Sonn & B. Bishop (eds) *Psychological Sense of Community: Research, Applications, and Implications*, pp. 291–318. New York: Plenum.

Pew Research (2021) Social networking fact sheet. Available at https://www.pewresearch.org/internet/fact-sheet/social-media/ (accessed November 17, 2023).

Putnam, R. (2001) *Bowling Alone: The Collapse and Revival of American Community*. New York: Simon & Schuster.

Roberts, J. (2023) Where does Gen Z spend the majority of their time online? Available at https://later.com/blog/gen-z-social-media-usage/#:~:text=Morning%20Consult%20reports%20that%2038,differences%20when%20using%20social%20media (accessed November 17, 2023).

Seemiller, C. & Grace, M. (2019) *Gen Z: A Century in the Making*. New York: Routledge.

Statista (2023) Digital advertising in the United States. Available at https://www.statista.com/topics/1176/online-advertising/#topicOverview.

Stratten, S. (2012) *UnMarketing: Stop Marketing. Start Engaging*. Hoboken, NJ: John Wiley & Sons, Inc.

Stratten, S. & Stratten, A. (2016) *UnMarketing: Everything Has Changed and Nothing Is Different*. Hoboken, NJ: John Wiley & Sons, Inc.

Thompson, M., Ellis, R. & Wildavsky, A. (1990) *Cultural Theory*. Boulder, CO: Westview Press.

TikTok (2023) Kentucky fried secrets. Available at https://www.tiktok.com/business/en-US/blog/kfc-secret-menu-hacks (accessed November 17, 2023).

Trusov, M., Bucklin, R.E. & Pauwels, K. (2009) Effects of word-of-mouth versus traditional marketing: findings from an internet social networking site. *Journal of Marketing*, 73(5), 90–102.

Waisbord, S. (2001) Family tree of theories, methodologies and strategies in communication for development. Rockefeller Foundation. Available at http://www.communicationforsocialchange.org/pdf/familytree.pdf (accessed November 17, 2023).

Wischhover, C. (2018) As "dieting" becomes more taboo, Weight Watchers is changing its name. *Vox*. Available at https://www.vox.com/the-goods/2018/9/24/17897114/weight-watchers-ww-wellness-rebranding (accessed November 17, 2023).

4

Mobilizing Your Users

Learning Objectives

After reading this chapter, you should be able to:

1   Mobilize your social media users into action through strategic messages.
2   Understand how user-generated content empowers media users into action.
3   Create a mobilization social media strategy that encourages users to interact with your social media sites and engage in offline advocacy.

Introduction

Social media is designed for users to engage in dialogue and participate with each other online. However, the goal of most marketing campaigns is to get people offline and mobilize them toward real-life behavior change. Most notably, companies are hoping to prompt consumers to purchase their product. Previous chapters have demonstrated the potential of social media in equalizing relationships between previous institutions of power and everyday citizens (Neuhauser & Kreps, 2003; Raftery, 1991; Weisbrod, 1991). Though the relationship between consumers and marketers may never be equalized, social media is certainly changing expectations.

Strategic Social Media: From Marketing to Social Change, Second Edition. L. Meghan Mahoney and Tang Tang.
© 2024 John Wiley & Sons, Inc. Published 2024 by John Wiley & Sons, Inc.

Top-down diffusion messages can easily reach a large number of people. Though the potential for behavior change is not great, diffusion is the most secure way to control your messages. However, by always playing it safe, you may be missing the real potential of social media marketing. Community strategies allow media users the ability to provide feedback and communicate directly with each other about issues they are vested in. This increases the amount of identification that users have with a product and allows recommendations to come from a personal network, rather than a top-down source.

Participatory social media has transformed audiences into more educated, empowered, and motivated Internet users (Boulos & Wheeler, 2007). This change provides social media marketers an opportunity to make a huge difference in their consumers and the real world around them through mobilization approaches.

This chapter explores various methods for social participation. How can marketers get social media users offline and use social media to prompt real-life interaction, engagement, and promote products? Chapters 2 and 3 explained how most behavior change interventions fail because of the oversaturation of media, with very few options for user feedback and interaction. While traditional media is limited in its ability to encourage interpersonal dialogue and reach many people at the same time, social media can bridge this gap. By allowing users to take control over social media messages, everyday consumers could be transformed into lifetime brand advocates.

Social Media Mobilization

One of the greatest advancements of social media is the ability for collective action. Often, social movements fueled through new communication technologies are called cyberactivism, which changes the landscape of collective action (Eltantawy & Wiest, 2011). Howard (2011) defines *cyberactivism* as the act of using the Internet to advance a political cause that is difficult to advance offline. This concept of collective action has been studied for half a century, guided by the *resource mobilization theory*. Though often criticized, the premise of resource mobilization theory is that desire, dissent, and attitude change are not enough to spark social change, but resources such as time, money and organizational skills are critical for a successful social movement (Jenkins, 1983; McCarthy & Zald, 1977).

Mobilization is defined as the process by which candidates, parties, activists, and groups induce other people to participate (Rosenstone & Hansen, 1993). Mobilization research generally examines large social movements and activism and deals with the planning, execution, and facilitation of these actions. Mobilization is an important concept to turn to if you are interested in inciting behavior change through social media messages because the premise for any successful behavior change through media messages requires both the advancing of media messages and an execution/facilitation strategy.

It is not enough to simply pique someone's interest in your product. While in isolation your message may be interesting enough to prompt behavior change, unfortunately consumers are bombarded with media messages all day. Users will read your direct social media message while waiting at the bus stop, on their way to work, while simultaneously answering emails and looking at a friend's Instagram pictures. By the time they have any free time, they have heard hundreds of additional requests and have forgotten all about your message. Thus, marketing practitioners must provide enough resources to make mobilization as easy as possible right when consumers first encounter your message.

While social media has undoubtedly reinvented activism, it has also made it easier for users to hide behind a screen. Malcolm Gladwell (2010) argues that the weak ties of social connections seldom lead to high-risk activism. This is partially due to the comfort that users feel when sticking to their technology and the discomfort when leaving it to experience new and uncertain behaviors. Social media makes it easy for users to diffuse messages, but harder for these messages to have a lasting impact on human behavior change.

Universities often struggle with this premise in their recruitment efforts. To experience university life, students must complete a comprehensive, arduous, and sometimes expensive application process. For years, university recruiters have attempted to bridge this gap through media messages that promote community. They disseminate brochures showing current students "just like you" have a great time in their facilities. However, rather than diffusing information about a student "just like you," why not use social media to encourage students to have those experiences prior to being admitted as an official student? Admission offices are now seeing the power of using social media to prompt individuals to put down the brochure, come to campus, and attend free open houses, sit in on classes, shadow faculty, and try out facilities like state-of-the-art rock-climbing walls. These experiences do so much more for individual decision-making processes than a single brochure. It is clear that media messages cannot compete with a great real-life experience.

For decades, mass media was primarily used as a vehicle to get the message out to hundreds of thousands of people (Stone, 1993). This process has been dubbed "push and pray" in the marketing realm (Stratten, 2012). As we learned in Chapter 2, push-and-pray marketing (Figure 4.1) is when practitioners try to reach as many users as possible

Figure 4.1   Push-and-pray marketing.

Figure 4.2   Pull-and-stay marketing.

(cold calling, radio broadcast, television commercials, email spam) in the hope that a small portion of that audience will follow through with the request in the message.

Nonetheless, social media allows us the chance to use media for critiquing, disrupting, and organizing. Why not provide users the chance to utilize the media in a way that they choose? Pull-and-stay marketing (Figure 4.2) allows practitioners to use media to listen and engage conversations. Here, users opt into receiving media content from an organization. This facilitation will bring the right consumers to you with a strong sense of trust and connection. Handing control over to users will empower them toward much larger and more impactful behavior change tactics. Let us examine how Chinese government shifts their Weibo social media strategy from push-and-pray to pull-and-stay marketing to alter behavior change practices in digital messages.

Traditional Chinese media channels are known for using didactic hard persuasion to communicate with citizens (Zhang *et al.*, 2023). However, given the rise of Weibo, a popular social media microblogging site, official Chinese media channels have been forced to adopt their communication strategy to fit the softened emotional tone of digital users. Rather than pushing prescriptive hard propaganda and coercion messages that people have come to expect in print and television news, Chinese state-run social media have adapted much softer emotional mobilization messages through their Weibo accounts. This communication invites users to follow the accounts as a resource in local and national dialogue, leading toward strong trust and connection. Ultimately, this trust will result in stronger behavior change, as users feel more in charge of their media content. As such, Weibo was a primary social media outlet for Chinese government to disseminate information about COVID-19 protocols.

Social media provides the tools for mobilization, by connecting individuals with a larger social network that feels the same way and ready to take action. It has distinct inherent properties for facilitating real-life participation. One of the oldest social media platforms, Meetup.com, is built on the premise of interest-based networking. Individuals with the same interests can find each other, locate based on proximity, and facilitate real-life gatherings that would have otherwise been very difficult to organize. The website's tagline describes Meetup as "neighbors getting together to learn something, do something, share something," which clearly demonstrates the power of social media to get people offline and create interpersonal experiences.

Boyd (2011) explains how social media technology enables user action through its design of three types of integrated affordances: profiles, friends list, and tools of communication. Profiles constitute the space where conversations, both synchronous and asynchronous, take place. These profiles allow individuals the opportunity to create their identity, whether real or idealized. Here, users can provide as much information as they choose and tell others what they feel is most important about themselves and their interests.

Social connections that users choose to opt into are the most critical part of social networks, as simply creating a social networking profile does not constitute a social experience. Often, users who create profiles but do not follow or participate with others' posts are called media lurkers (Crawford, 2009). They do not contribute or take anything from social media, and thus have little value to marketers.

Often there is great hype and excitement surrounding the release of a new social networking site, such as BeReal. However, regardless of the innovative features for network and connection of the new social media platforms, early users who migrate to the social platform may find little use and value in the sites given the limited friend connections that they have. Until a person establishes online connections with other users, there is not much they can do to enjoy a new platform. A social media site is only as good as the people we can connect with. That is why it is so difficult to launch a new successful social networking platform that can compete with the more established ones, such as X (formerly Twitter) or Instagram.

In addition to user profile and friends list, the tools of communication are really what allow users to communicate and organize themselves in a public or semi-public forum. These structures allow people to connect to the local and global and lead to collective outcomes (Enjolras *et al.*, 2013). These communication structures also provide some regulation to the spaces of communication. Without regulation, communities are likely to succumb to spam and "trolls," persistent posters of malicious or purposefully distracting comments (Gowers & Nielsen, 2009).

Once these structures are put into place (profiles, friends list, and tools of communication), the possibilities for mobilization are endless. The result of these features creates a more empowered and motivated action, as users do not feel as though they are being forced or prompted to do something. The action is the result of users' own ideas, collaboration, and efforts. These collective outcomes are the most powerful kinds of behavior change and should be the goal of every social media marketer.

The Power of User-Generated Content

We have discussed in great length the inverse relationship between control and participatory messages. The more control you have over the message, the less participatory it proves in nature. However, it is important to note that these are not mutually exclusive entities. A social media message should be good at message diffusion, community, and mobilization.

We have also discussed how participatory means promoting the greatest likelihood for human behavior change. *Participatory communication* includes any process through which people define themselves, what they need and how to get there, through dialogue (Byrne *et al.*, 2005). It utilizes dialogue that leads to the collective solutions to problems. Social media provides a great resource for this initial step.

It is very easy to go into a community and tell individuals what they should do. However, if you are searching for a lasting and even permanent behavior change, this is not the best persuasion tactic. In a study by Husain and Shaikh (2005), a village was given condoms free of cost. While many users took advantage of this opportunity, researchers found that the likelihood of using the condom increased if the individual had to pay for it, rather than receiving it for free. This is consistent with the premise of participatory communication because by purchasing the condom an individual is taking part and becoming an advocate for the cause. Individuals want an egalitarian solution and to be a part of the change (Dutta, 2006). Active participation is critical to the readjustment of structural forces that exist as the core of the problem. Social participation, a combination of mass dissemination and media engagement, has proven the most efficient and effective way to spark behavior change in communication and development literature (Waisbord, 2001). Here, media users are addressed in a bottom-up manner, rather than talked down to by media messages (Gray-Felder & Deane, 1999; Morris, 2003).

Sterne (2010) describes social media participation in marketing as providing consumers the opportunity to visit, click, retweet, post, comment, rate, and bookmark products. While this type of transactional feedback interaction is important, it also mirrors the same traditional top-down communication process (Bandura, 2004). Users have much more to offer than simply interacting with predetermined text. Allowing users to engage in transactional feedback is not enough to ignite permanent behavior change, especially in a media context where this type of engagement is the norm for today's media users. Social media marketing must mirror the same trends and involve participant dialogue and user engagement in every step of the process, including product and message design, transforming consumers into message advocates (Waisbord, 2001). You need to encourage consumers to move beyond content participation and move toward content creation.

In previous chapters, we have talked about that individuals learn best through modeling the behaviors of their own culture and environment. While some of these behaviors are learned through media messages, most of our behaviors are learned from direct observation of those in our interpersonal lives and our own lived experiences. We used the example of learning not to touch a hot stove to demonstrate how once you live out the experience of getting burnt, there is little message diffusion or community persuasion that will convince you to touch the hot stove again. The goal of social media marketing should thus be to provide users with a real-life lived experience. This strategy will prove stronger than other more diffusion and community-centric messages.

Marketers have used this "real-life experience" strategy to market products for years. This is why infomercials urge you to try their product out for free with no commitment.

This strategy is built on the premise that your real-life experience during the trial period will provide you with positive schemata of reference and to return the product would create great dissonance. Once users have a pleasant experience with a product, it is difficult to turn away. Research shows how simply allowing consumers to experience touching a product significantly increases their likelihood to purchase (Citrin *et al.*, 2003).

Of course, this creates challenges for social media marketers. It is impossible to allow Internet users to have a real-life lived experience online. Therefore, marketers should stop using the medium to tell users how wonderful their product is but should instead encourage users to sign offline and try the product out for themselves as easy as possible.

Heilman *et al.* (2011) investigated the power of in-store free samples of food products and their influence on subsequent purchasing behavior. Results of their study demonstrate how providing free real-life samples of food significantly increases the likelihood of shoppers buying a product that they otherwise would not have purchased. There was an even greater likelihood of a customer purchasing the food if a person was interacting with consumers in addition to the free sample. This finding is consistent with the idea of an interpersonal network influencing behavior change. Marketers must use social media as a space for consumers to share their real-life experiences with their personal network through community approaches.

Consumers like to be in control of their own media consumption. Uses and gratifications research shows how user characteristics and personal motivations influence exposure and consequent attitudes (Haridakis & Rubin, 2005). Users select media that gratify their needs, and the more motivated they are by that gratification, the stronger the experience. (We will discuss more about uses and gratifications research and social media uses in Chapter 5.) This includes a user's locus of control (Potter, 1988).

Locus of control is a trait personality that reflects one's conceptualization of who controls the events in one's own life (Haridakis & Hanson, 2009). Those who believe that they hold power over external circumstances are more internally controlled. Those who believe that things such as fate, luck, and other people act as controllers of their lives prove more externally controlled (Levenson, 1974). Locus of control has also been positively associated with the amount of media consumption and involvement in social activities (Levenson, 1974). It is an incredible tool for mobilization. Therefore, it makes sense to turn to locus of control when interested in behavior change through media messages.

The goal of social media messages should be to make your community feel as though they have a strong locus of control. Singhal and Rogers (2003) explain how most communication interventions fail because technocrats design them based on their own personal view of reality. Instead, you should allow for true participation, where users, individually and collectively, are able to reflect on their social situation and articulate their own discontent and action. One way to achieve this is through user-generated content (UGC).

Today, hundreds of millions of Internet users are self-publishing consumers. As discussed in Chapter 2, UGC fulfills three requirements: (i) is published on a publicly accessible website or on a social networking site accessible to a selected group of people;

(ii) shows a certain amount of creative effort; and (iii) needs to have been created outside of professional routines and practices (Kaplan & Haenlein, 2010). One of the largest and oldest UGC social media sites, YouTube, promotes users to "Remember that this is your community! Each and every user of YouTube makes the site what it is, so don't be afraid to dig in and get involved" (Van Dijck, 2009). However, it was not until the fastest growing social media app in history, TikTok emerged, that everyday users really began participating more in social media video creation (Koyak, 2021). Given the ease and structure of the TikTok video creation process, it became easier for everyday users to share their creative efforts without needing strong video editing skills. Mobilization requires a small ask of users to ensure strong participation.

Unlike diffusion and community strategy, mobilization most often occurs on a user's own social media page, rather than through dialogue on a brand or organizational account. Having users share with their own social network makes the experience much more authentic and memorable. They get interaction and feedback with the people that they know and hold the strongest connections with. Based on this information, the following mobilization action plan can be put into place.

Mobilization Action Plan

There are four steps toward maximizing an action in users through social media.

1 Ensure that your social media allows users to create their own user profiles, connect with friends, and provides tools of communication where users can share and organize themselves. This can either be done on an existing social media site (such as Instagram or TikTok) or a new application designed specifically for your organization and customers.

2 Encourage participatory communication that allows users to define themselves, their needs, and the resources needed to get there. Communicate with them often, but do not control conversations. Really listen to what your consumers are saying. Allow conversations to emerge naturally from your consumers.

3 Treat your consumer like an informed person, not a passive audience that needs information. Provide enough resources so that if they invest time or resources, they can make decisions on their own. This will create a stronger locus of control and will transform consumers into stronger brand advocates. Ask their opinions often and treat them like the experts of your organization.

4 Prompt social participation, where you are combining social media content with interpersonal behaviors. This can be done utilizing UGC. Allow your consumers to participate in "real-life" offline behaviors, such as creating a video, sharing pictures, voting in a poll, or developing a product. Mobilization campaign hashtags are a great tool for tracking these conversations.

Clearly, creating social media content becomes a much more powerful part of our schemata for interpretation. Once your consumers invest their own time, energy, and sometimes even money, the stakes are higher. These efforts become a part of their life experience and personal identity, and thus play a critical role in brand advocacy.

Offline Brand Advocacy

The purpose of any social media campaign should be to encourage message creation by users. As a social media marketing practitioner, you should constantly encourage users to comment, respond, and interact with your content. In addition to this online participation, your consumers may get so vested in this community that they become brand advocates offline as well.

One company that has been able to integrate their online and offline marketing is Cadbury Chocolate. The chocolatier is most known for their milk chocolate Easter crème eggs. To promote the product during its peak spring season, Cadbury created a Worldwide Hide mobilization campaign. The global Easter egg hunt allows users to hide a virtual purple egg anywhere in the world through the digital Google Maps Street View Platform interface (Cadbury, 2023). They can then send a personalized clue to a friend or family member, and when found, the hider can choose to send a real egg to their loved one. The campaign follows a bottom-up communication model, with users deciding when and where the eggs will be hidden. Additionally, the campaign is synchronous and requires users to be more active in the information exchange process. This real-life campaign creates a much stronger schemata for participating consumers to associate with the Cadbury brand.

Every social media campaign, regardless of the purpose, should urge users to do the same. You want your product to be a part of your consumers' everyday experiences. Mobilization extends beyond just clicking and interacting. It is about asking users to generate new content and to share it as part of their own message. The opportunity for mobilization is only possible if companies are willing to give up control of their brand narrative and allow users to not only participate but also design, create, and produce media content. As such, mobilization campaigns tend not to run year-round. Instead, organizations plan for a timed social media mobilization campaign during select times of the year. Cadbury holds the global egg hunt each Easter for only a few weeks. Mobilization takes great effort and really leaves a lot of brand control in the hands of users. Given the decrease in control, mobilization requires a strong and trusted mission statement. For mobilization to be successful, your consumers must understand the authenticity of your brand, identify with the lifestyle, and want to share it with their own network. With this type of strategy, a Cadbury chocolate egg can become a tool for connection.

TOMS shoes also effectively integrates online and offline in their marketing strategy. TOMS is built on a *contributory consumption* business model, where if a customer purchases a product, the organization donates something to a cause. TOMS calls this a "One for One" model, where an individual purchases a pair of shoes, and the company gives a pair of shoes to a person in need. Beyond a great brand narrative (CEO Blake Mycoskie traveled to Argentina, where he saw children living without shoes and decided to do something about it), TOMS has been able to integrate the mission of philanthropy and strong user locus of control in every piece of their marketing strategy. TOMS sends customers a flag of their logo with every shoe purchase and asks customers to take a picture and share their personal story of giving, whether it has to do with TOMS shoes or not. Rather than focusing their marketing on the purchase of shoes, TOMS has centered their brand on a lifestyle and social movement. Their website states:

> TOM is not a single person, it is the idea that the decisions we make today can echo into the future. If you believe in finding adventure while building a better tomorrow, you're TOM. If you shop consciously, volunteer with an organization that is changing lives, take part in creating a sustainable future or help raise awareness of issues affecting lives across the globe – you are TOM (http://www.toms.com/i-am-tom).

The TOMS social media brand strategy encourages consumers to do good things in real life, capture it on photo or video, and then share it on TOMS social media sites. The brand and its customers often share pictures using the hashtag #weargood to share TOMS shoes out in the wild. Though this campaign is not directly selling shoes, it is making their customers feel emotionally attached to the brand and creating a strong community among customers that are taking control over the brand narrative. Images shared with the TOMS Instagram channel is saved in a "TOMS by you" Instagram story highlight (Figure 4.3). This of course comes with great risk, as you are leaving your social media account open for customers to say whatever they want, using your campaign hashtag. If they are unhappy with your product, this will come through in their messages. Social media shifts power to consumers, which can be very powerful, or detrimental, to your brand.

The importance of community cannot be understated in the mobilization process. TOMS customers purchase shoes because the brand represents the way they construct their own identity and the role that they play in the world around them. They do not feel as though TOMS is just another shoe company that is trying to sell them an item for profit. They feel a strong locus of control about their purchase because TOMS allows them to control the brand narrative. Wearing TOMS identifies a person as a philanthropist willing to put their money toward a social cause. TOMS is not selling to customers; customers are TOMS because TOMS has given them the freedom and tools to share personal stories of how they have interpreted the mission into their own lives. Each of these real-life experiences makes customers feel more emotionally invested with the brand. This transforms the consumption process into a much more emotional experience. Moreover, customers can share their experience online through social media so that their personal network can witness the community movement. Undoubtedly, these images and videos hold great pathos, and the community would want to join in.

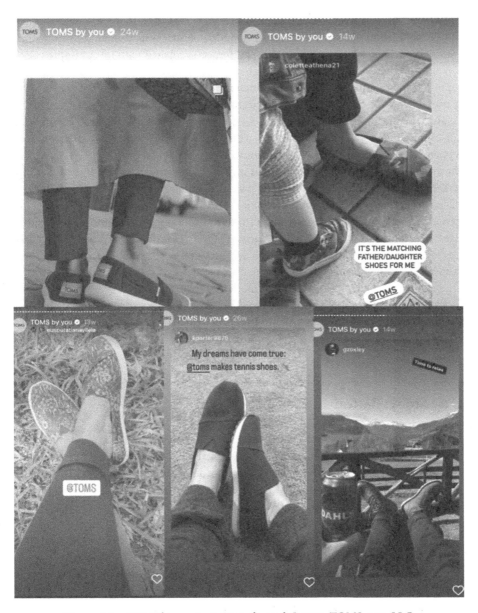

Figure 4.3 TOMS by you Instagram channel. Source: TOMS.com, LLC.

Most every organization would benefit more from messages that were tied to practical real-life mobilization efforts. These could include volunteering, donating money, signing a petition, or writing a letter. Often, these can be accomplished with just a simple click of a button as awareness-only techniques. Imagine spending an entire afternoon volunteering at a chemotherapy treatment center. How much more powerful would that experience shape your user's behavior than sharing an awareness hashtag on a social media post? This is especially true in causes that already have a strong, tightly knit community. Through more action-oriented mobilization approaches, your message will transform users into more interested, knowledgeable, and vested advocates for your brand.

The synchronous mobile tools utilized in mobilization campaigns lead to real-life impact. Since February 2022, when Russia invaded parts of Ukraine, over 7 million people have been displaced in Europe's largest refugee crisis since World War II (Rosenblat, 2022). Social media has proved a vital tool for mobilizing refugees with transportation, accommodations, and other services. Kobiety za Kółko (KZK), which translates to "Women Take the Wheel," is a Facebook group dedicated to providing transportation and meetups to Ukrainians fleeing from the war. With social media communication, users were able to quickly form a community and coordinate in real time during a crisis. The group's membership reached over 100,000 users with more than double offers and requests for hosting. The structural ease for creating such a strong mobilization community requires synchronous social media messages and a community that is willing to participate in bottom-up communication.

Case Study: BeReal

BeReal is a mobile social networking app that emerged where users are prompted to share one authentic snapshot each day of their life. Each day, the app sends a notification at a random time where users have two minutes to take a photo with a mobile phone's front and back camera that is shared with friends. It is impossible to predict what time the app will send a notification to plan your day accordingly. Therefore, some days users can share the best part of their day if the timing aligns, but most days, the notification catches users during ordinary moments of their lives that they would not otherwise share with their social network.

BeReal also created structural features to mitigate the lurking behavior of users on other platforms. Users who do not actively participate and share a photo each day are unable to view posts from others in the network (McCluskey, 2022). Therefore, it is impossible to only participate on the days when you are engaged in fun socially desirable activities without missing out in the content from friends.

BeReal grew widely popular among Gen Z, with more than 22.8 million downloads (McCluskey, 2022). Here, you can see how tweaking social media structures and interface options transforms how people utilize various social media platforms.

Media users are attracted to more authentic content where they can create and share without competing with professionals. Users respond positively to the less staged content being shared on BeReal, as it alleviates the pressure of sharing only the perfect highlight moments of your day.

The synchronous structure of BeReal does not allow for photo editing or more frequent sharing by users. Images shared on BeReal tend to be less posed and feature mundane pieces of users' day. Thus, it is being touted as the anti-Instagram. What you see on BeReal is what is actually happening in users' lives. It is difficult to work around this structure as a brand or organization. However, given the popularity of BeReal, many have tried.

Paid brand advertising is not permitted on BeReal, making it a challenge for companies to profit on its popularity. Nonetheless, many brands use the app to share synchronous coupons with followers. While alternative social media platforms, like Instagram, spend large number of dollars working with highly curated influencers to promote a product, BeReal offers a much more authentic and affordable structure. Synchronous content sharing can be more transparent to users, as they are able to see the actual people and processes behind a brand and the people that it attracts.

Discussion questions

1   What structural qualities of BeReal may attract (or not attract) you to use the app?
2   Creating emotional real-life experiences for users is one of the biggest indicators of mobilization success. How could a less filtered BeReal post facilitate stronger social media mobilization?
3   Think about utilizing social media to build your personal brand. Would you use BeReal? How could you incorporate less filtered social media posts into your personal branding strategy?

Summary

Think of the most influential moments in your life – the experiences that shaped you as a person, and the stories that you tell over and over. Chances are these are not scenes that you watched on TV or a website that you visited. We are not most influenced by the technologies in our lives, but by our experiences and the people closest to us.

If your goal as a social media marketing/communication practitioner is to have your product or message become an intricate part of others' lives, you must provide opportunities for them to experience it for themselves. Social media has many affordances that make this type of real-life mobilization easier than ever. The technologies aid better planning and easier execution and facilitation of action.

In addition to utilizing social media to prompt users to gain experience with your product, you must also use it as a space to create and share. UGC is critical to the transformation of users into message advocates. Message diffusion allows users to comply with a request. Community gives them a space to ask questions or post feedback. Mobilization is the only way for users to have a voice willingly and permanently in your campaign.

Before moving to a participatory strategy, you must be confident that the customer experience with your product will be positive. This does not mean that your goal as a marketing practitioner is to please everyone. In fact, this is impossible in today's digital media landscape. However, if you are finding that the negativity accounts for most of the feedback you are receiving, it is time to reign in the participatory features and start from the beginning. Reevaluate your brand's mission statement, authenticity, and transparency. Companies should be constantly monitoring and evaluating their community and feedback (more on this evaluation process can be found in Chapter 12).

As discussed in previous chapters, using media to ignite behavior change exists on a tricky continuum. Strictly diffusing messages allows you to have tight control over what is being said about your product. However, it has a lousy return on investment in terms of sparking behavior change. Allowing others to experience your product and speak on your behalf through strict participation means a much stronger vehicle for behavior change. However, this provides you with little control over what is being said. It is important to find a balance (Table 4.1).

The best social media strategies are not those that only use participation and mobilization-centric approaches; there should be a three-pronged social media strategy in combination with diffusion, community, and mobilization approaches. It is up to you to determine which tools you are going to use to accomplish your goal.

Now that we understand the most important functions of social media (diffusion, community, and mobilization), it is time to turn our attention to the users and messages involved. How has social media transformed audiences into active users for behavior change? How do social media structures influence user behavior? How does social media encourage more active engagement than traditional media? What tools help generate user participation? We will explore these questions and more in the next four chapters as we look at social media users and messages.

Table 4.1   Mobilization: Inducing individuals to participate with your social media campaign through real-life action.

Pros	Cons
Users highly identify with media messages	Targets individuals, not a mass audience
Transforms consumers into brand advocates	Requires established brand recognition and trust
Strongest behavior change yield	Loses control over messages

Key Takeaways

1 Social participation, a combination of mass dissemination and media engagement, provides users with real-life lived experiences and has proven the most efficient and effective way to spark behavior change.
2 Mobilization requires more than just interest. Marketers must use social media to make planning, execution, and facilitation of action as easy as possible for users.
3 Give consumers a strong locus of control by allowing them to create and generate content in every step of the process, including product and message design. This will pull consumers in, not push messages out, and transform consumers into brand advocates.
4 Cyberactivism should go beyond awareness only. Be sure that a tangible action is tied to your messages, corresponding to your initiative's goals.

References

Bandura, A. (2004) Health promotion by social cognitive means. *Health Education and Behavior*, 31, 143–164.

Boulos, K. & Wheeler, S. (2007) The emerging Web 2.0 social software: an enabling suite of sociable technologies in health and health care education. *Health Information and Libraries Journal*, 24, 2–23.

Boyd, D. (2011) Social network sites as networked publics: affordances, dynamics and implications. In: Z. Papacharissi (ed) *A Networked Self: Identity, Community and Culture on Social Network Sites*, pp. 39–58. New York: Routledge.

Byrne, A., Gray-Felder, D., Hunt, J. & Parks, W. (2005) Measuring change: a guide to participatory monitoring and evaluation of communication for social change. Available at http://www.communicationforsocial-change.org/pdf/measuring_change.pdf.

Cadbury (2023) Worldwide hide. Available at https://worldwidehide.cadbury.co.uk.

Citrin, A.V., Stem Jr, D.E., Spangenberg, E.R. & Clark, M.J. (2003) Consumer need for tactile input: an Internet retailing challenge. *Journal of Business Research*, 56(11), 915–922.

Crawford, K. (2009) Following you: disciplines of listening in social media. *Continuum: Journal of Media and Cultural Studies*, 23(4), 525–535.

Dutta, M. (2006) Theoretical approaches to entertainment education campaigns: a subaltern critique. *Health Communication*, 20(3), 221–231.

Eltantawy, N. & Wiest, J.B. (2011) Social media in the Egyptian revolution: reconsidering resource mobilization theory. *International Journal of Communication*, 5, 1207–1224.

Enjolras, B., Steen-Johnsen, K. & Wollebaek, D. (2013) How do social media change the conditions for civic and political mobilization? Available at http://www.academia.edu/1353639/How_do_social_media_change_the_conditions_for_civic_and_political_mobilization.

Gladwell, M. (2010) Small change: why the revolution will not be tweeted. Available at http://www.newyorker.com/magazine/2010/10/04/small-change-malcolm-gladwell.

Gowers, T. & Nielsen, M. (2009) Massively collaborative mathematics. *Nature*, 461(7266), 879–881.

Gray-Felder, D. & Deane, J. (1999) Communication and social change: a position paper and conference report. New York: The Rockefeller Foundation. Available at http://www.communicationforsocialchange.org/publications-resources?itemid=14.

Haridakis, P. & Hanson, G. (2009) Social interaction and co-viewing with YouTube: blending mass communication reception and social connection. *Journal of Broadcasting and Electronic Media*, 3(2), 317–335.

Haridakis, P. & Rubin, A. (2005) Third-person effects in the aftermath of terrorism. *Mass Communication and Society*, 8(1), 39–59.

Heilman, C., Lakishyk, K. & Radas, S. (2011) An empirical investigation of in-store sampling promotions. *British Food Journal*, 113(10), 1252–1266.

Howard, P.N. (2011) *The Digital Origins of Dictatorship and Democracy: Information Technology and Political Islam*. Oxford: Oxford University Press.

Husain, S. & Shaikh, B. (2005) Stalling HIV through social marketing: prospects in Pakistan. *Journal of the Pakistan Medical Association*, 55(7), 294–298.

Jenkins, J.C. (1983) Resource mobilization theory and the study of social movements. *Annual Review of Sociology*, 9, 527–553.

Kaplan, A.M. & Haenlein, M. (2010) Users of the world, unite! The challenges and opportunities of social media. *Business Horizons*, 53(1), 59–68.

Koyak, B. (2021) Meet TikTok. *Laurus College*. Available at https://lauruscollege.edu/meet-tiktok/.

Levenson, H. (1974) Activism and powerful others: distinctions within the concepts of internal–external control. *Journal of Personality Assessment*, 38, 377–383.

McCarthy, J.D. & Zald, M.N. (1977) Resource mobilization and social movements: a partial theory. *American Journal of Sociology*, 82(6), 1212–1241.

McCluskey, M. (2022) BeReal won't save us from social media – yet. *Time* Available at https://time.com/6201636/bereal-popularity-challenges.

Morris, N. (2003) A comparative analysis of the diffusion and participatory models in communication for development. *Communication Theory*, 13(2), 225–248.

Neuhauser, L. & Kreps, G. (2003) Rethinking communication in the e-health era. *Journal of Health Psychology*, 8, 7–22.

Potter, J. (1988) Perceived reality in television effects research. *Journal of Broadcast and Electronic Media*, 32(1), 23–41.

Raftery J. (1991) Faster access to modern treatments? Analysis of guidance on health technologies *BMJ*, 323(7324), 1300–1303.

Rosenblat, C. (2022) For women fleeing Ukraine: social media is a lifeline. *Dame*. Available at https://www.damemagazine.com/2022/06/13/for-women-fleeing-ukraine-social-media-is-a-lifeline/.

Rosenstone, S. & Hansen, J. (1993) *Mobilization, Participation, and Democracy in America*. New York: MacMillan.

Singhal, A. & Rogers, E. (2003) *Combating AIDS: Communication Strategies in Action*. Thousand Oaks, CA: Sage Publications.

Sterne, J. (2010) *Social Media Metrics: How to Measure and Optimize Your Marketing Investment*. Hoboken, NJ: John Wiley & Sons, Inc.

Stone, S. (1993) Getting the message out: feminists, the press and violence against women. *Canadian Review of Sociology and Anthropology*, 30, 377–400.

Stratten, S. (2012) *UnMarketing: Stop Marketing. Start Engaging*. Hoboken, NJ: John Wiley & Sons, Inc.

Van Dijck, J. (2009) Users like you? Theorizing agency in user-generated content. *Media, Culture, and Society*, 31(1), 41.

Waisbord, S. (2001) Family tree of theories, methodologies and strategies in communication for development. Rockefeller Foundation. Available at http://www.communicationforsocialchange.org/pdf/familytree.pdf.

Weisbrod, B. (1991) The health care quadrilemma: an essay on technological change, insurance, quality of care, and cost containment. *Journal of Economic Literature*, 29(2), 523–552.

Zhang, C., Zhang, D. & Shao, H. (2023) The softening of Chinese digital propaganda: evidence from the *People's Daily* Weibo account during the pandemic. *Frontiers in Psychology*, 14, 1–12.

Part II

Social Media Users and Messages

5

Social Media Uses

Learning Objectives

After reading this chapter, you should be able to:

1 Explain active audience theories, such as uses and gratifications, social cognitive theory, and mood management, and be able to identify opportunities and challenges when marketing to target social media users.
2 Identify individual and cognitive factors that influence social media use.
3 Analyze social media user profiles and understand how to utilize them for effective social media marketing.

Introduction

Part I of this book introduced social media functions and three strategies for creating messages: diffusion, community, and mobilization. Regardless of which combination of approaches you use in your social media strategy, all marketing should begin with a thorough audience analysis. This chapter will help in that process by explaining why people use social media, identify individual and cognitive factors that influence social media use, and pinpoint opportunities and challenges you may face when using social media to reach and influence users.

Strategic Social Media: From Marketing to Social Change, Second Edition. L. Meghan Mahoney and Tang Tang.
© 2024 John Wiley & Sons, Inc. Published 2024 by John Wiley & Sons, Inc.

Social media has aided more user-centered communication, brought increased sense of community, and prompted more positive participatory behavior change. Your social media users can simultaneously receive a sales message from their Facebook page, share thoughts (positive or negative) about your company on X (formerly Twitter), and provide suggestions for your next product line via your official website. They may also accidently encounter a pin board on Pinterest, make their purchase directly through the affiliate link, and re-pin it to make more people aware of their "likes." In today's social media landscape, your social media users may even become your brand advocates by actively creating and distributing content about your brand, product, and service on Instagram to not only their friends and family, but thousands of fellow social media users.

While technologies like artificial intelligence and customized recommendation could still guide or constrain people's content choices, social media has transformed passive audiences into more active participants that can endorse products directly in the marketplace. Thus, as a social media marketer, you should encourage more direct communication with your consumers and build customized user content. Since many factors can impact people's social media use, you first must identify a range of factors that explain how marketing content is consumed on social media, as well as what motivates your consumers to make purchasing decisions.

Transforming Passive Audiences to Participatory Users

In today's digital marketplace, social media users act as *prosumers*, or individuals who consume and produce content at the same time (Ritzer & Jurgenson, 2010). As you may have already noticed, the dynamic nature of social media makes your consumers interact with the medium in a much more direct and personalized manner than traditional media. Thus, you should aim to provide your consumers with a personalized experience and seek to achieve a thorough understanding of why and how they use your social media content and how such uses would influence their purchasing decision. What works well to persuade one individual may not be successful on another. Everyone consumes social media messages for reasons that are unique, yet specific to the context and life situation. It is important for you to consider your social media users as individuals, rather than a macro unit of aggregated mass (Potter, 2009). *What* to disseminate to the users is just as crucial as *how* to get the information to them when designing a social media strategy.

Active audience theories explain why people choose to use media. These theories adopt a psychological viewpoint and suggest that media users are active and goal-directed, and they make a rational choice to use media content to satisfy their personal needs and desires. While these theories do not consider how media and societal structures guide user behavior (which we will discuss in Chapter 6), they seek to answer the question what people do with media (Katz *et al.*, 1974).

To social media marketers, active audience theories point out that user activity is prevalent in today's media environment as the experience lends itself to a convergence culture wherein individuals have more choices and control on what, when, where, and how they consume media content (Ruggiero, 2000; Sundet & Ytreberg, 2009). A few illustrations of active audience theories that may help you understand how individual motivations, moods, personality, attitude, preferences, and demographics can influence social media use (Akar & Topcu, 2011), include uses and gratifications theory, social cognitive theory, and mood management theory.

Uses and gratifications theory

Uses and gratifications theory explains how people use media to satisfy their needs. The theory is based on five fundamental characteristics proposed by McLeod and Becker (1981), including:

> First, audiences are active. Second, media use is goal directed. Third, media use fulfills a wide variety of needs. Fourth, people can articulate their reasons for using the media. And fifth, the gratifications have their origins in media content, exposure, and the social context in which exposure takes place. (Potter, 2009, p. 142)

Researchers suggest that the social and psychological origins of needs lead to different patterns of media use (Katz *et al.*, 1974).

Specifically, the uses and gratifications theory identified two orientations that explain why people use media: instrumental media use and ritualistic use. According to Rubin (1984, p. 67), "*instrumental media use* reflects more active patterns of using media content to select information from realistically perceived messages. *Ritualized media use* reflects fewer active patterns of using the media to fill time and relieve boredom." While academia has debated the active/passive role of media users, it seems trivial for marketers to participate in this conversation. A more important question for social media marketers to answer is what motivates consumers to use what types of social media content. How can they develop effective social media messages to serve their consumers who have different motivations and goals?

Let's imagine that you were watching the Oscars award show on television. In the meantime, you were also actively tweeting your thoughts and predictions of who will take home an award. During the commercial break, you decided to fill the time by skimming through X posts. You see a post discussing Lady Gaga's elegant Versace gown. The dress captured your attention, and you immediately retweeted the post, pinned it on Pinterest, and began to actively search for more information about Versace. This scenario indicates how both instrumental and ritualistic motivations influence our media use. People do use a medium both purposefully and out of habit (Cooper & Tang, 2009). We will talk more about the relationship between motivations and social media use in the next section.

Social cognitive theory

Social cognitive theory has been widely applied to explain many stages of media choices, including the initial adoption, content selection, and habitual behavior. The theory suggests that outcome expectations, self-efficacy, and self-regulation are the conscious factors that determine human behavior (LaRose, 2009; LaRose & Eastin, 2004). *Outcome expectations* refer to both positive outcomes and negative consequences that enact the behavior, including novel, social, activity, monetary, self-reactive, and status outcomes (LaRose & Eastin, 2004). Novel outcomes refer to using media to find new information or features. Social outcomes suggest that people use media for social support, sense of belonging, and relationship development. Activity outcomes are like entertainment motivations, while monetary outcomes indicate that media use can help save time and money. Self-reactive outcomes refer to using media to pass time, and status outcomes suggest that people use media to get respect and values (LaRose & Eastin, 2004).

Self-efficacy indicates the belief in one's capability to perform a task (LaRose & Eastin, 2004). You should note that self-efficacy is different from actual skill level or previous experience, but simply reflects users' confidence level in their ability to use a media product/service. *Self-regulation* is a process that incorporates three stages: self-observation, judgmental process, and self-reaction (Bandura, 1991). It's believed that people observe their behavior, compare the behavior with social norms, and then decide whether to repeat the behavior or change it (LaRose & Eastin, 2004).

As a social media marketer, you need to be aware that social media use is based on the mutual influence of outcome expectations, self-efficacy, and self-regulation. Let's imagine that your client is planning a wedding. You introduce her to Pinterest because you believe that Pinterest provides a structure that can help meet her unique social and status expected outcomes (using social media structures for social media marketing will be discussed in Chapter 6). She can use Pinterest to follow your newest products, trend must-haves for a spring wedding, communicate with other brides-to-be, share with friends and family, and retell her experience with thousands of people via the virtual community. These are all the possible benefits of following your Pinterest page.

In the meantime, you need to build your customer's self-efficacy with those who have never used Pinterest before. Here, you help your customers connect with their friends and social networks, link them to the boards they would like, encourage them to join social groups with which share the same interests and passion, and reinforce the positive values they would get via your continuous conversations with them. As suggested by the social cognitive theory, your clients' initial exposure to a new social media endeavor may be led by your recommendation or their previous experience with a similar site. However, it is the perception of their future use of the endeavor that determines their adoption and continuous use.

Mood management theory

Mood management theory suggests that individual's media choices vary with their moods (Zillmann, 1988). There are many reasons why individuals turn to media during emotional situations. When people are excited, they are likely to select a more relaxing media outlet. Bored people, on the other hand, seek to find stimulating content. People who are stressed prefer to consume calming programs. Men tend to use media for distraction when they are in a bad mood, while women tend to watch sad movies to mediate their moods (Nolen-Hoeksema, 1987). In general, people like to consume media content with a positive tone and tend to avoid any message that generates disagreeable feelings (Knobloch-Westerwick, 2007). Therefore, you should set up a positive and pleasant tone in your social media messages. Most of your consumers simply wishes to use social media for fun.

It is also important for social media marketers to match their messages with the context and their consumers' mood. This requires practitioners to stay up to date on important public sphere issues. For example, maybe your consumers were very excited about the Argentina–France game in the 2022 World Cup. If most of your consumers were from Argentina and fans of Lionel Messi, they probably looked for a way to express their national pride. This context provided a great opportunity to connect with your Argentina consumers via social media. Before and during the game, you could have created engaging visuals and videos about the World Cup on Instagram and Tiktok, kept up with the game in real time to show your support, and celebrated with them when Argentina scored a goal and won the champion. These actions allow you to take part in the conversation that is already taking place and will make you seem more like a human and less like a brand. Remember that identification is crucial to behavior change. It is important that your social media messages adapt to the real-life experiences and moods of your consumers. Social media should be a place to have fun with your consumers.

An example of such is American Heart Association's "Keep the Beat Challenge" on TikTok. In February 2021, the nonprofit organization invited TikTokers to post themselves moving and dancing to popular songs on TikTok (Tabas, 2021). Instead of "lecturing" about the risks of heart diseases and the importance of research from the American Heart Association, the campaign simply asked people to have fun and share their love of dance on social media. As a result, the campaign reached 34,000 followers and more than 246,000 likes, which helped the nonprofit build an increased sense of community. Additionally, it mobilized users to share heart-healthy activities on their own social networks. This example demonstrates the importance of knowing your social media users while simultaneously satisfying their needs and moods via your social media strategy.

Predicting Social Media Use

The COVID-19 pandemic has impacted every aspect of society, including the museum business. Many museums were forced to close for an extended amount of time to the public in 2020 due to the public health restrictions. They had to be creative on how to engage their audiences. The Getty Museum, a museum located in Los Angeles that aims to inspire curiosity about and enjoyment of the visual arts, took advantage of the stay-at-home orders by providing their patrons things to do during the pandemic.

In March 2020, they started a playful social media challenge inviting its patrons to re-create their favorite art in Getty utilizing just a few objects at home (Waldorf & Stephan, 2020). Within days, Getty's patrons submitted thousands and thousands of photos of their recreated arts on X (formerly Twitter), Facebook, and Instagram. For example, they recreated *Still Life with Apples* with home pottery and gin, and restaged Jacques-Louis David with a fleece blanket and duce tape. A 6-year-old girl and her family used pasta, boiled eggs, brown paper bag, and a couple of basil stems to recreate the artwork *Imaginary Insect, Tulip, Spider, and Common Pear* (Waldorf & Stephan, 2020).

This fun (maybe ironic) social media challenge not only guided numerous traffic to Getty's website and social media pages but also created a bright spot for all during a tough time, which could ultimately lead to a long-term bond between the organization and its members. This example illustrates how you can successfully engage with your customers emotionally and create not only a fun experience but also a connected community. Taking time to get to know your consumers is the first step.

Individual factors of target consumers have long been considered in marketing campaigns. Gender, age, income, ethnicity, and/or sexual preference make consumers use different media, and hence make various purchasing decisions (Sewell, 1992). Who we are directly influences what media we choose to use and which communication we seek to pursue. For example, Pinterest is considered a more female-oriented social media. TikTok is for younger users. WhatsApp is popular among people in Asia and Europe. For this reason, you need to conduct demographic analysis of your target consumers. Age, gender, education, socioeconomic status, ethnicity, and occupation are all important data any marketer should obtain about their consumers before developing their marketing strategy. It is important for you to research the appropriate social media platform to best reach your target consumers. Often industry research will surprise you. Never guess media behavior of your target audience. Use reputable media research to make strategic decisions about how, where, and when your audience is online.

Personality is also a predictor of media consumption (Zillmann, 1988). Researchers suggest that there are five personality traits: neuroticism (sensitive/nervous vs. secure/confident), extroversion (outgoing/energetic vs. solitary/reserved), openness (inventive/curious vs. consistent/cautious), agreeableness (friendly/compassionate vs. cold/unkind), and conscientiousness (efficient/organized vs. easy-going/careless). This is often abbreviated to *OCEAN* (*o*penness, *c*onscientiousness, *e*xtroversion, *a*greeableness, *n*euroticism). Media use can be explained by the personality continuum OCEAN (Jenkins-Guarnieri *et al.*, 2012; Rammstedt & John, 2007).

For example, extroverted people tend to choose activities that provide direct social contact (Argyle & Lu, 1990). Introverts like to use text-based media because text-based media can provide them a sense of control. People who are anxious and moody are likely to use media to escape. Those who are more neurotic prefer objective messages (Finn, 1997; Krcmar & Strizhakova, 2009). When developing a social media campaign, you not only need to understand your consumers' personality but also give your social media campaign a personality. Then, find the social media platforms that can best carry the personality and reach consumers who share or appreciate the personality, as it is getting increasingly important to humanize a brand in today's digital environment.

Wendy's, an American fast-food company, now has 3.9 million followers, due to its unique social media approach. The company is known for its sassy brand voice. Its Twitter (renamed X in 2023) strategy stayed true to the branding by using a playful approach that cracks jokes and calls out its competitors (McKinnon, 2023). For example, in March 2017, Wendy's retweeted McDonald's tweet "Today we've announced that by mid-2018, all Quarter Pounder burgers at the majority of our restaurants will be cooked with fresh beef," by adding its lead "@McDonalds So you'll still use frozen beef in MOST of your burgers in ALL of your restaurants? Asking for a friend." The company also remains the playful tone when interacting with its consumers on social media. For example, a follower tweeted Wendy's "@Wendys how do you feel that people build your restaurant besides a McDonalds?" Wendy's replied, "Even in the worst places, it's nice for people to have hope." This unique social media "personality" not only makes Wendy's the most innovative company in the social media category (McKinnon, 2023) but also helps it increase sales. What you can learn from Wendy's is to give your brand a personality and stay true to your brand voice when creating social media messages. We are going to discuss how to give your campaign a personality in more detail in Chapter 10 when we talk about social media marketing strategies.

In addition to demographics and personality traits, cognitive factors also predict which media we choose to use (or not use). These cognitive factors include, for example, motivations, attitudes, self-efficacy, and preferences. Compared to individual factors (demographics and personality), cognitive factors are less fixed and can change from time to time. They set up internal boundaries for our media use and other social behavior. For example, your consumer may have a desire to visit your company's TikTok account because they are outgoing and extroverted, but their attitude toward your TikTok account will ultimately decide whether they will use it. If they do not like the constant pushy videos about your product on TikTok, or if they hold a negative attitude toward the increasing amount of social media advertising in general, users will not visit your TikTok page, no matter how outgoing they are.

As mentioned earlier, attitude is a cognitive factor that predicts social media use. When consumers hold a negative attitude toward your page, they stop visiting it (Akar & Topcu, 2011). Researchers suggest that attitudes toward online media are based on attitudes toward elements other than the media itself (Wang *et al.*, 2002). An advertisement, a picture, or a message on your social media page can influence your consumer's opinion about the entire page. People have personal preferences and primarily consume media materials that fit their tastes. Therefore, it is important to carry out solid audience research to know your consumers' likes and dislikes. Many social media monitoring tools now allow you to assess people's attitudes toward your company. We will talk more about these tools in Chapter 12.

Four motivations – intrinsic motivation, identified regulation, external regulation, and automotivation – can influence how and why your consumers use social media (Ryan & Deci, 2000). *Intrinsic motivation* refers to the reason that simply comes from the satisfaction and pleasure of using the media itself. For example, your consumers may watch a YouTube video just for fun. *Identified regulation* indicates that people use media because they believe that the media can be beneficial to them in the long run (Ryan & Deci, 2000). They choose to use the media for the reward. For example, you may use Coursera to take an online social media marketing course, because you believe the course can put you ahead in the social media marketing field. Identified regulation helps to explain why users utilize certain media.

External regulation suggests that people use media to avoid a negative outcome or to seek external rewards (Ryan & Deci, 2000). The difference between identified regulation and external regulation is that when people use media for external regulation, they feel that they have no choice but use the media. Nonetheless, when people use media for identified regulation, they feel that they have free choices, and they use the media because they want to. For example, you may participate in an online discussion board because your professor requires you to do so. People can also use a medium without a clear motive. They may use the medium simply because it is available. We call this type of behavior *automotivation* (Ryan & Deci, 2000).

Your social media messages must align with your consumers' motivations and be able to satisfy their individual desires. Motivations are not necessarily equal to the gratifications people obtained from using the media. The uses and gratifications theory defines gratifications sought and gratifications obtained. *Gratifications sought* are the reasons for using the media, whereas *gratifications obtained* are the results after using the media (Krcmar & Strizhakova, 2009). People may seek out social media for social uses but end up being lonelier after spending hours on Facebook. Thus, social is the "gratification sought," while passing time may become the "gratification obtained."

Mismatched campaigns can lead to negative outcomes that offer disincentives for social media use and hurt product sales in the long run. Let's say you are now in charge of the Facebook page of Lifetime Fitness, a popular gym in the United States. Your customers wanted to learn about weight loss tips and how to maintain a healthy lifestyle (i.e., basically to seek identified regulation) from Lifetime Fitness's Facebook page. If they successfully obtained this information after the initial exposure, they would be satisfied and would go back to your page. However, if they found that the Facebook page were full of ads for various nutrition and equipment products, their identified regulation motivation would not be satisfied, which would discourage them to revisit the page, and ultimately influence their purchasing decision of gym membership. As a social media marketer, you want to use identified and/or external regulation as your communication strategy, or simply make using your social media site an automatic behavior of your consumers.

Self-efficacy is another cognitive factor that influences social media use. As mentioned earlier in this chapter, self-efficacy is not equal to the actual technology skill, but rather about users' personal belief in their ability to use the media. People with high self-efficacy generally are more willing to adopt and use new media, while those with low self-efficacy tend not to do the same. Positive previous experience generally enhances one's confidence in ability to repeat the behavior. However, it is the self-reflection, rather than the objective skill, that guides or constrains people's social media use (LaRose, 2009). Social media marketers thus need to positively affect their consumers' self-efficacy mechanism.

HubSpot is a leading company in the United States that provides marketing tools for businesses. The company has used a content creation plan that reflects what their clients want. When HubSpot writes articles on social media, they tag their articles based on their clients' experience level and develop different materials to match their clients' interests and skill levels. HubSpot's interface is very easy to use. They make sure that the site prominently displays like, share, email, print, and comment widgets next to each article/message. These all help enhance HubSpot users' self-efficacy and make them continuously use the site.

In addition to creating user-friendly content display, making your content part of your consumer's daily routine will lead to a successful social media marketing endeavor. Habit has a big impact on human behavior. Researchers suggest that over half of all media behaviors are habitual (LaRose, 2009; Wood *et al.*, 2002). Over time, morning browsing Instagram may become a habit, independent of the content posted on Instagram. Morning, being an environmental cue, leads users to Instagram. Instagram use is then no longer a conscious decision but an automatic behavior. We will discuss more about how to aid an automatic behavior via structural factors in Chapter 6.

Understanding your consumers is the first step toward a successful social media campaign. Below is a step-by-step action plan to help you get to know your consumers.

Know Your Consumers Action Plan

1 Be certain to gather basic demographic information (e.g., age, gender, education, income, and geographic location) about your consumers, and choose the social media platforms that can reach target users.
2 Use research to conduct a more in-depth audience analysis to understand your consumers' interests, passions, personality, and, more importantly, why they would use your social media messages. Then, develop your social media messages to match their interests and personality in order to satisfy their desires.
3 Enhance your consumers' self-efficacy by guiding them to materials at their skill/knowledge level and making your social media messages easy to navigate.
4 Use social media monitoring tools to track people's attitudes toward your campaign and brand.

Social Media User Profile

Before you start a social media campaign, you may want to answer the question: Who are the social media users that I am likely to attract? When Pew Research Center first began tracking social media user profile in 2005, only 5% of the adults in the United States used social media. Today, 72% of all Americans use some type of social media. The social media user base has become more representative of the population (Pew Research Center, 2021). Worldwide, there were 4.76 billion social media users in 2023 (Kemp, 2023); and these social media users engaged with 6.6 various social media platforms (Dean, 2021). Slightly more females than males use social media. About 84% of young adults, 81% of 30–49-year-olds, 73% of 50–64-year-olds, and almost half of 65+ year-olds are social media users (Pew Research Center, 2021). This suggests that social media is used by people with various occupations, education, and income today.

Different social media sites, though, attract different types of users. Facebook is still the most popular social media platform, with almost 3 billion users worldwide (Facebook, 2023). Facebook is also one of the few social media sites that can reach older demographics, as more than half of the Internet users aged 65 years or older use Facebook (Dixon, 2022a). Thus, it is a great mass (social) media platform for you to send marketing messages with a general appeal. In addition, you should note that Facebook is a global media. More than 85% of Facebook users come from outside of the United States (i.e., the company's location; see Osman, 2022). India, Indonesia, Brazil, Mexico, Philippines, and Vietnam all have more than half million active Facebook users (Kemp, 2023). Thus, Facebook could be an effective social media platform for you to reach a global consumer base, people in Asia in particular. Overall, Facebook is a great platform for reaching the mass, developing trust, and building a community. Nonetheless, the average Facebook page engagement rate is 0.07% (Kemp, 2023), thus may not be your designated platform for interaction.

X (formerly Twitter) is a micro-blogging site. About 23% of US adults use X (Pew Research Center, 2021). X adoption is high among younger people. The largest group of global X users are 25–34 years old (i.e., 38.5%). In addition, 24% of the X users are younger than 24 years old (Dixon, 2022b). More than 60% of X users are male (Martin, 2023). Until today, X is still the major social media platform for people to stay up to date with news and events, thus you may want to take advantage of X's short-form, real-time nature to provide quick updates and feedback. Live tweeting and creating event hashtags may be a part of your X strategy (Martin, 2023). One of the biggest challenges of using X to disseminate social media messages is the short shelf-life of tweets. For example, there were 20,000 tweets every second during the 2022 World Cup (Martin, 2023). X is a great place to provide up to date information but may not be the best place for permanent message diffusion.

Instagram is one of the most-visited social media sites globally, with more than 2 billion active monthly users (Newberry, 2023). It is also Generation Z's (16–24 years old) favorite social media. In addition, your female consumers aged 25–34 years also prefer Instagram more than any other social media platforms. Geographically, India, the United States, and Brazil have the most Instagram users around the world. Instagram is a photo-heavy social media. Feeds are displayed in chronological order, so users tend to share photos that are happening now. Instagram has been believed to be an effective tool for carrying photo ads for marketers (Smith, 2014). If you're considering creating Instagram ads, you can potentially reach 1.32 billion users on the main feed, 996 million via Instagram stories, and 758 million on Reels (Newberry, 2023). Instagram analytics will help with your ad placement. We will talk more about social media monitoring in

Chapter 12. It is also important to know that just 0.1% of Instagram users only use Instagram. More than half of the Instagram users are on TikTok, and 81% of TikTokers also use Instagram (Newberry, 2023). Thus, you should consider your cross-platform content strategy. Make sure your content on each social media platform is unique and relevant because you're likely reaching the same people across different social media platforms. Furthermore, while Instagram is a great tool for disseminating visual products, it does not allow you to organically connect with consumers. It is up to consumers to choose who they would follow in their feed.

LinkedIn, launched in 2003, is a social media platform that aims to help users build professional networks. It currently has 900 million users in 200 countries (Ruby, 2023). The platform also tends to attract people with a college degree or higher and those with a household income of more than $US75,000 (Duggan *et al.*, 2013). Most LinkedIn users are Millennials, male, and business professionals (Shepherd, 2023). LinkedIn is a unique social media platform, with users quite different from other social media sites, and thus could be an effective tool for marketers interested in B2B communication and/or targeting professionals or people with relatively higher levels of education and income. Indeed, 75% of the B2B marketers use LinkedIn for their marketing efforts (Shepherd, 2023). LinkedIn content tends to be more polished (and consequently less interesting). Compared to other social media platforms, users do not visit LinkedIn as often.

Pinterest is a social media platform designed for users to organize bookmarks based on their interest. It is a more female-oriented site. More than 76% of Pinterest users are female, and only 17% of Pinterest users self-identified as male (Dixon, 2023). Pinterest users also skew toward people with relatively higher levels of education and social economic status. Most of the Pinterest users are loyal and active to the platform. Pinterest is an effective social media platform that targets audiences based on "who they are" (e.g., their interests, passions). One of the biggest challenges of Pinterest is that it is difficult to track pins and users. Thus, it may not be the best social media site for local small businesses to market their products.

TikTok was the most downloaded app in 2021. As a video-sharing site, TikTok is one of the most rapidly growing social media sites with over 1 billion active monthly users and 650,000 new users joining daily (Cyca, 2022). Along with Instagram and Snapchat, TikTok is one of the most favorite social media sites among Generation Zers. More females than males use TikTok. TikTok is also the most engaging social media app by far. The majority of TikTok users go to the platform to find funny and entertaining content.

In no way is this an exhaustive list of social media platforms, but these are most commonly used social media sites by businesses and nonprofit organizations (Tabas, 2021). As a practitioner, it is important for you to stay up to date on the greatest trends in technology. The most popular social media platforms are those with user-friendly interfaces. Therefore, it should not be too difficult to learn how to create and maintain any emerging social media platform. That is why this book focuses on social media functions through behavior change theory, rather than platform-specific recommendations.

Furthermore, the best social media practitioners use a cross-platform approach, because your consumers rarely choose just one space to share and receive content. According to the current Hootsuite Social Media Trends Report, 18–34-year-olds use 8 social media sites every month. Your TikTok users are also on Facebook, Instagram, and YouTube (Cyca, 2022). Thus, it is important that you are not creating one message to share identically across all platforms. Instead, social media marketers need to be aware of the reciprocity relationships between different social media sites; think of all the social media tools available and develop an integrated social media campaign to deliver messages effectively and efficiently.

Case Study: WeChat

This chapter discussed how different individual and cognitive factors influence social media uses and how knowing your consumers will lead to a successful social media campaign/product. One such example is WeChat ("Weixin" in Chinese), a popular Chinese social media app. WeChat is a social media product, like WhatsApp in the United States or Line in Japan, which allows users to send messages, share news and pictures via their mobile phone. It was first introduced to Chinese users in 2011. Today, WeChat has 827 million users in China and over 1.3 billion worldwide. Tencent, the Chinese social media company that owns WeChat, is now worth more than US$450 billion on the Hong Kong exchange (Yahoo Finance, 2023).

WeChat's success is the result of the thorough approach that it takes to understand its users. The platform's initial strategy is to target on young, urban smartphone owners and aims to provide these users an "all-in-one-platform" app. It offers a wide range of functions from sending a baby photo to friends, making phone calls, getting news, watching funny videos, paying for utility bills, to finding a cab on the street. WeChat is more than a combination of Facebook, Instagram, TikTok, X (formerly Twitter), Snapchat, and eBay. Users can do almost anything via WeChat, which makes the platform particularly appealing. With unlimited choices available to media users today, individuals are doing whatever they can to reduce "search cost." If they can get all they want from one platform, why bother to find other options. This helps to explain the success of WeChat, particularly its user base expansion from young adults to broader population.

WeChat is also easy to use. Its interface (Figure 5.1) and all the functions are designed to be straightforward and convenient to users. For example, WeChat allows users to record messages by simply holding on one button and talking, which saves the trouble of typing Chinese characters on the phone. When people read news on WeChat, instead of sending them to the news organization's official website, WeChat links them to the news source's URL within its own in-app browser, which is more viewable and visually pleasing. Users rarely need to leave WeChat to open a mobile

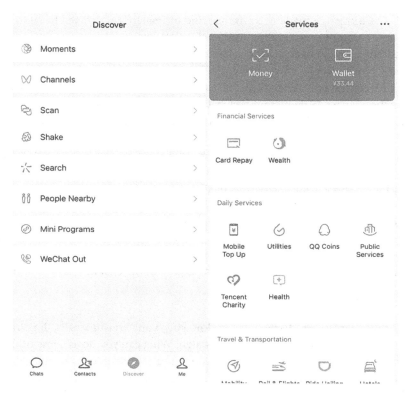

Figure 5.1 WeChat interface. Source: WeChat.

browser no matter if they want to watch videos or make a purchase, which is not only convenient to users but also helps WeChat keep the user flow. WeChat's "Moment" feature allows users to post status updates and share short-length videos in just a couple of clicks. Because WeChat makes everything so easy to do and significantly enhance its users' self-efficacy, it has become the norm for Chinese people's media use.

WeChat also strives to match users' cultural norms and satisfy their social needs. For example, WeChat's "Qiang Hongbao" campaign (i.e., Red Envelope campaign) allows users to send and receive red envelopes virtually through online banking. Red Envelope is a traditional Chinese culture that includes a monetary gift that Chinese people give to family and friends during holidays. To evoke an exciting and suspenseful mood, WeChat further allows users to put a sum of cash in the Red Envelope and then distribute the money randomly among a group of recipients the user set up (Horwitz, 2014). For example, if you want to give a total of $50 to Sarah, Maxx, Fiona, and Tracy, WeChat will assign this money randomly to these four people. Maxx may be the lucky one who will get $30, Fiona will have $10, Sarah $8, and Tracy will just get $2. The campaign made users excited and ultimately encouraged them to spend more time and money using the social media platform.

In addition to addressing users' social needs, WeChat has become a part of users' routine. Chinese people rely on WeChat's "functional" features for booking flights and trains, ordering taxi, processing online transactions and electronic payment, and more. During the COVID-19 pandemic, WeChat was used for prevention of infection. People can submit their health reports and scan a health code to enter public places using WeChat (Li *et al.*, 2021). These "functional" features not only further satisfy WeChat users' niche needs but also train them the habit of using WeChat for "everything," which could ultimately bring financial benefit to Tencent in the long run.

One big takeaway from the success of WeChat is that you should make your social media product a part of your users' everyday routine and habit. Since WeChat targets mobile users, it is always with people no matter they are at work, waiting for their food in a restaurant, or taking the subway. When your social media product becomes a part of people's daily life, it will be easier for you to make a behavior change, whether that behavior is a purchasing decision or a positive social change.

Discussion questions

1   In this chapter, we discussed how knowing your consumers is the first step toward a successful social media campaign. What can you do as a practitioner to ensure that you know as much as you can about your consumers? How did WeChat achieve this goal?
2   How does WeChat's structural features fit into their users' needs, interests, and moods? Is it possible to integrate WeChat to accommodate every characteristic of its users?
3   What elements of WeChat make it a part of Chinese people's daily life? Do you think WeChat will be equally successful in other countries?

Summary

This chapter focuses on social media users. Specifically, it explores factors that influence how and why your consumers use social media and identifies marketing opportunities and strategies to reach your social media users. Active audience theories (uses and gratifications, social cognitive theory, and mood management) suggest that media users are active and goal directed and make a rational choice to use media content to satisfy their needs and wants. Media users have a greater control over their media choices than ever before. Thus, it is important for you to consider your consumers as an individual, rather than an aggregated mass. Facing an abundance of media options, you must provide your consumers a personalized experience and be aware how technologies may guide or constrain their attention and content choices.

Both individual characteristics and cognitive factors can influence social media use. Different types of people use different social media platforms. Your consumers may make their social media choices based on "who they are." It means that you want to use the social media platforms that your target consumers use and give your social media campaigns a personality.

There are four motivations – intrinsic motivation, identified regulation, external regulation, and automotivation – that explain people's social media use. Media users today do use various social media for various purposes. It is important for your social media messages to fit your consumers' motivations and be able to satisfy their wants. Please remember that motivations are not equal to gratifications obtained. Mismatched campaigns can lead to negative outcomes that offer disincentives for social media use.

You also need to present your consumers with social media materials based on their knowledge and experience levels, since self-efficacy can both guide and constrain human behavior. In addition, this chapter has suggested that social media use can be a habitual behavior. Making your brand and/or social media product a part of people's daily life should be your ultimate goal. Developing environmental cues could be crucial to encourage automatic use of your social media messages. Many structural factors, such as availability, access to media technologies, and infrastructures provided by the industry and society, can guide (or constrain) user flow. Let's explore how you could use structures to influence consumer behavior in Chapter 6.

Key Takeaways

1 When consumers gain increasing power over their media use, tailoring your social media marketing campaign to your consumers' needs, moods, and interests is important.
2 Conduct a thorough and accurate audience analysis before any social media endeavor. Both individual characteristics (i.e., demographics and personality) and cognitive factors (i.e., attitude, motivations, self-efficacy, and habit) influence how and why your consumers use your social media messages.
3 Keep your social media messages/product simple and easy to use. Often, people choose to use a media simply because it is convenient. Guide your consumers to materials that match their skill/knowledge levels. Training your consumers' self-efficacy is important for them to adopt and continuously use your product/service.
4 Use a special occasion/context to develop a social media campaign. Make your consumers excited about your campaign and put them into a positive mood to share. Most often, your consumers are using social media for fun. Only the marketers who successfully engage consumers emotionally can influence their purchasing behavior.

5   In today's multimedia environment, marketers need to notice the reciprocity relationships between different social media platforms. Use all the social media tools available to you and develop an integrated social media marketing campaign.
6   Ultimately, your goal is to make your social media product/your brand a part of your consumers' daily lives. When it becomes a part of their everyday life rituals, you do not need to sell your product/service anymore.

References

Akar, E. & Topcu, B. (2011) An examination of the factors influencing consumers' attitudes toward social media marketing. *Journal of Internet Commerce*, 10, 35–67.

Argyle, M. & Lu, L. (1990) The happiness of extraverts. *Personality and Individual Differences*, 11, 1011–1017.

Bandura, A. (1991) Social cognitive theory of self-regulation. *Organizational Behavior and Human Decision Process*, 50, 248–287.

Cooper, R. & Tang, T. (2009) Predicting audience exposure to television in today's media environment: an empirical integration of active-audience and structural theories. *Journal of Broadcasting and Electronic Media*, 53(3), 1–19.

Cyca, M. (2022) 23 Important TikTok stats marketers need to know in 2023. *Hootsuite*. Available at https://blog.hootsuite.com/tiktok-stats/ (accessed November 17, 2023).

Dean, B. (2021) Social network usage and growth statistics: how many people use social media in 2022. *Backlinko*. Available at https://backlinko.com/social-media-users (accessed November 17, 2023).

Dixon, S. (2022a) Facebook usage reach in the United States 2021, by age group. *Statista*. Available at https://www.statista.com/statistics/246221/share-of-us-internet-users-who-use-facebook-by-age-group/ (accessed November 17, 2023).

Dixon, S. (2022b) Twitter: distribution of global audiences 2021, by age group. *Statista*. Available at https://www.statista.com/statistics/283119/age-distribution-of-global-twitter-users/ (accessed November 17, 2023).

Dixon, S. (2023) Pinterest: distribution of global audiences 2023, by gender. *Statista*. Available at https://www.statista.com/statistics/248168/gender-distribution-of-pinterest-users/#:~:text=Pinterest%2C%20founded%20in%202009%20andover%2017%20percent%20were%20male (accessed November 17, 2023).

Duggan, M., Ellison, N.B., Lampe, C., Lenhart, A. & Madden, M. (2013) Demographics of key social networking platforms. Available at http://www.pewinternet.org/2015/01/09/demographics-of-key-social-networkingplatforms-2/ (accessed June 8, 2016).

Facebook (2023) http://www.facebook.com.

Finn, S. (1997) Origins of media exposure: linking personality traits to TV, radio, print, and film use. *Communication Research*, 24, 507–529.

Horwitz, J. (2014) Chinese WeChat users sent out 20 million cash-filled red envelopes to friends and family within two days. Available at https://www.techinasia.com/wechats-money-gifting-scheme-lures-5-millionchinese-users-alibabas-jack-ma-calls-pearl-harborattack-company/ (accessed June 8, 2016).

Jenkins-Guarnieri, M.A., Wright, S. & Hudiburgh, L.M. (2012) The relationship among attachment style, personality traits, interpersonal competency, and Facebook use. *Journal of Applied Developmental Psychology*, 33, 294–301.

Katz, E., Blumler, J.G. & Gurevitch, M. (1974) Utilization of mass communication by the individual. In: J.G. Blumler & E. Katz (eds) *The Uses of Mass Communications: Current Perspectives on Gratifications Research*, pp. 19–32. Beverly Hills, CA: Sage.

Kemp, S. (2023) Essential Facebook statistics and trends for 2023. *Datareportal*. Available at https://datareportal.com/essential-facebook-stats#:~:text=Number%20of%20Facebook%20users%20in (accessed November 17, 2023).

Knobloch-Westerwick, S. (2007) Gender differences in selective media use for mood management and mood adjustment. *Journal of Broadcasting and Electronic Media*, 51(1), 73–92.

Krcmar, M. & Strizhakova, Y. (2009) Uses and gratifications as media choice. In: T. Hartman (ed) *Media Choice: A Theoretical and Empirical Overview*, pp. 53–69. New York: Routledge.

LaRose, R. (2009) Social cognitive theories of media selection. In: T. Hartman (ed) *Media Choice: A Theoretical and Empirical Overview*, pp. 10–31. New York: Routledge.

LaRose, R. & Eastin, M.S. (2004) A social cognitive theory of internet uses and gratifications: toward a new model of media attendance. *Journal of Broadcasting and Electronic Media*, 48(3), 358–377.

Li, J., Zhou, L., Heijden, B.V.D., Li, S., Tao, H. & Guo, Z. (2021) Social isolation, loneliness and well-being: the impact of WeChat use intensity during the COVID-19 pandemic in China. *Frontiers in Psychology*, 10(12), 707667. doi: 10.3389/fpsyg.2021.707667.

Martin, M. (2023) 29 Twitter stats that matter to marketers in 2023. *Hootsuite*. Available at https://blog.hootsuite.com/twitter-statistics/ (accessed November 17, 2023).

McKinnon, T. (2023) Wendy's brilliant twitter strategy and its top 22 best tweets. *Indigo Digital*. Available at https://www.indigo9digital.com/blog/wendystwitterstrategy (accessed November 17, 2023).

McLeod, D.M. & Becker, L.B. (1981) The uses and gratifications approach. In: D.D. Nimmo & K.R. Sanders (eds) *Handbook of Political Communication*, pp. 67–99. Beverly Hills, CA: Sage.

Newberry, C. (2023) 34 Instagram stats marketers need to know in 2023. *Hootsuite*. Available at https://blog.hootsuite.com/instagram-statistics/ (accessed November 17, 2023).

Nolen-Hoeksema, S. (1987) Sex differences in unipolar depression: evidence and theory. *Psychological Bulletin*, 101, 259–282.

Osman, M. (2022) Wild and interesting Facebook statistics and facts. *Kinsta*. Available at https://kinsta.com/blog/facebook-statistics/#:~:text=Facebook%20Statistics%20on%20Data%20andabout%20300%20petabytes%20of%20data (accessed November 17, 2023).

Pew Research Center (2021) Social media fact sheet. Available at https://www.pewresearch.org/internet/fact-sheet/social-media/ (accessed November 17, 2023).

Potter, W.J. (2009) *Arguing for a General Framework for Mass Media Scholarship*. Thousand Oaks, CA: Sage.

Rammstedt, B. & John, O.P. (2007) Measuring personality in one minute or less: a 10-item short version of the Big Five Inventory in English and German. *Journal of Research in Personality*, 41, 203–212.

Ritzer, G. & Jurgenson, N. (2010) Production, consumption, presumption. *Journal of Consumer Culture*, 10(1), 13–36.

Rubin, A. (1984) Ritualized and instrumental television viewing. *Journal of Communication*, 34(3), 67–77.

Ruby, D. (2023) 108 Important LinkedIn statistics for 2023. *DemandSage*. Available at https://www.demandsage.com/linkedin-statistics/ (accessed November 17, 2023).

Ruggiero, T.E. (2000) Uses and gratifications theory in the 21st century. *Mass Communication and Society*, 3(1), 3–37.

Ryan, R.M. & Deci, E.L. (2000) Self-determination theory and the facilitation of intrinsic motivation, social development, and well-being. *American Psychologist*, 55(1), 68–78.

Sewell, W.H. (1992) A theory of structure: duality, agency, and transformation. *American Journal of Sociology*, 98(1), 1–29.

Shepherd, J. (2023) 40 Essential LinkedIn statistics you need to know in 2023. *Social Shepherd*. Available at https://thesocialshepherd.com/blog/linkedin-statistics (accessed November 17, 2023).

Smith, C. (2014) Here's why Instagram's demographics are so attractive to brands. Available at http://uk.business.insider.com/instagram-demographics-2013-12?r=US&IR=T (accessed June 8, 2016).

Sundet, V.S. & Ytreberg, E. (2009) Working notions of active audiences: further research on the active participant in convergent media industries. *International Journal of Research into New Media Technologies*, 15(4), 383–390.

Tabas, J. (2021) How nonprofits can use social media to increase donations and boost visibility. *Forbes*. Available at https://www.forbes.com/sites/allbusiness/2021/03/06/how-nonprofits-can-use-social-media-to-increase-donations-and-boost-visibility/?sh=ef374b42bb7e (accessed November 17, 2023).

Waldorf, S. & Stephan, A. (2020) Getty artworks re-created by geniuses the world over. *Getty*. Available at https://www.getty.edu/news/getty-artworks-recreated-with-household-items-by-creative-geniuses-the-world-over/ (accessed November 17, 2023).

Wang, C., Zhang, P., Choi, R. & D'Eredita, M. (2002) Understanding consumers' attitude toward advertising. *Paper presented at the 2002 Annual Meeting of the Eighth America's Conference on Information Systems*.

Wood, W., Quinn, J.M. & Kashy, D. (2002) Habits in everyday life: thought, emotion and action. *Journal of Personality and Social Psychology*, 83, 1281–1297.

Yahoo Finance (2023) Tencent holdings limited. Available at https://finance.yahoo.com/quote/TCEHY/.

Zillmann, D. (1988) Mood management through communication choices. *American Behavioral Scientist*, 31, 327–340.

6

Active Within Structures

Learning Objectives

After reading this chapter, you should be able to:

1 Explain active within structures theory and the dynamic model of exposure and understand constrained active use of social media.
2 Define social media structures and explain how structures can guide and/or constraint social media use.
3 Identify the appropriate social media structures to create effective campaigns.

Introduction

Chapter 5 explored how social media users are more active and selective in content consumption and discussed how individual psychographic factors such as motivations, moods, preferences, and demographics influence your consumers' social media use. We learned that as a social media practitioner, you should design campaigns based on a thorough audience analysis, create social media messages to feature interests, cultural values, and life experiences of your target consumers, and stimulate an appropriate emotional mood. However, there is little you can do as a marketer to control consumers' personal preferences, life experiences, moods, and other individual psychological factors. We also learned

---

Strategic Social Media: From Marketing to Social Change, Second Edition. L. Meghan Mahoney and Tang Tang.
© 2024 John Wiley & Sons, Inc. Published 2024 by John Wiley & Sons, Inc.

structures of time, access, interactive features can influence social media uses. As a social media marketing practitioner, the questions you may want to ask are: Is Monday 10 a.m. the best time to send a paid ad via Twitch? Can your consumers in Eritrea access your Instagram content via mobile? How can you use tagging and hashtags to guide your consumer attention? Can any features lead your social media users to make a direct purchase of your product? This chapter, thus, focuses on the structures of social media technology, something you have control, and discusses how you can use these structures to guide social media uses to better meet campaign objectives.

With only 24 hours in a day, your consumers simply cannot use all the media content available to them. They purposefully or incidentally use media and social structures to find the messages that satisfy their needs and desires. As Nobel laureate Herbert Simon (1971, p. 40) observed, "A wealth of information creates a poverty of attention, and a need to allocate the attention efficiently among the overabundance of information sources that might consume it." There are many opportunities for you to use structural strategies to guide consumers' navigation of social media messages. To begin, let's focus on a couple of newest and most innovative theories that systematically examine media users in today's dynamic environment.

Active Within Structures

In Chapter 5, we discussed how active audience theories help you understand that your social media users are selective and make media choices based on their needs and preferences (Reiss & Wiltz, 2004). Different from active audience theories, structural theories see media users as more passive in consuming media, and suggest that media use, including social media use, is influenced by structural features such as time availability, access to media technologies, and infrastructures provided by the technology and society (Webster *et al.*, 2006). For example, researchers pointed out that evenings typically have higher TV ratings than mornings, because more people have time available to watch TV. Esports users who have access to ultra-responsive gaming equipment spent more time in gameplay because their access to the technologies allows them to make quick decisions in seconds (Stubbs, 2017).

The relationship between individuals and structures, indeed, has been illustrated by a British sociologist, Anthony Giddens, in his *structuration theory* (Giddens, 1984). Giddens suggested that individuals and structures interact with each other; individual agents act within the social system, while the repetition of their acts reproduce the structure. Advocating Giddens' structuration conceptualization, Webster (2014) proposed the *Dynamic Model of Exposure*. The theoretical framework explains how individuals engage with media and what influence their behaviors. The theory points out that media users are agents "who recursively drew upon structured media resources. As they do, they both reproduce and change the media environment" (Webster, 2017, p. 357). Researchers suggest that individual predispositions, such as needs, preferences, moods (things we have discussed in Chapter 5) can be motivators for media use, but media choices are also to some degree a result of media and social structures (Tang *et al.*, 2023).

Another theoretical approach that integrates active-audience theories with structural theories is the *active within structures approach*. This theoretical approach conceptualizes today and tomorrow's media users as "active within structures" (Cooper & Tang, 2009) and posits that individuals actively seek media content within internal and external structures. *Internal structures* refer to cognitive structures that guide or constrain media use, such as motivations, attitude, and habit strength, while *external structures* refer to the relatively hard constraints of environmental/contextual factors that influence media use, such as time availability, access to technologies, and infrastructures provided by the technology, industry, and society. This perspective highlights the role of active choice in convergent media environments, while acknowledging the continuing influences of habit and structure. As Cooper and Tang (2009, p. 416) suggest:

> With hundreds of television channels and millions of websites currently available to many media users, individuals may even seek structure as a way to deal with the vast multitude of content and media options available. This may be manifest in decisions to pay for one type of content or delivery system over another, or to self-impose limits on media use. Thus, structure should not be viewed as a "passive" characteristic of media use, but rather as one of several valid influences on media use.

The takeaway from these important audience theories is that you should consider the various kinds of media users with differing levels of participation along this active–passive dichotomy. For example, your boss, who oversees many individuals and must be very organized, may prefer a technological device with easily synchronized calendar applications. Meanwhile, a social teenager may be more interested in a technological device that has camera features, making it easy to edit and send images to friends. Today, your consumers seek to actively structure their preferences, and if the structure of your social media site/campaign makes it too difficult to participate, they will go elsewhere. As what the active within structures approach suggested, individual characteristics, internal structures, and external structures interact with each other to influence media use. We have learned in Chapter 5 how individual factors and internal structures influence social media use. Now, let's focus on the external structures.

Audience availability is one of the most powerful structural determinants of media use. Years of industry practice tell us that Thursday night generally has the highest rating because most people stay at home watching TV on Thursdays. More people watch TV in January and February than in the summer. The total television audience size varies predictably by hour of the day, day of the week, and week of the year because of audience availability (Webster *et al.*, 2006). TV programmers have applied this understanding to their scheduling practices by putting different types of programs into different parts of the day.

While social media is available to users on a 24/7 basis, Beyers (2004) suggests that audience availability still plays a role in the online world. For example, in the morning (6 a.m. to 8 a.m.), people tend to check emails and have a quick read of news. From 8 a.m. to 5 p.m., they are likely to go online for fun. In the evening, your consumers may have more interests in looking for product information and doing online shopping. Thus, you should place different content at different times of the day.

In addition, because of audience availability, practitioners must also post at different times on different social media platforms. For example, the best day to post on Instagram is Saturdays, while the worst is on Mondays. The best times to post on Instagram are mid to late evening and mid to late afternoon, while you should not post on Instagram from 6 to 9 a.m. (Needle, 2023), as consumers tend to have limited time to check Instagram in the morning. Instagram Chief, Adam Mosseri, also suggests that you may want to only post two feed posts per week, but two stories per day, to build a following (McLachlan & Cohen, 2023). If you use Facebook, you should also post in the late afternoon and evening. Like Instagram, Fridays and Saturdays will generate more attention to your posts, while Sundays will be the worst day for you to post on Facebook.

However, the best time to post on text-based social media, such as X (formerly Twitter), is morning, from 9 a.m. to noon (Needle, 2023). During these times, your consumers may have some scattered time available to get quick information, news, and even product updates. While it's easy to tweet, practitioners should limit posts to no more than five times a day (McLachlan & Cohen, 2023). For LinkedIn, a professional social networking site, the best times to post are Mondays, Wednesdays, or Tuesdays during work hours. You will not generate much user engagement during the weekends on LinkedIn.

In terms of the video platforms, such as YouTube and TikTok, the best times to post are from 6 to 9 p.m., followed by 3 to 6 p.m., because your consumers have more time available to watch videos. Saturdays and Fridays are the best time to post on these video platforms. There are fewer people on video sites on Tuesdays and Mondays (Needle, 2023). Hopefully, you can see how structural factor – user time availability can play a role in impacting your social media campaign. As we encourage you to use a cross-platform strategy, you may want to use a social media content calendar to schedule your posting on various platforms. We will discuss how you can use a social media content calendar for your benefit in detail in Chapter 10 when we discuss various social media marketing strategies.

In addition to time availability, the kinds of technologies and services owned by your consumers can guide specific media use. Your consumers can choose to use a certain medium simply because one device is available over another (Tang & Cooper, 2012). Most people now access social media sites via a mobile device. Popular social media sites, such as X (formerly Twitter), were designed with a "mobile first" principle. Platforms like Snapchat are only available on mobile. Mobile use even dominates the use of LinkedIn, a professional social networking site (Broadband Search, 2023). As such, it is important to highlight a "mobile first" strategy when you develop social media messages. Understanding the mobile infrastructure and design and developing content for the on-the-go are essential for social media marketers. In Chapter 11, we will discuss mobile marketing and e-commerce in detail.

Habit/repertoire is a structural factor that has received less attention but plays an essential role in social media use. Researchers suggest that more than half of media behaviors are habitual (Wood *et al.*, 2002). You may notice from your own media use that it is largely driven by routine with little conscious thought. Each morning you probably habitually check a few websites. Maybe it is your email, a news site, and one or two social media platforms such as LinkedIn and X. This is where you get all the information that you feel is necessary before starting your day. It would be almost impossible to prompt you to check a sixth or seventh website and break your routine in the morning. Therefore, if someone wanted to reach you, they should not spend too much effort doing it through an alternative website but should find a way to include their content via one of these routine sources.

Despite the endless options online, your consumers tend to revisit the sites that they just accessed and browse a small cluster of similar pages frequently to gratify their specific needs quickly and with little effort (Webster, 2014). You need to make sure that your social media messages are incorporated into your consumers' media use routine and become a part of their daily lives. This is why having a social media presence on the platforms where your consumers routinely access content is critical. Practitioners must integrate a social media content calendar into campaign planning to distribute messages around the same time each week. Connecting social media campaign/messages to things, people, topics, and issues with which your consumers are already familiar is vital. Building habits for your consumers is more crucial for your business than ever before.

Friskies (a cat food company) and BuzzFeed's Dear Kitten campaign demonstrates how businesses could use routine and sense of familiarity to increase brand awareness and enhance consumer engagement. The campaign videos simply featured an older housecat teaching a little kitten how to be a cat. This campaign reached more than 7 billion monthly global content views (Qualls, 2017). In addition, more than 20 million people subscribed the Buzzfeed's YouTube page. These cat videos also sparked a TikTok buzz, with more than 3.5 million views for the hashtag, #DearKitten (Bredava, 2022). The success of this campaign highlights the importance of knowing your consumers and embedding your messages into your consumers' routine and comfortable zone to reduce their perceived cognitive load. Watching cat videos is fun, and it is something your consumers have already opted into on their personal social media feeds.

Social media structures (e.g., hashtag, chat, search, and recommendations) also impact social media use. For example, before 2016, there was only a "like" button on Facebook. If you were sad about a post, or if you were surprised, you had to leave comments, which required more effort. Now, you can simply press a reaction button (i.e., love, care, haha, wow, sad, and angry) to express emotions more than "like." Facebook provides a much easier and effortless structure for their users to interact and communicate with each other. We will discuss these social media structures in detail in the next section and explain how these features guide social media use and engage social media users. As for now, it is important to consider the active within structures process when developing your social media messages. This should be completed through a four-step action plan.

Active Within Structures Action Plan

1   Be sure to post your social media messages at different times with different frequencies on different social media platforms. Put your consumers' time availability into consideration. Post when your consumers are ready and already use the platform for the type of messages.

2   Continue to push a mobile-first strategy for your social media campaigns. Be sure to understand mobile infrastructure and develop content consumable for on-the-go.

3   Build your consumers' habits. Make your social media messages a part of their routine. This includes encouraging your consumers to provide personalized registration early in the social media process, so they can readily access your information later; posting regularly on the platforms where your consumers have already used; connecting your social media messages to things/topics/issues with which your consumers are familiar in order to reduce cognitive clutters. Once habit is formed, media use will become automatic behavior rather than an active decision.

4   Use social media structures to get your existing users' attention and draw new consumers to your campaign, which ultimately will increase your brand awareness and loyalty.

Let's imagine that a close friend of yours is diagnosed with a scary illness. You would most likely feel scared, anxious, and have little control over the situation. You will probably seek as much information about the illness as possible online. Community health forums such as Caringbridge, a social media site for ongoing information exchange about medical conditions, may help fulfill your immediate need to actively seek information about the diagnosis. Once registered on Caringbridge.com, you will be guided through the process of connecting with a group of people by the embedded site structure. Such a connection structure pulls you to keep coming back. After a while, visiting Caringbridge becomes a part of your daily afternoon routine. You may find yourself visiting the site when you have time available, even after your friend recovers.

This example mirrors the active within structures process. The media routine starts with an active choice. During the initial exposures, external structures and the content provided by the site encourage the use and gradually make the use a habit, forming an internal structure. When such an internal structure is formed, the use becomes an automatic behavior and the active drive fades. Individuals, internal structures and external structures interact with each other, which in turn influences social media use.

The Role of Structure

Structure is a crucial yet elusive concept in social science (Sewell, 1992). It has been defined as hard rules and resources that place constraints on individual action (Giddens, 1984). Structure is active and multidimensional and acts as a valid factor that constrains but also guides media use. With the overwhelming amount of information available today, your consumers are increasingly relying on the infrastructures provided by media and society to find content that enacts their preferences (Cooper & Tang, 2009; Webster, 2014). This section introduces various *social media structures* that can be used in your social media campaigns to engage social media users, including hashtag, search, recommendation, profile, message/chat, endless scrolling, and connection to group/people.

Hashtag

Hashtag is one of the earliest and most important structures for any social media platform. It refers to using the pound symbol (#) to link related social media content together around a certain topic (MacReady, 2022). Hashtags make it easy for social media users to find content that interests them. People may see your social media messages simply because they're browsing tweets with the same hashtags you've used in your message. Hashtags provide social media users with a convenient way to navigate through overwhelming abundance of information, which in turn can change how user attention is distributed. As such, social media marketers must be able to strategically use hashtags to raise brand awareness, drive conversations, and enhance user engagement (MacReady, 2022).

Probably one of the most important reasons for social media marketers to use hashtags is to help your target consumers find you (MacReady, 2022). For example, if you are a newborn baby photographer, you may want to use some of the top Instagram hashtags like #love, #happy, or #cute on your Instagram posts (Molenaar, 2023). Someone who follow those hashtags may see the baby photos you posted in their Instagram feed, and then become your followers and potential consumers. Research indicated that on average, including a hashtag on your Instagram post could increase 29% interactions; while using hashtags in tweets can increase user engagement by 100% (Campbell, 2023).

Hashtags can also help you keep up with trends and breaking news and hint opportunities for creating a viral social media campaign. Many brands have also used hashtag challenges to show their support for social issues, demonstrating their brand voice and mobilizing consumers into actions behind important causes or issues (see Chapter 4). For example, Dove, a beauty product company, launched a #ShowUS hashtag challenge in 2019, which encouraged people to show beauty in various forms to challenge the stereotypes of beauty images. The campaign reached 1.6 million people worldwide. And the hashtag #ShowUs was used more than 7 million times across social media platforms in a year. Hopefully, you can see how using hashtags can strategically guide user attention and engage social media users to create social buzz. Please also note that when it comes to hashtags, less can be more. Limit the number of hashtags you use and only use relevant and specific ones (Campbell, 2023; MacReady, 2022).

Search

Search has been one of the most used digital media structures. It helps Internet users find preferred information quickly and easily by entering key words and choosing from a list of results (Earnheardt *et al.*, 2008). Research has demonstrated how the ranking of the search results can influence the "findability" of online content (Pan *et al.*, 2007). That's why businesses and organizations have focused on increasing their SEO (search engine optimization) and employed search engine marketing (Khoo, 2020).

Social SEO is also important. Almost 100% of the social networking sites provide a search feature. Social SEO refers to "adding text-based features like captions, alt-text, and closed captions to your posts to help people browsing social platforms easily find your content" (Newberry, 2022). As more social media users actively seek their preferred content, you should give attention to "search" in order to get your content seen (Newberry, 2022).

Recommendation

There are two types of recommendation system: implicit recommendation and explicit recommendation. *Implicit recommendation* is based on observation, such as times viewed, the number of "likes," times shared, and the "favorites" list. *Explicit recommendation* is based on numerical ratings such as average ratings, "one to five stars," and scales ranging from 1 to 100 (Knobloch-Westerwick *et al.*, 2005; Sundar & Nass, 2001; Thorson, 2008).

Like/Favorite/Ratings are commonly used recommendation systems within the social media context. Research found that 64% of social media sites include a like/favorite or ratings feature (Tang, 2013). Platforms like Twitch allow users to employ donation and subscriber icons to indicate their recommendation (Tang *et al.*, 2023). These recommendation structures not only help consumers reduce search costs and find their preferred product information efficiently but also enhance user engagement (Weller, 2015). Researchers pointed out that there is an endowment effect with utilizing the recommendation structures (Montag *et al.*, 2019). Your digital media users tend to actively seek impersonal influence and trust each other's recommendation when consuming media messages (Knobloch-Westerwick *et al.*, 2005; Pan *et al.*, 2007; Sundar & Nass, 2001; Thorson, 2008). That's why the participatory approach discussed in Chapter 3 is crucial to your social media strategy.

Share is one of the unique and foundational structures of social media (Kietzmann *et al.*, 2011). It allows social media users to interact. One reason that TikTok can reach 1 billion active monthly users is because they make content easy to share (Geyser, 2022). The Duet and Stitch features of TikTok allow users easily collaborate with each other, share content, and participate in a trend by just clicking a few buttons (Geyser, 2022). Apple's Shot on iPhone campaign is an example of how businesses can take an advantage of the share structure. The company invited iPhone users to share images captured with their iPhones on TikTok, Instagram and other social media platforms. The campaign is not only gone viral within the general public, but also attracted attention of celebrities, such as Selena Gomez and Lady Gaga. As a result, the first round of the campaign led to more than 6.5 billion impressions, highlighting the power of social sharing (Bredava, 2022). It demonstrates why brands should strategically use "share" to increase its visibility and enhance user engagement.

Content-based recommendation is used by social media sites to provide more personalized recommendations (Adomavicius & Tuzhilin, 2005). Content-based recommendation systems, such as DailyLearner or Stumble Upon, offer users a list of items/content similar to those they have already seen, preferred, or purchased in the past. Facebook also employed such advanced recommendation models. It not only recorded what people "liked" but also how long users spent on a certain post or a certain type of posts. Facebook can then show users only what they like based on the machine learning algorithms they developed, to keep users on the platform (Montag *et al.*, 2019).

Collaborative filtering systems such as Amazon and Netflix provide recommendations based on what a person "like you" may prefer. These structures apply stereotyped web consumption to predict an individual's tastes and find matching peers for each social media user (Adomavicius & Tuzhilin, 2005; Webster, 2011). If you think these recommendation systems would work for your products/organization, you may consider adopting one.

Advertising is a more traditional form of recommendation. Social media, like Facebook, X (formerly Twitter), and Pinterest, have been characterized to provide excellent brand engagement and development opportunities. Researchers suggest that digital ads can potentially influence the amount of awareness that each message/product attracts (Hargittai, 2000). Your consumers must learn about the existence of your product/social media messages before they can choose to use them. The awareness sets up the boundaries for your consumers' media choice (Napoli, 1999; Webster, 2011). This helps explain why almost 90% of social media sites link to Facebook and X (formerly Twitter) to increase awareness. In the online environment, your consumers are purposefully or incidentally exposed to banner ads, popup ads, paid links, and other indirect ad messages such as sponsored content, promoted tweets, or Google pay-per-click links. Thus, you should utilize various recommendation systems to increase awareness and guide consumer flow to your messages. We will discuss social media ads in greater detail in Chapter 9 when we talk about social media business models.

User profile

User profile is a unique structural character offered by most of the social media sites. More than 95% of social media sites allow users to create their personal profiles (Tang, 2013). A profile generally includes personal information such as name, pictures, and interests. On Facebook (Figure 6.1), users can upload their pictures, share personal information

Figure 6.1   Facebook's interface. Source: facebook.com/zuck.

(birthday, marital status, etc.), contact (phone number, email address, web page, IM ID, home address, etc.), interests (favorite books, movies, music, TV shows), as well as values and beliefs (political affiliation, favorite quotes). For TikTok, users can upload their profile photo, choose a nick name, and write a short bio (i.e., 80 words or less).

Other niche social media sites, like Gaia, allow users to customize profiles by creating avatars representing themselves in many ways, including skin tone, hair style, race (e.g., human, vampire, and elf), and outfits. Online personification is often the first step in social media use. Allowing your consumers to create unique profiles leads to more user-centered communication and can become an effective tool to make your site a part of your consumer's daily routine.

Messaging/chat

Messaging/chat is an important social media structure that highlights the social, participatory, and synchronous feature of social media. Facilitating conversations among individuals and groups is a fundamental feature of social media (Kietzmann *et al.*, 2011). More than

90% of social media sites provide a chat function and allow individuals to send private messages and make public comments (Tang, 2013). This structure gives you a great opportunity to develop one-on-one conversations, incorporate a direct feedback mechanism, and allow your consumers to freely express their opinions.

Facebook is a great example of a social media platform with various messaging/chat structures. Many heavy Facebook users may log onto Facebook every morning and stay on for the entire day, using the site as background noise. While there are many appealing components to the Facebook design, most of the Facebook content is asynchronous in nature, allowing users to catch up at any point throughout the day. The more synchronous chat feature prompts users to stay tuned in nonstop in case someone needs to reach them. In 2020, Facebook introduced Messenger Rooms for live video chats that allow users to invite a group of people to fully participate in live conversations. Instagram and WhatsApp have also developed similar structural features (Keefe, 2022). Twitch offered a "bit" feature that allows esports users to send a message that includes animated emotes to show support (Tang *et al.*, 2023; Twitch, 2020). Such structures make social media a combination of mass communication and interpersonal communication, create a space for a synchronous sharing experience, and demonstrate the unique social perspective provided by social media.

Endless scrolling/auto-play

Endless scrolling/auto-play is a structural feature that can create an immersive experience for social media users. Many social media sites like Instagram and Pinterest provide unlimited content that aim to make users go along with the flow to forget about time while using the platform (Montag *et al.*, 2019). Video sites like TikTok also include an auto play feature. As soon as users open the app, the videos will start playing one by one (Geyser, 2022). It is important to understand how influential these structures are to social media consumption. For example, you may plan to check TikTok quickly for a recipe before dinner. However, at the end of this short video, TikTok automatically plays another video that features Snoop Dogg (your favorite singer)'s billionaire bacon. As soon as the bacon video ends, Snoop Dogg's music video of *Drop It Like It's Hot* starts. Before you know it, two hours of your day are gone. Endless scrolling and auto-play could be an effective way in guiding user flow and keep your consumers staying in your social media community.

Connection to groups/people

Connection to groups/people is a unique feature and probably one of the most important structures leading to the success of your social media strategy. For many social media sites, one of the first steps is to ask users to identify their friends, groups, and interests, and connect them to their personal social network. By asking users to connect to groups, friends, and those sharing the same interests or problems, social media optimizes user engagement and helps build a community.

There are different types of groups in the social media landscape. Support groups, such as Caringbridge mentioned previously in this chapter, allow people to share ideas, knowledge, and advice. Social groups, like Meetup, make it easy for social media users with similar interests to make friends, social, and plan events. Insider groups, such as HubSpot, generally provide exclusive access to content on an invite-only basis (Keefe, 2022). Connecting with social media groups and getting to know the group members are the cornerstone of your users' social media experience.

In sum, social media structures – hashtags, search, recommendations, profile and groups, endless scrolling/streaming, and message/chat – change how attention is distributed and thus have a tremendous impact on guiding social media use. As a social media practitioner, you should well use these structural features when developing your social media campaigns.

Recognizing Constrained Active Choices

Social media leads to increased social support, more user-centered communication, and increased user selectivity. It has even been dubbed the instrument of ultimate individualism, and it has been suggested that social media use is solely determined by needs, wants, and preferences (Jenkins, 2009; Litt, 2012). We have learned in this chapter that social media use is a constrained active choice. Structures of time, access, and resources can influence your consumers' social media use. For example, while mobile access to social media has become a norm in the United States and many other countries, still about three-in-ten adults do not own a mobile device in Venezuela, India, and the Philippines (Silver *et al.*, 2019). In addition, researchers found that minorities often played console games because they have less frequent access to a personal computer or fast Internet connection (Tang *et al.*, 2023). As a social media practitioner, it is important for you to give attention to these less-often considered media and social structures (e.g., access to technologies, cost) and put media consumption habit, "lifestyle," and popular culture into consideration when developing your social media campaigns, particularly if your campaign will target different geographic areas in the world.

Constrained active choice means that in today's ever-complex media environment, it is impossible for us to be fully aware of all the available social media platform choices. Our awareness sets the boundaries for our media choice. Most of us only have knowledge of a limited number of social media sites and tend to browse a few popular ones frequently. As Chris Anderson (2006) noted, findability is more crucial than availability in today's marketplace.

Constrained active choice also suggests that social media structures provided by the technology and society could guide user attention. As mentioned in the previous section, structures such as hashtags can lead or mislead user attention to a handful of popular topics/messages over many other available choices. Even your most active consumers will purposefully use these structures to get quick and convenient information. While users can actively choose how and what they use in theory, exposure to niche content is constrained.

Constrained active choice further refers to individual's self-constraints and routine. Habits and repertoire play a significant role in influencing social media use. Your consumers become their own content managers when faced with endless choices. They actively decide their media use pattern, such as checking Instagram after every coffee break, and they purposefully choose to use or not to use certain content at certain times of the day, such as no news before bed. While these decisions are active choices at first, over time it becomes cognitive structures that your consumers impose to manage and constrain their lives. Your consumers cannot use every media and all content in 24 hours. Whether consciously or unconsciously, they are structuring and constraining their media use.

Overall, this chapter suggests that social media use is a constrained active choice. Your consumers are always free to use social media messages according to their needs and preferences. Nonetheless, the physical and virtual boundaries that exist within a media routine play an important role in determining social media use and should be considered when developing your social media strategy.

Case Study: Spotify's Wrapped Campaign

This chapter highlighted the active within structures process of social media use. The media routine typically starts with an active choice, while external structures can encourage (or constrain) the use. The repetition of active preferences will then reconstitute themselves as habits and routines that will ultimately structure future behavior and choices (Webster, 2014). Spotify's Wrapped campaign highlights such an active within structures process, pointing out how businesses can use both consumers' psychographic characteristics and structures to enhance engagement and build awareness.

Spotify, an audio streaming site, started Spotify Wrapped campaign in 2016, to provide users a personalized review of their most listened songs, musicians, and music genres for the year (Woods, 2022). Users can also see how their music highlights coincided with their life events in the year (Bredava, 2022). Spotify also encouraged its users to share their musical highlights on social media, such as Instagram Stories, and TikTok, and tag their favorite artists. Through years, Spotify Wrapped has not only become a holiday tradition for its users but also a hot topic on social media (Woods, 2022). During its launch month in 2016, the campaign has been mentioned in over a million tweets (Bredava, 2022). In 2020, 90 million people shared Spotify Wrapped (Shalvoy, 2021). In 2021, tweets about Spotify Wrapped increased 461% compared to 2020. In 2022, the first three days of Spotify Wrapped campaign brought more than 400 million tweets (Woods, 2022). The campaign is now something that users expect and look forward to each year.

Spotify's Wrapped campaign addresses its users' active needs of having fun, wanting to share, and showing who they are. The personalization of everyone's music story, along with marking songs that accompanied them in their lives, creates the initial drive for the continuous use of Spotify. It is evident that Spotify users want to share their story with family and friends and further connect with artists and other fans.

In addition to matching the campaign to users' needs and wants, Spotify utilizes social media structures to create the buzz around the campaign. The campaign consists of a series of visuals for each user, along with an invitation that asks them to share their personalized music stories on social media. To optimize social sharing, the information came in an easily shareable format (i.e., appealing visuals) with quick links to repost on various social media platforms, like TikTok, Snapchat, and WhatsApp (Woods, 2022). By encouraging the use of tagging and hashtags, the campaign drew more people who want to try this experience (Bredava, 2022).

Building user habit and making the campaign a part of people's routine are also key to success. Spotify showed listeners their "Year in Review" around the same time every year (i.e., early December) (Figure 6.2). The format of Spotify Wrapped also stays the same every year. The annual campaign provides the familiarity, which nurtures user habits. For many people, it has become an end of the year ritual (Woods, 2022). Exploring and sharing their most important musical highlights has been a part of Spotify users' lives. The power of repetition should never be understated in social media storytelling and strategy.

It is important to note that today's media users, digital natives in particular, have more than abundant choices in terms of media consumption. Thus, marketers need to develop social media campaigns that not only address consumers' active needs but also make social media messages fit the structural constraints of the platform, funnel consumers to the content, and utilize structures to nurture habits. The ultimate goal is to make your product and service a part of your consumers' lives. To this end, Spotify Wrapped provides a successful example of a social media campaign that fully considered the interplay between active choice, habit, structures, and social media consumption. While Spotify Wrapped surely satisfied its users' needs, the strategic use of social media structures made the campaign viral.

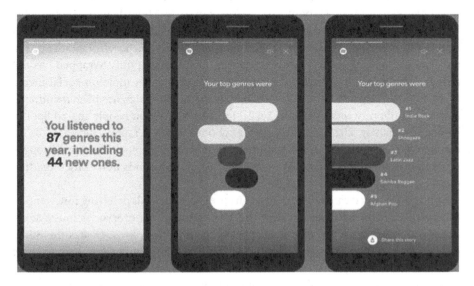

Figure 6.2   Spotify wrapped. Source: Spotify AB, https://newsroom.spotify.com/2021-01-12/4-tips-to-make-the-most-of-your-2021-wrapped/ (last accessed September 26, 2023).

Discussion questions

1   How did Spotify utilize structures to build a viral social media campaign? Do you think their approach is successful? Could the approach be applied to other social media campaigns?
2   If you oversaw the creation of a future Spotify Wrapped campaign, what would you keep the same? What would you change? Why?
3   Think about a social media campaign you have seen, which put the interplay between consumer preferences/needs, habit, and structures into consideration. Connect the lessons we learned about diffusion, community, and mobilization to explain why the campaign is a success.

Summary

This chapter highlights the crucial role that structure plays in social media uses. Specifically, the active within structures theoretical approach explains how we actively use media content within internal and external structures. There is little you can do to control your consumers' personal preferences, life experiences, moods, personalities, and other individual psychological factors. However, you can gain a solid understanding of how to utilize social media structures, such as hashtags, recommendations, search, and grouping, as well as environmental and societal structures like time, location, contexts, and culture to guide your consumer preference and content consumption.

This chapter also suggests that social media users increasingly access multiple portals from the same organization/brand/company. Despite the hype and promise associated with social media marketing, you need to achieve a more accurate understanding about how to effectively use social media messages to reach and influence consumers by fitting in with your existing marketing plan. This can be done by considering omnichannel content management, rather than focusing on medium-specific strategies.

Knowing your consumers is the first step toward developing successful social media messages. Hashtags, search, recommendations, user profile, connections to groups, endless scrolling, and chat/messages provide important contextual cues that can direct and/or constrain your consumers' social media use. Without a comprehensive understanding of your consumers and the infrastructures and constraints that they work within, messages can prove scattered, repetitive, and useless. Social media strategies must reflect an understanding of the interplay between active choice, habit, and structures. Chapters 5 and 6 have provided you with a complete picture of your social media users. Now let's turn our attention to how to create social media messages that encourage user engagement and community building in Chapter 7.

Key Takeaways

1 Active within structures is a nuanced theoretical conceptualization of social media users. Achieving a comprehensive understanding of your consumers is the first step toward developing successful social media marketing strategies. Social media campaigns should reflect an understanding of the interplay between active choice, habit, and structures.
2 Social media structures – hashtags, search, profile, message/chat, connection to groups/people, endless scrolling, and recommendations – play an important role in social media use. Making good use of these structures and creating social media messages that fit to the infrastructure and design of the medium are crucial.
3 Habits, self-constraints, and routine help determine social media use. Thus, you need to find and use contextual and structural cues to encourage habit formation and build brand loyalty.
4 Facing convergence, you must consider omnichannel content management, rather than isolating your social media strategy to a single medium.

References

Adomavicius, G. & Tuzhilin, A. (2005) Toward the next generation of recommender systems: a survey of the state-of-the-art and possible extensions. *IEEE Transactions on Knowledge and Data Engineering*, 17, 734–749.

Anderson, C. (2006) *The Long Tail: Why the Future of Business Is Selling Less of More*. New York: Hyperion.

Beyers, H. (2004) Dayparting online: living up to its potential? *International Journal on Media Management*, 6(1–2), 67–73.

Bredava, A. (2022) 17 Awesome examples of social media marketing. *Search Engine Journal*. Available at https://www.searchenginejournal.com/social-media-marketing-examples/380202/#close (accessed November 17, 2023).

Broadband Search (2023) Mobile vs. desktop internet usage (latest 2023 data). Available at https://www.broadbandsearch.net/blog/mobile-desktop-internet-usage-statistics (accessed November 17, 2023).

Campbell, S. (2023) Hashtags statistics 2023: Twitter, Instagram, Facebook & LinkedIn. *The Small Business Blog*. Available at https://thesmallbusinessblog.net/hashtags-statistics/ (accessed November 17, 2023).

Cooper, R. & Tang, T. (2009) Predicting audience exposure to television in today's media environment: an empirical integration of active-audience and structural theories. *Journal of Broadcasting and Electronic Media*, 53(3), 1–19.

Earnheardt, A.C., Earnheardt, M.B. & Rubin, R.B. (2008) Development and test of an Internet search evaluation measure. *Ohio Communication Journal*, 46, 45–72.

Geyser, W. (2022) What is TikTok?: everything you need to know in 2023. *Influencer Marketing Hub*. Available at https://influencermarketinghub.com/what-is-tiktok/ (accessed November 17, 2023).

Giddens, A. (1984) *The Constitution of Society: Outline of the Theory of Structuration*. Berkeley, CA: University of California Press.

Hargittai, E. (2000) Open portals or closed gates: channeling content on the World Wide Web. *Poetics*, 27(4), 233–254.

Jenkins, H. (2009) *Confronting the Challenges of Participatory Culture: Media Education for the 21st Century*. Cambridge, MA: MIT Press.

Keefe, C. (2022) Our top 10 social media engagement hacks for 2020. *WordStream*. Available at https://www.

wordstream.com/blog/ws/2020/07/30/social-media-engagement (accessed November 17, 2023).

Khoo, J. (2020) When to use social media and when to use search engine marketing. *Forbes*. Available at https://www.forbes.com/sites/theyec/2020/02/10/when-to-use-social-media-and-when-to-use-search-engine-marketing/?sh=2615646430cd (accessed November 17, 2023).

Kietzmann, J.H., Hermkens, K., McCarthy, I.P. & Silvestre, B.S. (2011) Social media? Get serious! Understanding the functional building blocks of social media. *Business Horizons*, 54, 241–251.

Knobloch-Westerwick, S., Sharma, N., Hansen, D.L. & Alter, S. (2005) Impact of popularity indications on readers' selective exposure to online news. *Journal of Broadcasting and Electronic Media*, 49(3), 296–313.

Litt, E. (2012) Knock, knock. Who's there? The imaged audience. *Journal of Broadcasting and Electronic Media*, 56(3), 330–345.

MacReady, H. (2022) How to use hashtags in 2023: a guide for every network. *Hootsuite*. Available at https://blog.hootsuite.com/how-to-use-hashtags/ (accessed November 17, 2023).

McLachlan, S. & Cohen, B. (2023) How often to post to social media in 2023. *Hootsuite*. Available at https://blog.hootsuite.com/how-often-to-post-on-social-media/ (accessed November 17, 2023).

Molenaar, K. (2023) The ultimate list of trending hashtags on every platform (2023). *Influencer Marketing Hub*. Available at https://influencermarketinghub.com/trending-hashtags/ (accessed November 17, 2023).

Montag, C., Lachmann, B., Herrlich, M. & Zweig, K. (2019) Addictive features of social media/messenger platforms and freemium games against the background of psychological and economic theories. *International Journal of Environmental Research and Public Health*, 16, 2612.

Napoli, P.M. (1999) Deconstructing the diversity principle. *Journal of Communication*, 49(4), 7–34.

Needle, F. (2023) The best times to post on social media in 2023. *HubSpot*. Available at https://blog.hubspot.com/marketing/best-times-post-pin-tweet-social-media-infographic#:~:text=According%20to%20our%202022%20surveyday%20to%20post%20is%20Friday (accessed November 17, 2023).

Newberry, C. (2022) Social SEO: how to help people find you on social media. *Hootsuite*. Available at https://blog.hootsuite.com/social-seo/ (accessed November 17, 2023).

Pan, B., Hembrooke, H., Joachims, T., Lorigo, L., Gay, G. & Granka, L. (2007) In Google we trust: users' decisions on rank, position, and relevance. *Journal of Computer-Mediated Communication*, 12, 801–823.

Qualls, A. (2017) Dear kitten: the marketing power of cat videos. *Drury University Social Media Strategy*. Available at https://dusocialmediastrategy.com/2017/05/dear-kitten-marketing-power-cat-videos/ (accessed November 17, 2023).

Reiss, S. & Wiltz, J. (2004) Why people watch reality TV. *Media Psychology*, 6, 363–378.

Sewell, W.H. (1992) A theory of structure: duality, agency, and transformation. *American Journal of Sociology*, 98(1), 1–29.

Shalvoy, J. (2021) Spotify unwrapped: inside the company's biggest marketing campaign. *Variety*. Available at https://variety.com/2021/music/news/spotify-wrapped-marketing-shares-1235139981/ (accessed November 17, 2023).

Silver, L., Smith, A., Johnson, C., Jiang, J., Anderson, M. & Rainie, L. (2019) Mobile connectivity in emerging economies. *Pew Research Center*. Available at https://www.pewresearch.org/internet/2019/03/07/use-of-smartphones-and-social-media-is-common-across-most-emerging-economies/ (accessed November 17, 2023).

Simon, H. (1971) Designing organizations for an information-rich world. In: M. Greenberger (ed) *Computers, Communications and the Public Interest*, pp. 40–41. Baltimore, MD: The Johns Hopkins Press.

Stubbs, M. (2017) Get the gear that esports pros use to become the best in the world. *Forbes*. Available at https://www.forbes.com/sites/mikestubbs/2017/12/25/get-the-gear-that-esports-pros-use-to-become-the-best-in-the-world/#7ef5dd8f5d12 (accessed November 17, 2023).

Sundar, S. & Nass, C. (2001) Conceptualizing sources in online news. *Journal of Communication*, 51(1), 52–72.

Tang, T. (2013) Is structure relevant any more: preliminary development of a new measure of social media structures. *Paper Presented at the Eastern Communication Association Annual Conference*, Pittsburgh, PA.

Tang, T. & Cooper, R. (2012) Gender, sports, and new media: predictors of viewing during the 2008 Beijing

Olympics. *Journal of Broadcasting and Electronic Media*, 56(1), 75–91.

Tang, T., Cooper, R. & Gandolfi, E. (2023) Interactive within structures: understanding ethnicity, esports uses and effects. *Howard Journal of Communication*, 34(4), 353–371. doi: 10.1080/10646175.2023.2179903.

Thorson, E. (2008) Changing patterns of news consumption and participation: news recommendation engines. *Information, Communication and Society*, 11, 473–489.

Twitch (2020) Bits. Available at https://www.twitch.tv/bit (accessed November 17, 2023).

Webster, J.G. (2011) The duality of media: a structurational theory of public attention. *Communication Theory*, 21, 43–66.

Webster, J.G. (2014) *The Marketplace of Attention: How Audiences Take Shape in a Digital Age*. Cambridge, MA: The MIT Press.

Webster, J.G. (2017) Three myths of digital media. *Convergence: The International Journal of Research into New Media Technologies*, 23, 352–361. doi: 10.1177/1354856517700385.

Webster, J.G., Phalen, P.F. & Lichty, L.W. (2006) *Ratings Analysis: The Theory and Practice of Audience Research*, third edition. Mahwah, NJ: Lawrence Erlbaum Associates.

Weller, K. (2015) Trying to understand social media users and usage: the forgotten features of social media platforms. *Online Information Review* 40(2), 256–264. doi: 10.1108/OIR-09-2015-0299.

Wood, W., Quinn, J.M. & Kashy, D. (2002) Habits in everyday life: thought, emotion and action. *Journal of Personality and Social Psychology*, 83, 1281–1297.

Woods, K. (2022) Spotify wrapped: what marketers can learn from the viral campaign. *Sprout Social*. Available at https://sproutsocial.com/insights/spotify-wrapped/ (accessed November 17, 2023).

7

Social Media Messages for Engagement

Learning Objectives

After reading this chapter, you should be able to:
1   Understand the theory of dialogic communication and apply it to a strategic social media strategy.
2   Define online engagement and virtual communities and understand their benefits to marketers.
3   Manage and maintain a dialogic loop with media users.

Introduction

Previous chapters have stressed the importance of encouraging user participation with social media content to yield the most effective results for desired behavior change. Chapter 6 explained how active media users can be limited or guided by the structures provided by the social media sites that they visit. This chapter provides practical advice on which features work best for user dialogue and feedback, even when consumers are dissatisfied with their online user experience.

People utilize social media to fulfill various gratifications. They access information, share content, and communicate with family and friends, both private and public in nature. Think

Strategic Social Media: From Marketing to Social Change, Second Edition. L. Meghan Mahoney and Tang Tang.
© 2024 John Wiley & Sons, Inc. Published 2024 by John Wiley & Sons, Inc.

about the last product that you purchased online. What was that process like? How did you find the website you purchased from? Did you read customer reviews before deciding? What types of feedback, if any, did the website ask of you after you made the purchase? These are all important considerations that your consumers consider each time they make purchase decisions online.

Consumer expectations have changed dramatically over the past decades. Rapid technological convergence, greater connectivity, enhanced interactive capacity, and increased organizational capability are making the information economy visible for everyday consumers (Butler & Peppard, 1998). The one or two retailers available in their immediate proximity no longer bind consumers. Instead, they use technology to help make consumption decisions that work best in their lives, whether the focus is on price, fair trade, quality of product, or speed of delivery.

These purchasing decisions are complex and extend along a continuum of problem-solving decisions, including categories such as price, perceived risk, experience, involvement, and information content. For the smaller ticket items that have less influence on their day-to-day lives (e.g., picture frames or a new t-shirt), people tend to seek less information, experience, and involvement in the purchase process. However, if people need to make big changes or a substantial investment in their lives, they tend to rely on a more purposeful and involved information-seeking process. Past brand experience becomes much more important for these decisions. That is why so many individuals stick with one brand of electronics or cars that they already know and trust.

Customers now have expectations for accessing and leaving feedback on the products they purchased and used. Searching through this feedback, you may come to the same resolution as other marketing professionals: customers are most likely to leave online feedback when they are incredibly satisfied or dissatisfied with a product. The everyday average user is less motivated to write an online review. This often leaves professionals feeling discouraged from providing participatory structural features. After all, why prompt users to engage if there is a greater chance that users will respond negatively?

This chapter explains how to encourage participatory dialogue on social media that will help facilitate positive and useful feedback from social media users. It first provides a theoretical understanding of how public dialogue is best for both marketers and consumers. Next, it demonstrates the importance of virtual communities in sustaining online engagement. Finally, it provides tips for responding to dissatisfied online consumers and maintaining an effective dialogic loop.

The Theory of Dialogic Communication

Part I of this book explains the importance of igniting participatory media users in social media messages to prompt behavior change. However, Chapter 6 demonstrated how social media users are limited and guided through the structural features available. Encouraging participation requires more than just providing users with functional social media structures for dialogue but needs a shift in the way we view the role that media users play in the communication process.

Habermas (1984) describes dialogue as the coordination in good faith of a plan for action. This suggests a cooperative communication process where organizational leaders are not hyper-focused on disseminating messages and selling products to consumers as one would see in a top-down diffusion model. Today's consumers expect brands to value their business and feedback. After all, every consumer carries millions of retailer options in their pocket. Communication is essential to the success of any social media strategy in today's marketplace.

True participation means working with and by the people, not working on or working for the people (Servaes, 1996). Yes, social media practitioners are trying to reach a consumer to sell a product or increase numbers, but what makes social media unique is its potential for users to access, participate, determine, sharpen, and manage content (Singhal, 2004). It is time that marketers stop selling to consumers and begin engaging them in a truly participatory manner.

Each year, companies spend a great deal of energy and money in marketing design and research. This includes both qualitative measurements (e.g., focus groups, direct observation, interviews) and quantitative measurements (e.g., survey and controlled experiments). Each of these requires skilled researchers, which can cost a significant amount of money. On average, a focus group research project can cost $4000–12,000 (Gell, 2023). While these are effective measures for creating and sustaining products, each comes with its own sets of challenges and drawbacks.

For example, one of these methodologies – focus groups, which has a long history in marketing research – tends to rely heavily on the moderator. Lack of leadership or control can lead to problems with focus group research (Gibbs, 1997). In addition, focus group research often fails due to *groupthink*, the psychological phenomenon in which people strive for consensus within a group (Irving, 1972). Another popular research method, survey research, could also be problematic because of low response rates and sample reliability (Reichheld, 2003). Moreover, these research efforts can succumb to what is known as the *Hawthorne effect*, where research subject answers are influenced by the presence of the researcher. Most often, participants give answers that they feel are desired, not what they actually believe to be true. They may say that a product is more useful than it proves in their everyday lives, because of social desirability. Clearly, user and marketing research is a difficult, expensive, and challenging task. More information about alternative research methods will be discussed in Chapter 12.

Social media allows many opportunities to provide immediate feedback, without the presence of a researcher to influence responses. While companies would pay a great deal of money for this type of information in marketing research, they often try to mitigate and control responses as much as possible due to the public nature of social media. Freire's theory of dialogic communication and action explains why these ideas and opinions should be valued rather than feared.

The *theory of dialogic communication and action* explains the importance of transactional communication for sustaining relationships through social media. It is defined as a type of relational interaction, where ideas and opinions are negotiated through communication exchanges (Kent, 1998). In other words, though the two parties do not have to agree on an absolute truth, they must be willing to reach mutually satisfying opinions. Here, dialogic communication is a product, not the process. The facilitator of communication is vested in both sides of the communication process, rather than the self-serving interest of marketing.

Stoker and Tusinski (2006) explain how dialogic communication aims to persuade likeminded publics by transforming dialogue into two-way asymmetric communication. The goal is to facilitate interactivity between an organization and the public. Dialogic communication demonstrates how they can work together to build more innovative ideas and a longer sustaining relationship and is often considered a more ethical way of conducting public dialogue and public relations.

Social media users expect dialogic communication functions when they engage in the platform. There are many structural features that organizations can include to promote dialogic communication on social media, including dialogic loop, usefulness of information, generation of return visits, ease of interface, and the conservation of visitors (Russell, 2008). Often, these can be achieved by employing the social media structures discussed in Chapter 6.

It is also important to search your brand information and feedback beyond your own social media pages and see what people are saying about your business. Respond to these customers. Just because they did not communicate with you directly, it does not mean that they would not want to hear from you. If there is something wrong with the direction of the dialogue, it is likely that something is wrong with the product. While this type of feedback would have cost thousands of dollars in traditional marketing research, social media allows consumers to let you know that your product is unsatisfactory for free before you continue to produce more of the same. Moreover, there is a chance for you to respond to your consumers' dissatisfaction to show how much you care and value their feedback. Social media marketing is about building and maintaining relationships.

Focus on promoting dialogue where people contribute in ways that others will want to hear. Rather than providing feedback in silos or discussion forum threads, prompt innovative options for participation: Have contests; ask for pictures; allow people to share user-generated videos. Organizations must provide much more than the product that customers have paid for. Your social media strategy should be based on a positive, fun, niche experience for users, not just a place where they come to learn about a product.

As a social media marketer, you should also adopt the role of facilitator, promoting an environment of nonjudgmental dialogue and active listening (Griffin, 2009). Such a cooperative, two-way, ethical communication practice requires neither side to attempt to control the communication process (Habermas, 1990). Do not try to change your consumers. Instead, change your product until it meets and exceeds their expectations. If this is not your goal, then you are not engaging in the mindset that meets the values of true participation.

Social Media Engagement and Virtual Communities

True participation should be the goal of any social media campaign. We have discussed the importance of a change in assumptions regarding the perception of social media users. Communication with them is no longer, nor has it ever really been, a top-down diffusion process. This hurts your brand and disengages consumers from participating further. User feedback is a critical asset for any organization. It is important to take as many steps necessary to encourage engagement between consumers and organizations. This is how long-lasting relationships are formed.

While this book focuses on social media, it is impossible to ignore the impact business websites have on the conversations happening on social networks. Since most diffusion posts link customers to a brand's website, practitioners must constantly monitor what that experience is like for consumers. As mentioned previously, there are many structural elements that an organization can add to their social media platforms to encourage dialogic communication, including dialogic loop, usefulness of information, generation of return visits, ease of interface, and the conservation of visitors (Russell, 2008). Each of these features help users engage and feel as though they are an intricate part of a community.

A *dialogic loop* is one of the most important features that social media users are beginning to expect from organizations. This includes ways in which users exchange messages with the source of an organization. If consumers have a question about your product, they should not have to leave your social media platform to send a query. There should be more than one structural feature that allows asynchronous (e.g., Twitter replies) and synchronous (e.g., instant chat) answers on your site. Indeed, many consumers tweeted businesses when they have a concern and/or encounter a problem.

It is important that the information you provide about your organization and product proves useful to consumers. Employ narrative structures to build brand authenticity and be transparent about every stage of the production, product dissemination, and price. One great way to provide useful information to users is to allow other members in the community to share reviews and experiences with your product. Sohome, a furniture and home décor company, did so by asking customers to share how they used Sohome's products for home decoration on Instagram. By asking customers to share real-life images of Sohome's products (Tran, 2023), the company encourages a dialogic loop, which in turn enhances user engagement with the brand.

If you are selling a shirt that runs smaller in size, it is better to have other reviewers state this so that consumers can negotiate this information in their purchasing decision. Maybe this will prompt them to order a larger size, or maybe they will order a different shirt altogether. Regardless, you are keeping them on your site because they feel as though you are being authentic and transparent about your product information. In fact, you can gain from having poor reviewed products available on your site. This allows customers to make informed decisions about purchasing higher-rated products. Customers prefer having a greater amount of information about products, rather than dealing with returns or exchanges later. Thus, do not filter negative feedbacks to only include positive comments. Otherwise, you may come across looking nontransparent and lacking authenticity. Remember from Chapter 2 that the theory of social penetration explains how an increase in self-disclosure leads to an increase in trust. Trust is a critical ingredient for social media engagement and community.

Prompting users to return to your social media pages is a difficult task. Current satisfied customers are at the top of the buying hierarchy (Stratten, 2012). It is best to nurture relationships with the customers that you already have than spend time and money chasing new customers. If your product is strong and their experience is positive, they will spread the word to their personal network and continue coming back for future purchases.

One way to encourage return visitors is to turn your social media page into a community. Facilitate conversations so that consumers who are interested in your product will want to come back and participate, even if they are not interested in buying a new product. If you notice a regular user has not visited in a while, reach out and let them know they are missed. Use social media to ask questions, update often, and prompt users to share. Make your space a place where people are happy to associate their identity with. Think about the types of content that would excite users to participate in conversations.

Don't make users frustrated when they visit your site. The ease of interface has a lot to do with how satisfied customers feel when they visit your page and whether they come back. This does not mean that you need to have the most technologically advanced page. In fact, it means quite the opposite. Keep your design simple and make sure that it aligns with your brand authenticity. Apple's website is a simple white background with gray font. This matches the simple and minimalistic style of their products. UNICEF's website uses colors of the globe: blue, green, and white. This is consistent with their logo and globalized development vision for children. Choose one or two fonts and colors and stay consistent throughout. Ensure that every page on your site has easy-to-find links where users can ask questions and get to the home page. Users should be able to get to the home page from any point on the website.

Be careful with *CAPTCHA* (*c*ompletely *a*utomated *p*ublic *T*uring test to tell *c*omputers and *h*umans *a*part), an application where users are required to type the word or numbers shown on an image to advance to the next step (Cui *et al.*, 2010). While these forms are a great way to minimize spam messages for you, they can be difficult to read, and users can become frustrated with the process.

All of these prove effective ways to ensure the conservation of visitors. It may be worthwhile to ask your users for some information about themselves while they first visit your social media site. As mentioned in Chapter 6, many social media platforms asked users to create a profile. Many companies also make users register their email address before being able to look at products.

The brand Joss and Main is a home décor members-only company. It requires users to register an email address and create a home portfolio before they can access content. The daily deal pioneer Woot makes users register their email address and hometown before they can browse. Zulily, a site that sells goods for mothers and children, requires a username, password, and email address for membership. While these strategies may lose some users upfront, the ability to learn more information and follow-up with consumers may lead to greater sales. Nonetheless, you should note that your customers do not like having to register with websites, even when checking out, let alone checking in (Charlton, 2007). You want users to return to your site because they had a positive experience, not because you bounded them by follow-up emails. So, find a balance between this push and pull of media content.

Humans function through habit and marketers know this. Companies all over the world are trying to determine how to get users to make their business a part of their regular online routine. Target Corporation is known for recruiting shoppers during the biggest transitional periods of their lives, such as graduation, marriage, and, most importantly, parenthood. These are dynamic periods of life where consumers are already going through substantial changes, and so it is likely to change purchasing patterns as well. New parents may appreciate the convenience of purchasing groceries and clothing in one stop, even if it means buying different products than they did prior to baby. If practitioners can entice customers to visit their store during these transitional periods through coupons or promotions, they may come back for life out of convenience.

Great sales, products, and promotions are excellent ways to tempt users into visiting your social media pages. You can set up user-friendly interfaces that save preferences, purchases, shipment, and payment information. People are much more likely to purchase a product if they only must press one button than if they must fill out fields each time. However, the key to transforming customers into lifelong brand advocates is to make them feel as though they belong to your community. You want consumers to form relationships and become emotionally invested with your community.

Online engagement is an essential ingredient to this process. *Online engagement* is a dynamic and sustained relationship from users to a brand that communicates brand value (Mollen & Wilson, 2010). This is only possible if you have a clear sense of your vision. If you are not certain of your brand authenticity, there is no way you can expect your consumers to know. Go back to Chapter 2 and help determine what makes you unique from other competitors in the marketplace.

There are many ways to encourage true participation from users in your social media strategy. This could be done via a five-step action plan.

True Participation Action Plan

1　Set up structural features to promote dialogic communication, including dialogic loop, usefulness of information, generation of return visits, ease of interface, and the conservation of visitors.

2　Provide a narrative that clearly outlines your brand authenticity. Be as transparent as possible about production, product distribution, and price.

3　Allow consumers to share reviews directly on your social media pages. Respond quickly to unsatisfied customers, but don't filter or censor. Having a few negative reviews can actually benefit a brand, provided the majority of comments are positive.

4　Use social media to facilitate conversations that are consistent with the lifestyle of your target consumers. Don't use this space to sell products. Instead, ask questions, update often, and prompt users to share information that is useful and speaks to them.

5　Ensure that your product interface is easy to use. Only use CAPTCHA forms if necessary and ask users questions on signing in to save their preferences, shipment, and payment information. Use this information to follow-up with consumers, especially during transitional periods in their lives.

There are many ways to engage consumers via social media. One of the best approaches may seem counterintuitive, and that is not to think of social media as a way for you, as a brand, to communicate with your community members. Instead, think of your social media as a place for your consumers to communicate with other consumers. Allow structural features that enable consumers to reach out to you if they would like to, but also allow a safe space where they are able to create materials on their own and communicate with other members of the community about issues of importance to them. Be sure that sources of engagement are authentic, relevant to the users, provide an emotional connection between members, and fulfill a narrative structure for and with your consumers. This hands-off approach is difficult, especially since you lose some control over the conversation. In addition, it will not work for every business and every product. This strategy requires a brand with a trusted history and strong authenticity. Nonetheless, it promotes independent satisfaction and helps build community (Krause & Coates, 2008).

Consider why consumers have chosen your social media platform and the types of things that they are likely to be interested in. It is possible that your product speaks to a certain aspect of their lifestyle and identity that is difficult to find in interpersonal settings. Play to these emotions. These are the types of conversations you should facilitate through social media because your users will want to engage.

One example of a company that has done this well is the Swedish furniture company IKEA. Its target consumers are likely on a budget, but still interested in home design and do-it-yourself projects (most furniture purchased in IKEA requires some level of do-it-yourself assembly). To engage with its target consumers, IKEA introduced a Pinterest search campaign during the back-to-school seasons, encouraging college students to find ideas to make their dorms fashionable with manageable cost (Xue, 2022). The campaign used structures, such as pins with keywords "dorm creativity," "dorm ideas," to make their content easy to find. Through these simple structural features, IKEA made it easy for users to communicate with each other, share their own projects, which in turn facilitates dialogic communication.

The campaign shows how you can encourage true participation on social media. Consumers would be interested in using IKEA's Pinterest board at many stages of the consumption process. They may want to use the site before making a purchase to see how they could use IKEA furniture to make their dorm organized. They could visit the site once they have purchased the furniture to see ideas for how it should be arranged in a room. They could also use the board to share their own completed projects. No matter how consumers prefer to use the site, IKEA has incorporated a structure where they are not telling users what to talk about. Instead, they offer an opportunity for consumers to check into the social media site and communicate with other people according to their own needs.

In 2021, IKEA and Pinterest teamed up and launched "Renocations," an AI-powered tool that aims to help IKEA customers find inspiration for their next home renovation projects (Leasca, 2021; see Figure 7.1). This tool starts with asking users to take a quick and fun quiz to determine their interests and identify "who they are." The quiz questions include: If you

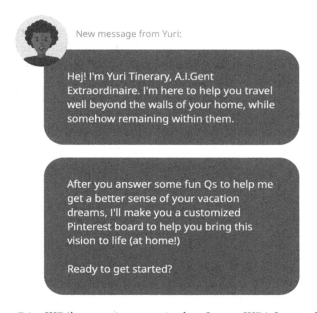

Figure 7.1   IKEA's renocation campaign bot. Source: IKEA Systems B.V.

could be anywhere, where would you be? (beach, nature, or city); what are your favorite activities to do there? (go swimming, read a book, etc.); and Is there a room in your house where you also feel free and relaxed? (living room, bedroom, backyard, etc.). The "Renocations" tool then create a Pinterest board based on the answers with pins of themed looks and individual products that can turn the consumer's home into their dream getaway place (Leasca, 2021). IKEA's "Renocations" shows how you can use *gamification* or utilize game thinking in a non-game context to engage users and solve problems (Zichermann & Cunningham, 2011). The fun quiz used by the IKEA's Renocations campaign is a great way to hook users into coming back and staying engaged. The best uses of gamification are those that are authentic to the purpose and shared vision of the virtual community.

Virtual communities are groups of people with common interests and practices that communicate regularly and for some duration in an organized way over the Internet through a common location or mechanism (Ridings & Gefen, 2004). This allows users the chance to personalize their online experience even more through character identification. Virtual communities allow discussions to evolve into the feelings and connections of personal relationships. They tend to be asynchronous in nature, but an emerging trend of synchronous communities has emerged where users meet in real time through cyber-face to cyber-face social interactions (Hill *et al.*, 1995).

Some asynchronous online discussion forums are just places for individuals to meet and talk without any sense of belonging or consistency among group members (Ridings & Gefen, 2004). These do not necessarily meet the requirements of a virtual community. Members should feel part of a larger social group, have ongoing exchanges with other members, and sense lasting relationships with others. It may take repeat positive experiences and periods of disengagement before members realize the value of community membership. There are only so many online communities that individuals can make a part of their regular routine. The more your community brand and your consumer's values align, the more invested they will feel toward your organization.

Creating a virtual community is an important step for any social media marketing strategy. This will help foster relationships between users and the organization. It will keep users vested in the connections that they have made, push innovation forward and keep your consumers coming back. Remember that virtual communities require much more than the technological capability for communication. Authenticity and sincere facilitation play a huge role in how invested users feel.

The Dialogic Loop

The goal of social media marketing is to form relationships with consumers. The importance of customer loyalty in organizational sustainment cannot be understated. Loyal customers mean more than someone who routinely buys products from a company. These customers may only be doing so because it is the simplest option available or because there is no alternative available. However, in a business climate that is constantly evolving, social media marketers cannot rely on these motivations.

Many takeout and delivery restaurants have begun utilizing mobile apps to allow users to order takeout food online without ever speaking with the customer. By signing up for an account on its mobile app, customers can store their address, payment information, and past purchases for future use. This process is much easier for customers because they can order food without remembering a phone number, menu, or digging their credit card out of their wallet. Furthermore, it mitigates some level of human error in getting the order and address correctly. When this technology first became available, customers may have only had one or two options for ordering via mobile. Perhaps every time they wanted to order food for delivery, they returned to your restaurant not because they felt loyal or liked your food the best but because the structural features made it the easiest process.

Sure enough, time has passed, and more and more takeout and delivery restaurants have had mobile apps. This is where customer loyalty plays a larger role than ease of use. Customer loyalty is one of the most important drivers of economic growth for a company (Reichheld, 2003). One of the most critical features for ensuring customer loyalty is the dialogic loop. If done correctly, customers will feel as though they are valued within the community. If done poorly, you may have lost their business forever.

There are many structural features that you can include in your social media platforms to ensure a dialogic loop. These include commenting and responding to your consumers in a timely manner; providing links to your company's website and other social media pages; offering regular updates; and using replies and mentions to facilitate communication with stakeholders (Wang & Yang, 2020). Fortune 500 companies have already used these structures to capture user attention. They also took their consumers' personal interests, thoughts, and suggestions into consideration when interacting with them on social media to make consumers feel recognized and cared (Wang & Yang, 2020).

It is imperative that you make it as easy as possible for customers to communicate with you. Allowing opportunities for your social media users to send messages directly to your organization, vote on issues, share their concerns, and fill out surveys identifying priorities and expressing opinions on issues helps customers see how much you care (Taylor *et al.*, 2001). However, they should never be included unless someone is able to respond in a timely manner. There is nothing worse than taking the time to query an organization and never hearing back.

Be sure to have an expert available who knows the product and brand well. Remember that customers can communicate with one another and so have a policy about how you are going to handle certain scenarios and stick to it. Do not give one customer special treatment over another. Through prompt replies to concerns and questions, customers will begin to feel a sense of relational trust and commitment to the brand. These relationships should not only serve the public relations goals of an organization but should also incorporate the interests, values, and concerns of users (McAllister-Spooner & Kent, 2009). Many companies have begun using personalized names of employees to answer customer questions.

Have a question while using Skype? Simply tweet @PeteratSkype and you will receive a prompt reply. This helps humanize the public relations process.

In the book *Unmarketing*, Scott Stratten (2012) explains a five-step process for dealing with angry customers through social media.

1   Have an existing strategy in place. While every query should be handled on a personal level, there should be consistency across organizational policies and mission statements. This information should be transparent and easily found in the company website.
2   Acknowledge the customer's dissatisfaction. Let them know that you received their complaint and that you understand their frustrations.
3   Clarify the company policy and why the user may have had the unsatisfactory experience that they encountered. This is not the time to place blame on the customer, but to ensure that the negative experience will not happen again.
4   Present a resolution that satisfies both the customer and the organizational policy and mission statement.
5   Social media allows companies to check back with customers after a resolution has been made to ensure they are satisfied with their customer service experience. This allows you to continue communication with the customer and let them know that their business and feedback are important to you.

Responsiveness does not simply mean getting back to individuals; messages should be personalized to the query, be timely in nature, and involve specially trained response personnel (Gustavsen & Tilley, 2003). No one expects every customer who comes to your social media site to be completely satisfied. However, it is imperative that your organization has a customer service strategy to handle unsatisfied customers.

Today, customers play a critical role in the communication process and the success of your social media strategy. Increased effective dialogue is the key for making your customers feel valued and engaged. If your values do not align with the values of the theory of dialogic communication, this will come across in your customer service practices. True participation through social media is imperative for organizational sustainment.

Case Study: Roblox

Social media provides alternative spaces for communication among and between diverse communities. Much scholarly research investigates potential uses of virtual communities regarding issues of identity and relationship building (Nisbett, 2006). With no proxemic physical space limitations, virtual communities make engagement easy and help build long-lasting relationships between members. One of the examples of such virtual communities that well use gamification is Roblox.

Roblox was first introduced to the public in 2006 as an online gaming platform that allows users to create, share, and play games developed by other users (Tornow, 2023). Roblox provides users with different tools and resources to create games (e.g., Lua programming language). It also serves as an online community for users to communicate with other players, connect with existing offline friends, and join groups (Aoki, 2023). Today, Roblox has 220 million active monthly users. Each day, more than 67 million people play Roblox worldwide (Tornow, 2023). As Roblox's mission statement indicates, the platform aims to "build a human co-experience platform that enables billions of users to come together to play, learn, communicate, explore and expand their friendships" (Roblox, 2023).

Through years, Roblox has evolved from a gaming site to a virtual community (Aoki, 2023). The platform provides many features that encourage true participation. Such features include chat boxes for players to easily communicate with each other; a friend request feature that connects users with their existing social networks, which can potentially bring new users to the platform; and team focused games to enhance community building (Ochukwuma, 2020). In addition, Roblox's developer forum allows users to exchange information and tips for creating and playing games. Its talent hub presents a channel for users to find one another to build mutual experiences (Tornow, 2023).

Roblox has also tried to make the community more "lifelike" (Tornow, 2023). For example, every Roblox user must create an avatar to represent themselves on the platform. Their avatars can now display natural facial expression to provide users a more immersive and realistic experience (Tornow, 2023). Roblox users can also buy and sell stuffs they created via its marketplace. There are also live virtual concerts for Roblox users (Aoki, 2023).

In addition to being "lifelike," Roblox was designed as a space that extends beyond the real world. Think of a person you know who is shy in their everyday life. Roblox provides a space where she or he may feel more comfortable communicating with others through their avatar. Perhaps a person is wheelchair bound but has always dreamt of becoming a professional basketball star. She or he can create an NBA basketball game and be a basketball player to play with Lebron James.

It should be noted that all the games on the platform are user generated. Roblox doesn't tell users what to create, what to play, or what to talk about. They simply offer tools and provide a library of user-generated content for users to have their own experiences (Aoki, 2023). For the most part, Roblox communities are built, developed, and controlled by the users. For this reason, they hold great potential for engagement (Neumayer & Raffl, 2008). Research demonstrates how behaviors from virtual worlds will translate to the real world. This connection may be due to how highly users identify with their personal avatar and their success in forming real social relationships with other avatars.

Recognizing the immersive and interactive experiences created by Roblox, many businesses and organizations have now included Roblox as a part of their communication strategy (Brown, 2022). Gucci, a luxury fashion brand, created a "Gucci Garden" experience on Roblox. When people enter Gucci Garden, their avatar will become a mannequin without gender or age and then wander through different themed rooms that feature Gucci's virtual products. The visitor's aviator can then purchase and wear exclusive Gucci virtual items in the experience (Roblox, 2021). There are many instances (including Gucci Garden) where demonstrations on Roblox translate into real-life behaviors. It is evidenced that the cyberspace mimics the real world much more so than other text- and image-based social media sites. Roblox is a great example of a social media platform that uses the principles of dialogic communication to foster true participation among members of its online community.

Discussion questions

1   What features of Roblox allow you to have a dialogic communication with other users? Could marketers use these Roblox features to engage consumers and create a stronger sense of community?
2   Roblox is a decentralized space, where users control most of the content. Based on this understanding, where would it fall on our diffusion–participation continuum? What opportunities and challenges does this extend to you as a social media practitioner?
3   Roblox has pushed to create more "real-life" experiences for its users. In addition to live virtual concerts, what online and offline activities would you recommend Roblox to develop to enhance community building for its users?

Summary

This chapter focuses on ways to construct social media messages to ensure online engagement between organizations and their customers. These messages are bound by the structure opportunities available on social media and the mindset in which they were produced. Social media practitioners must monitor the experience users have as they transition between social networks and business websites, especially for diffusion posts. The theory of dialogic communication teaches us the importance of user feedback, and how true participation is critical for social media marketing success. Though this feedback will not always be positive, it is necessary to maintain a dialogic loop where users feel as though they are listened and valued. True participation and cooperation between users and the organization will prove mutually beneficial.

This chapter also discusses many asynchronous and synchronous options for online engagement. Many factors can help you decide whether to use a synchronous or asynchronous approach for long-term behavior change. There are benefits and challenges for each. It is best to have both options available for users to choose which they are most comfortable with. There is no question that synchronous communication is the future of social media marketing. However, it is most important to ensure that you do not have the option for dialogic loop unless you are 100% confident that someone is going to respond to user queries. Determine what works best with your current schedule and staff and create the features accordingly. Knowing who you are is crucial to mobilize users toward true participation.

As discussed throughout the book, social media's premise rests in its ability to empower and engage users via interactive conversation. Thus, many social media efforts focus on building trust and creating a community. Social media can serve as a great branding and marketing tool and bring unforeseen opportunities to individuals, organizations, and society. However, it is difficult to create an authentic message for a company's brand if one is unable to create an authentic, aware personal brand. Thus, let's turn our attention to how social media can help build personal brand in Chapter 8.

Key Takeaways

1   True participation is more than just the structural ability for two-way communication. It includes a cooperative process working with and by the people.

2   Freire's theory of dialogic communication and action is a more ethical relational interaction, where ideas and opinions are negotiated through communication exchanges with the goal of reaching mutually satisfying opinions.

3   Structural features that promote dialogic communication via social media include dialogic loop, usefulness of information, generation of return visits, ease of interface, and the conservation of visitors.

4   Virtual communities hold great potential for fostering dialogic communication, forming a dynamic and sustained relationship, and making consumers feel part of a larger social group.

5   Dialogic loop features allow unsatisfied users to query organizations and allow organizations the opportunity to respond. These features include easy to find contact information, links to your organization's website and other social media pages, and using replies and mentions to facilitate communication with stakeholders.

References

Aoki, T. (2023) Roblox is creating a trusted global virtual community of metaverse. *LinkedIn*. Available at https://www.linkedin.com/pulse/roblox-creating-trusted-global-virtual-community-metaverse-aoki/ (accessed November 17, 2023).

Brown, S. (2022) What second life and Roblox can teach us about the metaverse. *MIT Management Sloan School*. Available at https://mitsloan.mit.edu/ideas-made-to-matter/what-second-life-and-roblox-can-teach-us-about-metaverse#:~:text=Key%20points%20include%20the%20importanceenter%20the%20metaverse%20than%20others (accessed November 17, 2023).

Butler, P. & Peppard, J. (1998) Consumer purchasing on the Internet: processes and prospects. *European Management Journal*, 16(5), 600–610.

Charlton, G. (2007) Hidden charges and poor usability deter online shoppers. Available at http://econsultancy.com/us/blog/718-hidden-charges-and-poor-usabilitydeter-online-shoppers (accessed June 8, 2016).

Cui, J., Mei, J., Zhang, W., Wang, X. & Zhang, D. (2010) A captcha implementation based on moving objects recognition problem. In: *2010 International Conference on E-Business and E-Government (ICEE)*, pp. 1277–1280. Piscataway, NJ: IEEE.

Gell, T. (2023) How much does a focus group cost? *Drive Research*. Available at https://www.driveresearch.com/market-research-company-blog/how-much-does-a-focus-group-cost-focus-groups-syracuse-ny/ (accessed November 17, 2023).

Gibbs, A. (1997) *Focus Groups*, 19. Social Research Update.

Griffin, E. (2009) *A First Look at Communication Theory*. New York: McGraw-Hill.

Gustavsen, P. & Tilley, E. (2003) Public relations communication through corporate websites: towards an understanding of the role of interactivity. *PRISM*, 1(1), 1–14.

Habermas, J. (1984) *The Theory of Communicative Action. Vol. 1. Reason and the Rationalization of Society*. Boston: Beacon Press.

Habermas, J. (1990) *Moral Consciousness and Communicative Action*. Cambridge, MA: MIT Press.

Hill, W., Stead, L., Rosenstein, M. & Furnas, G. (1995) Recommending and evaluating choices in a virtual community of use. In: *Proceedings of the SIGCHI Conference on Human Factors in Computing Systems*, pp. 194–201. New York: ACM Press/Addison-Wesley.

Irving, J. (1972) *Victims of Groupthink: A Psychological Study of Foreign-policy Decisions and Fiascoes*. Boston: Houghton, Mifflin.

Kent, J. (1998) Building dialogic relationships through World Wide Web. *Public Relations Review*, 24(3), 321–334.

Krause, K. & Coates, H. (2008) Students' engagement in first-year university. *Assessment and Evaluation in Higher Education*, 33(5), 493–505.

Leasca, S. (2021) Ikea and Pinterest teamed up on a new tool that will help turn your home into a vacation-worthy destination. *Travel & Leisure*. Available at https://www.travelandleisure.com/style/ikea-renocation-pinterest-boards (accessed November 17, 2023).

McAllister-Spooner, S. & Kent, M. (2009) Dialogic public relations and resource dependency: New Jersey community colleges as models for Web Site effectiveness. *Atlantic Journal of Communication*, 17(4), 220–239.

Mollen, A. & Wilson, H. (2010) Engagement, telepresence and interactivity in online consumer experience: reconciling scholastic and managerial perspectives. *Journal of Business Research*, 63(9), 919–925.

Neumayer, C. & Raffl, C. (2008) Facebook for global protest: the potential and limits of social software for grassroots activism. In: *Proceedings of the 5th Prato Community Informatics and Development Informatics Conference*. Available at http://cirn.infotech.monash.edu/assets/docs/prato2008papers/raffl.pdf (accessed June 8, 2016).

Nisbett, N. (2006) The internet, cybercafés and the new social spaces of Bangalorean youth. In: S. Coleman & P. Collins (eds) *Locating the Field: Space, Place and Context in Anthropology*, p. 129. London: Bloomsbury Publishing.

Ochukwuma (2020) Communities in Roblox. *University of Chicago*. Available at https://voices.uchicago.edu/202003sosc20224/2020/07/09/communities-in-roblox/ (accessed November 17, 2023).

Reichheld, F. (2003) The one number you need to grow. *Harvard Business Review*, 81(12), 46–55.

Ridings, C. & Gefen, D. (2004) Virtual community attraction: why people hang out online. *Journal of Computer-Mediated Communication*, 10(1). doi: 10.1111/j.1083-6101.2004.tb00229.x.

Roblox (2021) The Gucci Garden experience lands on Roblox. Available at https://blog.roblox.com/2021/05/gucci-garden-experience/ (accessed November 17, 2023).

Roblox (2023) Corporate overview. Available at https://ir.roblox.com/overview/default.aspx#:~:text=Corporate%20overviewexplore%20and%20expand%20their%20friendships.

Russell, A.E. (2008) *An analysis of public relations and dialogic communication efforts of 501(C)(6) organizations.* Doctoral dissertation, Ball State University, Muncie, IN.

Servaes, J. (1996) Participatory communication research from a Freirian perspective. *Africa Media Review*, 10, 73–91.

Singhal, A. (2004) Empowering the oppressed through participatory theater. *Investigación y desarrollo: revista del Centro de Investigaciones en Desarrollo Humano*, 12(1), 138–163.

Stoker, K. & Tusinski, K. (2006) Reconsidering public relations' infatuation with dialogue: why engagement and reconciliation can be more ethical than symmetry and reciprocity. *Journal of Mass Media Ethics*, 21(2–3), 156–176.

Stratten, S. (2012) *Unmarketing. Stop Marketing. Start Engaging.* Hoboken, NJ: John Wiley & Sons, Inc.

Taylor, M., Kent, M. & White, W. (2001) How activist organizations are using the Internet to build relationships. *Public Relations Review*, 27(3), 263–284.

Tornow, N. (2023) Enabling creation of anything, anywhere, by anyone. *Roblox*. Available at https://blog.roblox.com/2023/03/enabling-creation-anything-anywhere-anyone/#:~:text=At%20Roblox%2C%20our%20vision%20iscenter%20of%20everything%20we%20do (accessed November 17, 2023).

Tran, L. (2023) 8 Inspiring social media marketing examples to learn from. *Flockler*. Available at https://flockler.com/blog/8-inspiring-social-media-marketing-examples-to-learn-from (accessed November 17, 2023).

Wang, Y. & Yang, Y. (2020) Dialogic communication on social media: how organizations use Twitter to build dialogic relationships with their publics. *Computers in Human Behavior*, 104, 106183. doi: 10.1016/j.chb.2019.106183.

Xue, K. (2022) How IKEA uses digital campaign to deliver purpose-driving messages to its customers. Medium. Available at https://medium.com/marketing-in-the-age-of-digital/how-ikea-uses-digital-campaign-to-deliver-purpose-driving-messages-to-its-customers-b27dba85afe6#:~:text=In%20this%20campaign%2C%20Ikea%20usesas%20an%20idea%20starter%20while (accessed November 17, 2023).

Zichermann, G. & Cunningham, C. (2011) *Gamification by Design: Implementing Game Mechanics in Web and Mobile Apps.* Sebastopol, CA: O'Reilly Media.

8

Social Media for Personal Branding

Learning Objectives

After reading this chapter, you should be able to:
1 Understand the potential of social media in personal branding efforts.
2 Identify your public/private brand identity and integrate into a personalized social media brand strategy.
3 Determine which social media pieces are appropriate to incorporate into a digital portfolio to showcase your digital skills.

Introduction

Chapter 7 discussed how to apply the theory of dialogic communication to a social media strategy. We learned that social media has made it necessary for communication specialists to engage virtual communities and maintain a dialogic loop with their media users. This chapter focuses on identifying your personal niche persona to transform your social media presence into a strategic public/private digital brand. Before you can create an authentic message for a company/organization's brand, you should be able to create an authentic, purposeful personal brand, that helps to connect with your social media users. It is important

Strategic Social Media: From Marketing to Social Change, Second Edition. L. Meghan Mahoney and Tang Tang.
© 2024 John Wiley & Sons, Inc. Published 2024 by John Wiley & Sons, Inc.

to use social media to reflect upon yourself as a social media user. Regardless of your career aspirations, this public/private identity will showcase your skills and help future employers identify with your authenticity as a potential colleague.

According to a recent research report, over 90% of employers screen potential candidates' social media pages during the application process (Ahearn, 2020). Social media allows candidates the ability to showcase who they are and the skills that they offer. Many employers have begun to expect candidates to carry a digital presence, especially in media industries. According to the Harris Poll's survey, about one in five employers will not call a person for an interview if they can't find them online (Cotriss, 2023). Social media provides employers the opportunity to see the digital skills identified in a resume in action. Additionally, personal social media accounts provide a glimpse into the personal side of candidates beyond what is outlined on a resume. Thus, it is important to be mindful of how personal social media use impacts career advancements and how you can better control your own social media branding efforts.

Despite the potential of social media to fuel career development, it can be difficult for individuals to start personal branding efforts via social media. One challenge is that they view certain social media platforms (e.g., Instagram) as suitable for private communication and other social media platforms (e.g., LinkedIn) as more catered to their professional identity. This chapter encourages readers to think beyond these platform silos and curate an omnichannel approach to personal branding to identify a niche public/private identity that is suitable for professional Plan A goals. To begin, let's define personal branding and identify concepts related to a public/private identity.

Personal Branding

Anderson (2006) developed the long tail theory to demonstrate how latent commodities are more exciting to consumers because they do not appeal to the mass audience, but instead set us apart from others. Your greatest passions and interests are what make you a niche commodity. Just as these long tail markets are more valuable to digital businesses, specialized niche passions and skills are more valuable in career development. *Personal branding* is defined as the process of developing, harnessing, and classifying personal information and providing a comprehensive narrative for others to easily understand one's identity (Jacobson, 2020). It is the specific feelings, perceptions, and expectations people associated with you. Personal branding is not simply marketing yourself, but presenting your voice, values, personality, and an authentic self (Barnhart, 2023).

Social media is an effective tool in this creation, as individuals can utilize various interactive platforms to tell and manage narratives related to their niche identity. For example, Pokimane, a Twitch streamer, has utilized TikTok, Instagram, X (formerly Twitter), and YouTube to build her personal brand as a friendly, skilled, and knowledgeable gamer with a sense of humor. Her willingness to interact with followers has also been part of her brand narrative. Gary Vaynerchuk, an entrepreneur, author, and speaker, also uses social media to build his personal brand as someone knowledgeable in business and marketing with a passion for inspiring people to find ways to success (Brand Credential, 2023). Lionel Messi, a renowned soccer player, has a clear and consistent narrative across all social channels as a talented, team-first athlete with humility- and family-oriented values (Digital Resource, 2023). This strong personal brand makes him the second most followed athlete on Instagram with 440 million followers (Leyland, 2023).

Developing personal brand is critical to today's career advancement. However, very few have truly defined their personal brand. According to an industry survey, only 15% of people have a clear personal brand, and less than 5% create content that is consistent with their personal brand (Llopis, 2013). How well can you articulate who you are? A SWOT analysis about your strengths, weaknesses, opportunities, and threats can help you identify your personal brand (Pestle Analysis, 2022). Ask yourself, "what hobbies/interests will you spend hours doing with friends or when no one else is around? what are you better at than anyone else? Which achievements are you most proud of? What do you want to be known for?" (Cooper, 2022). These questions can lead you to a clear assessment of who you are, and how you could build your personal brand.

Challenge yourself to think about what you uniquely bring to your industry and community. Write down the top things you would expect others to think about you. Focus on who you truly are and want to be (Llopis, 2013). This may be challenging at first. Luckily, there are many steps that you can take to build your personal brand identity.

Public/Private Identity

There are countless narratives of individuals losing their career over something that they said or posted on social media. Often, students are warned of the dangers of posting personal artifacts on social media, as there is a certain permeance to our digital footprints. While it is true that future generations should be mindful of data privacy (Keenan, 2020), they could also utilize social media platforms to lend connections and showcase their digital skills. As such, users engage in a privacy paradox.

A *privacy paradox* explains how users can claim to be very concerned about their privacy but still share personal information online and take little steps to protect their personal data (Barth & De Jong, 2017). One explanation for such behavior is the inevitableness of having a digital presence in today's convergent media environment. Many individuals grew up with their own guardians' sharing photos and updates of their personal lives, including first baby steps, yearly school photograph updates, or college acceptance announcements. Social media is a key mechanism for communication and connection in today's digital age. Participating in social media requires a user to give up some message control and privacy constraints, though users today can determine for themselves the level of responsibility they opt into when they participate with social media.

Privacy is difficult in a digital climate of constant surveillance. Users don't always have control over what information gets shared about their lives. Friends or family can share personal photos without permission. As such, the open nature of social networking sites is often called a "semi-public" space by their very construct (Barrett-Maitland & Lynch, 2020). Content can be shared with an intended private group of people but also viewed by individuals outside of that group. This convergence of public and private is largely unavoidable when users engage with social media.

As discussed in Chapter 3, private sphere issues tend to center around family, relationships, goals, values, and health. Public sphere topics are related to civic activity, such as news, politics, weather, and sports (Habermas, 1991). Various social media platforms are built on different expectations of sharing regarding public and private issues. For example, X (formerly Twitter) describes itself as an online news sharing site. The structure of X encourages conversations surrounding public sphere issues and events. While users certainly share private sphere information on X, the structure of the platform aims to foster an environment for public sphere discourse. This is different than the structure of other social networking sites. For example, Snapchat describes itself as a fast way to communicate privately with friends. Once the friend directly receives the social media message, he or she could choose "disappear" your content. Snapchat provides a much more ideal social media structure for sharing private and personal details.

LinkedIn is a popular social networking site that focuses on professional public sharing. People utilize LinkedIn to showcase their industry skills and share updates on their professional journey. They also use the platform to connect with professional contacts in their current role, as well as reach out to prospective employers that work in sectors or positions above their current rank. Professional networking should balance these two places: current employment and future career advancement. As you build your digital brand, consider which platform best showcases the skills required for your Plan A career.

Your Plan A career is your dream job. What position would you love if money, location, or likelihood of advancement was not an issue? Many individuals are working toward a specific role or position in a company. This Plan A career should be the focus of your personal branding effort. Highlight the skills that you already have that would make you a strong candidate for the position. If you don't believe that you would be a good candidate, why should anyone take a chance on you?

For example, maybe your dream job is to own a digital marketing firm with multiple clients and employees. However, you are not in the place professionally to begin such an endeavor. Instead, you are working as an entry level social media practitioner for a small business. Rather than defaulting to the requirements of your current role, utilize social media to connect with other practitioners who are having your Plan A career. Highlight the skills that you already have that would make you a strong future owner of a digital marketing firm. Don't limit your connections with individuals that you know thus far in your interpersonal journey. Use social media to grow your network and make important virtual connections.

It is important to note that marketing yourself in your Plan A career should not be deceitful. Ensure that you are not overstating your qualifications. Use social media to connect and research what it will take you to get to the next level in your career. Don't allow your professional Plan A brand to shape haphazardly. Follow industry trends in your Plan A career. Share articles with your network. Add your own perspective on trending topics. Eventually, your followers will grow, and with careful content curation, you will begin to be seen as an expert in your Plan A career. Be strategic about the connections that you make. Craft it and use it, fostering a particular audience and achieving a particular impact (Smith, 2022).

The structure of LinkedIn makes it an appropriate social media platform for sharing more public and cherry-picked information about your professional journey. Today's converged media climate requires personal branding to extend into both public and private realms of your identity. In addition to curating a strong purposeful Plan A career in your personal branding, it is imperative that you also provide a personal glimpse into private sphere passions. Allowing prospective employers to catch a glimpse into the fun side of your life will help them determine what kind of fit you are for their team.

Professional resumes share a great deal of detail about the professional trajectory of a person. However, they do little to shed light into the personality or hobbies that individuals engage in their free time. Two prospective employees can have almost identical list of professional skillsets. Often, by the time an organization gets to the interview stage, it means that the small list of potential candidates is all qualified for the position. The goal of the interview is to see which candidate they personally connect with. Providing personal information earlier in the selection process puts you at an advantage by setting yourself apart from other candidates early on. By the time you reach the interview stage, the interviewers already feel like they know you.

Today's employers are looking for a social presence that illustrates creativity, engagement in a community, or a level of expertise (Casserly, 2012). You should never share anything embarrassing on your social media. You should also not leave out the most critical elements of your personal character. Hobbies, interests, passions, relationships, and the way you spend your free time are all important personal pieces that shape your professional self. Erasing every trace of your private sphere life does not benefit your professional development. Today's employers expect you to have a digital history. Erasing all your social content could imply to interviewers that you have something to hide (Cotriss, 2023).

When curating a personal branding social media presence, please be mindful and strategic about how you shape your persona for people outside of your private sphere circles (Smith, 2022). Be strategic about which aspects of yourself to include in your public/private identity. The more targeted and niche you can make your public/private identity, the clearer your personal brand becomes. Once you begin your personal branding efforts, it becomes difficult to change. After all, everyone agrees that shared online content holds some level of permanency. This first step is important.

Your public/private identity should include your Plan A professional career aspiration, as well as two private sphere passions that shape who you are (e.g., I am a social media practitioner who likes to explore local hiking trails and play with my border collie). Again, these passions should not be inappropriate or embarrassing. They should be niche passions and provide insight into how you spend your free time. This combination of one public, two private passions should be the foundation of your personal brand.

You should also be aware that the public audience for a personal branding effort can be anyone. Today's digital environment allows users from all over the world to engage your social media content. It is difficult to know the bounds of your social media users (Ravn et al., 2020). Your job is to curate content that is very clearly defined and tagged for a specific niche subculture. Conducting thorough audience research about who would be attracted to such niche content will help define your personal brand and grow your social media users appropriately.

Take time to research your potential audience segmentation. Audience segmentation defines your audiences, including demographics, psychographics, and geographic areas. As we learned in Chapter 5, audience research is the first step for any social media endeavor. Before you start to develop stories, strategies, and partnerships, you need to ask who your core audiences are, what problems they want you to solve for them, and what skills you bring to the table. Understand the needs and challenges of your audiences to build meaningful connections (Barnhart, 2023). Consider what types of relationships you wish to develop with them and the best channels to use to facilitate such interactions. All are important to your personal brand viability. When utilizing social media to build a personal brand identity, it is critical to have a strong action plan in place.

Personal Branding Action Plan

1   Understand who you are (e.g., your unique strengths, weaknesses) and be specific about what niche qualities you bring to your Plan A career.
2   Curate content that includes two private-sphere passions that you have in your personal life, as well as one professional area that you hope to rise as a practitioner.
3   Identify a potential group of users for your social media content. What needs do these users have and what content would they easily be drawn toward?
4   Know your target consumers. Use the audience analysis methods discussed in Chapters 5 and 6 to gather information about your core audiences' interests, passions, personality, and, more importantly, why they would consume your social media content and what they want you to do for them.
5   Decide the social media platforms that you wish to utilize in your strategy. Be careful that you don't include too many accounts that you are unable to develop consistent content but incorporate an omnichannel approach to personal branding.
6   Finally, develop a strategy with consistent storytelling around your public/private identity across all social media channels.

Omnichannel Personal Marketing

Today's social media users rely on mobile technology to curate an engaging and on-the-go experience. Users switch between social media apps to access various friend groups, online communities, and sources of news. A typical social media user today interacts with 6.6 different social media platforms (Ruby, 2023). The process is simple, as each app automatically stores user login and password information, allowing them to move freely between various social media sites in a seamless, unified experience, regardless of the channel used (Piotrowicz & Cuthbertson, 2014). This multichannel approach to social networking is referred to as an *omnichannel experience*. It is important that personal branding efforts take advantage of the omnichannel environment when curating a personal brand narrative.

With such a plethora of social media options in today's digital world, it can be difficult to choose which to include in your own omnichannel strategy. In general, personal branding requires much more diffusion efforts than a brand or organizational strategy. After all, the point of a personal brand is to share information about yourself to build your professional social network. However, there are still many opportunities to use social media to create posts that showcase your unique skills and characteristics through community and mobilization approaches.

Four key channels that help integrate a diffusion approach with more community and mobilization include a personal website, Google Alert, LinkedIn, TikTok, and/or Instagram.

Personal portfolio website

Professional resumes allow individuals to list their professional skills, education, and experiences. However, the industry report shows that an average position receives about 118 applications (Wise, 2022). This surplus of applications makes it difficult for candidates to stand out against other equally qualified applicants. Moreover, a digital media position requires a backpack of communication skills that are difficult to measure in a text-only resume. Digital portfolios allow candidates link examples of digital creations directly to their resume.

A personal portfolio allows you to show, not just tell, your digital skillset. These portfolios can be housed on a simple personal branding website that you include near the top of your resume through a direct link. There are many templates that work well for creating a personal portfolio space, including WordPress, Squarespace, or Wix. The colors, logos, and tone of your personal branding website are important, as you will utilize them throughout other omnichannel social media platforms. Think carefully about what style you most identify with and the type of positions that these choices may attract.

Every personal portfolio website should include a personal description page where you share your story and passion for the industry. These narratives should outline your public/ private identity. A full resume is not necessary on the personal website, as they do not take the place of your resume submission. Use your portfolio to focus on the digital skills that you bring to the industry, rather than a list of jobs that you have had in the past. Finally, be sure to remove any personal security information such as your address and phone number. Make it easy for users to contact you through an email or web form.

The goal of a personal branding website is to have a diffusion space where users are directed toward from all social channels in your omnichannel strategy. A link to your personal branding website should be included in the biography section of each social media channel. This landing page gives users the opportunity to interact with all social media pages that are used in your personal branding efforts. The more opportunities users have to interact with these pages, the less likely they will be to look for more personal digital spaces that you do not include.

Do not feel compelled to include everything that you have ever created on your personal portfolio website. In fact, less may be better. These digital selections should be cherry-picked among projects that showcase your best work. Every skill that you list on your resume should have a corresponding example on your digital portfolio. The personal portfolio website should be considered a permanent piece to your branding effort. Even if you are happily employed in your dream job, there are still many benefits to keeping your personal website active. Strategically curating your personal brand will lead to upward mobility (Jacobson, 2020) by bolstering your industry ethos and show your value to the industry. There is always room for additional networking. As your skills evolve, so should the skills portfolio sections of your website.

Google alert

In an Omnichannel environment, it can be difficult to keep track of all the digital spaces where you have a profile. Even on social media platforms where you do not have an account, other users are free to share information and link their content to your name. For better or worse, when potential employees search your name in a search engine, such as Google, these associations will shape their assumptions about who you are and the benefits and risks you bring to their organization. Be proactive in monitoring for updates when your name is mentioned online.

Many monitoring software can crawl the Internet for updates surrounding keywords. Given the simple and free process of creating a Google Alert, and Google's popularity as the leading search engine, it is the preferred tool for such monitoring. Google Alerts will search the Internet and notify users when their keyword appears, who is mentioning it, and which sites it recurs in. When setting an alert on google.com/alerts, users can set parameters regarding alert frequency, language, search region, and the amount and type of notifications users wish to receive. Users can also opt into synchronous notifications as they happen, or they can select to opt in to once-a-week emails with a summary of all mentions. Google alerts can drastically cut down the amount of time you spend planning and researching what is associated with your name in the context of personal branding (Thakker, 2022).

Consider the name for how you wish to brand yourself and make that name consistent across all channels related to your personal branding. Will you use a middle initial to brand yourself from other individuals with the same name? What possible misspellings of your name might potential employers use when searching? Of course, the more keywords you create Google Alerts for, the more notifications you will receive each week. Over time, you can narrow the associations that are most useful to track.

LinkedIn

There is no better space to connect with digital media professionals than through the social media platform, LinkedIn. The site has 52 million people searching for jobs each week, with 101 job applications submitted every second (MacReady, 2023). Even if you are not actively seeking employment, LinkedIn still proves itself as the leading site to connect and interact with industry leaders. The structures of LinkedIn make it easy for you to share your experiences, skills, connections, and links to alternative channels. The platform is filled with people looking to connect with others with similar professional passions.

As true with all media related to marketing, consistency is the key. Be sure that your LinkedIn home profile includes a clear headshot and the public/private identity that you used on your personal branding website. Use LinkedIn to brand yourself with your current and past employers, as they will be most suitable for endorsing your skillset. In addition to connecting with those you know interpersonally, don't be afraid to use LinkedIn to connect with leaders in the industry you most admire. It is not unusual for business networking to occur on LinkedIn. Find individuals who have the job or position that you aim for. Pay attention to the news and content that they share.

Optimize your LinkedIn profile so that other users are easily able to find you. Add captivating headlines, include relevant keywords, fill in the "About" section of your page, and be specific about the skills and services you provide (Chan, 2022). Join relevant subgroups and communities. In addition to diffusing information, be an active participant of a LinkedIn subculture community. Share news that is relevant to your industry. And comment and share updates from others whom you are connected.

Active sharing professional updates will help bolster your ethos, as these efforts allow others to see that you are passionate about the industry and keep up with the latest industry trends. Of all the platforms recommended for your omnichannel personal branding strategy, the structure of LinkedIn permits the strongest opportunity to showcase your writing skills. While LinkedIn is based on professional networking, it does not need to be a space void of personality. It is still appropriate to use the platform to share personal updates related to your public/private identity.

TikTok

TikTok is the fastest growing existing social media platform with more than 800 million active members. The app allows users to produce and share short creative videos between 15 and 60 seconds (TikTok, 2023). While the social media platform began as a space to share simple, silly music videos, today the biggest brands and entrepreneurs have found great success leveraging this massive user base to grow their personal brand.

Taking time to create a meaningful and consistent content on TikTok will expose you to a larger user base than other platforms. Be sure that your TikTok content strategy uses the same niche public/private identity. Rather than trying to use the channel to showcase various sides of your identity, create multiple profiles for each niche passion. The case study below illustrates one user who successfully built two vastly different viral TikTok accounts based on multiple interests. You can rise as a TikTok influencer quickly with a narrow and targeted personal branding strategy.

Unlike your LinkedIn account, TikTok videos can be a bit less professional. Use this channel as an opportunity to show a more personal side of yourself. Capitalize and participate in the latest Internet trends. Create short, digestible snippets, and share information about your expertise using trending and relevant hashtags. You can also mobilize people to try different TikTok challenges. The smaller request that you are asking of your TikTok audiences, the most likely they are to follow through. Try to always bring the topic of your videos back to your public/private identity. As your audience base grows, there is an opportunity to collaborate and connect with other creators or brands to get your name out to an even larger user base that will follow you to other channels in your personal branding strategy.

Instagram

There is a reason why the rise of Instagram as a preferred social media platform coincided with the rise of social media influencer marketing. The platform provides a unique opportunity for you to curate a highly controlled branded presentation of yourself. Instagram is a great platform to utilize when trying to drive traffic to your personal branding website, establish yourself as an expert on a niche topic, grow your followers, and share everyday stories. The multiple structures of Instagram allow for more public curated, permanent diffusion pieces of your brand, as well as more interactive and vulnerable private creations.

Begin setting up your Instagram account with a clear and consistent bio. Share your public/private identity here. Take time to carefully curate the grid, or social media posts, of your Instagram. Over time, these social media projections become a permanent story that new users will scroll through to get a sense of who you are. You may even consider sharing photos that have a consistent color scheme or topic selection. These should be considered more permanent pieces of your personal brand. Be mindful that not every post needs to speak to the totality of your public/private identity. The idea is that over time, your Instagram grid will be a showcase of who you are.

Once you have an established Instagram grid, you can turn your attention to the story structure on the Instagram platform. Instagram stories allow you to share static photos or short videos that disappear in 24 hours. Often, these posts are more immediate topics or events, and less curated, more authentic pieces of the day. Instagram stories are where your current active followers can learn more about how you spend your time. Here, you can showcase the more vulnerable and authentic pieces of yourself. Use stories to show a peek behind the curtain of who you are on a deeper level (Henderson, 2021). The more authentic pieces that you share via Instagram stories, the more users will engage with your content. Instagram stories allow a less-public forum for people to send messages and comments to you regarding your content. They also allow you to mobilize users through Q&A or polls.

This more private and intimate communication with your social media users results in stronger parasocial relationships. Over time, you and your Instagram followers will begin to trust and view each other on a deeper level if you are willing to share private pieces of your identity and engage people. The best way to become an Instagram influencer in your subculture is to engage other users in your niche community. Follow other users who share similar content. Utilize keywords and hashtags to find them. Learn from their posts, but do not copy. Remember, you are a niche commodity based on your unique passions and skills. Determine what gap you can fill in the current Instagram market. If you are authentic enough in your personal branding efforts, other influencers will view you as a possible collaborator, not competitor.

Authenticity and entrepreneurship are the two guiding principles of personal branding (Arriagada & Ibáñez, 2020). When developing an omnichannel strategy, you must focus on finding your unique value proposition and the reason that social media users should pay attention to you, rather than someone else. Consider your personal mission and vision and what you can uniquely offer to your Plan A career community. Developing a personal branding strategy is both art and science. Start with your public/private identity, conduct audience research, and create a cohesive storytelling plan through an omnichannel approach. Below is a case study of one such user.

Case Study: Rahul Rai

This chapter discusses the many benefits of building a public/private identity in your social media personal branding effort. You should utilize an omnichannel approach to curate a digital presence that showcases your digital skillsets and allows a glimpse into who you are as a person. Rahul Rai is a Bollywood actor who built a mindful social media presence that transformed his career (MacNeill, 2020).

During the COVID-19 quarantine, Rai took time to develop two social media brands on TikTok: One as his acting portfolio, @therealrahulrai (4.9 million followers) and the other as a niche passion, financial literacy @thelaymaninvestor (556.7k followers) (Danial, 2022). These channels were built in addition to his existing personal website, Instagram, and LinkedIn accounts. While these existing channels proved already strong outlets for highlighting his strengths as an actor, it wasn't until Rai purposefully created his own community and fan base by leveraging TikTok's viral structures (Bhavani, 2021) that he rose as a financial expert and social media influencer. These social media personal branding efforts have allowed Rai to take more control over his career and utilize the platforms for additional income (see Figure 8.1).

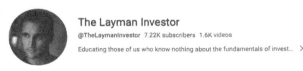

Figure 8.1   Screenshot. Source: The Layman Investor/www.youtube.com/c/TheLaymanInvestor/ last accessed September 26, 2023.

One interesting takeaway from Rai's case study is his ability to draw followers around two very distinct passions: acting and financial literacy. These two niche brand identities require a switch in storytelling that demands a strong understanding of what each audience wants most. Through a quick peruse of Rai's TikTok accounts, you will see a much sillier persona on @theralrahulrai and a much more serious tone on @thelaymaninvestor. This clearly illustrates the importance of using social media to "niche down" on topics that you are passionate and knowledgeable about. The consistency of the videos via each account helped build his brand as an expert in both topics. Rai explains how "knowing your strengths and how to use them is paramount for social media success" (MacNeill, 2020).

Hope you can see the importance of building cohesive stories around your unique passion via Rai's success. The authenticity of your stories may not be apparent right away, but over time, your ability to curate social media stories around your passion will build a unique brand that sets you apart from your competitors. As your social media users grow, your digital presence will eventually transform into an expertise in the content area. Being authentic with your niche passion and knowing your audience will set you apart as an influencer.

Discussion questions

1   Your public/private identity is the first step toward developing a personal branding strategy. Consider your own public/private identity. What possible talents or skills could you focus on through social media personal branding?

2   Rai's success is largely due to his ability to cater content to two distinct niche audiences. What tools do social media provide to understanding what each audience is looking for in content?

3   Rai credits much of his success on the ability to consistently curate new content. Where can you turn to gain new ideas for social media content surrounding your public/private identity?

Summary

This chapter focuses on developing a personal brand through an omnichannel social media approach. Specifically, it defines a public/private identity and discusses the importance of creating a cohesive strategy for professional growth. We have learned that personal branding extends beyond sharing professional insights about your current job. Combining your Plan A career goals with two private sphere passions will help potential employers gain a stronger sense of who you are and the digital skillset that you uniquely bring to the table. This connection will set you apart from other candidates with similar skillsets.

Social media provides the opportunity to connect with future employers on a more intimate level, as well as build a presence where you become a niche influencer on your chosen area of expertise. Understanding your online message consumers and potential market are imperative to building success. Today's media users no longer rely on the same gatekeeping industry structures. Consistent and informed content creation helps develop a digital portfolio that can transform into a career. Understanding your potential audiences and delivering catered content is a huge advantage.

Conduct research to determine which platform works best with your audiences and topic. A strong audience analysis will help to determine what would attract people to your content. Connect with industry leaders to see how they are using social media and the language and culture that they develop. Don't copy their efforts but determine how you can fit into the community and offer something new based on your unique public/private identity.

Carefully curate a brand that you will use across your personal branding efforts. What colors, aesthetic, tone, and details will you highlight? Once these pieces are established, it is difficult to rebrand without losing your followers. Since your personal brand should transcend your career, you want it to be fluid and grow with your progress, rather than restarting at each career phase. Even though it can be exciting to get started, take time to plan these details before beginning your content creation.

In this chapter, we have also learned that no one existing social media platform fits all. There are many benefits to utilize an omnichannel approach where people get a sense of your public/private identity through multiple social media platforms that are linked to a personal branding website. Creating a personal portfolio website allows you to showcase your digital skills, share your story as a practitioner, and create a "home base" where individuals can reach out from other platforms. It is important to use consistent branding of your name and identity throughout all social channels and set up a Google Alert accordingly to monitor your online presence. This will allow you to be notified when any updates are made online associated with your identity.

Creating a public/private profile on social platforms such as LinkedIn, TikTok, and Instagram will help position you as a leader in your niche community. LinkedIn allows more professional projects and connections with industry leaders in your Plan A career. It also provides the best structure for written updates regarding your personal brand. TikTok allows you to best leverage a social media algorithm to grow followers by creating consistent short-form content. Instagram is a more intentional and curated social media platform that you can utilize to grow as a niche influencer.

As discussed throughout the book, social media's premise rests in its ability to empower and engage users via interactive conversations. Thus, instead of using social media simply to talk to people about how wonderful you are, become a source of targeted information. Leverage the interactive structures of social media to form real connections. Social media can serve as a great marketing tool and bring employment and other unforeseen opportunities. Part III of this book will explore opportunities and challenges in social media marketing and business models. The next chapters will explore how social media allows businesses to target smaller consumer segments and sell a wider range of products, as well as explain how to develop market analysis and evaluate social media success.

Key Takeaways

1   Today's employers are expecting candidates to have a digital presence. Take time to develop a carefully curated omnichannel personal branding strategy.
2   Individuals can advance their career trajectory by using social media to become a leader in a niche community.
3   Integrate a combination of public and private self in your personal brand to set you apart from your competitors.
4   Consistent storytelling around niche content will help build an audience and brand you as an expert of a given field.
5   Be innovative, embrace the conceptualization of "all possible," and welcome all the unforeseen opportunities brought by integrated new media technologies in your personal branding efforts.

References

Ahearn, T. (2020) Survey reveals personal branding activities most valued during hiring process. *ESR*. Available at https://www.esrcheck.com/2020/06/03/survey-personal-branding-activities (accessed November 17, 2023).

Anderson, C. (2006) *The Long Tail: Why the Future of Business Is Selling Less of More*. New York: Hyperion.

Arriagada, A. & Ibáñez, F. (2020) "You need at least one picture daily, if not, you're dead": content creators and platform evolution in the social media ecology. *Social Media + Society*, 6(3), 2056305120944624.

Barnhart, B. (2023) The complete guide to personal branding. *Sprout Social*. Available at https://sproutsocial.com/insights/personal-branding/ (accessed November 17, 2023).

Barrett-Maitland, N. & Lynch, J. (2020) Social media, ethics and the privacy paradox. *Security and Privacy from a Legal, Ethical, and Technical Perspective*, 49.

Barth, S. & De Jong, M.D. (2017) The privacy paradox—investigating discrepancies between expressed privacy concerns and actual online behavior—a systematic literature review. *Telematics and Informatics*, 34(7), 1038–1058.

Bhavani, D. (2021) You have to play the game of leverage. *The Hindu*. Available at https://www.thehindu.com/entertainment/rahul-rai-content-creator-actor-interview-actors-must-play-game-of-leverage/article34905759.ece (accessed November 17, 2023).

Brand Credential (2023) Personal branding case study: a look at Gary Vaynerchuk's brand. Available at https://www.brandcredential.com/post/personal-branding-case-study-a-look-at-gary-vaynerchuks-brand (accessed November 17, 2023).

Casserly, M. (2012) Social media and the job hunt: squeaky-clean profiles need not apply. *Forbes*. Available at https://www.forbes.com/sites/meghancasserly/2012/06/14/social-media-and-the-job-hunt-sqeaky-clean-facebook-profiles/ (accessed November 17, 2023).

Chan, G. (2022) 5 Ways leaders can grow their personal brand on LinkedIn. *LinkedIn*. Available at https://www.linkedin.com/business/marketing/blog/skills/ways-leaders-can-grow-their-personal-brand-on-linkedin (accessed November 17, 2023).

Cooper, R. (2022) *The 12 Attributes of Extraordinary Media Professionals*. Lanham, MA: Rowman & Littlefield Publishing.

Cotriss, D. (2023) Keep it clean: social media screenings gain in popularity. *BND*. Available at https://www.businessnewsdaily.com/2377-social-media-hiring.html (accessed November 17, 2023).

Danial, K. (2022) TikTok content creation machine. *Interest Diva*. Available at https://www.youtube.com/watch?v=qL0SEA0v4no (accessed November 17, 2023).

Digital Resource (2023) Messi as a social media personality: how to be like him. Available at https://www.yourdigitalresource.com/post/messi-social-media-personality (accessed November 17, 2023).

Habermas, J. (1991) *The Structural Transformation of the Public Sphere: An Inquiry into a Category of Bourgeois Society*. Cambridge, MA: MIT Press.

Henderson, G. (2021) How to brand yourself on Instagram. *Digital Marketing Blog*. Available at https://www.digitalmarketing.org/blog/how-to-brand-yourself-on-instagram (accessed November 17, 2023).

Jacobson, J. (2020) You are a brand: social media managers' personal branding and "the future audience", *Journal of Product & Brand Management*, 29(6), 715–727.

Keenan, K. (2020) Millennials, generation X and baby boomers all care about online privacy. *Internet Innovation*. Available at https://internetinnovation.org/op-eds/millennials-generation-x-and-baby-boomers-all-care-about-online-privacy/ (accessed November 17, 2023).

Leyland, K. (2023) Sports stars on Instagram: who has the most followers. *National World*. Available at https://www.nationalworld.com/news/people/instagram-followers-most-sport-cristiano-ronaldo-4064521 (accessed November 17, 2023).

Llopis, G. (2013) Personal branding is a leadership requirement, not a self-promotion campaign. *Forbes*. Available at https://www.forbes.com/sites/glennllopis/2013/04/08/personal-branding-is-a-leadership-requirement-not-a-self-promotion-campaign/?sh=1404c626226f (accessed November 17, 2023).

MacNeill, M. (2020) Build your personal brand with TikTok. *Relevant Business*. Available at https://relevant-business.com.au/build-your-personal-brand-with-tiktok/personal-branding/ (accessed November 17, 2023).

MacReady, H. (2023) 47 LinkedIn statistics you need to know for 2023. *Hootsuite*. Available at https://blog.hootsuite.com/linkedin-statistics-business/ (accessed November 17, 2023).

Pestle Analysis (2022) How SWOT analysis in personal development helps you build self-confidence. Available at https://pestleanalysis.com/swot-analysis-in-personal-development/ (accessed November 17, 2023).

Piotrowicz, W. & Cuthbertson, R. (2014) Introduction to the special issue information technology in retail: toward omnichannel retailing. *International Journal of Electronic Commerce*, 18(4), 5–16.

Ravn, S., Barnwell, A. & Barbosa Neves, B. (2020) What is "publicly available data"? Exploring blurred public–private boundaries and ethical practices through a case study of Instagram. *Journal of Empirical Research on Human Research Ethics*, 15(1–2), 40–45.

Ruby, D. (2023) Social media users in the world. *DemandSage*. Available at https://www.demandsage.com/social-media-users/ (accessed November 17, 2023).

Smith, M. (2022) Personal branding: the what, why, and how. *Constant Contact*. Available at https://www.constantcontact.com/blog/personal-branding/ (accessed November 17, 2023).

Thakker, A. (2022) What are google alerts and how do they help businesses? *Infidigit*. Available at https://www.infidigit.com/blog/what-are-google-alerts/ (accessed November 17, 2023).

TikTok (2023) Defining your brand. Available at https://www.tiktok.com/creators/creator-portal/en-us/tiktok-content-strategy/defining-your-brand/ (accessed November 17, 2023).

Wise, J. (2022) Average number of applicants per job in 2023. *Earth Web*. Available at https://earthweb.com/what-is-the-average-number-of-applicants-per-job/ (accessed November 17, 2023).

Part III

Social Media Marketing and Business Models

9

The Long Tail and Social Media Business Models

Learning Objectives

After reading this chapter, you should be able to:

1 Explain the theory of the long tail and be able to identify the opportunities and challenges of marketing toward a latent consumer.
2 Define a business model and identify its key components.
3 Understand how to transform consumers into a niche commodity through social media and determine factors that influence business model development.

Introduction

The creation and implementation of a marketing strategy help organizations examine specific objectives and identify ways to reach their consumers over a long-term period. This involves careful research of the brand, consumers, and product market. Part II of this book highlighted the importance of prioritizing social media users and messages in this process. While this is a necessary first step in the marketing process, it is important that practitioners identify, anticipate, and satisfy customer expectations through a purposeful business model.

Strategic Social Media: From Marketing to Social Change, Second Edition. L. Meghan Mahoney and Tang Tang.
© 2024 John Wiley & Sons, Inc. Published 2024 by John Wiley & Sons, Inc.

Often, communication specialists are not as familiar with various business strategies as they are with communication persuasive appeal theories. A combination of both is crucial for the development of successful social media strategies.

Part III of this book focuses on how social media has changed existing business models, identifies emerging marketing strategies for your business, as well as suggests ways in which you can evaluate and predict marketing outcomes through formative research. A strong understanding of these areas will put you ahead of other social media communication specialists in the field. This is crucial to the long-term development of any organization or brand.

It is also important for organizations to integrate the design, implementation, and evaluation of marketing strategy and business models into day-to-day operations. It is not wise to segment these tasks into various departments. Communication will not seem cohesive and may result in a public relations nightmare for a company. This is especially true in today's digital age when every employee and customer has unlimited opportunities through social media as a mouthpiece for your organization.

The primary purpose of a business model is to help a company reach goals. Often, that goal is to increase revenue. As we learned in previous chapters, it is not enough in today's marketplace to simply have a strong product. Social media makes it necessary for companies to foster relationships with consumers. This chapter further explains how social media has changed the marketplace, defines a business model, and pinpoints the business and societal opportunities brought by social media.

Theory of the Long Tail

One of the most consistent elements of the traditional marketplace is the *power–law distribution*. A power law is a statistical relationship between two quantities, where one quantity varies proportionally based on the fixed power of the other. While the concept is quite complex, the main idea is that a small change in one quantity can give rise to a proportional change in the other quantity (Bar-Yam, 2011). The formula for a power–law distribution is shown in Figure 9.1.

This distribution is very important to strategists because it helps to explain some regularity in the properties of a complex system. Companies prefer regularities in consumer purchasing behavior because it provides some control over predicting the future of products and revenues. It is not just businesses that follow power–law distributions. Many natural and human systems also follow the same patterns. For example, the frequency of earthquakes is

$$p(x) = \frac{\alpha - 1}{x_{min}} \left(\frac{x}{x_{min}} \right)^{-\alpha}$$

Figure 9.1   Power–law distribution. Source: The author.

inversely related to their intensity, and the proportion of income distribution in society is inversely related to the amount of income (Jones & Kim, 2012).

Economists have found a significant power–law distribution in businesses, where significant profit can be made from selling a small number of popular items (Fenner *et al.*, 2010). This is especially true for media products, such as books, music, and movies. Traditionally, companies have been able to make a profit by only providing consumers the opportunity to purchase a small number of "hits" rather than a larger quantity of inventory.

Mass hits are included at the front of the distribution tail and reach a large number of consumers. More niche products are at the narrow, back end of the tail, and appeal to a much smaller latent market. The tail gets longer and longer, and the ability for marketers to profit on this inventory is traditionally lower (Jenkins *et al.*, 2013).

Economists often refer to this as the *80/20 rule*, where businesses appeal to 80% of the population by offering only 20% of the available products (Brynjolfsson *et al.*, 2011). Consider for a moment when you shop at a grocery store (which only carries a limited number of products available in the market). Chances are you walk through the grocery aisles and can purchase most of the products that you need. Moreover, there are enough selection options that you feel fairly informed about the decisions you make. The available inventory can keep consumers relatively happy, while also maintaining a profit.

Based on the 80/20 rule, the grocery store achieves this balance by only stocking a limited number of the possible products available in the market. These products are those items that are used most often by the masses. If you were attempting to find an ingredient for a recipe that is less appealing to the masses, you may have trouble finding it at the regular grocery store. Items not offered are a part of the *latent market*. These are products that cannot be profitably sold in traditional stores because they are not popular enough to recoup the cost of stocking it on the shelves (Spencer & Woods, 2010). Shelf space is expensive, and there is only so much available. The result of markets being dominated by a small number of best-selling products has often made it difficult for niche products to break through.

While business models have been developed based around traditional notions of power–law distributions, new technologies have changed the marketplace. Digital media and e-commerce have transformed our notion of shelf space. It is important for you to rethink traditional business models to make your organization fit for the future. One of the biggest shifts in thinking has been the theory of the long tail.

Today's digital world offers a lower cost of distribution, especially with the opportunities of e-commerce. Products are no longer bound by the constraints of physical shelf space and other bottlenecks of distribution. Anderson (2006) explored this phenomenon and developed a new business model for today's marketplace called the *theory of the long tail* (Figure 9.2), which explains how businesses can profit from a larger amount of niche products by using alternative distribution channels.

Not only are businesses able to profit from these niche sales, but the volume of latent commerce can collectively exceed the sale of a lower volume of hits. Marketers can make

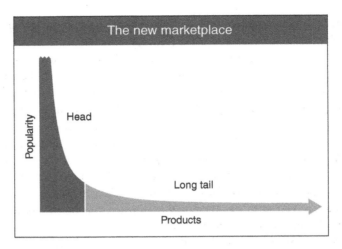

Figure 9.2   The long tail. Source: Reproduced with permission of Chris Anderson.

increased (or at least the same) revenue by selling to latent consumers than if they sold to the masses. Traditional businesses have only been able to stock the most appealing inventory because space is expensive. Online retailers, such as Amazon, can stock an unlimited selection of products. Given additional choice in products, consumers can gravitate toward those less popular niche products (Anderson, 2006). Therefore, it is important for social media practitioners to consider shifting their business model from targeting a mass market to a niche. Social media makes this more possible than ever before.

Let's consider the music industry for a moment. If you could determine the music inventory available in a traditional big box store, you likely be bound by the 80/20 rule. You would only have a limited amount of shelf space, so you would decide to stock the artists that prove most appealing to the masses, which would ensure the greatest number of sales.

An important transitional period in the music industry was in 2005, when Walmart was still America's largest music retailer and accounted for about one-fifth of music sales in the nation (Anderson, 2005). The most popular song in 2005 was Mariah Carey's *We Belong Together* (Billboard, 2005). Because of the song's mass appeal, Walmart personnel would certainly ensure that this album was available for purchase by giving it maximum shelf space.

Customers who purchased Mariah Carey's album from Walmart were likely satisfied with this stocking decision. They probably enjoyed the song when it was played on their local radio station, so when they went to the store to make a music selection, it was an appealing purchasing decision. If they didn't like the song on the radio, they would likely choose to purchase a different available album from an artist that they preferred more. If they went home and ended up not liking their purchasing choice, Walmart also offered the opportunity to exchange the album for one of their other items in stock. Overall, customers felt fairly satisfied that they were able to make informed decisions about their music purchases.

While this traditional business model was working for customers and businesses alike, digital media was about to change everything. The year 2005 was the first year that the number of legally downloaded digital singles outsold the physical products available in stores (Leeds, 2007). Customers were turning toward online music distributors, such as iTunes, to add songs to their personal music library rather than purchasing CDs from big box stores. They were no longer bound by the inventory of music selection that was decided by an outside agency. This shift provided a new opportunity for developing artists and independent labels.

Digital music changed the economics and players in the music industry (Anderson, 2006). Suddenly, artists were not competing for a finite amount of shelf space, for example, of the estimated 30,000 new albums released each year, Walmart stocked an average of 750. Through social media, rising artists were able to produce, collaborate, share, and sell their music at a relatively low cost. They no longer needed to appeal to a mass audience but were able to produce music that was authentic to their style, because hopefully, somewhere, there was a latent market that it satisfied.

In 2008, Spotify, a digital music streaming platform, was launched to provide songs, podcasts, and other audio products free of charge. Users can choose to listen to their customized playlists online free (with advertisements). Spotify Premium offers customers a paid, commercial-free, offline, and online listening experience (Spotify, 2023). Spotify users can also follow their favorite artists, discover new music based on their preferences, and share music with friends. They can see what music their friends are engaging and send songs to each other virtually any time (Andronico, 2022). The social factor not only makes the music listening experience immersive but also offers opportunities to many niche artists.

The latent market shifted power from the label producers to the artists and consumers. For the first time in history, audiences had unlimited access to every artist, genre, and song available online. This unlimited access to music made it easier for audiences to determine music styles that fit their own unique preferences and tastes. Maybe fans of Mariah Carey became aware of less popular artists through the recommendation structure of iTunes, or via the songs shared by their friends on Spotify. E-commerce makes it just as easy to purchase a song produced and uploaded from someone's basement, as it is to listen to songs on streaming platforms distributed from a major studio label.

The real potential of the long-tail business model resides in the emotional gratifications that consumers receive after making a latent purchase. Remember that businesses are not just able to profit from these niche sales, but the volume of latent commerce can collectively exceed the sale of a lower volume of hits (Anderson, 2006). Why is it that consumers were spending more money collectively on latent music products than they were on mass hits? The answer is simple: Consumers believe that their purchasing decisions are an extension of their individual identities.

Owning a Mariah Carey album does say something about a person's musical preferences. However, when there are only 750 available music options, the selection of Mariah Carey does not make a consumer significantly different from another consumer. One would not get that excited to learn that a stranger also likes Mariah Carey, especially since her song was the most popular hit on the radio. Therefore, this lack of differentiation makes the purchasing experience far less satisfying than if a consumer feels their selection is unique, highly personalized, and tailored toward their individual preferences.

Consider a musical group or artist that you enjoy and follow that no one in your own social network is aware of. Chances are you believe that your affinity for this music sets you apart from your friends. Your fandom for this artist becomes a large part of your identity. You may be more likely to follow that artist's social media updates, wear their t-shirt, or stop a stranger on the street that you see also sharing in your niche musical preference.

Latent commodities are more exciting to consumers because they do not appeal to the masses; they set us apart from our social network. We do not like being seen as identical to other consumers. It is likely that your greatest passions and interests have transformed you into a niche commodity. Are you an avid runner? Regular athletic shoes sold at the local big box store may not fulfill your unique needs. Niche stores that sell specialized running products, such as attire, hydration packs and safety gear that are not necessary for the everyday consumer may be your go-to place. Research demonstrates that consumers are willing to pay premium prices for niche products and subsequently make recommendations to others based on these latent purchases (Batte *et al.*, 2007). This gratifying experience transforms consumers into brand advocates for niche products. These are more than just products: They are an extension of ourselves.

Consumers prefer to be a part of something special and unique. It is important to note that business models based on the concepts of the theory of the long tail are only successful if practitioners know how to best use social media to target specific online consumers that are interested in a latent product. Otherwise, the same limited consumer base binds organizations as traditional in-store retailers. A strong understanding of a business model and its key components is important.

Developing a Business Model

A *business model* explains how your organization works (Magretta, 2002). It serves as a foundation for managers and communication specialists to share their understanding of the business with different stakeholders, helps to maximize strengths and alleviate weaknesses of your company, and is extremely important to a business's long-term viability (Hayes & Graybeal, 2011). You might think of the process of developing a business model similarly to how you would plan a party. You need to decide what's the occasion, who you would like to invite, how you could reach them, what you would provide in the party, what the desired outcome would be, and how much the party would cost (Bennett, 2013).

"Business model" is an often-misused term. Many have defined the term as a revenue model or a business statement about how a company can monetize consumers and make a profit (Cha, 2013; Stewart & Zhao, 2000). Here, the focus of the business model is on increasing revenue streams. However, business models should cover all matters of interest, including your business's value proposition, consumers, market position, distribution strategies, cost structure, and so on. Robert Picard (2000), a media economist, suggests that business models do more to examine the underlying characteristics that make commerce in the product or service possible. Business models should include various stages of a business, including conception, foundation, and financial flow. A business model is a living document that decides your company's marketing, pricing, distribution, customer relationship, revenue, and product development strategies.

There are seven components that you need to consider when developing a business model: (i) your business/product's value proposition; (ii) customer segments; (iii) competitive strategy; (iv) marketing strategy; (v) revenue streams; (vi) cost structure; and (vii) organizational development (key partners, resources, and activities) (Figure 9.3). Overall, your business model needs to answer two questions: What you can offer to your consumers and how will you achieve this?

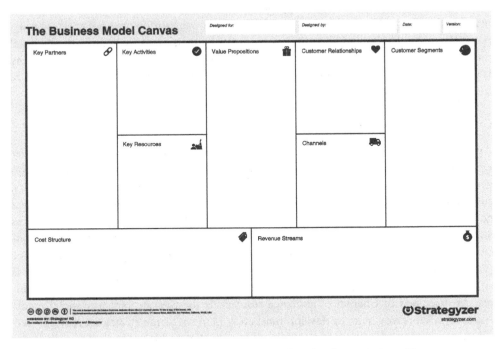

Figure 9.3 Business model canvas. Source: Reproduced with permission of Strategyzer.

Value proposition

Value proposition is one of the most important components of a business model. *Value proposition* defines the values that a business creates to fulfill the needs of consumers. Think about what you can offer to your consumers. Know why your consumers need your product/message, and why they are willing to pay (Hayes & Graybeal, 2011; IMT, 2013). This construct, rather than revenue streams, is the heart of your business model. It is always important to know your key competencies and build your marketing strategies, revenue model, cost structure, and partnership upon this value proposition.

Many approaches can help define your company's value proposition. Generally, you will start the process with an educated guess. Your value proposition could rest on the scope of your business, key features of your product/service, the cost structure, pricing strategies, customization, service delivery, and so on (Cha, 2013; IMT, 2013). For example, TikTok's value proposition is to provide a social and entertaining platform for people to watch and share short videos. Xing's (in Germany) value proposition is to help users build professional networks. Pinduoduo's (in China) value proposition is to provide lower prices to their customers for daily deals. TripAdvisor offers customer reviews and recommendations for traveling. Douguo, a Chinese recipe sharing site, received US$10 million in funding because it shares 10,000 recipes online and via mobile every month (Russell, 2012).

When identifying your own value proposition, consider the elements surrounding your brand authenticity (discussed in Chapter 3). Your value proposition does not need to be big, but instead should simply tell your customers the benefits of using your business/social media product, and why they cannot get the same benefits from your competitors. The key is to think about your value proposition first and revenue streams second. This will ensure a long-term commitment from your consumers.

Customer segmentation

Another crucial component of a business model is customer segmentation. *Customer segmentation* defines your consumers, including demographics, psychographics, and geographic areas. *Demographics* refers to quantitative information on your consumers, such as age, gender, education, race, marital status, income, and occupation. *Psychographics* goes beyond numeric information to offer qualitative data on your customers, such as attitudes, lifestyle, values, beliefs, needs, and wants. Both are crucial when identifying your customers. *Geographic areas* indicate where customers can find your product/service (Cha, 2013). Though social media makes most organizations a global marketplace, it is still important to frame messages according to the cultural norms of your target consumers. As discussed in Chapter 5, audience research is the first step for any social media endeavor. Before you start to develop marketing plans, revenue strategies, and partnerships, you need to ask who your core consumers are, what problems they want you to solve for them, and what their dream social media product would be.

Each successful social media product serves unique customer segmentation and differentiates their target consumers from existing businesses in the same market/category (Cha, 2013).

For example, LinkedIn's customer segmentation is college students and professionals who seek career development and networking opportunities, as well as companies/organizations who would like to recruit talents. Pinterest focuses on reaching female users who would like to share their passion and interests with others. Xiaomi, a social mobile phone service, identified its customer segmentation as young adults who like fashion and are open to new experiences, but cannot afford expensive products (Shih *et al.*, 2014).

Do as much as you can to step into the role of your customers when developing your business model. Try to go beyond stereotyping them but conduct research to best understand their attitudes and behaviors. We have discussed factors that influence your customers' social media use and purchasing decisions in Chapters 5 and 6. Begin with your educated guesses, and then get out of the building, meet your customers, and take efforts to engage them in your business plan. In addition to identifying who your target consumers are, you also need to consider other questions related to your customers. For example, how are you going to keep and grow your customers? What types of relationships do you want to develop with them? What channels would you use to respond to their concerns both before and after sales? All are important to your business's long-term viability.

Competitive strategy

When developing a business model, you also need to specify your competitive strategy. The term *competitive strategy* refers to an analysis of your competitors who are doing similar business or selling the same type of products/services in the market. Knowing your competitive environment and competitive advantages is necessary before you start thinking about how to sell your business to consumers, partners, and other stakeholders.

Many marketing firms start their marketing efforts by conducting a *SWOT analysis*, i.e., an investigation of a product/service's strengths, weaknesses, opportunities, and threats. An effective business model should be able to maximize your strengths and lighten your weaknesses. Before you reach out to your customers (existing or potential), ensure that your product/service is superior to your competitors and identify areas for improvement. Research to see if there are underserved segments in your market. What are possible threats? And be sure to consider the larger economic environment, policy change, technology innovation, and/or new players who may enter your market. Give attention to your major competitors and know the market share for each, including their value propositions and the price of each of their products. Use social media to track their customers' concerns, compliments, and complaints, because your competitors' customers today could be your customers tomorrow (and vice versa).

Marketing strategy

Marketing strategy is also a component of your business model. Nielsen found that an average consumer only took 13 seconds to purchase a brand in store and 19 seconds online (Beard, 2015). How can you make the most of these 20 seconds? This period should be the highest priority to consider when developing your marketing strategies.

Marketing strategies explain how a business reaches its consumers and brands itself. Your marketing strategies should be simple, clear, and vivid. Think about what you want your consumers to think about your brand in 20 seconds. Focus most of your research, marketing, and evaluation efforts here.

Let's take 20 seconds to think about the company Disney. You are likely to immediately think about Mickey Mouse, Disney movies, rollercoaster, and perhaps the happy experiences you had at the Disney theme parks/shops growing up. If you think about GEICO (i.e., an American insurance company), you may think about their green spokes lizard. When you think about Walmart, you may think about the yellow smiling face, low price, and one-stop shopping. There are limited details that your consumers will think about in 20 seconds. Your marketing strategies should focus on the elements of your brand that "easily come to mind" (Beard, 2015). Start with your value proposition, and then make it memorable. We will talk more about marketing strategy in Chapter 10.

Revenue stream

As business owners and marketers spend more money on social media, they become more concerned with monetizing social media products and endeavors. There is no doubt that revenue stream is a key component of a business model. The *revenue model* defines how a business makes revenue and monetizes its product/service (IMT, 2013). Revenue streams for social media businesses range from traditional advertising, subscription, sales, and transaction fees to the newer models, such as freemium model, affiliate revenue, crowdfunding, and virtual goods. As we have learned, business models go well beyond identifying revenue streams. However, understanding how a business makes money and generates ROI is important.

Advertising is the most-applied revenue stream. Social media advertising includes both direct and indirect ads. Like the ads displayed on traditional print media, some social media platforms like Facebook place domain ads and banner ads. YouTube also uses direct ads, both display ads and 15-second or 30-second in-stream video ads, to generate revenue. Ad revenue brought US$28.8 billion to YouTube. The social media platform takes 45% of this advertising revenue and gives the other 55% to the video creators who generate the ad sale (Hutchinson, 2022). In addition to direct ads, indirect ads, such as X's (formerly Twitter), promoted tweets that brought US$12 per user to the platform. Yet, when Elon Musk purchased Twitter (now renamed X) in 2023, he aimed to generate 50% of the revenue from subscriptions (Hutchinson, 2023).

Subscription revenue model has been used by digital media companies/services who charge users for quality niche content. For example, Netflix charges $8.99 to access its basic service. The *Wall Street Journal* charges readers $9.75 a week to access financial/business news on its digital platforms. While the subscription model has gained popularity among social media businesses, they constantly face the challenge that users who are not used to or willing to pay for online products/services. This is especially true for digital natives who are used to having many free online content options. As such, the freemium strategy was introduced for businesses that rely on digital subscription to make a living (Anderson, 2010).

The *Freemium model* is a revenue model introduced by Chris Anderson, creator of the long tail theory, suggesting that a company offers its basic service for free, but charges those who would like to access premium service/content. The hope is that after users try the basic/limited version for free, they would adopt the paid version if they like the basic one (Anderson, 2010). For example, LinkedIn provides the basic service to consumers for free, but charges US$39.99 per month for premium job seekers; US$59.99 per month for all-purpose premium business professionals; US$99.99 a month for salespeople; and more than US$8,999 a year for recruiters (Smulders, 2023). While most LinkedIn users still pay nothing to connect with colleagues and professional networks, a portion of its customers choose to pay extra to generate better opportunities to find jobs or gain business leads. These premium subscriptions account for 20% of LinkedIn's total revenue.

E-commerce is another revenue source used by many businesses in today's digital era. Facebook started to sell virtual goods in 2008. Users can buy and send virtual flowers and virtual balloons to their friends directly on Facebook, and this brought in more than US$30 million to Facebook in just its first year of service (Social Times, 2008). Twitch, a live streaming platform for gamers, sells virtual good – "bits," for users to support their favorite streamers via cheers and/or virtual gifts. The popular Chinese social media site WeChat (see Chapter 5) allows users to send virtual goods, even virtual money to each other. Roblox, a gaming platform we discussed in Chapter 7, also encourages users to create and sell virtual items, including accessories, clothing, tools, avatar customization options, etc.

Other revenue streams that can be applied to social media businesses include transaction fees and affiliate fees. The *transaction fee model* refers to a model that allows social media businesses to make money from facilitating or executing transactions (Enders *et al.*, 2008; Laudon & Traver, 2007). Generally, this type of transaction is called an *exogenous transaction*, suggesting that social media platforms facilitate selling of third-party content/products/services to users and enable transactions between social media users (Enders *et al.*, 2008). Well-known businesses like eBay, Alibaba (China), qoo10.sg (Singapore), and snapdeal.com (India) all rely on transaction fees for their operation.

The *affiliate model* suggests that businesses generate revenues by driving traffic to another company's website and/or providing leads for other businesses to sell products (Laudon & Traver, 2007; Loayza, 2009). Google made its entire business based on driving traffic to other companies. Many successful independent bloggers can make a living from providing affiliate links on their blogs. It is important for social media businesses to use multiple revenue streams and adopt a hybrid revenue model.

Cost structure

For many organizations, the goal of doing business is profit optimization. When considering profit, we must include both revenue and cost. Thus, cost structure is also a component of your business model. While most business owners spend a lot of time considering revenue streams, relatively less attention has been given to cost. You should think about the average cost to produce, deliver, and sell a product. What would be your biggest cost to run the business? Which costs are fixed, and which costs would be variable? Cost leadership is particularly crucial for social media businesses. As digital competition continues to saturate the marketplace. Those who can produce the product that satisfies consumers' needs at the lowest cost will win consumers.

Many people believe that their cost for social media marketing/communication should be zero because we do not need to pay for using most of the social media sites. However, it is important to note that social media is not free. Effective social media endeavors require both financial and human resources. There are also opportunities to engage customers through giveaways and promotions. Thus, examine your budget and consider how much cost you can afford to improve and maintain your social media efforts.

Organizational development

Finally, your business model should address the plan for carrying out these concepts. *Organizational development* defines how a business organizes the tasks that will need to be done (IMT, 2013). It includes several major components, such as a business's key partners, resources, and activities. After you know who your consumers are, what you can offer them, and how you can monetize them, it is time to think about how you will actually conduct the business. Who are your key partners? Suppliers? How can you locate them? What resources would you need to do your job? The resources could include physical, financial, and human resources. The finishing line of developing a business model is to decide what you would do yourself and what you would need others to do.

It is also important to note that while determining ROI is a growing concern for businesses' social media endeavors, the goal of some social media platforms/efforts is to provide a free service to users. As we discussed in the previous chapters, social media opportunities rest in behavior change and the role it plays in community building and user engagement. If the entire premise of social media is the ability to hold a conversation online, would not a successful social media endeavor be to engage the intended users through interactive dialogue rather than top-down diffusion? Thus, instead of generating revenues, many companies choose to use social media as a platform to enhance customer relationship, build a community, establish brand expertise, and/or aid behavior change. In Part IV, we will further discuss social media's function in empowering users and aiding behavior changes for social good. There we will see how social media can go beyond direct ROI to change a company's entire structure.

Developing a business model is both art and science. Start with your guesses, then test the model, and refine it constantly. Below is a step-by-step action plan to develop your business model.

Developing a Business Model Action Plan

1 Understand who you are (e.g., your unique strengths, weaknesses) and be specific about what unique problems you could help your customers to solve. Identify what customers' needs your product/service can fulfill that other similar businesses cannot.
2 Know your most important consumers. Use the consumer analysis methods discussed in Chapters 5 and 6 to gather information about your core consumers' interests, passions, personality, and, more importantly, why they would use your social media product and what they want you to do for them.
3 Decide your revenue model. You may use more than one revenue stream, or simply decide to use your social media products to generate "social good" (rather than ROI). Determine and communicate how you can produce ROI.
4 Finally, explore the most successful operations for conducting your unique business. Identify the necessary components for achieving your goals (e.g., key partners, resources, suppliers).

One Business Model Doesn't Fit All

Hopefully, the most important takeaway from this chapter is that your business now can move beyond an "either or" conceptualization but consider "both and" and "all possible." An integrated approach can utilize the strengths and alleviate weaknesses of each traditional business plan and find a path for your business in today's convergent media environment.

According to the theory of the long tail, targeting your latent consumers is an important shift for businesses in today's digital environment. However, there are things to consider about the theory before implementing latent consumers into your business plan.

Questioning the long tail

The theory of the long tail is based on the idea that "niche media content is able to accrue value at a different pace, on a different scale, through a different infrastructure and on the basis of different appeals than the highest grossing commercial texts do" (Jenkins *et al.*, 2013, p. 238). While this has certainly resulted in users having more access to a diverse array of media content than ever before, it is important that the societal impact of this phenomenon is not overstated.

One of the first caveats to consider is the type of media users most likely to purchase a niche product. Research demonstrates that heavy media users who engage in most of the media content are more likely to seek latent commodities than light and casual social media users (Jenkins *et al.*, 2013). While finding niche products online does not require a high level of competency, it seems to be done most often by those with greater access, infrastructure, and online experience. It is important to understand the online habits of your target consumers before integrating the theory of the long tail into your business plan.

Second, the impact of the long-tail market on society can be overstated as idealistic for producers and consumers alike. Virtually anyone can engage in e-commerce, transforming power from traditional media producers to everyday consumers. While digital media has certainly advanced opportunities for minority products, money still matters, especially when it comes to media institutions. While the potential for an independent latent market to break through exists, overtaking a well-established business with a large marketing budget still proves to be the exception.

As such, it is important to follow the four pieces of cautionary advice below for those interested in profiting from the long-tail market (Elberse, 2008).

1   Continue to include hits in your management strategy, as a few mass appeal items go a long way. Digital media has provided the opportunity for marketers to introduce the possibility of additional sales, but the common denominator products still matter.
2   Ensure that production cost of latent products is as low as possible. Distribution that appeals to only a small specific consumer base is risky. The more one minimizes the cost of this risk, including resources and time of production, the better.
3   Market your most popular products to a mass audience and use low-cost social media to target the latent market. There is still a place for both traditional and new revenue streams. Distribute messages according to the size of the potential consumers.
4   While newer inventory will be available at a faster rate than ever before, do not forget to include old hits in your marketing strategy. Newer is not always better. Products can now virtually live forever and present a real opportunity for profit if the appropriate market is found.

These suggestions should help guide decisions about the business and marketing strategies of your organization in an ever-changing media landscape. We will discuss how to integrate old with new in Chapter 18. Before that, it is important to understand the many factors that can influence your business model development.

First, the type of your business largely determines your business model. If you work for a traditional business that provides professionally made products, you may rely on advertising, subscription, and/or use social media as a marketing tool (rather than revenue generator) to reach target consumers and build brand awareness and credibility. If your business is based on niche market and user-generated content, you may want to consider the freemium model, affiliate model, and selling virtual goods. Research suggests that fun products and friendly services that require little research from the user end are the best fit for social media businesses (Duboff & Wilkerson, 2010). The value proposition is the fundamental factor that decides your business model.

As always, you want to consider your target consumers. Are you selling products/services to individual consumers or other businesses? B2B (i.e., business to business) companies tend to rely on social media to generate revenue and actively measure ROI, while B2C (i.e., business to consumer) marketers are more likely to use social media to build consumer trust and/or reduce marketing and distribution cost (Duboff & Wilkerson, 2010).

Consumers' willingness to pay can also influence your business model. *Willingness to pay* is defined as the maximum price consumers would like to pay based on their perceived value of the product/service (Wertenbroch & Skiera, 2002). Willingness to pay is a constant challenge faced by social media business owners and marketers, since paying money is inconsistent with the "free culture" of online media consumption. Nonetheless, willingness to pay is a precursor of many revenue models, including the subscription, freemium, and e-commerce models. Economists and marketers suggest that people only pay for "superior, timely, original content" (Clemons, 2009). Why would users pay for anything less? In addition, consumers prefer to use virtual currency (e.g., Robux in Roblox) and/or micropayment to pay for online transactions (Hayes & Graybeal, 2011; Hsee *et al.*, 2003).

Consumer size is important to determine your business model. Broadcast networks have charged advertisers millions of dollars because they can reach a mass audience (e.g., 90% of the US population). For years, reach has been used as a primary measurement for evaluating a marketing effort. In the social media era, customer size is particularly important for businesses that utilize the advertising, affiliate, and transaction models. Having the ability to generate a large amount of web traffic is vital to attracting advertising dollars, transaction fees, and other revenues. Companies targeted on niche consumers (e.g., hyperlocal news organizations) should not use advertising as their primary revenue source.

Moreover, consumer trust can drive revenues for businesses. For example, the affiliate model rests solely on the level of consumer trust (Hayes & Graybeal, 2011; Loayza, 2009). Using such a model, your goal is to drive traffic to other companies' websites (and lead to sales). If people do not trust you, they will not visit the sites or buy the products that you recommend. Nonetheless, it is important to disclose the revenue source to your consumers. Remember from Chapter 2 that transparency is the first step toward building trust.

Furthermore, perceived risk may influence your business model. Whenever you ask customers to connect their financial information (i.e., bank/credit card information) to your site, perceived risk is involved. Products/services with higher prices and those that could be dangerous to use (e.g., health products) are generally associated with more perceived risks and require more consumer trust (Duboff & Wilkerson, 2010). Research suggests that consumers need to trust the product, company, and technology before they are ready to make an online transaction (Van Baalen *et al.*, 2005). Thus, only after you obtain consumer trust, will e-commerce, virtual goods, and transaction models fit your business.

As you can see, many factors influence your business model development. Ultimately, you need to choose the model based on your unique strengths and balance the different operations of your business (Berman *et al.*, 2006). More importantly, please remember that one model does not fit all, which indicates that you should use all revenue streams appropriate for your business. Do not limit your options. Maybe none of the existing business models that we have introduced here fit your business, but some of these concepts may work. That is why this book is not concerned with platform-specific approaches, but instead focuses on providing a strong understanding of how social media inspire human behavior change. The ability of social media to offer boundless choices has changed our traditional thinking of business models and the marketplace. Therefore, be innovative, test your ideas, prepare to shape your model, and embrace all the opportunities and challenges brought by social media.

Case Study: Livestream Shopping

This chapter talks about how traditional marketplace has followed the power–law distribution model. Only popular items were carried and sold to customers as they tend to bring large amount of profit to businesses. However, digital technologies have reduced the production and distribution costs and have brought about the possibility of generating profits for niche products. The latent market led to unforeseen business and societal opportunities. One of such examples is China's livestream shopping.

Livestream shopping is a combination of live video streaming and online shopping where hosts present products in an entertaining manner and users can watch the video, ask questions, and make a purchase directly via the livestream (Baird, 2023; Pollard, 2021). First introduced in 2016 by Alibaba, a giant e-commerce platform in China, livestream shopping has reached more than 460 million users and generated US$327 billion revenue in 2022 (Baird, 2023; Chi, 2022). Every month, more than 9 million livestreams are launched on Douyin (Chinese version of TikTok), which can sell 10 billion pieces of products, ranging from snacks to cosmetics to cars (Chi, 2022). Top international brands, such as Louis Vuitton and L'Oréal, have also used livestreams to market their products in China (Pollard, 2021). Livestream shopping is a clear illustration of the theory of the long tail and has disrupted the marketplace with how people buy and sell goods in China.

The success of livestream shopping in China is due to a strong business model built upon a thorough understanding of value proposition and customer segmentation. Probably one of the most important value propositions of livestream shopping is interactivity. Live streamers/hosts speak directly to online shoppers. Shoppers can ask questions and make requests (e.g., ask the host to try a shirt on to show them the product from different angles) via informal chat, and the hosts respond these questions/requests in real-time. Often, these livestream hosts call individual customers by name, as they were old friends. In return, customers show the intimacy with sending animated pink hearts or messages like "I missed you, too" to the hosts (Wang, 2023). The interactivity of livestream shopping makes the purchasing experience unique and highly personalized. Gradually, customers become fans of the streamers, and eventually, brand advocates.

Livestream shopping's value proposition also rests on its entertaining value. China's livestream shopping is a show. The streamers often tell jokes and/or personal stories in an energetic way to hold audience attention (Baird, 2023; Wang, 2023). Jiaqi Li, a top streamer, often put various lipsticks on his lip, with his catchphrase "Oh my god, buy it" to stimulate the excitement (Pollard, 2021). Many streamers also use the urgency appeal by providing limited time offers to create hype. Some people may watch a streamer throughout the entire evening in order to purchase the limited deal (Baird, 2023).

The success of livestream shopping is also due to its product-market match. When livestream shopping was first launched in China, Chinese consumers have already been mobile-oriented. They were already accustomed to using mobile to chat, social, shop, and consume media content. Since the introduction of livestream shopping, many Chinese digital media platforms, such as Douyin, Kuaishou, and Taobao, have already included video streaming, interactive chatbox, and built-in payment features, making livestream shopping in China convenient and familiar to consumers. In addition, in China, influencer recommendations tend to have a greater influence on purchasing decisions than anywhere else in the world. This is a culture where community input is highly prioritized. Collectivist cultures such as China are highly concerned with others in their network, well above their own individual needs. They see themselves as part of a larger community. They believe that what is satisfying to others will most likely be satisfying to them.

There is no doubt that livestream shopping brought many opportunities to niche products and average people. There are more than 20,000 agencies in China, which each manage multiple livestream influencers (Pollard, 2021). Most of these influencers are less-known people. They are farmers, shop assistants, factory owners, teachers, and tour guides. For example, Jiaqi Li was a shop assistant in a makeup store before becoming a top livestream shopping influencer. He has 47 million followers on his Taobao livestream room (Pollard, 2021; Wang, 2023). On the Single's Day (i.e., November 11) in 2021, Jiaqi attracted 250 million viewers and sold $19 billion worth of goods during the day. Yonghao Luo, another top livestream shopping influencer, was an English teacher. He attracted 48 million viewers to his first livestream via Douyin and made $15.4 million that day (Chi, 2020). Livestream shopping based on the long tail model could make anyone an entrepreneur, transforming power from traditional conglomerates to everyday consumers.

Seeing the growth of livestream commerce in China, NBC Universal made its livestream shopping debut in November 2021. Snap invested in augmented reality technology to enhance consumers' online shopping experience (Pollard, 2021). YouTube and Amazon have also initiated their livestream shopping efforts. Facebook introduced Facebook Shops during the pandemic, while Google, Shopify, Walmart, among others all allowed consumers to buy products featured via live streams (Ruether, 2022). However, these efforts have struggled to attract American consumers. Thus, many including Facebook and Instagram abandoned their livestream shopping efforts (Wang, 2023).

One takeaway from China's livestream shopping case is the importance of building a business model around your unique niche strengths. Only when you understand your consumers, and you are authentic with your brand, can opportunities thrive. As we have discussed throughout this chapter, while the long-tail market has brought many business and societal opportunities, one model doesn't fit all. Your success depends on your ability to leverage your product/service's unique value proposition.

Discussion questions

1   Your value proposition is the first step toward developing a successful business model. What is the value proposition of China's livestream shopping? In your opinion, what will be the next stage of livestream shopping?
2   Livestream shopping has been successful in China. However, American consumers did not immediately react warmly to the platform. Why is it less successful in the United States? If livestream shopping would like to work on its global appeal in the future, what would you suggest being its local integration strategy in your country?
3   Livestream shopping has made many average people celebrities and entrepreneurs. If you were going to start a livestream shopping show, how could you leverage your unique value to make it successful?

Summary

This chapter examines traditional notions of business models and how they have been impacted by new media technologies. A strong understanding of the industry's business trends should help guide future decisions about product revenue and consumer relationships for social media practitioners.

Under the traditional notions of power–law distribution, businesses make distribution judgments based on the idea that they could appeal to 80% of the population by offering only 20% of the available products (Brynjolfsson *et al.*, 2011). This strategy worked well for many decades and was consistent with the business model of advertising to the masses. However, as digital media and e-commerce allowed for the cost of production and distribution to decrease, latent markets began emerging, providing new profit possibilities for organizations.

The theory of the long tail teaches us new possibilities for businesses to capitalize on the collective sale of niche products. While this latent market has less demand than bestselling hits, it can collectively make up a rivaling market share. The long-tail model has advanced many opportunities for niche products to compete in the marketplace and has given consumers unlimited choices when it comes to product selection. This benefits the producer, consumer, and retailer alike.

The real value of a niche commodity has more to do with the purchasing experience than it does with the potential revenue. We have learned how consumers prefer to buy these niche commodities because they serve individual interests and passions. The purchasing experience becomes an extension of personal identity. Your consumers feel as though they are making an investment in themselves when they make latent purchases. This is how your consumers are transformed into brand advocates.

This chapter also identifies key components of a business model. We have learned that a business model is not the same as a revenue model. A business model acts as a conceptual tool to guide your company's operation (Osterwalder *et al.*, 2005) and consists of seven components: value propositions, customer segments, competitive strategy, marketing strategy, revenue streams, cost structure, and organizational development. The business model should rest in your product/service's value proposition. Understanding your customers and knowing how to operate your business are as important as determining your business's revenue streams.

As business owners and marketers invest more in social media, they aim to monetize their social media users. Several revenue streams can be applied to social media businesses, including advertising, subscription, freemium, affiliate, transaction, and virtual goods. Facing today's competitive marketplace, it is important for a social media business to use multiple revenue sources and discover new revenue generators.

In this chapter, we have also learned that no one existing business model fits all. You need to find one that works best for your business. Many factors can influence this decision, including the type of your business, user size, consumer's willingness to pay, and consumer trust. It is also important to note that the functions of social media exceed ROI. As discussed throughout this book, social media's premise rests in its ability to empower and engage users via interactive conversation. Thus, instead of using social media simply to talk to consumers about how wonderful your business is, it become a source of targeted information. Leverage the interactive structures of social media to form real connections. Social media can serve as a great marketing tool and bring unforeseen opportunities. Let's explore more about social media marketing strategies in Chapter 10.

Key Takeaways

1　The power–law distribution has dominated the conceptualization of traditional business models. However, as digital technologies have reduced the costs of production and distribution, latent markets began emerging.
2　The theory of the long tail identifies the possibility of increasing profit by focusing marketing efforts on niche latent consumers, rather than a mass appeal.
3　Consumers are willing to pay premium prices for niche products and are more likely to make niche recommendations to others. These latent purchasing experiences transform consumers into brand advocates but are only possible if consumers can find your product.
4　A one-size-fits-all business model is not available for social media businesses. Finding your unique value proposition and product–market match is the most important factor when developing your business model.
5　Social media is not built for short-term sales. The advertising model may not be the best fit for all social media businesses. Find the niche revenue streams (e.g., freemium, virtual goods, affiliate) for your business. Use multiple revenue streams and control cost to realize profit maximization.
6　Be innovative, embrace the conceptualization of "all possible," and welcome all the unforeseen opportunities brought by technology.

References

Anderson, C. (2005) The long tail: Chris Anderson's blog. Available at http://www.longtail.com/the_long_tail/2005/07/americas_record.html (accessed November 17, 2023).

Anderson, C. (2006) *The Long Tail: Why the Future of Business Is Selling Less of More*. New York: Hyperion.

Anderson, C. (2010) *Free: How Today's Smartest Businesses Profit by Giving Something for Nothing*. New York: Hyperion.

Andronico, M. (2022) I ditched Spotify for apple music for 2 weeks: here's why I'm going back. *CNN Underscored*. Available at https://www.cnn.com/cnn-underscored/electronics/apple-music-vs-spotify (accessed November 17, 2023).

Baird, N. (2023) Livestream shopping is not going to take over e-commerce. *Forbes*. Available at https://www.forbes.com/sites/nikkibaird/2023/03/05/livestream-shopping-is-not-going-to-take-over-e-commerce/?sh=46acb04f1c61 (accessed November 17, 2023).

Bar-Yam, Y. (2011) Concepts: power law. Available at http://www.necsi.edu/guide/concepts/powerlaw.html (accessed November 17, 2023).

Batte, M.T., Hooker, N.H., Haab, T.C. & Beaverson, J. (2007) Putting their money where their mouths are: consumer willingness to pay for multi-ingredient, processed organic food products. *Food Policy*, 32(2), 145–159.

Beard, R. (2015) Make the most of your brand's 20-second window. Available at http://www.nielsen.com/us/en/insights/news/2015/make-the-most-of-your-brands-20-second-window.html (accessed November 17, 2023).

Bennett, S. (2013) Paid, owned, earned: a strategic business model for effective social media marketing. Available at http://www.adweek.com/socialtimes/social-media-party/477660 (accessed November 17, 2023).

Berman, S., Abraham, S., Battino, B., Shipnuck, L. & Neus, A. (2006) Navigating the media divide: innovating and enabling new business models. Available at http://www-935.ibm.com/services/us/gbs/bus/pdf/g510-6551-02-mediadivide.pdf (accessed November 17, 2023).

Billboard (2005) 2005 Billboard music award winners. Available at http://www.billboard.com/articles/news/60428/2005-billboard-music-awards-winners (accessed November 17, 2023).

Brynjolfsson, E., Hu, Y. & Simester, D. (2011) Goodbye pareto principle, hello long tail: the effect of search costs on the concentration of product sales. *Management Science*, 57(8), 1373–1386.

Cha, J. (2013) Business models of most-visited U.S. social networking sites. In: A. Albarran (ed) *The Social Media Industries*, pp. 60–85. New York: Routledge, Taylor & Francis.

Chi, S. (2020) Smartisan's founder sets new sales record. *China Daily*. Available at https://global.chinadaily.com.cn/a/202004/02/WS5e85860fa310128217283f05.html (accessed November 17, 2023).

Chi, S. (2022) Users of live streaming e-commerce increase. *China Daily*. Available at https://www.chinadaily.com.cn/a/202211/24/WS637edee8a31049175432ba87.html (accessed November 17, 2023).

Clemons, E. (2009) Business models for monetizing Internet applications and web sites experience, theory, and predictions. *Journal of Management Information Systems*, 26(2), 15–41.

Duboff, R. & Wilkerson, S. (2010) Social media ROI: marketers are seeking to answer the "greatest question". *Marketing Management*, Winter, 33–37.

Elberse, A. (2008) Should you invest in the long tail? *Harvard Business Review*, 86(7–8), 88.

Enders, A., Hungenberg, H., Denker, H. & Mauch, S. (2008) The long tail of social networking: revenue models of social networking sites. *European Management Journal*, 26, 199–211.

Fenner, T., Levene, M. & Loizou, G. (2010) Predicting the long tail of book sales: unearthing the power-law exponent. *Physica A: Statistical Mechanics and Its Applications*, 389(12), 2416–2421.

Hayes, J. & Graybeal G. (2011) Synergizing traditional media and the social web for monetization: a modified media micropayment model. *Journal of Media Business Studies*, 8(2), 19–44.

Hsee, C.K., Yu, F., Zhang, J. & Zhang, Y. (2003) Medium maximization. *Journal of Consumer Research*, 30, 1–14.

Hutchinson, A. (2022) YouTube generated $28.8 billion in ad revenue in 2021, fueling the creator economy. *Social Media Today*. Available at https://www.socialmediatoday.com/news/youtube-generated-288-billion-in-ad-revenue-in-2021-fueling-the-creator/618208/ (accessed November 17, 2023).

Hutchinson, A. (2023) Twitter implements its 50% ad reduction incentive for twitter blue subscribers. *Social Media Today*. Available at https://www.socialmediatoday.com/news/twitter-implements-its-50-ad-reduction-incentive-for-twitter-blue-subscrib/647078/ (accessed November 17, 2023).

IMT (2013) 8 Key elements of a business model. Available at http://imtebiz2013.blogspot.com/2013/10/8-key-elements-of-a-business-model.html (accessed November 17, 2023).

Jenkins, H., Ford, S. & Green, J. (2013) *Spreadable Media: Creating Value and Meaning in a Networked Culture.* New York: New York University Press.

Jones, C.I. & Kim, J. (2012) Exploring the dynamics of top income inequality. Available at http://isites.harvard.edu/fs/docs/icb.topic1118825.files/Jones_Nov19.pdf (accessed November 17, 2023).

Laudon, K.C. & Traver, C.G. (2007) *E-commerce: Business, Technology, Society*, third edition. Upper Saddle River, NJ: Prentice Hall.

Leeds, J. (2007) Plunge in CD sales shakes up big labels. Available at http://www.nytimes.com/2007/05/28/arts/music/28musi.html?_r=4&oref=slogin&oref=slogin (accessed November 17, 2023).

Loayza, J. (2009) 5 business models for social media start-ups. Available at http://mashable.com/2009/07/14/social-media-business-models/ (accessed November 17, 2023).

Magretta, J. (2002) Why business models matter. Available at https://hbr.org/2002/05/why-business-models-matter (accessed November 17, 2023).

Osterwalder, A., Pigneur, Y. & Tucci, C.L. (2005) Clarifying business models: origins, present, and future of the concept. *Communications of the Association for Information Systems*, 16, Article 1. Available at http://aisel.aisnet.org/cais/vol16/iss1/1 (accessed November 17, 2023).

Picard, R.G. (2000) Changing business models of online content services: their implications for multimedia and other content producers. *International Journal on Media Management*, 2(3), 60–68.

Pollard, J. (2021) How livestream shopping works in China. *Asia Financial*. Available at https://www.asiafinancial.com/explainer-how-livestream-shopping-works-in-china (accessed November 17, 2023).

Ruether, T. (2022) Live commerce: how streaming is transforming shopping. *Wowza*. Available at https://www.wowza.com/blog/live-commerce-streaming-transforming-shopping (accessed November 17, 2023).

Russell, J. (2012) Chinese recipe sharing service Douguo serves up $8 million in fresh funding. Available at http://thenextweb.com/asia/2012/11/27/chinese-recipe-sharing-service-douguo-serves-up-8-million-in-fresh-funding/ (accessed November 17, 2023).

Shih, C., Lin, T.M.Y. & Luarn, P. (2014) Fan-centric social media: the Xiaomi phenomenon in China. *Business Horizons*, 57, 349–358.

Smulders, S. (2023). LinkedIn account types 2023: detailed comparison of all premium plans. *Expandi.Io*. Available at https://expandi.io/blog/linkedin-account-types/ (accessed November 17, 2023).

Spencer, R.W. & Woods, T.J. (2010) The long tail of idea generation. *International Journal of Innovation Science*, 2(2), 53–63.

Spotify (2023) About Spotify. Available at https://newsroom.spotify.com/company-info/ (accessed November 17, 2023).

Stewart, D.W. & Zhao, Q. (2000) Internet marketing, business models, and public policy. *Journal of Public Policy and Marketing*, 19(2), 287–296.

Social Times (2008) Facebook selling virtual gifts at $30–40 million/year rate. Available at http://www.adweek.com/socialtimes/facebook-selling-virtual-gifts-at-30-40-millionyear-rate/213389 (accessed November 17, 2023).

Van Baalen, P., Bloemhof-Ruwaard, J. & van Heck, E. (2005) Knowledge sharing in an emerging network of practice. *European Management Journal*, 23, 300–314.

Wang, V. (2023) The shining promise and dashed dream of China's shopping craze. *The New York Times*. Available at https://www.nytimes.com/2023/04/28/business/china-livestreaming-ecommerce.html (accessed November 17, 2023).

Wertenbroch, K. & Skiera, B. (2002) Measuring consumer willingness to pay at the point of purchase. *Journal of Marketing Research*, 39(2), 228–241.

10

Social Media Marketing Strategies

Introduction

Though social media offers many opportunities for businesses to market themselves to a larger global consumer base, the most successful companies are those able to utilize omnichannel social media platforms to better communicate with individual users. Chapter 9 discussed how this process works through the theory of the long tail, and the importance of having a full-scale business model that puts different stakeholders into consideration. This chapter aims to help you design a marketing strategy that works best for your goals across multiple media landscapes in a strategic manner.

Strategic Social Media: From Marketing to Social Change, Second Edition. L. Meghan Mahoney and Tang Tang.
© 2024 John Wiley & Sons, Inc. Published 2024 by John Wiley & Sons, Inc.

We have discussed how today's social media market is controlled by consumers. The best practitioners are those who are comfortable giving up some control so that consumers can mobilize experiences in a bottom-up manner that transforms them into lifelong brand advocates. This balance is complicated, and much of the behavior change theory that we have covered helps guide these decisions. While this knowledge will help you make decisions about individual social media messages, it is important to always have a broader understanding of how different social media platforms work together. Social media is a great resource for marketing practitioners, but it is just one piece of a larger campaign. Every successful social media campaign needs to be consistent with a company/organization's overall marketing strategy.

Therefore, this chapter provides tips for building an integrated marketing strategy for your business, explains how to use this strategy to create a branded experience for your consumers, and presents best practices of existing industries. While consumers have gained more control, practitioners are still able to make informed decisions about marketing strategy.

Transitioning from Traditional Marketing

The past decades have changed the field of public relations and marketing drastically. There are many myths being perpetuated by marketing practitioners that are just no longer true in today's digital media environment. According to Hanna *et al.* (2011), these myths include sentiments such as

- brand managers own and orchestrate their brands;
- companies use marketing communication to control their messages;
- consumers purchase products promoted by marketers;
- providing a forum for customers to talk is dangerous and risky.

Each of these myths illustrates the initial struggle of the industry to accept the new participatory role that consumers play in the marketing process. The role of social media marketing practitioners today focuses on communication and relationship building, rather than control and management. Marketing specialists have primarily adopted institutional tools (e.g., email), top-down diffusion message structures, including blogs and podcasts, as well as more technologically complex tools that cater to niche consumers, such as mobile messaging, virtual worlds, and gaming. One trend is that businesses continuously add popular social media platforms to their branding efforts without much regard for how they work within the larger communication system.

Consumers have been quick to adopt social media tools to communicate about their brand experiences. We see consumers turn away from traditional sources of advertising toward more immediate sources that they can access at their own convenience to make informed purchasing decisions. They perceive social media as a more trusted source of information regarding products and services (Mangold & Faulds, 2009). Thus, it is time for marketers to accept the reality that communication about their product is not primarily coming from their message distribution efforts. Consumers are talking to other consumers about their experiences on social media.

While social media provides new opportunities for marketers to talk at and with their consumers, one of the primary duties in today's marketing is to listen. *Listening* allows you to observe communication, feedback, and insight about your customer experiences from social media conversations (Solis & Breakenridge, 2009). Social listening offers many advantages that other quantitative research methodologies do not. Most importantly, listening can be free and does not require a lot of time or resources. There are two different types of listening that you can make: participant and unobtrusive listening.

Participant listening requires you to join a group and listen as an inside member. This can be done by directly asking your customers for feedback on social media about their experiences. You can also gain participant insights through feedback and comments that individuals make on your own social media sites. Here, your customers are aware that their comments are reaching the company/brand.

Unobtrusive listening requires you to be detached and not take an active part in the situation. This requires the marketing practitioner to search for conversations that are happening about the brand and/or product through social media platforms external to the company's own sites. When individuals are dissatisfied with your product, they will not necessarily only discuss their dissatisfaction with you. They may not include you in the conversation at all. Instead, they may discuss your product with their social networks without using tagging features. Fortunately, most social media sites allow practitioners the ability to search conversations through keywords and phrases. This search may offer more natural insights into how individuals are reacting to your product. We will talk more about social media listening in Chapter 12.

It is important to keep track of how consumers use technology to communicate about their brand experiences. Mangold and Faulds (2009) developed a communication paradigm to illustrate this communicative process in a convergent media environment (Figure 10.1). The diagram shows how several media platforms work together in a much larger process. Integrating social media into an omnichannel media climate is difficult and should not be done with little regard to resources and overall strategy. One way to ensure that you are harnessing all the benefits of social media is by using the applied strategic theory.

Applied Strategic Theory

Though your company likely already has a larger marketing campaign, it is important to consider the role of social media within the larger structure. The social media strategy helps you make sense of all available communication tools for your marketing endeavors and provides a predictable ROI that can be measured and improved upon in future years.

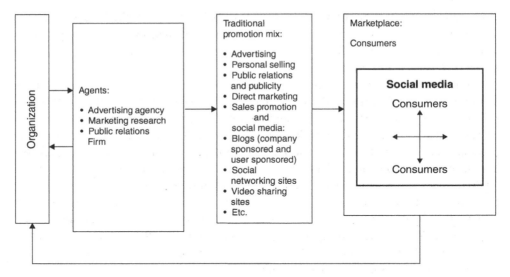

Figure 10.1   New communications paradigm. Source: Mangold and Faulds (2009)/Reproduced with permission of Elsevier.

When creating a social media strategy, it is important to consider a design framework that includes goals, target consumers, social media choice, resources, policies, monitoring, and activity plan for every communication platform (Effing, 2013). This seven-step design framework action plan is outlined here and elaborated in more detail in the following sections.

Design Framework Action Plan

1   Goals
2   Target consumers
3   Social media choice
4   Resources
5   Policies
6   Monitoring
7   Activity plan

Goals

Every company was created with some objective in mind. Hopefully, this objective extends beyond just creating an additional revenue stream. Perhaps you were working long hours at a job that you disliked. You decide to open your own Etsy shop with the hope of having more time at home to spend with family. This narrative helps set the tone for your company: you are a family–friendly company that values entrepreneurship and individual passions.

When determining the goals of your social media marketing campaign, consider your core business objectives and then link these objectives to desired outcomes and goals. These goals should be tangible and specific. Some could be monetary (e.g., make enough profit to pay the mortgage) but others should be on a larger scale (e.g., add "health and wellness" to the brand image). Consider what will make you most satisfied in the long term. Do you value mentorship/sustainability/health and wellness? Your brand authenticity can help you determine both short-term and long-term social media goals.

Once you have created your target goals, consider a practical action plan for how they can be actualized. It is likely that you will not be able to achieve all the goals initially. Rank-order them according to urgency and affordability. Maybe you would love to utilize 100% sustainable packaging with your product, but it would simply cost too much at this stage in your business. Determine what is most practical at the current stage, and as your business grows, so can your efforts toward this goal.

Target consumers

While traditional marketing strategies ask you to consider the consumers that are most likely to use your product, a social media practitioner should consider which consumers would likely be interested in each of your goals. You have already learned about how to conduct an audience analysis in Chapters 5 and 6. It is important that this analysis defines local priority populations, segmentation, and desired consumers (Effing, 2013).

Chapter 9 discussed how smaller, more narrow latent targets may increase your ROI. Though this is one major difference between traditional and social media marketing campaigns, it is important to note that you will still be utilizing traditional media efforts to market your business. Therefore, you will still need to determine who is your larger target consumers. We will discuss how to utilize various platforms and benchmarks for each type of consumers in a manageable manner below.

You will identify larger target consumers to reach through mass media messages (e.g., women, ages 25–54); a smaller niche consumer group to target through diffusion and community social media messages (e.g., mothers who enjoy yoga and live in southeastern India); and individual users (e.g., Kathy, who drives a Prius and composts her own food) to mobilize into lifelong brand advocates. For every goal, these three types of consumers (target, niche, and individual) should be identified.

Do not be frustrated if you cannot identify each of these three types of consumers for every goal right away. These should be informed decisions that come from research and experience. Chapter 16 will introduce the concept of the positive deviance audience that may help you identify these consumers. This takes some knowledge of who is using your product on their own. Remember that the digital marketplace is guided by consumer behavior, and often you must be patient and let actions happen organically to make the best strategic decisions.

Social media choice

Once you have identified the three types of consumers (target, niche, and individual), you will want to select appropriate social media channels and related content forms for each. Most media companies will provide statistical data about who is using their platform. Other resources, such as Pew Research Center, provide third-party research results on Internet user behavior. Do not just guess which social media your target consumers are accessing. Research external sites and conduct focus groups or surveys to learn more about consumer behaviors. This is one of the most important decisions that you can make as a social media marketer. After all, how successful can you be if your messages appear on a social media site that your target consumers never access?

A brief overview of social media user profiles is outlined in Chapter 5. This should be used as a guide but remember that the market is always in flux. Likely, the landscape and patterns are perpetually changing, and it is your job as a social media practitioner to stay up to date with trends.

Generally, X (formerly Twitter) is a great tool for businesses in need of multiple synchronous messages. Snapchat could be used to generate more timely and genuine conversations with your consumers (Wong, 2021). You can use LinkedIn to build brand ethos and enhance B2B relationships (Bottles & Sherlock, 2011). Video social media platforms such as YouTube, TikTok, and Instagram Stories and Reels can drive your brand awareness and bring products to life in an entertaining and engaging way. Social audio platforms such as Clubhouse and X Spaces allow you to listen to live conversations on specific topics and build your brand image as a leader in your niche (Wong, 2021). You can also use social discussion forums such as Reddit to answer your customers' questions and demonstrate your subject expertise. Try not to use Reddit to promote your products.

Consider whether your product would benefit through more visual, textual, or audio messages. There are many benefits and challenges for utilizing each social media platform. Eventually you will want to exist across multiple channels. However, you do not want to disseminate the same message on every social media. What is posted on your Instagram page should be different from what is posted on X. Remember that each social media serves a different function and has different users. You should also not open a social media account and then not update it regularly. Decide which platform makes sense initially, build and grow that user base, and then create additional spaces when you have the resources to do so effectively.

Resources

It is important to consider the requirements of running a successful marketing campaign. This includes financial investments, the expertise of your employees, and quality control of messages for your organization (Effing, 2013). Here, you want to be honest about the skill-set that you best bring to help reach your target goals, and what is still lacking that may prevent you from reaching them.

The great news is that social media provides an opportunity for success with less resources than ever before. However, this also means that you could unexpectedly become an online viral sensation without adequate resources to deliver the product. Since the highest ROI comes from current satisfied customers (Stratten, 2012), you want to ensure that you are not making existing customers frustrated with your product/service. Ensure that you are prepared for success.

Social media campaigns do not always require a large budget. However, you still want to have some resources for marketing, whether that goes into giveaways, promoted posts, or evaluation efforts. A general rule of thumb is that 10% of your gross annual income should be reinvested into marketing (Entrepreneur, 2010). However, financial resources are not the only considerations you should make.

Many practitioners who try to navigate the digital media landscape by themselves are experiencing fatigue that leads to their eventual demise. *Blogger burnout* is a phenomenon where first-generation successful bloggers are leaving the industry because they are overwhelmed by the task. We are seeing this more and more with social media practitioners whose jobs and responsibilities have ballooned with the digital landscape. There is great stress that comes when a passion transforms into a career. Many online professionals are unwilling to delegate tasks and feel as though that to be authentic, they must ensure that all social media messages come from the creator of the brand. Considering that the Internet never sleeps and constantly wants fresh content (Kurutz, 2014), this expectation is impossible. It is imperative that you surround yourself with individuals who share in your brand narrative and help manage the workload to prevent this fatigue.

Policies

Every organization must have guidelines for social media use, data privacy, restrictions, and ethical considerations (Effing, 2013). Though these are not the most interesting or glamorous pieces of social media marketing, they are essential to the success of any organization. It is important that these policies are established initially and not retroactively.

Social contract theory explains how members of society must give up some freedoms to reap the benefits of a functioning society. There are examples of this theory at play everywhere around us. For example, you follow traffic rules and regulations to prevent chaos on the roads. You enjoy the privilege of driving because you are willing to give up the freedom of doing whatever you want on the road. The same balance is true of social media.

You must set policies for how individuals within your company post social media messages, handle customer complaints, and offer promotions to customers. You do not want the service to change according to which individual a customer is communicating with at any given time. Policies should be clear, specific, and tangible. They should have a logical link to your mission statement. Employees and customers alike should be able to access these easily. A likely place for this distribution is on your company's homepage. Policies should be part of your transparency plan and diffusion strategy (discussed in Chapter 2).

Monitoring

Once messages are disseminated to your target consumers, it is important to measure behavior and effects. Your strategy should include informed decisions about which effects will be measured by which metrics (Effing, 2013). We will discuss specifics about monitoring and evaluation in Chapter 12. It is important that each of these stages (goals, target consumers, social media choice, resources, policies) is monitored periodically.

A social media marketing strategy is a dynamic process. You will never have a completed strategy that allows you to sit back and let it run on its own. It requires constant attention and research to determine whether current efforts are successful and what can be done to improve it. Otherwise, your campaign will become stale, and a more innovative organization will capture your customers' attention.

Activity plan

Your social media strategy should identify a clear timeframe that governs when projects and monitoring will take place (Effing, 2013). This includes individual social media posts, as well as broader strategic goals. The activity plan will help you to make mindful decisions about the roll-out of your campaign. It will also prevent you from feeling overwhelmed.

One way to manage social media posts is through a *social media content calendar*. This is a predetermined template that outlines all the necessary channels, resources, and messages and organizes them in a way that makes it easy to access information for dissemination when you need it (Sorokina, 2014). This is a day-to-day schedule that can be organized ahead of time about what messages are being published and promoted.

These postings can be organized through social media management software. With social media management software, you do not have to sign into multiple social media channels. *Hootsuite* is a popular social media dashboard that helps practitioners manage multiple social media channels through one platform (Hootsuite, 2023). Other available social media dashboards include Sprout Social, Sprinklr, and Buffer.

You may choose to designate a specific day of the week for a certain kind of post. For example, each Monday you could highlight a loyal fan on LinkedIn; Tuesday you could have a live X Q&A session with an expert; Wednesday you could share an entertaining video tutorial on TikTok; Thursday you could share a vintage picture of employees on Instagram using the Throwback Thursday hashtag #tbt; and Friday you could invite consumers to play a fun game together on Facebook. Here, you have a managed and consistent plan across platforms that consumers can recognize and participate with. It is important to supplement each account with additional content. Otherwise, subscribers to your Instagram account will only see #tbt posts. Timely synchronous posts will help you have conversations with customers and make you seem on trend and relevant with current events.

Though a social media content calendar may help you stay organized, it is important not to enable functions that automatically post content. You can use these resources to set up media messages ahead of time, but a real-life practitioner should be the one to hit the button to publish. Remember that the goal of social media is to facilitate dialogue. This becomes impossible if there is not an actual person on one end of the conversation.

Activity plan should highlight broader strategic goals as well. For example, you may decide to begin your social media campaign with a Facebook account before creating a TikTok channel. Having a longitudinal view of your social media activity will help you stay on track without getting lost in the day-to-day activity. This clear distribution timeline and benchmarks will help you determine when and where your marketing campaign will take place.

There are many moving parts to this activity plan. Four aspects of this interactive process should be repeated over time to optimize your social media strategy. Effing (2013) illustrates this fluid process by the social media strategy design framework (Figure 10.2).

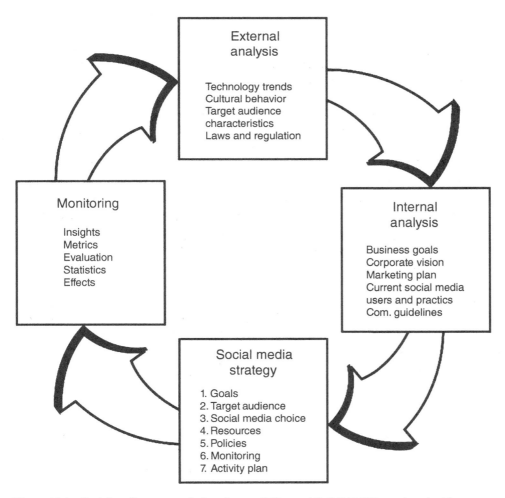

Figure 10.2   Social media strategy design. Source: Effing and Spil (2016)/Reproduced with permission of Elsevier.

This framework is most successful when senior-level sponsorship of the social media strategy is in place, organizations ensure a long-term social media commitment, and organizational behaviors are authentic to the real-life behaviors (Effing, 2013).

Now that we understand the strategy for creating, distributing, and monitoring social media marketing efforts, it is important to consider who should manage the strategy. A social media strategy is most successful when no single person is in control. Social media efforts should be an integrated portion of every employee position and should be managed by trained and qualified personnel (Bottles & Sherlock, 2011). By having individuals in every department who have been trained on company goals and policies and how to use social media in a mindful manner, the task of posting often and authentically will seem less daunting.

It is essential that each employee listens to what is being said about your brand anywhere on the Internet, not just within your own social media platforms. Be sure that all employees are comfortable responding to and engaging customers in a manner that is consistent with the authentic voice of the organization. This also means that you should hire individuals who present a clear and consistent voice on your social media sites that align with your brand narrative.

In the digital age, every employee becomes a public relations/marketing recruit. You must train each employee how to establish relationships by showing consumers respect, honesty, and enthusiasm and then nurture those relationships through authentic personal interactions (Bottles & Sherlock, 2011). On the other hand, while every employee should be able to utilize social media for the benefit of your organization, not everyone is trained in dealing with especially difficult customer service situations. Hire a designated person who handles these types of special circumstances. It is also important to note that while you want to value consumers and pay attention to their insights and opinions, you must also negotiate between constructive feedback and trolls. You will not be able to please everyone, and this becomes especially true with a global consumer base on an open platform for dialogue.

Integrating social media into an existing marketing strategy is imperative in today's omnichannel marketplace. Before doing so, ensure that you address the needs of your target consumers through social media. Understand how your target consumers utilize social media, as well as the costs, both financial and labor, associated with the process. Finally, be prepared for the changes that an effective social media marketing strategy will bring to your organization and consumers.

Branded Social Experience

Once you have a social media strategy in place, you may consider incorporating a branded experience into one or more of your goals. A *brand experience* is conceptualized as sensations, feelings, cognitions, and behavioral responses evoked by brand-related stimuli that are part of a brand's design and identity, packaging, communication, and environments. There are four dimensions to a brand experience: sensory, affective, intellectual, and behavioral (Brakus *et al.*, 2009). Social media provides opportunities to maximize each of these areas.

- *Sensory experiences* provide consumers with a real-life schema that they can reflect in the future. It gives them something to see, hear, taste, smell, and feel in association with your product. This is difficult to achieve online, but mobilization efforts discussed in Chapter 4 will help you create this brand dimension.
- *Affective experiences* allow customers to emotionally connect with your product. This requires a large amount of pathos, appealing to a part of your consumers' lives where they are already invested. Creating a sense of community, as discussed in Chapter 3, may help achieve an affective experience for your consumers.
- *Intellectual experiences* require consumers to put forth cognitive activity to carry out the call of your messages. While you want your social media messages to be clear and concise, you also do not want to patronize your consumers. The more thought and energy your consumers place in your message, the more invested they will feel (provided there is a positive outcome). This is one area where a diffusion strategy, as discussed in Chapter 2, may ignite permanent adoption.
- *Behavioral experiences* change consumers' real-life action. This could be an adoption of a new ritual or the cessation of an existing one. Here, you are utilizing social media to prompt real-life behavior change. This is consistent with the mobilization efforts discussed in Chapter 4. However, rather than concentrating on a single sensory experience (e.g., taste test), you are combining multiple ones to prompt a stronger frame of reference.

These four dimensions guide brand experiences. Your goal as a social media marketer is to speak to an existing set of social scripts that consist of expressions, actions, and other behaviors that result from emotion (Morrison & Crane, 2007). Emotion highly influences how consumers select products and transform into loyal advocates to a brand. It is the goal of a marketer to create and manage a positive emotional brand experience before, during, and after the brand purchase.

Morrison and Crane (2007) suggest first creating a well-designed and attractive atmosphere. This can be done in person and online through font and interface design. Customer loyalty will stem from the emotional brand experience during the service consumption process as customers interact with this design. Marketers should also continue communication after the point of purchase to establish trust and connections.

If customers associate positive emotions with your brand before, during and after purchase, it will result in brand advocacy. Brand advocacy leads to word-of-mouth marketing to external social networks. This leads to the highest ROI pillar of the hierarchy of buying (Stratten, 2012). Brand strategy is much more about "emotion share" than it is market share (Morrison & Crane, 2007). Thus, marketers should focus on innovation and customer-centric service to ensure the best possible customer experience.

Traditional marketing practitioners believe that they need to reach consumers through an array of noise from other competitors. Marketers have long used the metaphor of a funnel to illustrate consumer touchpoints: consumers start at the wide end of the funnel with many brands in mind and then narrow the brands down to a final choice (Edelman, 2010). There are many misconceptions regarding this customer decision-making process in today's social media era. Social media makes it easier for consumers to make informed decisions about products through self-seeking evaluation techniques. Therefore, it is time for your social media strategies to focus on customer service and brand experience, rather than raising awareness about products. Focus on the quality of your product and building a strong reputation. Once customers make an informed decision about a product and have a positive brand experience, they then spread positive word of mouth about the brand. This is where the brand awareness process takes place.

Taking TikTok as an example, the goal of TikTok's algorithm is to determine a curated stream of videos that appear on each user's "For You" page (Ashbridge, 2022; TikTok, 2023). The social media tries to only show content that users like. User interactions, video information, and device and account settings determine TikTok's algorithm, though the follower count or previous high-performing videos will not influence TikTok's recommendations (Newberry, 2023; TikTok, 2023). The platform aims to provide an equal opportunity for seasoned TikTok users and people who created their TikTok videos for the first time. Here, you see how social media prioritizes those aiming to create a brand experience than brands that simply aim to raise awareness through a push strategy.

Thus, you should use TikTok to enhance consumers' brand experience. Create content that is fun, real, and authentically connects with TikTokers. Find your niche and then tap into an existing TikTok communities using hashtags or becoming a part of a special interest group on the platform (Newberry, 2023). Engage with other TikTokers, comment on their videos, and reply to comments on your own videos (Ashbridge, 2022; Newberry, 2023): React, respond, and remix (TikTok, 2023). More than 60% of TikTokers said that they prefer seeing everyday people in TikTok ads. Authenticity is what motivated today's social media users to purchase a product. Building a brand experience is the key for today and tomorrow's social media marketing.

It is important to remember that social media marketing efforts are shaped by both technology and culture, and that the actions and creations of consumers are also influenced by these factors (Berthon *et al.*, 2012). Technology and consumer behavior are intrinsically linked. Be sure to create a social media strategy that encourages a brand experience through sensory, affective, intellectual, and behavioral branding, rather than simply focusing on building awareness and a higher ROI. Let's explore one social media campaign that capitalized on the relationship between technology and culture.

Case Study: Wendy's Keep Fortnite Fresh Campaign

In this chapter, we have learned that social media marketers should not just utilize the technology to diffuse information, but to create a brand experience. Social media marketing strategy should shift its goal from increasing brand awareness to transforming customers into brand advocates. Wendy's Keep Fortnite Fresh campaign is a strong example of this process.

Wendy's, an American fast-food company, has been known for its engaging, often witty, and humorous social media efforts. Its brand voice is distinct on social media, which effectively engage Wendy's target consumers – young adults who tend to frequently eat fast food (Commarts, 2023). The Keep Fortnite Fresh campaign (see Figure 10.3) has advanced Wendy's social media efforts to a new level, demonstrating how a brand can organically engage customers and build a brand experience.

In 2019, Fortnite, one of the most popular online games, introduced a new game mode, Food Fight, which features Team Pizza fights Team Burger. Wendy's saw this game as an opportunity to engage its target consumers, and thus launched the "Keep Fortnite Fresh" campaign. Here, the company created an avatar on Fortnite similar to its mascot Wendy. Wendy joined Team Pizza to declare a war on frozen beef in the game. Instead of playing against other Fortnite players (as most other players would do), Wendy's avatar focused on destroying freezers to highlight its brand "fresh, never frozen beef" (Vie, 2023). The company also livestreamed the gameplay on Twitch. Millions of people watched the streams and thousands of gamers began joining the game to destroy burger freezers in their own gameplays and sharing with their own

Figure 10.3   Screenshot of Wendy's "Keep Fortnite Fresh" campaign.

social networks (Commarts, 2023; VMLY&R, 2023). As a result, Fortnite developers removed burger freezers from the game. Wendy's gameplay has been watched for more than 250,000 times. Social media mentions of Wendy's increased by 119% across platforms (VMLY&R, 2023).

Wendy's "Keep Fortnite Fresh" campaign follows the action plan we've discussed in this chapter. It had a clear goal, aiming to re-highlight Wendy's core brand value – never use frozen beef. The campaign targeted on adolescents and young adults, who often play games and visit fast food restaurants. It chose a video game as the delivery channel for the campaign, which is innovative, engaging, and effective. The campaign only used limited resources to make a strong statement. Wendy's found an organic way to create this brand experience for its consumers without allocating a large budget to purchase traditional ads/sponsorships that may interrupt gameplays (which often annoy the audience). Instead of employing traditional marketing approaches, such as tweeting push messages to gamers, Wendy's "leveraged the game's storyline to drive its brand message" (Vie, 2023).

We have discussed how the actions and creations of social media consumers are influenced by both technology and culture (Berthon *et al.*, 2012). Wendy's "Keep Fortnite Fresh" campaign is a great illustration of this connection, demonstrating the brand's deep understanding of its consumers and contemporary culture (Commarts, 2023). Shifting away from sending push marketing messages, Wendy's did something cool and fun. Gamers then talked about it, shared the brand message, and may eventually become its lifetime brand advocates. The campaign brought nuances to traditional marketing approaches, thus won many prestigious marketing awards, such as the Grand Prix at the Cannes Lions Festival of Creativity, two gold awards at the Clios, and Adweek Project Isaac award. Industry leaders believe that this campaign goes beyond purpose-driven marketing and hints on the next marketing trend (Netimperative, 2019).

Discussion questions

1   Where do you see Wendy's successfully applying the marketing action plan in its "Keep Fortnite Fresh" campaign?
2   How well does Wendy's "Keep Fortnite Fresh" campaign speak to its target consumers? In your opinion, how would this campaign be more effective?
3   What future marketing trends do you see possibly aligning with the brand mission of Wendy's?

Summary

This chapter discusses ways in which the changing digital media landscape has influenced consumers, and how these changes should be incorporated into a social media marketing strategy. It is imperative that you understand how applied strategic theory fits into your overall marketing campaign and how to keep this up to date throughout the lifespan of your brand.

We have learned the importance of listening, both as a participant and as an unobtrusive entity. This must be done at every stage of the brand experience. It is crucial to keep track of how consumers use technology to communicate about their brand experiences. Please note that your customers may discuss your product/service with their social network without including you in the conversation. Marketers need to listen both within their own social channels and through social media external to the brand.

In this chapter, you have also learned that it is important to create a branded social experience. Social media can provide opportunities to maximize your customers' sensory, affective, intellectual, and behavioral experiences. It is more important to focus on the quality of your product and building strong relationships with your customers than simply increasing brand awareness.

Careful consideration must be made about goals, target consumers, social media choice, resources, policies, monitoring, and activity plan of your overall social media strategy. You will want to identify larger target consumers via mass media messages, a smaller niche consumer base through diffusion and community social media messages, and individual users to mobilize into lifelong brand advocates.

Engaging in mobile technologies is one way to mobilize consumers toward true participation. For the first time in history, users can interact with technology in any place, at any time in their lives. This creates many opportunities for social media marketers. We will explore these mobile techniques and how they can be beneficial for you and your consumers in Chapter 11.

Key Takeaways

1   Social media practitioners should not just utilize technology to communicate with consumers but also to listen to what they say about your product. This can be done through participant or unobtrusive means.
2   Marketers must integrate a social media strategy into existing marketing campaigns. The design framework should include goals, target consumers, social media choice, resources, policies, monitoring, and activity plan.
3   Social media strategy should include a brand experience that highlights sensory, affective, intellectual, and behavioral dimensions of the consumer experience. This will shift strategy attention from increasing brand awareness to transforming customers into brand advocates.
4   The actions and creations of social media consumers are influenced by both technology and culture. Therefore, they should be fluid and change with society.

References

Ashbridge, Z. (2022) How the TikTok algorithm works: everything you need to know. *Search Engine Land.* Available at https://searchengineland.com/how-tiktok-algorithm-works-390229 (accessed November 17, 2023).

Berthon, P., Pitt, L., Plangger, K. & Shapiro, D. (2012) Marketing meets Web 2.0, social media, and creative consumers: implications for international marketing strategy. *Business Horizons*, 55(3), 261–271.

Bottles, K. & Sherlock, T. (2011) Who should manage your social media strategy. *Physician Executive*, 37(2), 68–72.

Brakus, J.J., Schmitt, B.H. & Zarantonello, L. (2009) Brand experience: what is it? How is it measured? Does it affect loyalty? *Journal of Marketing*, 73(3), 52–68.

Commarts (2023) Keeping Fortnite fresh. Available at https://www.commarts.com/project/30531/keeping-fortnite-fresh (accessed November 17, 2023).

Edelman, D.C. (2010) Branding in the digital age. *Harvard Business Review*, 88(12), 62–69.

Effing, R. (2013) Social media strategy design. In: *Proceedings of the 2nd Scientific Conference Information Science in an Age of Change*, Institute of Information and Book Studies, University of Warsaw, Poland, April 15–16, 2013.

Effing, R. & Spil, T. (2016) The social strategy cone: towards a framework for evaluating social media strategies. *International Journal of Information Management*, 36(1), 1–8.

Entrepreneur (2010) Marketing. Available at http://www.entrepreneur.com/answer/222045 (accessed November 17, 2023).

Hanna, R., Rohm, A. & Crittenden, V.L. (2011) We're all connected: the power of the social media ecosystem. *Business Horizons*, 54(3), 265–273.

Hootsuite (2023) About us. Available at https://www.hootsuite.com/about (accessed November 17, 2023).

Kurutz, S. (2014) When blogging becomes a slog. Available at http://www.nytimes.com/2014/09/25/garden/when-blogging-becomes-a-slog.html?_r=0 (accessed November 17, 2023).

Mangold, W. & Faulds, D. (2009) Social media: the new hybrid element of the promotion mix. *Business Horizons*, 52(4), 357–365.

Morrison, S. & Crane, F. (2007) Building the service brand by creating and managing an emotional brand experience. *Journal of Brand Management*, 14(5), 410–421.

Netimperative (2019) Cannes Lions Winner: Wendy's wins social top prize for "Keeping Fortnite Fresh" campaign. *Digital Intelligence for Business.* Available at https://www.netimperative.com/2019/06/25/cannes-lions-winner-wendys-wins-social-top-prize-for-keeping-fortnite-fresh-campaign/#:~:text=Netimperative%20Toggle%20navigation-,Cannes%20Lions%20Winner%3A%20Wendy's%20wins%20social%20top,for%20'Keeping%20Fortnite%20Fresh'%20campaign&text=Burger%20Chain%20Wendy's%20scooped%20the,the%20evils%20of%20frozen%20beef (accessed November 17, 2023).

Newberry, C. (2023) 2023 TikTok algorithm explained + tips to go viral. *Hootsuite.* Available at https://blog.hootsuite.com/tiktok-algorithm/ (accessed November 17, 2023).

Solis, B. & Breakenridge, D.K. (2009) *Putting the Public Back in Public Relations: How Social Media Is Reinventing the Aging Business of PR.* Upper Saddle River, NJ: FT Press.

Sorokina, O. (2014) 5 Reasons why a social media content calendar is important for your business. Available at http://blog.hootsuite.com/how-to-create-a-social-media-content-calendar/ (accessed November 17, 2023).

Stratten, S. (2012) *UnMarketing. Stop Marketing. Start Engaging.* Hoboken, NJ: John Wiley& Sons, Inc.

TikTok (2023) Community guidelines. Available at https://www.tiktok.com/community-guidelines/en/ (accessed November 17, 2023).

Vie (2023) Wendy's reactive Fortnite social campaign. *Unlocked Meta.* Available at https://unlockedmeta.com/case-study/wendys-keeping-fortnite-fresh/#:~:text=The%20campaign's%20objective%20was%20to,frozen%20beef%20in%20the%20game (accessed November 17, 2023).

VMLY&R (2023) Keeping Fortnite fresh. Available at https://www.vmlyr.com/en-us/united-states/work/keeping-fortnite-fresh.

Wong, L. (2021) 9 Types of social media and how each can benefit your business. *Hootsuite.* Available at https://blog.hootsuite.com/types-of-social-media/ (accessed November 17, 2023).

11

Mobile Marketing and e-Commerce

Learning Objectives

After reading this chapter, you should be able to:
1   Encourage consumers to use mobile digital projections to bolster online identity.
2   Understand the role of peer influence and the concept of a "third place" in mobile marketing.
3   Implement a social media mobile strategy that generates return visits from users.

Introduction

Everyday decision-making is influenced by a multitude of factors: personality, mood, life experience, social networks, internal noise, external noise, and media structures. The way we negotiate the world around us is unpredictable and one of the most difficult tasks of a social media marketer. Communication philosopher Marshall McLuhan (1994) famously wrote that "the medium is the message." The characteristics of the media that carry content prove just as, if not more, important than the content itself.

Imagine arranging a lunch date with one of your friends with the message "We should grab lunch." How would this message be interpreted if delivered by stopping in-person by your friend's house unannounced? What if you emailed them the request? What if the message was sent through text message? The sense of urgency and timeline for carrying through the desired action would change depending on the media choice, even though the content of the message remains the same. If the message was received through text message, the recipient may think that the lunch date should happen soon. If received through email, a longer planning timeline may occur. Though this is not exactly what McLuhan meant with his statement, media platform choice has never been more important than in today's digital media landscape.

Mobile technology is spreading across the world and is undoubtedly changing the way we communicate with one another. Mobile phones are vastly popular due to their affordability, portability, easy personalization, and location-awareness capabilities (Kurkovsky & Harihar, 2006). Users can customize mobile phone features so that they are virtually unlike any other person's device. Chances are, if you lost your mobile phone, the person who finds it would not only be able to track it back to you through your personal contacts but also be able to make a pretty accurate guess about who you are based on some of your customization decisions. Even the brand of mobile device we choose to carry says a great deal about who we are and what we value.

Due to lower cost and faster infrastructure, mobile technology is spreading around the world at a faster pace than older technologies. Some of the most successful social media are mobile-oriented, such as Snapchat, Instagram, WhatsApp, TikTok, and VSCO. Users will not be able to use personal computers, if they want to communicate on the photo-sharing application – Instagram, the video-sharing platform – TikTok, the chat application – Snapchat, and the service review platform – Path. These applications require people to share content through mobile devices, encouraging them to synchronize their file sharing with real-life events. Though users can share older photos through Instagram (there is a popular hashtag #tbt, or throw back Thursday, for such occasions), this is not the intended purpose of the application. In fact, this is why users decide to alert other people that they are not following through with the synchronous norm (no one ever tags photos with #happeningright-nowthursday). This also explains the popularity of disrupting synchronous sharing photo apps, such as BeReal. Mobile technology is all about up-to-date synchronous communication. Traditional boundaries of time and space have been transformed with greater immediacy, and these changes influence effective marketing strategies.

In fact, more than 30% of American adults are almost constantly online (Perrin & Atske, 2021), and 15% of them are smartphone-only Internet users (Perrin, 2021). In addition, 75% of Americans self-reported feeling uneasy leaving their phone at home. On average, they check their phones 140 times a day (Keral, 2023). Mobile technology is engrained and routinized in users' daily activities, and it is important for marketing efforts to understand these habits. Thus, this chapter aims to explore how mobile technology influences consumer behavior and your marketing strategy. Specifically, it focuses on mobile digital projection, the influence of peers in a shared social journey, and strategies for generating return visits via mobile marketing.

Mobile Digital Projections

Computer-mediated communication (CMC) has been at the forefront of media research for decades. However, much changes when technology allows users to gain instant access to their network at any time and any place. *Mobile-mediated communication* (MMC) is a type of CMC that emphasizes mobility. As phones begin to converge with portable multimedia computers, and traditional media devices become more mobile, the distinction between these blurs.

Mobile technology is increasing the level of participation through social media features such as sharing, tagging, and AI-powered filtering (Pang, 2021; Siver et al., 2019). It is much easier to share what you are doing while you are in the moment than it is to remember hours later when you have returned home and are sitting in front of your personal computer. Mobile technology allows users to instantly share where they are, whom they are with, and whether they would like to invite others to join. As such, your consumers may expect more synchronous, less-polished marketing materials. Consider your own social media feed. How many brands that you are following share unedited Instagram stories of their day-to-day activities?

Mobile technology also provides spaces for users to share their own stories with the public, or with a network of carefully screened individuals. It is okay for social media to be a work in progress. Indeed, mobile social media uses are never in a final completed stage but are dynamic and has become a part of users' lives.

Individuals share their everyday lives through a process dubbed *digital projections*. Whether they are sharing a status, photo or video update, these digital projections are a way for people to construct their own identity through technology and share it with their network. Perhaps more than ever before, users have a say in how other people make sense of their lives. Of course, one cannot account for the sense-making process entirely.

If a social media user wishes to be associated with traveling, he or she could choose to share news articles from various locations around the globe, lodge recommendations, future dream trips, or photos from personal travels. They may also ignore sharing other aspects of their lives, such as sitting at home watching reruns of a favorite reality show. Social media allows us to choose to project the best of ourselves and keep other features private.

Though individuals can utilize mobile technology in a variety of ways, so long as they stay within the boundaries of the media structure provided. They still must work within many of the unwritten rules, expectations, and customs of communication. Research on digital projections demonstrates how increased sharing of photographs of oneself is correlated with a decreased feeling of intimacy from media users (Grenoble, 2013). While individuals connect through social media to receive life updates, there is a balance that must be struck between what constitutes too much sharing, and how much of it should be centered on the self. Thankfully, there are easy collaborative structures available, such as user polls or tagging.

This is not so different from the various other marketing rules that we have discussed thus far. Remember that social media is an outlet to market according to your own goals. Even if you, as a social media practitioner, are not selling a product, how can you still present a cohesive on-brand narrative? It is important to interact, engage, and participate with other users. Use the platform as a tool for dialogue surrounding issues that are important to you and your users. Share some pictures, but ask for, and comment on others, more.

Research demonstrates that the more individuals engage in these participatory activities, the more they entice further connections and participatory action. Continuous feedback should remain the keystone of social media, as individuals engage in identity management of their own profiles. Media users create a sense of who they are and the role that they play in society through collective feedback from their online communities. While social media users are aware of their own reputation management, they also hold an awareness of what their social networks are sharing online.

Online social narratives are hardly true depictions of our own selves. Users tend to post idealized versions of their lives, or only share when things are exotic and special. Consider the places where you or your friends have "checked-in" or shared the location of a real-life interpersonal event. Chances are, these are places that you don't mind being associated with. We hardly share ordinary run-of-the mill experiences through social media, despite a call for more authentic sharing.

Though the technology potential exists for mobile group communication, most mobile users utilize the technology for individual networking. This is the appeal of one-to-one mobile apps such as Snapchat. Snapchat is a mobile phone messaging application that was made popular by allowing users to send text messages, photos, videos, as well as make voice and video calls. When it was first introduced, the Snapchat message (i.e., snap) "disappear" upon opening in as few as 10 seconds to encourage more spontaneous and authentic sharing among users, which mitigates the permanence and public nature of other types of online communication. Today, Snapchat's "disappearing" function is an option. The platform wants to provide users more choices in terms of the "shelf life" of snaps to satisfy diverse user needs (Yurieff, 2017).

Smartmobs, or mobilization of the masses through mobile technology, is one of the first many-to-many features of mobile technology (Grob et al., 2009; Rheingold, 2003). This is where many users coordinate themselves at a particular place and time for an event. Often, these events are lighthearted and fun in nature, though sometimes they are arranged with hopes of raising awareness or protesting an event. Online group communication tends to be initiated by one person who invites a set of contacts to participate. However, some social media users find this annoying and do not accept or remove themselves from group conversation. A better way to initiate cohesiveness among a group is through tagging features (Grob et al., 2009).

Tagging features exist in many forms. In general, they link individuals to the purpose or event of the communication. Some tagging includes a text-based hashtag, or a character string proceeded by the # sign to signal topic organization, audience, or meaning (Efron, 2010). For instance, if you were attending the 2024 International Communication

Association convention, you may include the hashtag #ICA24 with all conference-related posts. This allows individuals who are interested in the conference, whether attending or not, to follow along. Tagging also includes labeling faces on pictures or bookmarking sites or contact lists under specific categories. In general, tagging helps people understand why they are being included in a message by seeing what they have in common with other people or designated topics.

Mobile communication does not mean that users must know each other interpersonally. Users who find each other through interest-based sites may not know each other very well at first, but through increased online interactions and sharing they could become quite friendly and begin to consider each other as important members of their lives. Some individuals choose to exchange their contact information and meet in real life. However, most mobile-specific social networks are designed specifically for the mobile community (Counts & Fisher, 2008). Just because users do not choose to meet in real life, it does not mean that real feelings and emotions do not develop. Often, individuals communicate more frequently through social media sites than they do with interpersonal-based friends.

We tend to have perpetual contacts with those we wish to see interpersonally in our everyday lives. While Instagram has check-in features and Google alerts you when others in your network are close by, researchers found that few use the features to meet up interpersonally. Using location-based settings helps users project the type of social person they are and holds potential for marketers to know more about their consumers' everyday experiences, but it is unlikely that someone in your network will see these notifications and consequently come and join you without an invitation.

Dodgeball was one of the first mobile social media designed as a location-based information distributor where users could meet up in-person with their friends. Users would broadcast their location through mobile devices by checking in, and their chosen social network would receive a text message regarding the location. Google purchased Dodgeball in May 2005, but has since rolled the technology into other platforms (Humphreys, 2007), none with great success. Mobile networking applications should be utilized to make organization and social experiences easier and more enjoyable. They alter social experiences, but rarely do they create them.

Because users carry and use mobile technology virtually anywhere, more and more information is shared about their daily lives. If you check in at a local coffee shop online, other stores on the same street can see this check-in and send a coupon asking you to try their coffee next time you're in the area. However, users are growing more and more concerned with privacy issues of location disclosure. Do we really want everyone to know where friends, family, and strangers are always located?

Mobile applications allow users the ability to capture and upload text, photo, voice, and video messages. Generally, users can alter settings to allow the public to view content or to restrict such content to permitted people. It does take some level of media literacy and communication competency to navigate through these permissions. The longer individuals grow with social media, the more competent they become.

Just because mobile technology allows you to share, realize it is not always appropriate or safe. While social media is a place for you to share your digital projections, remember that social media is about relationship building and transactional communication. A good rule of thumb is the 2:1 standard. You should interact and engage other users twice as often as you share information about your brand. Nevertheless, every organization is different, and undoubtedly your social media use will grow and change with you.

Peer Influence and a Shared Social Journey

There are more than 8 billion mobile phone subscribers worldwide today (World Economic Forum, 2022). Mobile networking technologies allow users to create, develop, and strengthen ties wherever they are, to keep in touch with acquaintances easier than at any other time in history, and hold potential for strengthening relationships with close family and friends.

Some research points to a new phenomenon where the technology hinders relationships. An increase in mobile technology use is found to limit the formation of new relationships we make (Ling, 2000). A possible reason for this change may be due to the way we utilize the technology. Often, we fill empty time between events or while waiting in line with mobile games, text messages, or social media. While this empty space may have previously been an opportunity to communicate interpersonally with others who are also waiting, we are now able to communicate with individuals already in our network through mobile technology. This is a much more comfortable communication situation for many than talking to strangers.

Look around next time you are in a group situation. Some individuals will be using mobile technology in isolation, making little eye contact, and ignoring interpersonal communication with those around them physically. Others will be using mobile technology to create a shared social journey with those they are with. They tag each other together in the real-time event; take pictures and comment online about the fun that they are having. Your friends' mobile communication may say just as much about them and their social life as your own.

As discussed, the term *"Third Place"* is a traditional designation for a public place that hosts regular, voluntary, informal, and anticipated gatherings of individuals beyond the realm of home ("First Place") and work ("Second Place") (Oldenburg, 1989). These are often popular restaurants, bars, or events. Here, social networks gather on a platform that is central to their sense of self and community. Individuals identify with the Third Place much more than they do other spaces where they may spend more physical time, such as work. Generally, the mood is upbeat and relaxed at the Third Place (Humphreys, 2007).

Mobile technology allows individuals to experience the Third Place with each other even if they are far away. Consider the "Third Space" posts that your own social network shares. You may be able to follow their experiences and get to know their new group of friends even though you have never met them. Despite not being physically present, you are able to share in your friends' journey and let them know that you care by commenting and sharing online.

Another phenomenon of mobile technology is called schedule softening (Ling, 2000). *Schedule softening* is where individuals engage in minimal preplanning rituals because they know that they will be able to reach the other party by mobile phone when it is closer to the actual time of the event. Users are also rearranging their schedules with minimal notice at an increased rate than before. For example, you may not feel bad about stopping at a store on your way to meet someone because you will be able to text them and let them know if you are running late. While individuals used to be more schedule conscious due to the lack of communication on the go, short-term changes in circumstances are becoming less of a faux pas today.

Different cultures and genders utilize mobile technology differently. African Americans are the most active group of mobile Internet users. They tend to use phones for job search, getting heath information and education content (Anderson, 2015). Females mainly use mobile phone for social purposes. They tend to form a larger group of contacts, interact more frequently with their social network via mobile than males, while male's mobile phone use is more diverse, such as watching movies, playing mobile games, etc. (Gutierrez et al., 2016). Older adults are emerging as the newest market for mobile social media. Particularly, their use of YouTube has grown in the past years (Faverio, 2022). People utilize mobile technology for social purposes and so it makes sense that their journey would be most like those within their race, gender, and age cohort.

Collaborative projections enable joint and simultaneous creation by many users (Kaplan & Haenlein, 2010). This is a great way to prompt your consumers to create new real-life experiences and share online. Mobile technology allows marketers to incorporate time and space into social media projects. There are many effective examples of how organizations utilize the synchronous nature of mobile technology to incite real-life behavior change in media users.

Urban Adventure Quest is a travel service that allows visitors to explore a city via an interactive mobile scavenger hunt game. Here, participants use their phones as a guide to find clues, answer questions, and complete challenges, which will lead them to different attractions in a city. The app also provides real-time feedback and allows users to compete against each other for an exciting and immersive experience. Mobile scavenger hunts are a great way to create life experiences and get users to share how much fun they are having with their social network.

The Liseberg Amusement Park in Sweden created a mobile game contest for people who wait in the long line for its popular roller coaster, the Helix. The mobile game allows people who're waiting in the line to play against each other. Every 15 minutes, the player with the top score will win a free express pass to skip the line to take the ride. By strategically utilizing mobile technology's synchronous nature, waiting is no longer boring (Byers, 2015).

In Brazil, Burger King launched the Burn That Ad campaign to promote its mobile app. Using augmented reality technology, Burger King customers can point their phone at the ad

Figure 11.1 Screenshot of Burger King *Burn that Ad* Campaign.

of Burger King's competitor (e.g., McDonald's), the ad will be on fire in real time (see Figure 11.1). The app will then turn into Burger King's ad and give the user a coupon for a free Whopper. The campaign was designed to create an interactive, playful, and memorable experience for users (Hirani, 2020). As a result, 400,000 ads were "burned" during the campaign period, and Burger King's in-app sales increased 54% (Hirani, 2020).

These are all great ways of getting customers involved in the digital projection process. Even though mobile phones are an individualized technology that serves the specialized and customized needs of each user, think beyond individual participation when using it in marketing strategies. Urge users to share, create, and make memories with their social networks. Consider the following action plan when creating a mobile strategy.

Mobile Strategy Action Plan

1 Develop an alternative social media strategy for mobile devices. Consider mobile-mediated communication features, such as localization, portable sharing, and synchronicity.
2 Allow users to tag friends and share posts with their own social network whenever possible. These collaborative structures will help create a stronger sense of community and speak to users' own gratifications for your product.

3   Incorporate location-based check-in features so that users can share their experiences with your brand with their own social network. Ensure that this experience speaks to the notion of the Third Place and will be something that they would want their online identity to be associated with.

4   Create collaborative campaigns where users contribute to a synchronous prompt, such as a scavenger hunt. Encourage them to leave their houses, have out-of-the-box experiences, and share photos or videos.

Generating Return Visits

Mobile technology is a shared social space for individual networks. Individuals are highly influenced by their social network and make purchasing and behavior change decisions accordingly. While mobile technology allows marketers the ability to deliver promotional information to consumers based on their individualized preferences and location, it would be more beneficial if they were able to prompt users to share their experiences with their social network, creating memories associated with a brand.

Often, businesses try to prompt people to visit stores by offering free products through mobile updates. However, research demonstrates that people are more persuaded, especially toward long-term behavior change, if they are involved in the information-seeking process, rather than just being given a coupon. Remember that emotion and engagement highly influence our everyday decisions. Commitment can be enhanced through building emotional value (Varnali & Toker, 2010). *Push text messages* are mobile alerts that applications send to update users with new content. While these are efficient and cost-effective, they tend to lack emotion and may not be as persuasive as marketers hope. In fact, many mobile users find those alerts disruptive and annoying. Free materials with no-strings-attached offers may even prompt consumers to devalue the products. Make customers work for coupons, even if it is through simple acts such as scanning QR codes or sharing offers with friends.

Most mobile advertisements are based on text messaging services, which is not a very emotionally engaging communication medium. Companies offer special deals if consumers opt-in to receiving text messages from the company. This is called permission marketing and is different from spam because it requires the recipient to agree to receive the messages (Bauer et al., 2005). What separates mobile marketing from other forms of new media is its ability to personalize and customize settings based on what works best for the user. Most companies are not utilizing mobile media to this potential and are sending impersonal messages that seem interruptive. Remember that customers will be interrupted much more by text-based messages because they will arrive by phone, not in an asynchronous platform such as email. Most individuals will see your message but will find it bothersome and not appropriate for what they are doing at the time and will associate the brand with this negative feeling.

One way to improve this marketing strategy is to personalize the type of messages that your consumers receive. Mobile marketing allows you the ability to learn a lot about your consumers' demographics, location, and interests (Scharl et al., 2005). Once you begin to gain a sense of what your consumers enjoy, construct the messages accordingly. The simplicity, affordability, and speed of mobile delivery make this type of target messaging possible. Address the recipients by name and ask them to participate in the process. Let them know that there is a human on the other end of the message.

The best way to ensure users continue engaging with your mobile campaign is to make it creative and entertaining (Bauer et al., 2005). Research demonstrates how these two constructs are the highest correlating factors with intentional customer return visits. While there is a slightly more addictive tendency with mobile technology than other types of media, marketers cannot solely rely on habitual routine for repeat use (Ehrenberg et al., 2008).

The medium is the message. While it is easy to make traditional Internet content friendly for mobile devices, mobile marketing requires more than just an interface change. Content and features should change according to the platform that users engage and the goals of the company. Mobile marketing also does not allow for the same richness of information as Internet marketing, so be sure to keep all information concise (Shankar & Balasubramanian, 2009).

Overall, commercially oriented marketing messages are less appealing than social and entertainment-related strategies (Grant & O'Donohoe, 2007). Users want to control over their mobile technology; after all, it is an incredibly important construction of self-identity. Aim for personalization of content, rather than sending interruptive messaging. Mobile marketing should encourage users to strengthen relationships with those in their networks by prompting new experiences, offering promotions when they are out together, and providing games to play when they are away.

Case Study: LINE

The process of engaging media users through social media constantly evolves as more users log on through mobile technology. In this chapter, we talked about the importance of keeping mobile content exciting and entertaining. Your mobile social media strategy should focus on culture, personalization, interactivity, socialization, and localization. LINE is such a mobile social media platform.

LINE was launched during the 2011 Tohoku earthquake in Japan as "a reliable line of communication" for family and friends to contact each other during crises (Sehl, 2021). Through years, it has evolved from a solely mobile messaging app to a social media hub for entertainment, social, and daily activities. LINE users can use the app to text, make audio and video calls, create and share stickers, make payments, order food, taxi, and other services, watch TV, listen to music, read comic books, and even consult with healthcare professionals (Ostaszewski & Kwan, 2017; Sehl, 2021). Today, LINE has more than 220 million users worldwide, with 92 million in Japan. It also generated US$2.36 billion revenue in 2021 (Iqbal, 2023).

LINE is successful because it provides users entertaining and engaging content. Built on Japanese users' passion on anime and emojis, LINE sticker (i.e., huge emoticons) was a driver of LINE's popularity since its debut (DMFA, 2023; Kang, 2016). The app created a series of animated and sound stickers of LINE characters like Brown the bear and Cony the bunny (see Figure 11.2). In addition, users can create their own stickers and share their stickers for free or sell them in exchange LINE coins. It is estimated that selling sticker packs brings LINE US$20 million revenue every month (Kang, 2016).

Gaming has also proven itself as one of the drivers of LINE's growth (DMFA, 2023). The most engaging games are those in which users compete and share experiences with their social network. Mobile games enhance the social

Figure 11.2   LINE sticker shop. Source: LINE Corporation.

experience, making it more enjoyable and interactive by allowing users to create new experiences when they cannot be together.

LINE's success is also because the platform has taken localization and cultural norms into serious consideration when developing its global strategies. For example, LINE created Lunar New Year stickers in Taiwan, and Ramadan celebrating and fasting stickers in Indonesia to help localize the app (Ostaszewski & Kwan, 2017). In Thailand, LINE introduced LINE Man, a service that provides 24-hour delivery for users in Bangkok. In Indonesia, LINE produced a mini sequel to a popular Indonesian romance movie when introducing a new LINE feature (i.e., reconnect long lost acquaintances in Indonesia). In Taiwan, LINE also collaborated with Watsons, a local health and beauty store, to allow Taiwanese to redeem LINE stickers for merchandise (Ostaszewski & Kwan, 2017). These efforts all demonstrate that LINE values culture, community, and localization, which in turn makes the app one of the most popular social media in Asian markets, particularly in Japan, Taiwan, Thailand, and Indonesia (Iqbal, 2023; Ostaszewski & Kwan, 2017).

LINE also excels in urging real-life experiences through mobilization. It started physical LINE stores in Taipei that sell LINE merchandises, such as plushies, clothing, and more (Ostaszewski & Kwan, 2017). Users are encouraged to visit the stores with friends and take selfies with LINE mascots and share the pictures on social media. It also introduced LINE Pay, which allows easy transition of money among its users and their contacts (DMFA, 2023). All these make LINE users feel the "social experience." LINE, thus, has become "a holistic lifestyle brand" (Ostaszewski & Kwan, 2017), rather than just a mobile messenger.

Clearly one of the benefits of social media platforms is the ability for users around the globe to communicate and interact with one another. For marketers, mobile social media like LINE provides more individualized options for sharing and participation from consumers. In addition, LINE demonstrates the importance of culture in how we share. In Asian countries where users tend to turn to their community as an influence in all decisions, mobile marketing allows them to be together for all decisions. It is important that structure, content, and culture all align to maximize satisfaction for users.

Discussion Questions

1   In your opinion, how has LINE put localization into its strategy and speak to different cultures? Do you think LINE could succeed if it would enter the North American market?

2   How could you use LINE to communicate about your identity in a positive manner? Specifically, how could you use mobile technology to share information about your third place experiences?

3   How influential do you feel stickers were to LINE's success? If you oversaw LINE's development team, what new features would you create to further enhance user engagement for LINE?

Summary

Marketers were just beginning to understand best practices for communicating with online users through social media when mobile technology exploded in popularity. Today, we know that the medium that carries online content alters the human behavior change process. It is important for social media marketers to be aware of the available technology and ensure that users are not prevented from participating in the process due to your message not being mobile-friendly. Marketing strategies should be inclusive of every type of online users, as there are opportunities and challenges with each new medium.

While mobile-mediated communication holds potential for increased participation and engagement between online users, it could also decrease the value of interpersonal communication. There has been much concern about a mobile world where everyone is looking down at their mobile devices and missing the world right in front of them. While it is important to keep mobile content exciting and engaging, the focus should really be on encouraging real-life experiences through mobilization.

Mobile marketing must focus on culture, personalization, interactivity, socialization, and localization (Bauer et al., 2005). These are all opportunities that were incredibly difficult to establish through traditional technology. GPS capabilities make traveling in foreign places simple and have provided independence to those directionally challenged people. Families are better able to coordinate schedules through simple phone calls or texts. People can share applications that synch calendars, grocery lists, and games of Scrabble.

This chapter focuses on how mobile users utilize technology to share their life experiences with personal networks. It is your job as a social media specialist to apply traditional theories to social media messages to establish customer loyalty and apply marketing strategy and business models to sustain growth. In fact, research measurements are one of the most vital factors in successful social media marketing. Now that we understand how to develop and implement social media business models and marketing strategy, let's turn our attention towards evaluation and research. Chapter 12 will focus on evaluating social media marketing. The ability to systematically monitor and evaluate marketing efforts will help you understand how and why individuals engage with your social media messages.

Key Takeaways

1   The characteristics of the medium that carries content highly influence the way consumers use and interpret the content itself. Therefore, marketing content should vary depending on the platform that consumers utilize.
2   Mobile-mediated communication is a type of computer-mediated communication that allows for unlimited mobility, faster infrastructure, and low-cost plans where users share, search, and interact with others.

3   It is important to incorporate structure, content, and culture in your mobile social media marketing strategy.
4   Social media users create digital projections of their lives through status, photo, and video updates. Mobile technology allows individuals to easily share experiences with each other in real time, even if they are far away.
5   Mobile marketing should encourage collaborative projects where users create and share real-life experiences with their personal network. Commercially oriented marketing messages are less appealing than social and entertainment-related strategies for your consumers.

References

Anderson, M. (2015) Racial and ethnic differences in how people us mobile technology. *Pew Research Center*. Available at https://www.pewresearch.org/short-reads/2015/04/30/racial-and-ethnic-differences-in-how-people-use-mobile-technology/ (accessed November 17, 2023).

Bauer, H.H., Barnes, S.J., Reichardt, T. & Neumann, M.M. (2005) Driving consumer acceptance of mobile marketing: a theoretical framework and empirical study. *Journal of Electronic Commerce Research*, 6(3), 181–192.

Byers, R. (2015) Liseberg amusement park has gamified a roller coaster line. *Trend Hunter*. Available at https://www.trendhunter.com/trends/liseberg (accessed November 17, 2023).

Counts, S. & Fisher, K. (2008) Mobile social networking: an information grounds perspective. In: *Proceedings of the 41st Hawaii International Conference on System Sciences*. Piscataway, NJ: IEEE.

DMFA (2023) Why is LINE the most popular social media app in Japan. *Digital Marketing for Asia*. Available at https://www.digitalmarketingforasia.com/why-line-is-the-most-popular-social-media-app-in-japan/ (accessed November 17, 2023).

Efron, M. (2010) Hashtag retrieval in a microblogging environment. In: *Proceedings of the 33rd International ACM SIGIR Conference on Research and Development in Information Retrieval*, pp. 787–788. New York: ACM Press.

Ehrenberg, A., Juckes, S., White, K. & Walsh, S. (2008) Personality and self-esteem as predictors of young people's technology use. *CyberPsychology and Behavior*, 11(6), 739–741.

Faverio, M. (2022) Share of those 65 and older who are tech users has grown in the past decade. *Pew Research Center*. Available at https://www.pewresearch.org/short-reads/2022/01/13/share-of-those-65-and-older-who-are-tech-users-has-grown-in-the-past-decade/ (accessed November 17, 2023).

Grant, I. & O'Donohoe, S. (2007) Why young consumers are not open to mobile marketing communication. *International Journal of Advertising*, 26(2), 223–246.

Grenoble, R. (2013) Posting too many Facebook "selfies" can hurt your real-world relationships, study says. Available at http://www.huffingtonpost.com/2013/08/13/too-many-facebook-photos-study_n_3749053.html?ncid=edlinkusaolp00000003&ir=College (accessed November 17, 2023).

Grob, R., Kuhn, M., Wattenhofer, R. & Wirz, M. (2009) Cluestr: mobile social networking for enhanced group communication. In: *Proceedings of the ACM 2009 International Conference on Supporting Group Work*, pp. 81–90. New York: ACM Press.

Gutierrez, J.C., De Fronseca, F.R., & Rubio, G. (2016) Cell-phone addiction: a review. *Frontiers in Psychiatry*, 7. doi: 10.3389/fpsyt.2016.00175.

Hirani, R. (2020) King over clown? *LinkedIn*. Available at https://www.linkedin.com/pulse/king-over-clown-burn-ad-burger-david-sp-brazil-2018-rohan-hirani/ (accessed November 17, 2023).

Humphreys, L. (2007) Mobile social networks and social practice: a case study of Dodgeball. *Journal of Computer-Mediated Communication*, 13(1), 341–360.

Iqbal, M. (2023) Line revenue and usage statistics (2023). *Business of Apps*. Available at https://www.businessofapps.com/data/line-statistics/ (accessed November 17, 2023).

Kang, J. (2016) What you need to know about LINE, one of the world's most popular messaging apps. *Forbes*. Available at https://www.forbes.com/sites/johnkang/2016/07/14/what-you-need-to-know-about-line-messaging-app/?sh=6561144559fc (accessed November 17, 2023).

Kaplan, A. & Haenlein, M. (2010) Users of the world, unite! The challenges and opportunities of social media. *Business Horizons*, 53(1), 59–68.

Keral, A. (2023) 2023 cell phone usage statistics: mornings are for notifications. *Reviews*. Available at https://www.reviews.org/mobile/cell-phone-addiction/#:~:text=Americans%20check%20their%20phones%20144minutes%20of%20receiving%20a%20notification (accessed November 17, 2023).

Kurkovsky, S. & Harihar, K. (2006) Using ubiquitous computing in interactive mobile marketing. *Personal and Ubiquitous Computing*, 10(4), 227–240.

Ling, R. (2000) Direct and mediated interaction in the maintenance of social relationships. In: A. Sloane & F. Van Rijn (eds) *Home Informatics and Telematics: Information, Technology and Society*, pp. 61–86. Boston: Kluwer.

McLuhan, M. (1994) *Understanding Media: The Extensions of Man*. Cambridge, MA: MIT Press.

Oldenburg, R. (1989) *The Great Good Place*. New York: Paragon House.

Ostaszewski, B. & Kwan, J. (2017) Localizing mobile apps: a case study of LINE Messenger. *Asia Pacific Foundation of Canada*. Available at https://www.asiapacific.ca/blog/localizing-mobile-apps-case-study-line-messenger (accessed November 17, 2023).

Pang, H. (2021) Identifying associations between mobile social media users' perceived values, attitude, satisfaction, and eWOM engagement: the moderating role of affective factors. *Telematics and Informatics*, 59, 101561. doi: 10.1016/j.tele.2020.101561.

Perrin, A. (2021) Mobile technology and home broadband 2021. *Pew Research Center*. Available at https://www.pewresearch.org/internet/2021/06/03/mobile-technology-and-home-broadband-2021/ (accessed November 17, 2023).

Perrin, A. & Atske, S. (2021) About three-in-ten U.S. adults say they are "almost constantly" online. *Pew Research Center*. Available at https://www.pewresearch.org/short-reads/2021/03/26/about-three-in-ten-u-s-adults-say-they-are-almost-constantly-online/ (accessed November 17, 2023).

Rheingold, H. (2003) *Smart Mobs: The Next Social Revolution*. Cambridge, MA: Perseus Books Group.

Scharl, A., Dickinger, A. & Murphy, J. (2005) Diffusion and success factors of mobile marketing. *Electronic Commerce Research and Applications*, 4(2), 159–173.

Sehl, K. (2021) What is the Line app?: everything brands need to know. *Hootsuite*. Available at https://blog.hootsuite.com/line-app/ (accessed November 17, 2023).

Shankar, V. & Balasubramanian, S. (2009) Mobile marketing: a synthesis and prognosis. *Journal of Interactive Marketing*, 23(2), 118–129.

Siver, L., Huang, C. & Taylor, K. (2019) In emerging economies, smartphone and social media users have broader social networks. *Pew Research Center*. Available at https://www.pewresearch.org/internet/wp-content/uploads/sites/9/2019/08/Pew-Research-Center_Emerging-Economies-Smartphone-Social-Media-Users-Have-Broader-Social-Networks-Report_2019-08-22.pdf (accessed November 17, 2023).

Varnali, K. & Toker, A. (2010) Mobile marketing research: the state-of-the-art. *International Journal of Information Management*, 30(2), 144–151.

World Economic Forum (2022) This infographic shows the rise of mobile device subscriptions worldwide. Available at https://www.weforum.org/agenda/2022/10/mobile-device-subscription-rise-technology/ (accessed November 17, 2023).

Yurieff, K. (2017) Snapchats no longer have to disappear after 10 seconds. *CNN Business*. Available at https://money.cnn.com/2017/05/09/technology/snapchat-new-tools/index.html (accessed November 17, 2023).

12

Evaluating Social Media Marketing

Learning Objectives

After reading this chapter, you should be able to:
1   Identify current social media marketing measurements and trends.
2   Understand the importance of a hybrid approach to evaluation research.
3   Incorporate audience reception research methodologies into your social media marketing strategy.

Introduction

Part III of this book discusses the many ways in which social media marketers must alter traditional marketing strategies to best meet the needs of a digital era. Chapter 9 discusses how the theory of the long tail changes a mass audience to a more latent niche; Chapters 10 and 11 illustrate how to incorporate strategic theory into marketing campaigns. Clearly, social media has dramatically changed the ways in which we produce and share media messages. In addition to this creation and dissemination process, the best marketers understand that research is the most critical indicator of success in strategy.

Strategic Social Media: From Marketing to Social Change, Second Edition. L. Meghan Mahoney and Tang Tang.
© 2024 John Wiley & Sons, Inc. Published 2024 by John Wiley & Sons, Inc.

Research is vital at every stage of a marketing strategy: creation, production, dissemination, and evaluation. This chapter explains how current social media marketing measurements have evolved and explores how the changing social media users require a more hybrid approach to data analysis. We will identify how holistic measures are more possible than ever before through social media. A strong social media strategy is necessary for marketers to design, analyze, make sense, and apply data analytic techniques. Monitoring and evaluation efforts can only be aided, never replaced, by new media technologies. Let us explore the many ways in which the industry has changed how we evaluate consumer behavior and the success of a marketing campaign in a social media era.

Current Social Media Marketing Measurements

Mass communication research is defined as the systematic study of media content, the forces that shape its creation, how and why people use media, and the impact of media content and media institutions on individuals and society (Folkerts & Lacy, 2003). Marketers utilize mass communication research methodologies to better understand how their media messages are interpreted by and influence consumers. There are many different paradigms and approaches to mass communication research.

Three of the most basic distinctions between research methodologies have to do with the type of questions asked, and the ways in which data is collected. All research can be categorized as quantitative, qualitative, or hybrid approach.

- *Quantitative research methodologies* emphasize systematic measurements through the gathering of numerical data and the generalization of findings across groups of people (Babbie, 2020). Quantitative data is collected through various methods, including surveys, experimental studies, and secondary data or technology-enabled data (e.g., social media monitoring data).
- *Qualitative research methodologies* seek to understand the psychological operations by observing a broad interconnected pattern of variables, rather than the strength of the statistical relationship of variables (Graziano & Raulin, 2004). Qualitative data is collected through focus group, participant observation, open-ended questionnaires, conversations, and textual analyses.
- *Hybrid research methodologies* are mixed methodological approaches that utilize both qualitative and quantitative data. The hybrid approach uses the strengths of each and alleviates the weaknesses. Today, data fusion and data integration, two types of popular hybrid research methodologies, have become a trend for audience analytics.

Some may believe that a more specialized understanding of research approaches is not necessary with today's technological landscape. There are numerous businesses, consultants, and platforms available that can help companies research their marketing strategy. Rather than learning the different methods and measurements themselves, companies believe that they can hire or use an external technological service to tell them what they would like to know. This section argues that research should be the core of any marketing strategy. A thorough understanding of research measures and evaluation is important to any social media practitioner.

Traditionally, the goal of mass media marketing campaigns has been to reach the highest number of consumers possible. Since mass media institutions are so intrinsically linked to advertising, ensuring that the largest mass audience was reached by messages was always central to strategies. You may remember from Chapter 2 that this approach is called "push-and-pray" marketing. It is an outdated mindset to strategic goals in social media marketing. Instead, social media practitioners should have optimum user engagement as the focus to their strategy.

This does not mean that large consumer numbers do not matter. We have explored the endless options that consumers have for accessing media content. In this saturated environment, practitioners must ensure that their brand rises to the top of search engine listings. It is becoming more difficult for consumers to find brands as more and more brands emerge in the marketplace. A strong search engine optimization (SEO) plan will help ensure that your company is easily findable.

SEO helps to drive traffic to a website by increasing the ranking of the site in results returned by a search engine. The results of Google's first page capture more than 70% of online traffic (McCormick, 2023). The first step in deciding your company's SEO strategy is to determine which niche keywords best fit your product and brand. These should include phrases that are broad enough to speak to your overall product, but specific enough to demonstrate what sets you apart from your competitors.

SEO is the art, craft, and science of driving traffic to websites (Davis, 2006). Understanding how various search engines compile a listing query is not as straightforward as it may sound. Very generally, search engines follow four basic mechanisms of Google: discovery of the meaning of websites, storage of links and page summaries, ranking of page importance, and return of results. This is often called DSRR (discover, storage, ranking, and return). A complete understanding of how to optimize DSRR would require much more space than this book allows. Fortunately, if you are interested in learning more about SEO, there are many resources available, such as *The art of SEO: Mastering search engine optimization* by Enge *et al.* (2023) and *Search engine optimization secrets* by Dover and Dafforn (2011). SEO concepts tend to stretch beyond the scope of a marketing practitioner. Thus, it may be wise to invest in an external agency to meet the demands of SEO.

Nonetheless, Google's free Analytics Academy is a quick guide for you to make sense of Google analytics data. Google measurements are primarily interested in the number and type of click-through links posted to social media sites. In other words, these measurements can help you understand how many consumers your message is reaching. You can even break your consumers down into segments according to age, race, gender, and geographic location. Since most websites and search engines model Google's design, it serves as a great starting place for understanding metrics.

It is also helpful for you to understand similar analytical programs for your social media sites. Facebook Insights is a free analytical tool that provides basic analytics about Facebook pages, posts, and users (Teyes, 2022). Meta Business Suite offers more comprehensive analyses and visual reports for Facebook and Instagram (Newberry, 2022). X Analytics (formerly Twitter) provides metrics about followers, impressions, engagement rate, link clicks, retweets, likes, and replies in a chosen period of time (e.g., the past 28 days). It also identifies top tweets, top mentions, top followers for your X account (Martin, 2021). If you have a TikTok business account, TikTok provides you four types of analytics – overview, content, followers and LIVE, all via its creator tools. TikTok analytics also tells you who your followers are, such as their gender, where they located, and when they used the app (Hirose, 2022).

LinkedIn also offers a native analytics tool that allows LinkedIn page admins to see insights about the page's visitors, followers, competitors, updates, leads, and employee advocacy. For example, its follower metrics shows who have interacted with a company's LinkedIn page. The competitor analytics hints on what the company is doing right, and areas of improvement compared to its competitors (MacReady, 2022). Based on these analytics, marketers can improve their campaign and enhance user engagement. Pinterest analytics includes audience insights, conversation insights, and trends analysis (Beveridge, 2022a). Pinterest business account owners can also see the number of users, impressions, and engagement of the account in the past 30 days. Snapchat Insights monitors and analyzes engagement on Snapchat. The analytics shows you the content sources your Snapchat users spent time with, the usage of AP lenses and filters, and characteristics of your users. It also tracks unique views, impressions, completion rates, and screenshot rates (Beveridge, 2022b).

These social media analytics all aim to help you understand your consumers, the opportunities for your business and product development, and enhance customer relationships and user engagement (Newberry & MacReady, 2022). In addition, these quantitative data can inform practitioners about competitors and show relevant industry and market trends. Sometimes, by tracking real-time sentiment, it is easy to spot on a crisis and address it efficiently (Newberry & MacReady, 2022).

Regardless of the goals of your social media marketing research, your analytics should focus on several aspects: (i) Sentiment: to understand what positive and negative things people talked about your product/service/brand. (ii) Questions: see if there are repetitive questions about your product/service. Answer those questions and be mindful about the opportunities brought by these questions. (iii) Trends: what are topics often shared by your consumers? Are there weekly or seasonal trends that you can use to create your social media massages/campaigns? (iv) Consumers: know about your consumer demographics, where they locate, when they use different social media platforms, and what they like to talk about. (v) Advocates: find your brand advocates. Get to know them, and build a community with your fans (Seiter, 2014).

We have learned in Chapter 10 that marketers need to research social media conversations about their product/brand through social media platforms external to their own sites.

As such, while each social media site's native analytical tool (discussed earlier) can provide you important insights about your users and messages on a single platform, it is important to conduct cross-platform analytics. Some measurement tools, such as Hootsuite, can track all your social media performance in one place. The tool allows you to monitor social media conversations, key words, mentions, and hashtags across 50 platforms (Hootsuite, 2023; Whalley, 2020). It then provides both real-time and longitudinal analytics on reach, engagement rate, impressions, likes, shares, clicks, saves, comments, video views, followers, profile visits, and website clicks across platforms and by each social media channel (Hootsuite, 2023).

Like Hootsuite, Sprout Social is a one-stop, paid, social media listening and analytics tool that allows users to track brand mentions, industry trends, customer sentiment, and competitor performance across multiple social platforms, such as Facebook, X, Instagram, YouTube, LinkedIn, Pinterest, Google Analytics, HubSpot, and TripAdvisor. It also provides reports on new trends around which marketers can tailor their social media messages (Watson, 2021). Netbase Social Listening & Analytics is a research tool that utilizes Natural Language Processing (NLP) for social conversation analytics. This powerful machine learning tool can collect data from hundreds of millions of daily social posts and more than 100 billion past posts across media platforms and generate research reports on trends, sentiments, customers, competitors, and influencers for a company (Newberry & MacReady, 2022). Brandwatch is another paid social media monitoring and analytics tool. It is based on AI technology, which allows users to track real-time conversations via 100 million unique data sources. The tool also provides tracking and analyses for 1.6 trillion historical online conversations (Brandwatch, 2023).

Hopefully, you can see how current social media research tools used by the industry can provide you both real time and longitudinal analyses that reflect attitudes, opinions, and trending topics. You can also obtain geo-targeting information for your campaign and identify top influencers. Each of these social media listening tools provides aggregate quantitative data of user behavior on social media and is perfect for a beginner interested in designing an evaluation strategy. Though analytics may seem to be highly statistical in nature, there is no need to feel apprehensive about making sense of the data, as these programs do a nice job of presenting the information in layman's terms.

Quantitative methodologies have primarily led the measurement industry. In general, FRY is what quantitative social media measurement has focused on (Blanchard, 2011). FRY refers to frequency (how often your target consumers are reached by your social media campaign), reach (how many people your campaign can reach), and yield (average dollar value per transaction). Blanchard (2011, p. 241) suggests that FRY represents the three ways that consumer behavior could be changed:

> You could convince people already buying from you to do so more often, you could convince more people to buy from you, and you could convince people who were already buying from you, without doing business more often, to spend a little more than they already were per transaction.

Other quantitative measurements include search, traffic, retention, brand metrics leads, sales, and profit (Hudspeth, 2012). We have discussed many of these metrics above. Here, the brand strategy is still to reach as large number of target consumers engaging with a social media message as possible. However, these objectives are like those of traditional mass media marketing. For decades, advertisers have been producing television commercials and hoping that they can reach the largest mass population possible. None of these measures account for the potential of the latent long tail market discussed in Chapter 9. Remember that there are various negotiations and levels to the consumer experience. If you can prompt behavior change through participatory means in your consumers, they are much more likely to be transformed into your brand advocates. These brand advocates hold a higher ROI than the "push-and-pray" model of mass media. A more sophisticated understanding of active audience research design may help you personalize the research process.

As we learned in Chapter 9, social media business models are not as concerned with reaching the highest number of consumers as traditional media. Instead, social media marketers are increasingly interested in the way their consumers interact with media messages, rather than only finding values in counting the number of followers or fans (DiStaso *et al.*, 2011). The quality of this interaction is key. This is consistent with everything we have learned about the value of participatory social media messages and mobilizing users.

Therefore, social media evaluation should mirror the assumptions of "pull-and-stay" marketing. Here, you use the medium to listen and engage in conversations to increase trust and connection (Stratten, 2012). Evaluation and measurement efforts need to link to helping practitioners design, produce, disseminate, and evaluate social media strategy. In addition, it functions as a great way to listen to your consumers and tell them that you care about them. While the current quantitative social media listening and data analytics tools are important and necessary for the success of any business, social media marketing evaluation efforts should also employ qualitative research to understand meanings, reasons, and relationships. We will discuss in detail one popular qualitative research method – focus group.

Building on the Focus Group

When designing a research strategy, it is important to know what methodologies help answer what types of questions. While quantitative research provides insights into a larger mass community, qualitative research is great for examining local or latent consumers. Since social media users are generally seen as more individual than homogeneous mass, it makes sense for social media research and evaluation efforts to turn towards more qualitative measures. Qualitative research can also help explain relationships, trends and patterns that emerge from quantitative measures (Garbarino & Holland, 2009). While quantitative research is great for identifying trends, until you know the reason behind them, there is little a practitioner can do to control change in behavior.

In the field of marketing, one of the most trusted and widely used research methods is focus group. *Focus group* is a controlled group interview of target consumers, usually consisting of 5–12 participants, that is led by a facilitator through a series of guided questions and topics (Entrepreneur, 2014). This is a great way for social media practitioners to capture user opinions quickly, understand nuances between members, and gain a sense of sentiments toward a new product.

Perhaps you are interested in increasing the number of female fans of your brand. You could bring in a group of 8–10 female followers of your Instagram account to interview in a focus group setting. A focus group discussion with this small group of females will allow you to hear their attitudes toward your brand through a conversation with each other. This helps to explain some of the behavior that you see on quantitative social media analytic metrics via a particular focus and explanatory lens. Focus groups are a great resource for exploring secondary niche audiences.

While focus group research can be very valuable for social media marketers, there are other qualitative methodologies that you can utilize to better understand how consumers make sense of social media messages. These methodologies include, but are not limited to, in-depth interviews, participant observation, textual analysis, and anthropological studies. Qualitative research methodologies tend to be more time-consuming and costly. However, these efforts are worth it because the research can provide a unique view into consumer behavior that you do not get with big data analyses alone. Paired together, marketers can achieve both broad and deep insights into consumer behavior.

There are many ways in which qualitative and quantitative research naturally work together. In fact, focus groups have become a favored method in recent years for researchers who are interested in combining qualitative and quantitative methodologies (Bernard, 2000). Focus groups complement surveys and big data analyses, rather than replace them, as they can help interpret results, especially when the meaning behind quantitative data is unclear. While survey research tells you what your consumers think, and social media listening tells you what your consumers did and talked about, focus groups are able to find out why your consumers feel the way they do and how they arrive at these feelings.

A hybrid evaluation approach is useful for every stage of the product process – design, production, dissemination, and evaluation – to ensure best results. The Johns Hopkins Bloomberg School for Public Health Center for Communication Programs (2007) defined *monitoring and evaluation* as the process of collecting key data related to program objectives and operations and analyzing these data to guide policy, programs, and practices. Here, you see how research must be done at every stage of the process, not just at the end when a product or message hits the market.

Furthermore, longitudinal, people-centered, qualitative methodologies can help researchers/practitioners capture the social, cultural, economic, and political dimensions of life (Singhal & Rogers, 2003). It is important that we now understand the role media users play in the interpretation process. Most evaluation research cannot reach comprehensive conclusions about consumers at all because they constantly construct their reality and self-identity through media text negotiations (Fiske, 1987). Media users are influenced by the text differently from one another depending on their consumption habits, motivations, and life experiences. Therefore, evaluations must move away from people as the objects of change and focus on more participatory methods, such as a focus on dialogue, cultural identity, and decision-making processes (Byrne *et al.*, 2005). This can be done through more holistic evaluation research that also includes efforts aimed at understanding how media users negotiate meanings (Petraglia, 2007). One of such methodologies for capturing the complexities of an active media user is audience reception research.

Audience Reception Approach

Often, marketers examine the media messages that have already been disseminated and wonder how they can shape them to trick consumers into following through with a desired behavior. Here, consumers are not seen as playing a very active role in the process. It is time to monitor consumers and evaluate social media marketing efforts through a more active process.

Audience reception research understands the active role that media users play. It considers three areas of media reception: (i) individual qualities and life experiences of media users; (ii) the meaning that users make during the moment of consumption; and (iii) subsequent decision-making processes. Audience reception research requires marketing practitioners to complete a strong audience analysis. By learning as much as possible about your consumers, they will begin to feel more like individuals, rather than a homogeneous mass. You should focus on the daily life of the family, social temporality, and cultural competence (Tufte, 2002).

Understanding how individuals live in a natural environment requires complete and thorough media ethnography. *Media ethnography* explores everyday media practices and life experiences and can understand culturally specific ways of how individuals live in the world around them.

Consider how you access and use social media in your own life. It is likely that you do not often sit down at a computer and log in to a social media platform such as Instagram and access nothing but Instagram content for the entire duration. Today's social media users are on the go. They access an array of media content, simultaneously, across a wide range of platforms and devices (often via mobile). This convergent environment must be taken into consideration by social media evaluation research.

In addition, participants today no longer need to leave their natural environment to participate in research studies. This becomes increasingly true with the recent technology advancements in Internet of Things (IoT) and artificial intelligence (AI). Wearable technologies, such as Apple Watch, Go Pros, VR headsets, smart jewelry, and other biometrics measurement tools, can collect real data of user behavior without interrupting their activities (Yasar & Wigmore, 2022). You can gather data about individuals as they live their lives. These are great technologies for capturing accurate user data in a more natural setting rather than controlled experimental research.

Today's marketing practitioners are interested in identifying how users engage across different social media platforms. Many technology-enabled measurement tools that attempt to account for cross-platform activity, such as Google Analytics, Sprout Social, Hootsuite, Brandwatch, provide a more nuanced understanding of how each of the platforms works with each other. As such, you can examine the entire media landscape to best understand cultural trajectories that may influence interpretation through various dimensions of inter-textuality. Though it is important that you create a separate social media strategy for each social media platform, monitoring and evaluation efforts should aim to understand how these platforms work with one another.

Be careful that you are not just examining how users are accessing your content on your own social media sites. It is also useful to see what other content is being accessed in com-bination with your messages. For instance, it may be useful to know that when consumers are looking at online information about Coca Cola, they are also looking at information about diabetes research. This will help you design a better product that serves the needs of your consumers.

Researchers have also identified media ethnography as a useful evaluation methodology as it transcends the relationship between media users and media content to explore social and cultural transformations (Tufte, 2002). Your consumers' media environment very much influences how they interpret media messages. Even the experience of looking at social media content from a mobile phone is very different from doing so on a desktop computer.

Once you have a strong sense of who your consumers are, and how they are using media in their own lives, it is important to complete a genre analysis of media content. Here, you examine the media message landscape and identify where different layers of primary, secondary, and tertiary media messages are distinguished from one another. This process provides a more holistic understanding of their relationship (Fiske, 1987; Tufte, 2002). While media ethnography examines how people use various technologies, genre analysis examines the many media messages to which users are exposed. Social media marketers need to identify pop culture media artifacts to see what consumers are finding the most pleasure in. They should also examine alternative media messages from organizations with similar objectives.

We have identified the processes for understanding the individual qualities and life experiences of your consumers. However, this is just one piece of the reception process. Next, you must try to understand the meaning that individuals make during the moment of consumption.

Social media marketers should ask questions about the dynamics between media messages and users and stop separating users from messages (Katz, 1988; Livingstone, 1991). It is also important for you to ask several questions: What key differences exist between users? How do different users negotiate meaning from media messages differently from one another? Holistic audience reception research shifts the emphasis from an analysis of the consumption process to an analysis of the meaning media users make of the media messages. These can be understood through a textual analysis of your media messages.

A *textual analysis* is a qualitative research method where researchers make an educated guess at some of the most likely interpretations that users may make of a media text. This is done to obtain a sense of the ways in which particular cultures live at particular times, how people make sense of the world around them, and the variety of ways in which it is possible to interpret reality (McKee, 2003). Here you see how media users are seen as a much more active entity where they negotiate media messages differently from one another.

The focus of a textual analysis is to determine how media users construct their reality and self-identity through media messages (Fiske, 1987). This method is not explicitly examining audience reception, but rather context about the themes and underlying messages in media content. The first step of a textual analysis is to identify themes and salient messages within a media message (Bernard, 2000). Next, these themes and messages help determine narrative structure, symbolic arrangements, and ideological potential of media content (Fürsich, 2009). Here, what is of interest is not the text itself, but what the text signifies (Curtin, 1995). While a textual analysis uncovers many of the possible interpretations, a complex relationship exists between interpretation, expectations, and media genres. That is why a textual analysis should be paired with additional qualitative research that focuses on user communication. Popular blogs and long-form user discussion forums are popular samples for a new media textual analysis.

When doing social media monitoring and evaluation research, marketers also need to consider the interaction between media messages and everyday life. Asking questions about what environment people consume messages in, and how that environment influences interpretation and subsequent behavior can do this. The most important part of this process is to get users talking and reflecting on their experiences.

Specifically, focus group discussions could be used when researchers are interested in gathering real-life data on issues that benefit from a group dynamic. Here, you can promote self-disclosure among focus group participants about what they really think and feel about a topic. Participants should be assembled with some common identifiable feature (e.g., gender, interest, belief, and attitude). This way, they identify with each other and are more open to reflect on the quality in their discussion.

In-depth interview discussions can be used when you are more interested in understanding what your consumers mean when they behave in a certain manner. Information gathered from multiple interviews allows practitioners to hear multiple perspectives on an event or issue. It is also a great tool to test emerging ideas about communicative action and sensitive messages/topics. With this method, you define a purpose for such conversations to occur, select certain social actors to advance the conversational purpose, and draw out cultural logistics that individuals employ in their everyday experiences of communicating (Lindlof, 1995). The most critical factor when conducting interview research is the ability of the researcher to perform a close reading of the transcript and draw conclusions once the interview is completed.

An added benefit of either of these methods is that your customers begin to feel valued by your brand. By allowing them to participate in the process, they feel more invested as a thought leader. This can easily be done through social media; just ensure that the process is personalized and allows for open-ended discussion. Predetermined questionnaires distributed by companies are impersonal and do not elicit the same fruitful results. Be open to what your consumers say and how they interpret your product. The following action plan can be used as a guide.

Audience Reception Research Action Plan

1 Research your consumers through a thorough audience analysis.
2 Conduct media ethnography to examine the various platforms and technologies that your consumers use and determine the many ways in which they work together.
3 Understand the various genres of media messages that your consumers use.
4 Complete a textual analysis of your own media messages to uncover possible interpretations and negotiations your consumers will form.
5 Interview consumers to learn about their own sense-making and subsequent decision-making processes.

Very little audience reception research based on monitoring and evaluation efforts exists. One reason for this discrepancy could be the lack of trained researchers that are comfortable with hybrid methodologies. Most institutions focus on either qualitative or quantitative measures. It is important that we begin educating future professionals on both approaches to social media marketing research. Integrative methodologies are key to a successful social media marketing monitoring and evaluation strategy.

Case Study: Walmart

Hybrid research methodologies can prove time-consuming and costly but may result in a strong ROI for an organization. This approach accounts for the active nature of media users. However, not all brands have the capacity or expertise to make sense of the big metric data that social media provides. Even if they have the resources, many companies do not have the employees who have been trained to understand how and why they should pair metric information with deep qualitative research findings. One company that has focused a lot of attention and money on getting this balance is Walmart, an American retail giant.

In 2011, Walmart purchased Kosmix, a holistic categorization engine that aims to organize the Internet information in a more hybrid manner than traditional search (Clifford, 2012). This engine categorizes Internet content into topics and presents the information as magazine-style pages. These pages do not just include informative links, but also related videos, photos, news, commentary, opinions, and communities. One of the greatest advantages of Kosmix is the ability to analyze big metric data and monitor more qualitative social media conversations.

Walmart named this research sector @WalmartLabs, which is now a part of Walmart Global Tech. The section has focused on identifying trends in customer conversations on social media platforms. It may seem unconventional for a retail store to obtain a search engine, especially when you consider the high price tag. This transaction cost Walmart an estimated $300 million (Clifford, 2012). However, the return can be great, when competitors are only able to complete qualitative or quantitative analysis on a smaller scale.

Walmart is proud of its evaluation efforts to meet the needs of their customers wherever they are. This includes a cross-platform approach, where they can see conversations of customers shopping in a store, browsing websites, or using their mobile apps. They aim to use the data-driven strategy to integrate the online and offline shopping experiences for their customers (Thomas, 2021). In addition, Walmart can see how consumers utilize various social media technologies to complete purchasing decisions and online transactions.

Walmart has also worked on data-driven, cross-media efforts. One example of its cross-platform efforts is the collaboration with Pinterest. Walmart launched the first large-scale shoppable recipes on Pinterest (see Figure 12.1), which allows customers add ingredients from the recipe they saw on Pinterest directly to their Walmart carts for purchase (Walk-Morris & Moran, 2021). In addition, a cross-platform partnership between Walmart and the Meredith Corporation provided customers with an AI-powered meal planning experience, including visual search, shoppable recipes, chatbot help, etc. (Walmart, 2021). Here, you can see how Walmart places less emphasis on reaching a homogeneous mass through "push-and-pray" marketing but employs a "content-to-commerce" means to reach its latent consumers (Walk-Morris & Moran, 2021).

Walmart Global Tech has also focused on developing and employing advanced analytics technologies to serve existing and potential customers. Its Global Data and Analytics team allows the company to develop and operate the data feeds, analytics tools, machine learning technology, algorithmic products, and infrastructure to support hundreds of developers, data scientists, and analysts (Thomas, 2021). The company understands the power of data analytics and has made it available to guide its strategic directions.

It should be noted that all the quantitative data is supported with a unique qualitative search feature. The trend function of @WalmartLabs helps the company see nuances in customer conversations, especially between geographical segments of population.

Figure 12.1   Screenshot from Walmart's Pinterest account.

This information is then used to expand reach into new consumer segments by driving traffic into product areas through a visual browsing experience. The technology examines conversations on various social media sites and search terms used by customers. It reports the level of buzz and overall consumer sentiments about products (Clifford, 2012). Walmart then uses the research results to determine which products, and how much, to carry in which stores.

The research team is also able to pinpoint the intricacies between American geographical cultures. One example of how research changes Walmart products is when research identified that consumers in California and the Southwest were most excited about a new spicy chip called Takis. The retailer was then able to introduce a similar private-label product into that market (Clifford, 2012). Rather than taking up shelf space in stores that are less interested, Walmart provides a different shopping experience for every population it serves.

Now, you see how Walmart can use hybrid research approaches, cross-platform data, social media listening, and cultural nuances to increase their ROI. By doing so, Walmart is closing the gap between data scientists and key marketing decision-makers who know consumer behavior well.

Discussion questions

1 Reflect on your own experience. Why is it important for big retail stores like Walmart to have unique research and evaluation team like Walmart Global Tech? How might this research put them ahead of their competitors?
2 One of the advantages of Walmart is the ability to categorize qualitative conversations on social media platforms. How might Walmart use this research to their advantage? How is this method of data collection different from predefined survey questionnaires delivered to customers after a purchase?
3 In your opinion, how could big retail stores use data to inform their new product development and innovative strategy? Why is this important in today's convergent media environment?

Summary

Social media evaluation is transitioning from a quantitative metric-driven only industry to a more user-centered holistic approach. You should consider utilizing both quantitative and qualitative research methods to understand how individuals are making sense of social media messages. These hybrid strategies should be implemented at every stage of the product process, including the creation, production, dissemination, and evaluation of media messages.

Perhaps the most effective way to understand user engagement is through an audience reception study. This is achieved through research centered on your consumers' real-life environment. Learn as much as you can about their individual attitudes, preferences, culture, and social networks. You should also conduct media ethnography to examine the various media that your consumers are accessing, and how they are working together.

Consider how social media is being consumed in today's convergent media landscape. Users are engaging multiple social media platforms simultaneously. Monitoring and evaluation efforts should not just analyze what consumers are doing on each platform but also measure how these platforms are interacting with one another. Cross-platform measurements are vital for understanding the totality of consumer behavior.

Practitioners must also examine various genres of social media messages. Not only focus on technology and devices but also examine the many different messages that individuals are exposed to each day. Be honest about how your product fits within this media landscape. This reflection should stem from a thorough textual analysis of your own media messages. Identify the underlying themes and messages in your content. Consider possible interpretations from various populations. This illustrates the distinction between treating the audience as a large mass and taking the time to consider the individual differences between them. Finally, allow users to retell their experiences with social media content to explain why and how they experienced the content. This dialogue will help you connect with your consumers, uncover rich outside-the-box thinking, and empower them to be your lifetime brand advocates.

In this section, we have learned new and traditional business models, marketing strategies, and evaluation efforts. The next section will focus on incorporating this knowledge into health initiatives, civic engagement, and global development. Part IV of this book will discuss ways in which social media practitioners are able to market their goods for social good. The future social media opportunities exist within a globalized society. Let us explore these opportunities together.

Key Takeaways

1   Social media measurements are beginning to place more value on user engagement and relationships than achieving a large mass following.
2   A hybrid approach to social media evaluation will provide the most complete view into the contextual cues of consumer behavior.
3   Today's technological landscape requires a cross-platform analysis of social media use.
4   Audience reception research will help explain how individuals make sense of media messages, identify differences between consumers, and provide nuances and opportunities for your business.

References

Babbie, E. (2020) *The Practice of Social Research*. Belmont, CA: Wadsworth.

Bernard, H. (2000) *Social Research Methods: Qualitative and Quantitative*. London: Sage Publications.

Beveridge, C. (2022a) Pinterest analytics 101: tips and tools to help you track your success. *Hootsuite*. Available at https://blog.hootsuite.com/pinterest-analytics-for-business/.

Beveridge, C. (2022b) Snapchat insights: how to use the analytics tool. *Hootsuite*. Available at https://blog.hootsuite.com/snapchat-analytics/.

Blanchard, O. (2011) *Social Media ROI: Managing and Measuring Social Media Efforts in your Organization*. Boston: Pearson Education.

Brandwatch (2023) Social listening. Available at https://www.brandwatch.com/p/demo-social-listening/?utm_source=google&utm_medium=cpc&utm_campaign=bw-na-demo-ppc-brand-en-exact-phrase&utm_content=Brand-Exact_/p/book-a-meeting/&utm_term=brandwatch&cq_src=google_ads&cq_cmp=19320211087&cq_term=brandwatch&cq_plac=&cq_net=g&cq_plt=gp&_bt=648436066046&_bk=brandwatch&_bm=e&_bn=g&_bg=143030636045&gclid=Cj0KCQjwyLGjBhDKARIsAFRNgW9VyaEG0aa0m75wYlmZtlSsNDsZ67gHvdZZeTTk9PwpbTwkwAKCNaEaAnQ2EALw_wcB.

Byrne, A. with Gray-Felder, D., Hunt, J. & Parks, W. (2005) Measuring change: a guide to participatory monitoring and evaluation of communication for social change. Available at http://www.communicationforsocialchange. org/pdf/measuring_change.pdf.

Clifford, S. (2012) Social media are giving a voice to taste buds. Available at http://www.nytimes.com/2012/07/31/ technology/facebook-twitter-and-foursquare-ascorporate-focus-groups.html?_r=0.

Curtin, P. (1995) Textual analysis in mass communication studies: theory and methodology. *Paper presented at the 78th Annual Meeting of the Association for Education in Journalism and Mass Communication*, Washington, DC, August 9–12, 1995.

Davis, H. (2006) *Search Engine Optimization*. Sebastopol, CA: O'Reilly Media, Inc.

DiStaso, M., McCorkindale, T. & Wright, D. (2011) How public relations executives perceive and measure the impact of social media in their organizations. *Public Relations Review*, 37(3), 325–328.

Dover, D. & Dafforn, E. (2011) *Search Engine Optimization (SEO) Secrets*. Indianapolis, IN: Wiley Publishing, Inc.

Enge, E., Spencer, S., Stricchiola, J. & Fishkin, R. (2023) *The Art of SEO: Mastering Search Engine Optimization*. Sebastopol, CA: O'Reilly Media, Inc.

Entrepreneur (2014) Focus group. Available at http:// www.entrepreneur.com/encyclopedia/focus-group.

Fiske, J. (1987) *Television Culture*. London: Routledge.

Folkerts, J. & Lacy, S. (2003) *The Media in Your Life: An Introduction to Mass Communication*. Boston: Allyn & Bacon.

Fürsich, E. (2009) In defense of textual analysis: restoring a challenged method for journalism and media studies. *Journalism Studies*, 10(2), 238–252.

Garbarino, S. & Holland, J. (2009) Quantitative and qualitative methods in impact evaluation and measuring results. Available at http://www.gsdrc.org/docs/open/EIRS4.pdf.

Graziano, A. & Raulin, M. (2004) *Research Methods: A Process of Inquiry*. Boston: Pearson.

Hirose, A. (2022) The complete guide to TikTok analytics: how to measure your success. *Hootsuite*. Available at https://blog.hootsuite.com/tiktok-analytics/.

Hootsuite (2023) What analytics does Hootsuite provide? Available at https://www.hootsuite.com/platform/ analytics.

Hudspeth, N. (2012) Building a brand socially. *Journal of Brand Strategy*, 1(1), 25–30.

Johns Hopkins Bloomberg School for Public Health Center for Communication Programs (2007) What is monitoring and evaluation? Available at https://www. k4health.org/sites/default/files/guide-to-monitoring-and-evaluating-health-information.pdf.

Katz, E. (1988) On conceptualizing media effects: another look. In: S. Oskamp (ed) *Television as a Social Issue*. Newbury Park, CA: Sage Publications.

Lindlof, T. (1995) *Qualitative Communication Research Methods*. Thousand Oaks, CA: Sage Publications.

Livingstone, S. (1991) Audience reception: the role of the viewer in retelling romantic drama. Available at http:// eprints.lse.ac.uk/999/1/AudiencereceptionPDFTODAY.pdf.

MacReady, H. (2022) LinkedIn analytics: the complete guide for marketers. *Hootsuite*. Available at https://blog. hootsuite.com/linkedin-analytics/.

Martin, M. (2021) How to use twitter analytics: the complete guide for marketers. *Hootsuite*. Available at https://blog.hootsuite.com/twitter-analytics-guide/.

McCormick, K. (2023) 10+ Free ways to get on the first page of Google. *Wordstream*. Available at https://www. wordstream.com/blog/ws/2020/08/19/get-on-first-page-google#:~:text=In%20fact%2C%20the%20 first%20pageto%206%25%20of%20website%20clicks.

McKee, A. (2003) *Textual Analysis: A Beginner's Guide*. London: Sage Publications.

Newberry, C. (2022) 3 Tools to use instead of Facebook analytics. *Hootsuite*. Available at https://blog.hootsuite. com/facebook-analytics-insights-beginners-guide/.

Newberry, C. & MacReady, H. (2022) What is social listening, why it matters + 14 tools to help. *Hootsuite*. Available at https://blog.hootsuite.com/social-listening-business/.

Petraglia, J. (2007) Narrative intervention in behavior and public health. *Journal of Health Communication*, 21, 493–505.

Seiter, C. (2014) The simple blueprint for social media monitoring: 10 unique insights to look for. *Buffer*. Available at https://buffer.com/library/guide-to-social-media-monitoring/.

Singhal, A. & Rogers, E. (2003) *Combating AIDS: Communication Strategies in Action*. Thousand Oaks, CA: Sage Publications.

Stratten, S. (2012) *UnMarketing. Stop Marketing. Start Engaging*. Hoboken, NJ: John Wiley & Sons, Inc.

Teyes, C. (2022) Facebook analytics: how to analyze your data. *Sprout Social*. Available at https://sproutsocial.com/insights/facebook-analytics/.

Thomas, M. (2021) Walmart Labs. *Query Sprout*. Available at https://querysprout.com/walmart-labs/.

Tufte, T. (2002) Soap operas and sense-making: mediations and audience ethnography. In: A. Singhal, M.J. Cody, E.M. Rogers & M. Sabido (eds) *Entertainment-Education and Social Change: History, Research and Practice*, pp. 399–415. Mahwah, NJ: Lawrence Erlbaum Associates.

Walk-Morris, T. & Moran, C.D. (2021) Walmart to use AR, shoppable content to connect brands with consumers. *Grocery Dive*. Available at https://www.grocerydive.com/news/walmart-to-use-ar-shoppable-content-to-connect-brands-with-consumers/609342/.

Walmart (2021) Walmart and Meredith Corporation partner to help families answer the universal question: What's for dinner? Available at https://corporate.walmart.com/newsroom/2021/09/08/walmart-and-meredith-corporation-partner-to-help-families-answer-the-universal-question-whats-for-dinner.

Watson, Z. (2021) Sprout Social vs Hootsuite: social media comparison. *Technology Advice*. Available at https://technologyadvice.com/blog/marketing/sprout-social-vs-hootsuite-comparing-two-social-media-standouts/

Whalley, B. (2020) The 12 best free social media monitoring tools for every marketing team. *HubSpot*. Available at https://blog.hubspot.com/blog/tabid/6307/bid/29437/20-free-social-media-and-brand-monitoring-tools-that-rock.aspx.

Yasar, K. & Wigmore, I. (2022) Wearable technology. *Tech Target*. Available at https://www.techtarget.com/searchmobilecomputing/definition/wearable-technology#:~:text=Modern%20wearable%20technology%20falls%20underenabled%20glasses%20and%20Bluetooth%20headsets.

Part IV

Marketing for Social Good

13

Social Media for Social Behavior Change

Learning Objectives

After reading this chapter, you should be able to:
1 Apply the principles of *We First* marketing to a social media campaign.
2 Examine the role of identification in the behavior change process.
3 Understand how the creation of a socially conscious strategy may lead to an increased return on investment.

Introduction

Together, we have examined the influence of social media on behavior change literature, perceptions of social media users, business models, and various marketing strategies. While these all point out the dynamic power of social media, perhaps nothing demonstrates as great a potential for global social change as the field of communication. The next five chapters will explore new media transformations in public health, civic engagement, communication for development, and entertainment education for social change.

Throughout each of these chapters, more will be understood regarding social media's role in transferring considerable power from traditional authorities to everyday citizens. Often, this is through social media's participatory features that encourage more transactional

Strategic Social Media: From Marketing to Social Change, Second Edition. L. Meghan Mahoney and Tang Tang.
© 2024 John Wiley & Sons, Inc. Published 2024 by John Wiley & Sons, Inc.

dialogue between users. We have discussed how users want more transparency and interactive opportunities from an organization's social media sites. Understanding these new demands of today and tomorrow's media users is imperative for any organization trying to find their niche in the marketplace.

The purpose of this chapter is to explore how consumers are entering the marketplace with new globalized motivations to build a better world. While not every consumer is interested in taking huge steps toward positive policy reform and more sustainable social structure, there are many ways in which the marketplace is changing through small day-to-day consumer purchasing decisions, both positively and negatively. Marketers have new opportunities to target these socially conscious consumers to make a positive change in society and increase their return on investment at the same time.

Socially conscious consumers are those who are mindful of the consequences of private purchasing decisions and choose products that minimize harmful effects and maximize long-run beneficial impact on society (Mohr et al., 2001). According to research, 55% of consumers are willing to pay more for eco-friendly brands (Ruiz, 2023). Digital media have allowed users to have increased knowledge regarding the products that they consume. This information creates expectations about social issues, such as the environment, and thereby encourages prosocial forms of consumption (Keum et al., 2004).

This chapter begins with an introduction to the *We First* marketing movement and explains how it benefits companies, consumers, and the planet alike. Second, we explore ways in which users can better make purchasing decisions in their daily lives and the responsibility that comes with the privilege of unlimited information access. Then, the chapter explains why humans inherently identify stronger with prosocial consumption practices, which can be better for a business's bottom line. Finally, it explains the Global Reporting Initiative and how business stakeholders are developing transparent and sustainable guidelines for corporate social responsibility programs.

We First

Social media is a critical tool for businesses looking to engage consumers who are interested in changing economic practices to create a better world. *We First* branding explains how social media gives consumers the chance to demand increased transparency into how the products they buy influence the world they inhabit (Mainwaring, 2011). For example, consumers are more aware than ever of the negative environmental impact of increased home package deliveries from online shopping. However, the normal buying and selling patterns of consumerism do not have to remain the same. Today, 58% of online consumers are willing to delay shipping time for fewer package deliveries (Pitney Bowes, 2021). Your digital media users are empowered by online information about which products are best for the environment, global societies, and future generations.

Mainwaring (2023) explains how businesses can work together in new ways to solve sustainable issues of our time, while still maintaining business growth. These purpose-led movements can positively shape culture and turn customers into collaborators and companies into impact leaders (wefirstbranding.com). These efforts extend beyond just fewer shipping boxes at consumers' doorsteps but transcend every stage of a product's production lifecycle, including sourcing, distribution, waste, and employment equity.

In the opening pages of *We First*, Mainwaring (2011) asks readers "Is this the world you want?" Today's free market capitalism is built on the idea of widespread and self-regulating wealth but has also transformed into a single-minded pursuit of profit for a small elite at the expense of the overall society (Mainwaring, 2011). The gap between rich and poor nations is growing, as well as the gap between rich and poor within these nations. There is a correlation between the information technology available in society and the increase in wealth for their economic future (Lucas & Sylla, 2003). Nations with better information access have growing economies, often at the expense of those that do not.

However, today's digitally connected world also provides a lens into these inequities. Everyday users can see photographs, videos, and hear stories from those who are negatively impacted by this system. About 84% of customers say that poor environmental practices will alienate them from a brand or company (Ruiz, 2023). Consumers are also able to see directly into the lives that they impact, both positively and negatively, through social media.

The theory of dependency suggests that the problems of the Third World would not disappear through economic development (Sood & Rogers, 2000) because the world is divided into three categories of societies: core, periphery, and semi-periphery. *Core societies* are wealthy, powerful, early developing societies that maintain independent economic diversity. *Periphery societies* are relatively weak and poor nations that are subject to control by stronger societies. *Semi-periphery societies* are somewhere in between and are attempting to industrialize to gain more independence (Bollen, 1983).

Generally, as peripheral societies develop and gain economic markets, core societies also benefit. This makes it more difficult for peripheral societies to minimize the economic gap because as they get richer, so do the core societies. Developed nations profit from commerce, while peripheral nations suffer from an unequal exchange process.

In some ways, digital technologies have increased this gap between the rich and poor (Lucas & Sylla, 2003). Companies are now able to hire employees anywhere in the world, which may lead to lower wages and decreased employee regulations. While this does create greater job opportunities for some regions of the world, corporations also increase profits due to the lower cost of operation. Thus, the wide profit gap continues.

Many companies find that the least expensive option is to manufacture products at the expense of environmental concerns and poor labor practices to keep sales costs low and competitive. China is the world's largest manufacturer. This has severe consequences on the land, which is not designed to support such heavy usage. In China's northwest region, one-third of the country's grassland has now turned to desert (Matisoff, 2013). Dust storms carry pollutants to surrounding areas, causing some of the most heavily polluted cities in the world.

Consumers play an important role in the mounting pressure on businesses to keep costs low. Mainwaring (2011) warns that unless something is changed about the ways in which all societies consume products, we will only secure short-term profit for the few at the expense of the environment and peripheral societies. Consequently, these changes will begin negatively impact the majority.

The shift from *Me First* thinking, where everyone is concerned with the single-minded pursuit of profit, to *We First* thinking, where all corporations, businesses, consumers, and citizens use capitalism as a driver of prosperity for the greater good, is more possible than ever before (Mainwaring, 2011). Social media provides the opportunity for individuals to connect around shared values and take action. Consumers are now sharing brand narratives, as well as their experiences related to the products that they purchase. We have become more mindful about the products that we buy, and if we take the time to realize the influence that our purchasing decisions have on the world in production, distribution, and profit stages, we can make small changes to fight against poverty, child mortality, clean water, renewable energy, climate change, and environment degradation (www.wefirstbranding.com).

There are many social media resources that consumers can turn to when making such a decision. Envimpact.org provides users with a composite environmental index that measures the life cycle of products and how much pollution is created to produce, use, and dispose of them. There is also a forum where users discuss other ways that they can get involved in local initiatives to help with the environment. LocalHarvest.org is a website where users can go and look up local organic foods that are grown and produced in their neighborhood. The Local Harvest blog discusses the benefits of eating local and organic and shares pictures from around the United States. LaborVoices.com provides workers the opportunity to anonymously report unfair working conditions, which helps guide employees to the best factories to work with and puts pressure on corporations to only supply their products through the most reputable manufacturers.

People around the world are using social media to share concerns and inform themselves about consumption decisions. Mainwaring (2011) identifies globalization, interconnectedness, complexity of problems, population explosion, environmental threats, power shifts, and demographics of change as the reasons individuals are moving toward *We First* consumption.

We receive information from all over the world each day, causing us to see ourselves and the role we play in society as larger than just our everyday community. Younger generations see themselves as a member of a globalized society with less borders and increased cross-cultural communication. A stronger and more reliant interconnectedness between societies comes with globalization. In sum, today we are more mindful about the community we live in and the impact this livelihood has on others.

The theory of dependency illustrates how the actions of one society hold consequences for others. For example, simply throwing trash on the ground directly impacts the appearance of your own community, but it also has deeper consequences for wildlife, water sources, and vegetation. This helps to demonstrate the complexity of economic inequity around the world.

World populations are growing at an alarming rate, and the planet cannot sustain the rapid growth. Two billion people are expected to be added to our global population by 2050 and an additional 1 billion more by 2100 (United Nations, 2019). The planet cannot sustain renewable energies, food production and clean water supplies, and the effects of increased pollution (Ehrlich & Holdren, 1971). By visiting a developing nation with the intention to build stronger infrastructure and bigger buildings and increase consumerism, the larger problems of the Third World are not solved. Moreover, it could further widen the gap between wealthy and poor societies. To a certain extent, every single human is responsible for the destabilization of ecological systems and use of renewable and nonrenewable resources.

While it may be easy for businesses to ignore these environmental threats, the general public cannot. Public concerns for environmental issues have steadily increased over the years (Dunlap, 1991). These environment concerns create environmental responsibility, a powerful driving force that motivates individuals to bear environmental responsibility and engage in pro-environmental consumption behavior (Yue et al., 2020). Individuals are more mindful than ever on issues such as climate change and carbon emissions. New technology allows consumers the opportunity to find information and communicate with businesses about their growing concerns. There has been a shift in power where businesses are no longer able to make decisions behind closed doors and must answer to the demands of everyday consumers. Companies today are also concerned with a more diverse demographic of consumers than in previous decades. Previously muted minority cultures now have a voice through social media.

Part III of this book discussed how social media created business opportunities for every market segment and niche consumers. While previous advertising efforts may have been focused on demographics with the most spending power, companies are now realizing the potential for marketing to all demographics. Based on all these changes, it has never been a better time to change our consumption and production habits. It is clear why *We First* consumption is the best approach for the environment, workers, and consumers. One of the most interesting findings to emerge from the last decade of marketing research is the possibility for businesses to increase profit through socially conscious marketing.

Traditional marketing research demonstrates how companies that associate themselves with a prosocial cause for a variety of reasons, including the ability to gain national visibility, enhance corporate image, promote repeat purchases, increase brand awareness, broaden customer base, and reach new market segments (Varadarajan & Menon, 1988). It can be a good economic decision for a brand to identify itself with a cause; however, profit should not be the sole reason for doing so. Mainwaring (2011) calls for *profit with a purpose*, where businesses build their brand and prosocial movement through their authenticity and the company's true values. There are many ways in which consumers can utilize social media to determine how authentic corporations are regarding their cause.

As we move forward with more conscious consumer purchasing decisions, much of the burden for change falls on everyday citizens. While large corporations can make more socially conscious decisions, they will not do so without pressure from consumers. The next section explores ways in which you can change your own daily purchasing habits to better align with the *We First* strategy.

Role of the User

One of the oldest ways in which businesses have aimed to improve the world around them is through corporate social responsibility programs. *Corporate social responsibility* (CSR) is the policy and practice of corporate social involvement to satisfy social needs through economic, legal, ethical, and philanthropic responsibilities (Lii, 2011). There are three types of philanthropic CSR: sponsorship, cause-related marketing, and philanthropy.

1   *Sponsorship* includes a strategic investment where resources (money, staffing, or facility) are given to an activity with commercial gain. Companies may sponsor a local sports team or help with a charitable event. These are great ways to boost brand images. Sponsorships often work best if there is a clear link between the product and the charity. For example, Nike's sponsorship of basketball superstar Lebron James makes sense, given both of their commitment to sport and athleticism. Many felt as though Coca-Cola's continued sponsorship of the Olympic Games is inappropriate because it led to increased junk food advertising toward children (Backholer, Zorbas & Martino, 2021).
2   *Cause-related marketing* is when a company promises to donate a certain amount of money to a social cause when consumers purchase products or services. For example, Primark's (RED) campaign donates 10% of all profits to the Global Fund to fight AIDS and ensure equitable treatment of diseases. However, many online communities are critical of the company's enormous overlay, marketing costs, and lack of nonprofit collaboration. The company has faced backlash for its inequitable sourcing of materials and unfairly paid workers (Cano, 2021). The best way to build a cause-related marketing strategy is to increase transparency to consumers regarding how much of the profit actually is donated and the tangible results of the initiative. This is where you see the benefits of a strong diffusion strategy.
3   *Philanthropy* is when a business donates to a cause simply to be a good citizen, without expectations for commercial or economic gain. More businesses around the world are allowing employees to take paid volunteer days to volunteer at the charity of their choice. This has resulted in better turnover rates, higher job satisfaction, and stronger employee enthusiasm (Baxter, 2013). Philanthropy also helps bolster business image around the community, as employees would likely spread volunteering efforts across many initiatives, not just the one or two causes that the head of the company chose.

There are many reasons why a company would choose to engage in CSR. Consumers who identify with a cause are likely to exhibit increased loyalty, repeat purchasing behaviors, spread positive word of mouth, and show increased resilience to negative information (Lii, 2011). While consumption often makes customers feel bad for spending money, especially if it is something they do not need, cause branding makes them feel satisfied because it appeals to the natural human impulse to help others. Moreover, consumers begin to associate the feeling of helping others with the brand and identify strongly with the mutual desire to help others. Research pointed out that married mothers are the most likely consumers to spend more for prosocial products (Laroche et al., 2001). This demographic has huge spending power and has always been the primary target for corporate advertising. Cause marketing is a great way to gain their long-term loyalty and trust.

More than 80% of the Fortune 500 companies market the CSR programs that they participate in, especially as marketing becomes more of a norm in business practices. Not all CSR programs are as altruistic as the brand makes them appear. In fact, there have been calls to end CSR programs, as they seem more focused on attracting new customers than integrating strategy into overall brand purpose and tangible good (Strandberg, 2019). Consumers must be wary of cause washing, green washing, and local washing from corporate marketing. These three marketing challenges have increased greatly over the past decade as more brands navigate consumer expectations for sustainability.

Generally, *cause washing* is associated with events where the number of units sold is correlated with an associated donation to the cause. Often, these donation numbers are miniscule or have established donation limits set ahead of time. In this case, it does not make a difference how many units consumers buy, though consumers feel as though they are making a difference by contributing. The website Think Before You Pink (www.thinkbeforeyoupink.org) provides a critical look into the feel-good cause marketing programs. They investigate the percentage of proceeds from pink breast cancer awareness products that goes toward cancer research. Often, the results are surprisingly low. The website also raises awareness about "pink" products that contain chemicals that may be linked to breast cancer.

Green marketing is trendy now, as businesses know that most consumers are willing to spend more for a product if they feel it is better for the environment than an alternative product. *Green washing* is when the environmental friendliness of a brand is overstated. Greenwashing.com has created an online index where users are able to post a product that they have seen being advertised as good for the environment, and other community members can rate it with a "thumbs up" or a "bogus thumbs down." Plastic water bottles that advertise being green for reducing carbon emissions are often at the top of the bogus list for making it appear that using plastic water bottles is a green thing to do.

Consumers are also willing to spend more money on products they feel are produced, manufactured, or grown locally (Brown, 2003; Su et al., 2019). There are many societal benefits to buying local. Local consumer spending keeps profits within the community where it is more evenly distributed than from large corporations. It also reduces environmental impacts due to a decrease in packaging and travel costs. Many companies are realizing that localness is becoming more important to today's informed consumers.

However, *local washing* is whenever a company makes a product appear more local than it is (Mainwaring, 2011). Often, there are no regulations about what it means to be a locally sourced product. In Des Moines, Iowa, the term means that the products come from within the state; the New Orleans' Crescent City market includes the whole Gulf Cost; while the Park Slope Food Coop in New York defines local as coming from within 500 miles (Food Print, 2020).

As a consumer with access to unlimited information online, it is imperative to begin investigating the types of products that you buy and their impact on the environment. Generally, consumers look for a logical fit between a brand and a cause. They want to clearly see why a brand chooses to invest in a social cause (Barone et al., 2007). The alliance must make sense, and if it does not and the cause is "washed," users will turn to social media to voice their outrage.

Consumers also want to see companies make investments consistent with their own values (Gupta & Pirsch, 2006). Identification is one of the most critical assessments consumers will make when selecting a cause. It is impossible for you to care about all causes, and so it is important to determine what is the most important to you and find corporations that align with your values. Once you have found companies that share in your philanthropy goals, purchasing behaviors will turn into habitual routines, and you will not even notice the change.

Perhaps you are interested in natural living but have always found it difficult to navigate natural products in big box stores. Shopping in traditional stores for natural products can leave consumers with little choice and higher-priced items. With a few minutes of Internet research, you are likely able to find hundreds of online and in-store options for retailers that only sell natural products. For instance, Thrive Market is an online retailer for thousands of natural and organic goods, including grocery, beauty, cleaning, and even pets. For a product to be available on Thrive Market, the company reviews the product standards on dimensions of quality, sustainability, and affordability. This retailer puts all natural options in one place, making it easier than ever to find natural products online that fit within your lifestyle and budget.

It would prove incredibly time-consuming to research every single product before purchasing. By choosing a small number of important causes that are unique to your life experiences, it will not take much effort to change your buying habits. Chances are there is a social media community that is dedicated to the same vision: Join, participate, and share your experiences. Even if you just change one or two habits, it will make a difference. Do not worry about causes that you are not enthusiastic about. There is a social media community out there filled with people who strongly identify with their goals and values. It is their job to spread awareness and put pressure on companies in support of their initiatives. Focus on the prosocial causes that you already esteem and the information and research you would enjoy receiving. Be a vocal and participatory member for the causes that you feel the most passionate about.

It is your job as a consumer to spread the word if you see something that does not align with your prosocial vision. If you walk by a business that markets themselves as "green" yet has recyclable materials in their dumpster, put pressure on them to make a change. They may appreciate the suggestion, as they are hopefully invested in their green marketing strategy. Amazon has taken active steps to contact outside vendors that receive negative feedback from customers about excess product packaging. They send engineers to help companies build better designs. This initiative boosts customer satisfaction, lowers shipping costs, and appeals to environmentally conscious consumers (Edwards, 2011).

Research has found that 30% of consumers claimed that they would give priority to pro-environmental products and services, but only 3% of consumers made green purchasing decisions (Yue et al., 2020). Changing consumption behavior is difficult. While individual users hold some responsibility in researching the products that they buy online, the more pressure we can put on businesses, the more they will voluntarily increase their standards for sustainability. It would be great to live in a world where individuals do not have to research every single product before purchasing because all businesses engage in ethical and long-term prosocial decision-making. Until then, it is our role and duty as consumers to be mindful about the products we buy.

We are all consumers of products. *We First* thinking encourages you to think about how your purchasing decisions influence the world around you. As a current or future social media practitioner, it is likely that you will have a say in future business strategies of the world. The next section explains the benefits of cause marketing, both on the world and on the company's bottom line.

We First Action Plan

1   Understand how to integrate your niche authenticity into cause marketing. Curate social media content that is consistent with this authenticity.
2   Consider a holistic Corporate Social Responsibility program that helps build social networks and connections at every stage of the production process.
3   Do not engage in cause washing by promoting deceitful corporate social responsibility. While cause marketing can increase your return on investment, that should not be the primary goal.
4   Increase transparency and dialogue surrounding cause marketing. Be forthcoming with how your business practices impact the cause, both positively and negatively.
5   Align your brand with other networks with similar goals and cause missions.

Identification Through Social Behavior

Mainwaring (2011) outlines a *consumer evolution process* toward more responsible consumption habits, which includes individual commitment, community engagement, promotion of values, driving awareness, thought leadership, building a community, and connecting communities.

Individual commitment is the stage in which consumers change their own habits through more mindful shopping. They use the Internet to gain product information and investigate the ways in which their habits influence the world around them. Next, they enter the community engagement stage. Here, they find online communities and participate in online conversations with like-minded individuals.

The third stage, *promotion of values*, is when consumers start to communicate with others in their network about their values, beyond those who already agree. They begin advocating through social media and taking real-life actions to push back on companies whose visions do not align. This leads to the driving awareness stage. Others outside of the cause encounter these messages, which leads to an increased awareness. The activist's individual social network becomes more knowledgeable about the cause, as well as targeted organizations and businesses. In this stage, the single vision has turned into a more collaborative effort among a network.

Eventually, consumers become leaders and advocates for the cause. They then enter the thought leadership process, where they generate arguments that others need to persuade the public. These can take the form of books, articles, interviews, videos, webinars, blogs, and social media posts (Mainwaring, 2011). This process leads to building a community where consumers organize people to take collective action. This can occur online or offline. Finally, they connect with other communities to synchronize efforts, which results in a strong social change movement.

It is imperative for consumers to research and investigate the products that they buy to understand the impact it is making on society. It is also a smart business choice for corporations to brand themselves authentically through prosocial behaviors. Humans identify emotionally with cause marketing, which can lead toward more loyal and long-term brand advocates. Social media professionals must take advantage of this opportunity and fulfill people's natural desire to positively impact the world.

Advertising has always engaged in lifestyle marketing, where messages tell consumers the latest indicators of self-worth and social distinction and what makes "the good life." Consequently, consumers engage in status-conscious consumption where we desire to purchase goods that meet these ideals (Keum et al., 2004).

We use consumption to brand ourselves and the roles we play in society. *Social identity theory* demonstrates how humans perceive themselves through their interactions with others, the status of their network, and support from institutions (Ashforth & Mael, 1989). These distinctions are traditionally formed based on the community in which we live. If you were unable to find acceptance in your local proximity, your social identity consequently suffered. Social media has provided a space where you are able to find community outside the boundaries of where you live.

Nonetheless, shared identity is something that is difficult, if not impossible, to achieve with brands and corporations. After all, if humans perceive themselves based on interactions, status, and support, there is a natural power difference in the consumption process. Consumers have always been at the bottom of the corporate relationship. Though a free-market society is built on the premise that everyday consumers play a role in what is available and how much products cost, the process is complex. Consumers are unlikely to feel as though they have power as they hand their money over to corporations.

Social media has made great strides in transforming this relationship. We have discussed how consumers now have participatory relationships with brands through social media. They are now able to access, share, and communicate with corporations. This helps consumers identify with businesses, as there is a real person responding (hopefully!) to social media messages. Consumers also have the digital tools and skills to create product reviews or become brand ambassadors within their social network.

Brands are also able to promote status in a way that members of our community are not. It feels very different receiving a message from a major corporation, especially one that you identify with, than receiving a message from your friend. We get excited. We share the experience with our network. This becomes a unique part of our life experience, and we feel valued by the brand. This is a brand's way of lending support, which increases identification even more.

Think of the prosocial cause that you strongly identify with. Is it cancer research? Environmental issues? Animal activism? There is a real-life experience that has made you passionate about that initiative. Maybe your mother was diagnosed with breast cancer, and you were able to talk to others going through the same scary experience. Online communities are formed based on these mutual experiences. Individuals who have never met in person are able to create and sustain relationships through these shared concerns Companies are now able to access these relationships and say, "I care about that too." Every time you walk by a product that has "gone pink" in support of breast cancer research, maybe you will think of your mother. This makes shopping a much more emotional experience. Hopefully, this message is delivered with an authentic narrative that extends beyond increasing profits.

Humans have a natural desire to make a positive impact on the world. Volunteering increases individual happiness, life satisfaction, self-esteem, and sense of control over life (Thoits & Hewitt, 2001). Consumers can experience some of the emotional benefits of giving that they would not typically receive through traditional consumption of goods. This purchase satisfaction is longer lasting as you feel positive about the cause each time it is used. These initiatives are also able to create a social experience, as people encounter others who have invested themselves in the same initiatives. This works best if a product is branded differently from traditional products, such as pink awareness ribbons or green sustainable products. Maybe every time you see someone wearing Primark Product (RED) item, you think more positively of them. They have branded themselves as someone who cares about a cause and is willing to purchase products to make a difference.

While there is much debate in the field about whether businesses are engaging in CSR activities solely for profit's sake, the positive potential for social change is there. Humans want others to associate them as someone who cares about the world. This desire can translate into purchasing products that are better for social good.

Case Study: Scout Canning

This chapter highlights the many ways in which consumers are putting pressure on businesses to create a more mindful and sustainable marketplace. It is important to highlight the many ways in which businesses are taking proactive initiatives by creating prosocial measures on their own. These businesses are disrupting the industry and paving the path toward capitalism that positively influence society.

Scout Canning, a North American craft seafood cannery founded in 2019, is one example of a business with an authentic desire for change. The mission of Scout Canning is to create responsibly source seafood. The business model of the company is built upon three key principles: (i) Consumers should know where their seafood comes from; (ii) all sourcing decisions should be mindfully made with consideration of the future health of our planet; and (iii) the company and its partners should focus on promoting biodiversity by working with a greater variety of species that have been deemed safe and abundant by third-party auditors (We First, 2023). The authenticity of these principles come through in all branding and marketing of the company.

This chapter has discussed how a company can increase trust with consumers by providing additional transparency about its production process. Scout Canning capitalizes on that through increasing information about where the fish was caught. Its packaging also includes a sourcing map that tells consumers what region their product originates (Figure 13.1). Though this transparency step may seem simple, it is the first of the canned seafood market to do so. Having this information helps consumers feel like they are consuming a higher quality product and not just artificial filler that is filled with preservatives. Consumers of the $27 billion canned seafood market value this information (We First, 2023).

The remaining two principles of Scout Canning are more important, as global production of fish and seafood has quadrupled over the past 50 years. The average person now eats almost twice as much seafood as half a century ago (Ritchie & Roser, 2021). Globally, humans are simply catching more fish than there are available,

Figure 13.1   Scout Canning website. Source: Scout / https://enjoyscout.com/collections/salmon/
products/wild-pink-salmon-4-pack / last accessed 26 September, 2023.

creating an unsustainable industry that is terrorizing the ocean ecosystem. When
consumers think of seafood distributors, they may think of these negative stories and
images of an industry depleting the environment. Scout Canning attempts to change
this association through their social responsibility initiatives.

The only way to create a more sustainable seafood system is for businesses to
engage in more ethical practices. Scout Canning has partnered with the Marine
Stewardship Council to set standards for sustainable fishing. This relationship
ensures that the fishes caught by the company comply with the standards of a
healthy ocean ecosystem. The company is not just doing the bare minimum to
comply with the rules and standards set forth, but they are actively involved in
creation and reform.

Moreover, Scout Canning engages in cause marketing by partnering with *1 Percent
for the Planet*, a campaign to help protect oceans and waterways by re-investing 1
percent of profits into climate action. This investment helps restore many of the most
high-risk and dependent populations of the fishing industry. The cause marketing
partnership benefits everyone, as research and action into saving the biodiversity of
the ocean ecosystem are important for the sustainability of the seafood industry.

This holistic business practice is consistent with the values of *We First* marketing.
Sustainability is the heart of the mission of Scout Canning. This disruption to the
industry changes the structure and power between companies and consumers.
Consumers can get a quality product that they can feel good about consuming. Here,
you can see how consumers identify stronger with companies that align their values.
The strategy proves successful, as Scout Canning products are now sold in over 2000
stores, including giant retailers such as Whole Foods and Wegmans.

Discussion questions

1   How does Scout Canning's initiative align with the principles of *We First* marketing?
2   In your opinion, what role does transparency play in the relationship between Scout Canning and its consumers? How does its vision help build trust with users?
3   Consider your own life experience. What is something in your life that you wish could be better. How could you use social media to help change some of these scenarios?

Summary

This chapter further demonstrates how organizations looking to incorporate prosocial marketing into their business strategies should highlight diffusion, community, and mobilization for consumers. There must be clear diffusion of information regarding the authenticity of prosocial initiatives. Companies should share their story about why they get involved with the chosen movement. There are numerous examples of companies successfully providing this narrative for consumers.

Brand narratives are very important to how consumers emotionally connect with your company. The McDonald's website shares the story of the first Ronald McDonald house opening in Philadelphia in 1974 and how it led to their mission to create, find, and support programs that directly improve the health and well-being of children (RMHC, 2023). Apple's website includes an interactive section where users can see a visual timeline for how every product is produced and distributed and why this transparency is important to them (Apple, 2023). Coca-Cola's website shares the personal experience of individual team members and their transformation from being hired, to their shared vision with the brand's commitment to partnership between business, government, and civic society (Knoll, 2013).

These narratives help consumers identify more strongly with the brand. It is also important for companies to provide as much transparency as possible about the production, consumption, and profit of their products. Remember that consumer trust increases with the amount of information provided by the company. It should be made as easy as possible for consumers to identify what societal impact the company is making.

Community is a critical part of the *We First* strategy. It is the responsibility of each consumer to determine which social issue they identify strongest with and join online communities that share in that vision. By becoming more mindful in product choice, consumers advance on the customer evolution process, which helps spread awareness and puts pressure on organizations to make more responsible production and distribution decisions. If we all used the power of collective community, it would take less research and mindfulness to make conscious consumer decisions.

Finally, mobilization is another essential element of the behavior change process. It is not enough for users to care about certain prosocial issues, but this concern must translate into real-life action. Every small mindful purchasing decision becomes a part of routine and habit. Eventually, these small changes evolve into personal advocates for social change. Social media makes it easier than ever to investigate the impact your purchasing decisions make on the world. Investigate sustainability and environment indexes and be willing to align your money with your value system. Mobilization allows consumers to join with other organizations and collaborate for change. These small real-life mobilization efforts will translate into substantial social changes.

When *We First* asked "Is this the world you want?," we likely all considered our own life experiences. There is something in all our lives that we wish could be better: a family member not to be sick; education not to be so expensive; more time to spend with friends. We can use social media to help change some of these scenarios. While it is always important to take a step back and look at what we can improve about our own lives, it is refreshing to see that future generations are taking the time to look at the lives and societies around them. It is probably the time to ask "Is this the world that *they* want? Is this the world that they *deserve*?" Your everyday actions hold a potential in making things better for everyone.

This chapter discusses ways in which the *We First* movement changes the structure and power between companies and consumers and explains the small changes that individuals can make to be more mindful of our environment and world. The next chapters will highlight ways in which social media could influence specific areas of our lives, including the public health industry, civic engagement, communication for development, and entertainment education for social change. It is not just communication and marketing practitioners that prove interested in these changes. Nearly every field has been impacted by changes in user communication and expectations through social media. Let's explore social media use in the public health industry in Chapter 14.

Key Takeaways

1   In an increasingly globalized society, it is difficult to ignore the way everyday purchasing decisions influence societies around us. This has caused consumers and businesses alike to start shifting decisions from what is in their best interests to what is best for society.

2   Social media is the key to *We First* thinking because it allows users to seek information, communicate with brands, and unite for collective action.

3   Brands are beginning to build prosocial programs in response to an increased consumer push. The most successful programs are those that are authentic, transparent, and accountable.

4   Users can do more research on the brands that they purchase. This investigation can uncover cause washing, local washing, and green washing of products by businesses looking to make a profit without an authentic concern for the cause.

5   Consumers are willing to spend more money on products that align with their own social values. This helps companies make a profit while making more responsible decisions and helps consumers brand themselves as prosocial conscious consumers.

References

Apple (2023) Apple and the environment. Available at https://www.apple.com/environment/.

Ashforth, B. & Mael, F. (1989) Social identity theory and the organization. *Academy of Management Review*, 14(1), 20–39.

Backholer, K., Zorbas, C. & Martino, F. (2021) Junk food companies have no place on the Olympic sponsorship podium. Available at https://intouchpublichealth.net.au/junk-food-companies-have-no-place-on-the-olympic-sponsorship-podium.

Barone, M., Norman, A. & Miyazaki, A. (2007) Consumer response to retailer use of cause-related marketing: is more fit better? *Journal of Retailing*, 83(4), 437–445.

Baxter, A. (2013) More companies encourage workers to volunteer, on the clock. Available at http://www.npr.org/2013/08/14/211961622/more-companiesencourage-workers-to-volunteer-on-the-clock.

Bollen, K. (1983) World system position, dependency, and democracy: the cross-national evidence. *American Sociological Review*, 48(4), 468–479.

Brown, C. (2003) Consumers' preferences for locally produced food: a study in southeast Missouri. *American Journal of Alternative Agriculture*, 18(4), 213–224.

Cano, L. (2021) What is Primark cares? Available at https://itslauracano.com/blog/what-is-primark-cares-lets-talk-about-greenwashing/.

Dunlap, R.E. (1991) Trends in public opinion toward environmental issues: 1965–1990. *Society and Natural Resources*, 4(3), 285–312.

Edwards, C. (2011) Wal-Mart joining Amazon to promote rage-free packaging: retail. Available at http://www.bloomberg.com/news/2011-11-29/wal-mart-joiningamazon-to-promote-rage-free-packaging-retail.html.

Ehrlich, P. & Holdren, J. (1971) Impact of population growth. *Science*, 171(3977), 1212–1217.

Food Print (2020) Local and regional food systems. Available at https://foodprint.org/issues/local-regional-food-systems.

Gupta, S. & Pirsch, J. (2006) The company-cause-customer fit decision in cause-related marketing. *Journal of Consumer Marketing*, 23(6), 314–326.

Keum, H., Devanathan, N., Deshpande, S., Nelson, M.R. & Shah, D.V. (2004) The citizen-consumer: media effects at the intersection of consumer and civic culture. *Political Communication*, 21(3), 369–391.

Knoll, J. (2013) My China residency and Coca-Cola. Available at http://www.coca-colacompany.com/coca-cola-unbottled/my-china-residency-and-coca-cola.

Laroche, M., Bergeron, J. & Barbaro-Forleo, G. (2001) Targeting consumers who are willing to pay more for environmentally friendly products. *Journal of Consumer Marketing*, 18(6), 503–520.

Lii, Y. (2011) The effect of Corporate Social Responsibility (CSR) initiatives on consumers' identification with companies. *African Journal of Business Management*, 5(5), 1642–1649.

Lucas, H. & Sylla, R. (2003) The global impact of the Internet: widening the economic gap between wealthy and poor nations? *Prometheus*, 21(1), 1–22.

Mainwaring, S. (2011) *We First: How Brands and Consumers Use Social Media to Build a Better World.* New York: St Martin's Press.

Mainwaring, S. (2023) *Lead with We: The Business Revolution that Will Save Our Future*. Dallas, TX: Matt Holt.

Matisoff, A. (2013) Manufacturing malady: The hidden cost of a product. Available at: http://asiasociety.org/education/students/global-topics/manufacturing-malady-hidden-cost-product.

Mohr, L., Webb, D. & Harris, K. (2001) Do consumers expect companies to be socially responsible? The impact of corporate social responsibility on buying behavior. *Journal of Consumer Affairs*, 35(1), 45–72.

Pitney Bowes (2021) How many deliveries are too many? Available at https://www.pitneybowes.com/us/blog/too-many-deliveries.html.

Ritchie, H. & Roser, M. (2021) Fish and overfishing. Available at https://ourworldindata.org/fish-and-overfishing.

RMHC (2023) Ronald McDonald house: Our history. Available at http://www.rmhc.org/our-history.

Ruiz, A. (2023) The round up. Available at: https://theroundup.org/environmentally-conscious-consumer-statistics/#:~:text=Sources-Key%20Statistics,feel%20that%20sustainability%20is%20important.

Sood, S. & Rogers, E. (2000) Dimensions of parasocial interaction by letter-writers to a popular entertainment-education soap in India. *Journal of Broadcasting and Electronic Media*, 44, 386–414.

Strandberg, C. (2019) Is this the end of corporate social responsibility? Available at https://www.greenbiz.com/article/end-corporate-social-responsibility.

Su, C.H., Tsai, C.H., Chen, M.H. & Lv, W.Q. (2019) US sustainable food market generation Z consumer segments. *Sustainability*, 11(13), 3607.

Thoits, P. & Hewitt, L. (2001) Volunteer work and wellbeing. *Journal of Health and Social Behavior*, 42(2) 115–131.

United Nations (2019) World population prospects. Available at https://population.un.org/wpp.

Varadarajan, P. & Menon, A. (1988) Cause-related marketing: a coalignment of marketing strategy and corporate philanthropy. *Journal of Marketing*, 52(3), 58–74.

We First (2023) Growth through purpose. Available at https://wefirstbranding.com/scout-the-future-of-mindfully-sourced-seafood/.

Yue, B., Sheng, G., She, S. & Xu, J. (2020) Impact of consumer environmental responsibility on green consumption behavior in China: the role of environmental concern and price sensitivity. *Sustainability*, 12(5), 2074.

14

Social Media and Health Campaigns

Learning Objectives

After reading this chapter, you should be able to:
1 Understand the activation theory of information exposure.
2 Apply concepts from the health belief model to a public health social media trategy.
3 Practice mobile reach to meet strategic marketing goals.

Introduction

Chapter 13 discussed We First strategy and explained how social media has transferred considerable power from traditional authorities to everyday citizens. For the healthcare industry, this includes understanding the power of physicians, hospitals, and insurance companies, and creating efforts that help empower patients, family, and communities for positive action. Health communication scholars have spent considerable efforts over the past decade determining the best way to disseminate and engage users interested in personal healthcare management. Many of the strategies discussed in this chapter are like the persuasive techniques outlined in Part I of this book. Ultimately, the strategy for establishing behavior change remains consistent regardless of the discipline or content that the message

Strategic Social Media: From Marketing to Social Change, Second Edition. L. Meghan Mahoney and Tang Tang.
© 2024 John Wiley & Sons, Inc. Published 2024 by John Wiley & Sons, Inc.

contains. However, it is important for social media and health communication specialists to understand these changes and the influence of access on the welfare of society.

Today, over 80% of Internet users seek health information online (Finney Rutten *et al.*, 2019). The health-centered websites are the number one resource for users interested in being more proactive with their personal healthcare management and cover everything from long-term illness, common colds, mental health, weight loss, or even skincare (McMillan & Macias, 2008; Stellefson *et al.*, 2020). Many people use the Internet as their primary source when seeking health information. Patients are now able to gather information from their home living room, or on the go through mobile technology. This convenient information access increases the public's knowledge, awareness, and empowerment regarding personal health issues. Moreover, it fuels a new expectation for patients to act, reinforce knowledge, and refute incorrect health myths (National Cancer Institute, 2001).

In addition to seeking health information online, social media provides opportunities for individuals to video chat with physicians, find a community with similar diagnoses, or ask for support from their current social network. While these may not seem like huge influences when it comes to the treatment and prevention of certain illnesses, they have drastically changed the amount and type of health communication the average patient engages.

Increased health communication provides individuals with more choices, both in their own personal healthcare management (Collins *et al.*, 2002) and in healthcare provider decisions and treatment advice (Haean *et al.*, 2008; Stellefson *et al.*, 2020). Health websites do more than just diagnose possible ailments, but also provide alternative treatment options and recommend various physicians in a patient's area of residency. All could lead to better health outcomes. Research demonstrates that patients who are more proactive in personal health management are more willing to follow treatment advice (Berry *et al.*, 2008; Kelly *et al.*, 2020). While it may be easy to dismiss what a physician has prescribed, it is less likely that an individual will ignore information sought through his or her own efforts.

It is possible that you have been using social media for health information without even realizing that you had crossed into the public health sector. Do you know someone who hates going to the doctor in your social network? Hopefully, you or someone else in the network encourage them to get regular check-ups. If they are still unwilling, social media proves a resource for information that may prompt them to seek treatment. While online information should never replace the expertise of a physician, it does change the amount of top-down power physicians previously held. Individuals hold more locus of control and accessibility over their health. Social media also allows the opportunity for many hard-to-reach patients to be seen by physicians through video messaging (Connolly *et al.*, 2021; Hawn, 2009), or simply allows an opportunity for patients to seek the information on their own through health communities and websites.

While there are many benefits to online health communication, it is presenting many challenges in the field of health communication. This chapter explores the theoretical underpinnings of personal healthcare decision-making, as well as the advances of digital healthcare. Additionally, we explore the benefits of increased information access and the challenges of misinformation and healthcare marketing.

Activation Theory of Information Exposure

Making decisions about personal healthcare management is complicated. Perhaps you have been lucky enough to go through life thus far without having the need to make decisions regarding your own health or, even more difficult, the healthcare of someone close to you. Think of a person that you know in your own social circle who smokes cigarettes, whether the behavior is social or habitual in nature. Do you believe that they are unaware of the many adverse effects of smoking? Chances are, if they grew up in today's public health information age, they understand that smoking tobacco puts them at greater risk for cancer, respiratory disease, cardiovascular disease, and death (Centers for Disease Control, 2013). Why would someone still choose to smoke if they know it is bad for them? The same is true for individuals who binge drink, don't exercise, or consistently make poor diet decisions. When you think about how social media can help people to navigate these important health choices, it is necessary to understand the complicated cognitive processes that humans undergo when it comes to their personal healthcare decisions.

Chapter 2 discussed how difficult it is to achieve permanent behavior change in individuals through diffusion-centric media messages. It is not enough to spread knowledge and awareness about a certain health issue. Yes, cigarette smoking is an unhealthy habit. What type of message would it take for this knowledge to transform into a tangible decision not to smoke? The answer is different for everyone. What works for one individual may not work for someone else. Skilled health communication experts have been developing strategies for other impacting factors in the way we make decisions regarding personal health management. This strategy will increase the likelihood of an individual receiving a public health message and following through with the requested behavior change.

Health communication is defined as the art and technique of informing, influencing, and motivating individual, institutional, and public audiences about important health issues (Ratzan *et al.*, 1994). Scholars and health communication specialists have focused on topics such as disease prevention, health promotion, healthcare policy, the business of healthcare, and enhancement of the quality of life and health of individuals within a community (US Department of Health and Human Services, 2000).

Effective health communication is essential to positive healthcare management (Collins *et al.*, 2002; Say *et al.*, 2006). Public health research states that lack of substance and vagueness of health communication may be linked to feelings of mistrust towards the source of messages (Collins *et al.*, 2002). If people do not understand what and why a message is being communicated with them, they are less likely to trust the motivations behind it. Have you ever received treatment advice from a physician that was too complicated to understand? Perhaps you have had the opposite problem, where a physician has used vague or oversimplified terminology. It is the duty of a health communication expert to ensure that health messages are constructed in an effective manner. The way that prescriptions are communicated is almost as important as the prescription itself. Unfortunately, most health communication is sent through diffusion strategies and do little to account for individual user nuances.

Say *et al.* (2006) investigated factors that influence patients' willingness to become involved in the health treatment process. The results of their study indicate that identification is vital to positive perceptions of health advice, as it makes patients feel as though they are a part of the decision-making process, igniting empowerment and a sense of control over their illness. This includes identification with the physician, as well as the treatment prescribed. Individuals want to feel as though they have control over their own body.

Social media can increase the way patients identify with physicians. *Cochrane Child Health* is a pediatric health community that utilizes social media in its communication with patients (Elliott *et al.*, 2020). Included in their health strategy is an active X (formerly Twitter) account, influencer communication, and an active blog written by active faculty and staff. Patients can navigate through the digital platform to seek out information relevant to their questions or illness. Posts include a photo and short biography for each author. These personal touches could help patients see their physicians as less intimidating experts that they are unable to relate with. People are likely to seek out physicians with similar life experiences, which could increase the quality of information exchange and their willingness to disclose their personal health issues.

This chapter demonstrates how decision-making regarding personal healthcare is not that different from other decisions that we make in our daily lives. Chapter 5 demonstrated how media consumers are active users who interpret media content according to their own experiences and needs. Therefore, it is important to learn the theoretical health communication models that health communication specialists have utilized to incite behavior change in participatory health media users. This includes the activation model of information exposure and the health belief model. As you learn about both, consider how they relate to the earlier concepts of diffusion, community, and mobilization approaches for behavior change.

Earlier we discussed how individuals growing up today are probably aware that cigarette smoking is dangerous to their health. While diffusion-centric awareness campaigns are important for spreading information, they do little to prompt permanent behavior change, especially for those already engaging in the behavior. The *activation model of information exposure* (Table 14.1) is designed to explain how individual levels of need require both activation and arousal. If messages do not meet these levels, individuals will experience a negative state and will turn away from the given source of information. Smokers may feel turned off by messages that are too information-heavy, or which portray users in a negative manner. Generally, collaborative and personalized messages prove most effective.

If adequate levels of activation and arousal are met, individuals will continue to expose themselves to the information (Donohew *et al.*, 1980). Today's health communication messages must not only fulfill individual need for information but also fulfill the need for

Table 14.1   Activation model of information exposure.

Characteristics	
Cl	Individuals vary in their levels of need for stimulation as a function of their inherited drives and learned needs based on rewarded and nonrewarded experiences. High sensation seekers have higher needs for stimulation than low sensation seekers
C2	In messages, stimulation is provided by formal features, including (a) fast action, (b) novelty, (c) color, (d) stimulus intensity, (e) complexity, and others, and by the verbal content, including dramatic qualities and emotional intensity
Laws (theoretical statements)	
L1	Individuals seek to achieve or maintain a level of activation at which they feel most comfortable
L2	Attention to a message is a function of (a) individual level of need for stimulation or cognition and (b) level of stimulation provided by a stimulus source (such as a message)
Deduced propositions	
L3	Individuals will attend to messages that fulfill their needs for activation
L4	Individuals will turn away from messages that fail to generate enough arousal to meet their needs for activation to seek more exciting stimuli
L5	Individuals will turn away from messages that generate too much arousal to seek less exciting stimuli
Explanandum	
E	Operational hypotheses, based on the propositions expressed in L3, L4, and L5, may concern exposure to information, attitude or behavior changes, or other variables

Source: Donohew et al. (1998). Reproduced with permission of John Wiley & Sons.

stimulation or entertainment (Donohew *et al.*, 1998). Without understanding this second need for entertainment gratification, health information will be lost on users. The most skilled communication professionals will understand how to structure content so that it serves both needs, as well as create enticing messages that individuals will want to seek in their daily lives.

More recent research into the activation theory of information exposure suggests that individuals satisfy their need for stimulation and entertainment when attending to a message *before* they seek to fulfill their need for information alone (University of Kentucky, 2001). If given the choice, people would rather spend their time with content that is entertaining than informative. However, public health service announcements tend to be oversaturated with information and bore users. Thus, individuals tend to shift attention towards more entertaining commercial sites, rather than government or research-based sources.

One critical concern is the quality of health information consumed and diffused online, especially as health communication and entertainment narratives begin to merge. We have discussed in Chapter 5 how media users are more purposeful and selective when consuming media content. They would access the information that best gratifies their emotional needs. Because online information is unregulated, there are many sites with public health misinformation, some promoting products and others outright scams. The amount of misinformation is ever growing, specifically misinformation on major public health issues such as vaccines and diseases (Morahan-Martin & Anderson, 2000; Suarez-Lledo & Alvarez-Galvez, 2021). Many healthcare professionals worry about the deadly consequences of spreading blatant misinformation online (Intlekofer *et al.*, 2012).

While it is impossible to examine how much influence this type of public health misinformation has on personal healthcare decisions, it is possible to change how existing reputable health information sources communicate so that they prove more appealing to users. Reputable health sources such as the Mayo Clinic have begun using storytelling techniques (e.g., Historias Mayo) to engage with niche communities regarding health issues (Hiatt, 2013; Ortíz Soto, 2020). Historias Mayo is a global storytelling campaign that uses X (formerly Twitter), YouTube and Facebook to follow the stories of Hispanic patients and physicians. This is a great way for a reputable health source to diffuse effective communication in a way that is appealing to everyday users.

Hopefully you are seeing the application of the marketing strategies discussed in previous chapters to health communication campaigns. Chapter 2 discussed the importance of including brand stories in your diffusion marketing strategy. The importance of including narratives in health communication is equally imperative to prompting behavior change.

Health Belief Model

The activation model of information exposure explained why individuals do not follow through with public health treatment advice, despite having the knowledge of the benefits of doing so. The *health belief model* (Figure 14.1) further explains this process and demonstrates how healthy behavior is dependent on two variables: the value placed by an individual on a particular goal and the individual's estimate of the likelihood that a given action will achieve that goal (Janz & Becker, 1984).

Before following through with a behavior change, individuals must actually have the desire to avoid illness or get well and believe that the behavior change being asked of them will help them to avoid or treat illness. If a cigarette smoker does not prioritize health or feels that quitting smoking will have little effect because they are exposed to second-hand smoke all the time anyway, a public health message will have little influence. The health belief model outlines many dimensions social media practitioners need to consider when creating health campaign messages (Janz & Becker, 1984).

First, you must consider the perceived susceptibility or the perceptions of personal vulnerability and risk to a condition. This proves difficult, especially in young adults, who may believe that they are invincible or that bad things will not happen to them. If they do not feel as though they will be impacted by the illness, they will not seek treatment.

You must also consider the perceived severity of contracting the illness. This happens when patients evaluate both medical and social consequences of contraction. Often, the effects of the condition on social interactions with friends and family mean more to a

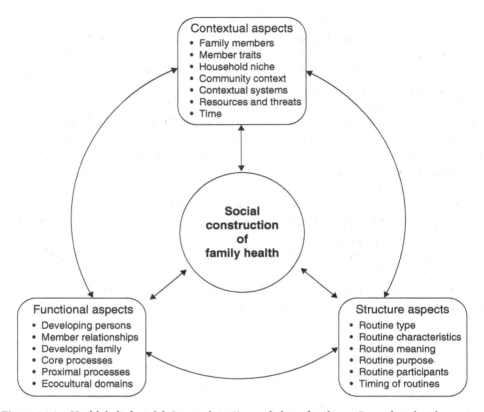

Figure 14.1   Health belief model. Source: http://www.diabetesfamily.net. Reproduced with permission of Ohio University.

person than disability or pain. With sexually transmitted infections, patients often get them treated to avoid embarrassment in locker rooms or so that future partners will not raise questions, not because of the dangers if left untreated.

It is important to consider the perceived benefits of following through with the behavior. While individuals may accept that they are susceptible to a condition, the desired action may not be greater than the perceived risk. Consider the pharmaceutical commercials that you see on television. What do you think when you hear the long list of potential side effects? Why would someone take a medication to cure restless leg syndrome if the medication may cause heart failure or even death?

Finally, and perhaps most importantly, it is necessary to consider the perceived barriers of following through with a health recommendation. Individuals will engage in a cost–benefit analysis, where they weigh the behavior change effectiveness against the challenges of following through, such as cost, time, or even social status. Many teen pregnancy initiatives struggle with the perceived barriers dimension, because even though young adults know that they can become pregnant through unprotected sex, are aware of the impact that this will have on the rest of their life and know that wearing a condom is not that expensive or difficult, they feel embarrassed or uncomfortable asking their partner when it is time.

Hopefully you can see how the health belief model is contrary to a more diffusion-centric model that suggests a lack of information is the reason individuals do not follow through with a suggested behavior change. This model demonstrates the relationship and connection between health behaviors, practices, and utilization of health services. It is easy to see how awareness-only campaigns are not very effective. If one was just to follow the diffusion of innovation strategy and raise awareness about the dangers and/or benefits of an action, it only tackles half of the health belief model. Instead, campaigns should motivate users through individual perceptions (evaluation of illness), modifying behaviors (demographic variables, perceived threat, and cues to action), and the likelihood of action (factors of recommendation) (Hochbaum *et al.*, 1952).

Moreover, individuals should also be able to easily pick out what behavior change is being asked of them. While there may be many steps a person could take, health campaigns should only choose one. Think of all the different possible ways an individual can stop smoking: immediate cessation, hypnosis, or the use of patch, gum, or e-cigarettes. The message will be much stronger if a social media campaign is clear and provides specific advice for the audience.

It is also important that this solution presents a tangible course of action at acceptable cost. People should not feel as though they will lose a part of their individual or social selves by carrying out the desired behavior change. Finally, all campaigns should promote feelings of competency to act while considering cultural factors, socioeconomic status, and individuals' previous experiences.

Social media provides a great platform to tackle some of these dimensions. It allows a networked community to create profiles based on their own individuality and interests and to network with others going through similar trials and encourages dialogue that is supportive and encouraging. One example of a public health campaign that utilizes social media for a very specific group of users is the suicide prevention charity CALM.

CALM launched their "Suicidal doesn't always look suicidal" campaign (see Figure 14.2) by featuring 50 portraits of people who have lost their lives to suicide (Henderson, 2023). The campaign is a compilation of photos and videos taken by loved ones that show the individuals smiling, laughing, and seemingly happy. The campaign encourages people to talk more about mental health and help remove some of the stigmas associated. The CALM website allows multiple outlets for these conversations, including a 24/7 webchat, phone number, Instagram, Facebook, and X (formerly Twitter) social media communities.

Another online health campaign, "That's Public Health," is a webisode series created by the American Public Health Association (APHA). The 20-part YouTube web series focuses on a range of issues related to public health, including climate change, gun violence, racism, and more (APHA, 2021). The webisodes are entertaining, with young, common denominator users in mind. The videos are created in short format, that can easily be shared on social media.

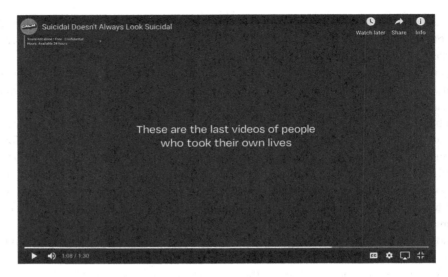

Figure 14.2   Screenshot from the YouTube CALM Campaign.

Public health campaigns have also turned to social media influencers to promote various health initiatives to younger users. The truth anti-tobacco #LeftWwipeDat campaign utilized endorsements from prominent influencers such as Grace Helbig, Harley Morenstein, King Bach, and more to show users that smoking does not make people look more attractive or cool, but in fact would cause online dating users to swipe past social profiles (Kostygina *et al.*, 2020).

Social media provides the ability for people to not just seek more information about the public health issues that are important to them, but to engage with others who are dealing with similar health problems. Public health practitioners can now use social media to diffuse their messages, create a community of public dialogue, and mobilize online media users towards a specific desired action. To create a successful health campaign, the following action plan has been developed from the activation model of information exposure and the health belief model.

Health Campaign Action Plan

1   Think about what is noteworthy to your health campaign's target audiences. Conduct a thorough audience analysis. Consider demographics, cultural traditions, and socioeconomic status of your target audience.
2   Balance between entertainment and information through narrative techniques.
3   Offer an appropriate incentive if your campaign audiences took action.

Mobile Reach

We have discussed many ways in which social media has transformed access, relationships, and outcomes that users have with their personal health management. One of the biggest game changers in the health industry has been dubbed mHealth, or text-based health campaigns.

mHealth is defined as emerging mobile communication and network technologies for healthcare systems (Istepanian *et al.*, 2006) and is set to profoundly change the health industry (Delgreco, 2009). Mobile technology has become an inexpensive and more efficient way for doctors and patients to communicate with one another. It is especially practical for patients who have limited access to traditional healthcare facilities.

The *short message service* (SMS) technology of mobile communication allows users to share written messages between handsets and has two main advantages over traditional phone calls: it is relatively inexpensive, and it is asynchronous in nature. You may remember from Chapter 7 that synchronous communication requires individuals to be gathered at the same time to communicate. Text message users do not have to read the message immediately to effectively participate in the communication process (Ling, 2005). This technology is ideal for physicians who may have small pockets of time between patients to access "held messages" that patients may have sent earlier in the day.

Several health campaigns have already been developed and are successfully using mHealth technology with patients. For example, STOMP (Stop Smoking Over Mobile Phone) was created to reach members attempting to quit smoking. It sends a series of motivational text messages to users over the course of 26 weeks when a patient is trying to kick the habit. This additional communication offers the advantage of anonymity and convenience, providing a cost-effective and scalable delivery method to reach a large number of smokers regardless of their location. mHealth can tailor messages to key user characteristics such as age, sex, and race, as well as link the patient with others for social support (Orr *et al.*, 2019).

Text-based health initiatives show promise in reaching many hard-to-access communities. Ameratunga *et al.* (2012) developed an intervention to reduce problem drinking and injury among hard-to-reach trauma patients in New Zealand by sending them messages over a period of four weeks following hospital discharge. The weight loss program Noom uses text messages to reach subscribers and send health tips throughout the day to help them with their weight loss goals (Noon, 2023). Textspot provides women the opportunity to receive funny text message reminders about taking their birth control pills (Textspot, 2023).

While mobile technology could bring new sorts of concerns, such as increased misinformation, patient confidentiality, and liability concerns for physicians, it provides opportunities for individuals to have equal access to healthcare information and be able to communicate with physicians in ways that are not entirely disruptive to their lives. The increased connectivity via mobile technology is a game changer for the health industry.

This chapter demonstrates the importance of incorporating communication theory into public health and behavior change initiatives. Beyond the need for information and awareness on public health issues, other factors, such as economic or sociostructural challenges, prevent individuals from carrying out a desired behavior change. The next generation will have better tools to access, engage, and treat patients. Social media and mobile communication will play an intricate role in this process.

Case Study: UK Government Response to COVID-19

The COVID-19 pandemic was declared a public health emergency by the World Health Organization in January 2020 (WHO, 2021). The virus is highly contagious through close contact transmission, causing global quarantine and travel restriction recommendations during early weeks of the outbreak. Information about the novel virus needed to be diffused to media users quickly and effectively. This guidance was new, and in many cases, information changed quickly as scientists learned more about the virus. For example, recommendations early in the pandemic that encourage people to sanitize mail and groceries that come into the homes changed within weeks of quarantine (NCH, 2023). COVID-19 proved the biggest communication and information challenge for public health officials in decades.

Given the rapid changing pace of the virus, official communication response needed to be direct and swift. Thus, popular social media platforms such as Facebook and Instagram were utilized as primary channels to diffuse public health information directly to citizens in efforts to stop the spread of the virus. One of the most innovative social media campaigns was created by the UK National Health Services. The campaign reached multiple demographics through seven different social media channels. Each platform required innovative niche content that would motivate specific users towards a specific call-to-action.

As the pandemic continued, the amount of misinformation and conspiracies shared on social media increased. It became difficult for users to filter through all social media conversations. COVID-19 was referenced on social media 40.2 million times from May 12, 2020, to May 18, 2020 (Gottlieb & Dyer, 2020). It was important for official public health channels to deliver pertinent information and speak directly to key users.

As such, UK's NHS used TikTok and Reddit to hold Q&A sessions with both young and older users. In addition, more niche and community information diffusion regarding local COVID-19 restriction details were disseminated through the Nextdoor social media platform. A face mask filter was created on Snapchat to interact with younger demographics, and a chatbot was developed through Google Searches to provide deeper, more tailored, information for those seeking. As a result, content drew over 95 million clicks to the NHS website (Kirk, 2022).

As the health belief model explains how healthy behavior is dependent on the value an individual places on a particular health goal and the likelihood perception that a given action will achieve that goal (Janz & Becker, 1984). Messages needed to be identifiable and relatable for different users. Social media played an important role as a primary source to provide the public with accurate public health information during the pandemic in United Kingdom.

Discussion questions

1   Based on the activation model of information exposure, at what stage of the COVID-19 public health campaign could users engage through a narrative technique? What role can social media play in this process?
2   How did the UK governmental response to COVID-19 encourage community participation? What are some possible ways could they have improved upon the engagement of the strategy?
3   In your opinion, when might it prove more beneficial to obtain public health information from a more diffusion-oriented website, rather than a community-oriented social media community? What are possible benefits that the community provides that the diffusion website could not?

Summary

Traditional healthcare models require patients to recognize that something is wrong with their current health, seek a physician for answers, and adhere to their treatment recommendations. Today's patients can access health information, communities, and alternative physicians at any point in this process, transforming them into more empowered, participating and active managers of personal healthcare (Couchman *et al.*, 2001; Roter & Hall, 2006).

The activation model of information exposure and the health belief model are just two of many health communication strategies that illustrate how complicated the process is for individuals to make decisions regarding their personal healthcare. Patients use social media to seek second opinions, research their own symptoms, and discuss questions with online communities. Social media provides many of these participatory features that allow individuals to share stories and find community with others. While these technological advances hold great potential for positive change, they can just as easily be used in an ineffective or damaging manner. As the activation model of information exposure demonstrates, individuals are primarily concerned with the emotional dimension of health messages. More efforts therefore need to be made to ensure that credible sources of health information are presented in ways that are understandable and entertaining to users. This is where storytelling and cultural narrative techniques should be utilized when implementing health campaigns.

Social media allows individuals the opportunity to participate in dialogue and form communities surrounding health issues. Whether you are a lifelong contributor or just stopping in to read other patient experiences, forums, discussion groups and topic blogs are a great way to feel less alone. Most cultures view health as a private sphere issue, something not openly discussed in public. Social media allows these conversations to happen anonymously, which is incredibly useful for taboo topics, such as sexual health, mental health, or addiction. It is also a great place to begin conversations, normalize health concerns, and shift public personas so that people feel more comfortable talking about these uncomfortable topics.

One of the greatest advances of social media is the ability to transcend virtual boundaries. Individuals do not live in isolation from one another. Social media allows communities to organize themselves and for individuals to find resources that they can use in their "real life." It is also a way to get families involved in the treatment of their loved ones. Finally, just as discussed in marketing, the goal of behavior change messaging is to turn everyday users into message advocates. Once individuals have successfully managed their own personal healthcare, social media provides an avenue for them to share their experiences with others who are just starting or struggling with their journey. These empowered users may be more meaningful to patients than physicians who simply prescribe but have not had the personal experience in dealing with the illness.

The future of healthcare has a great deal to do with infrastructure, insurance, and physician training. These have historically held powers in the healthcare industry. Hopefully, this chapter has highlighted the important role of social media and today's patients. For the first time, everyday patients are actively participating in their own treatment, and can aid in the treatment of others.

This book has hopefully highlighted the importance of diffusion, community, and mobilization when constructing social media messages. While these are important constructs for social media marketing, they also play a role in the way we make and manage all decisions. It is important to consider how these elements fit into the public health arena as well. Public health is often defined as "What we as a society do to assure the condition in which people can be healthy," including the planning and implementation of health communication (Capper & Sands, 2006). Clearly, a healthy public extends well beyond adequate medical treatment when an individual makes a trip to the physician. The following chapter will explore the importance of healthy civic engagement in society, and how our personal well-being is connected to the world and cultures around us.

Key Takeaways

1 Social media has transferred power from traditional healthcare practitioners to everyday patients by raising knowledge levels, providing more choices, and empowering patients.
2 The activation model of information exposure illustrates how making decisions about personal healthcare management is a complicated process that involves the need for activation and arousal.

3   The health belief model prompts practitioners to consider the perceived susceptibility, perceived severity, perceived benefits, and perceived barriers of following through with a health recommendation when designing public health campaign messages.

4   mHealth, or mobile communication and network technologies for healthcare systems, is profoundly changing the health industry by providing an inexpensive and more efficient way for doctors and patients to communicate.

5   Social media can allow a networked approach to provide public health information in otherwise hard-to-reach communities.

References

Ameratunga, S., Smith, E., Kool, B. & Raerino, K. (2012) Feasibility of a brief intervention delivered via mobile phone to reduce harmful drinking and injury among trauma patients in New Zealand. *Addiction Science and Clinical Practice*, 7(Suppl. 1), A92. Available at http://www.ascpjournal.org/content/7/S1/A92 (accessed November 17, 2023).

APHA (2021) Public health made easy. Available at https://www.apha.org/News-and-Media/News-Releases/APHA-News-Releases/2021/Public-health-made-easy (accessed November 17, 2023).

Berry, L., Parish, J.T., Janakiraman, R., Ogburn-Russell, L., Couchman, G.R., Rayburn, W.L. & Grisel, J. (2008) Patients' commitment to their primary physician and why it matters. *Annals of Family Medicine*, 6(1), 6–13.

Capper, S. & Sands, C. (2006) The vital relationship between public health and pharmacy. *International Journal of Pharmacy Education*, Fall(2), 1–3.

Centers for Disease Control (2013) Health effects of cigarette smoking. Available at http://www.cdc.gov/tobacco/data_statistics/fact_sheets/health_effects/effects_cig_smoking (accessed November 17, 2023).

Collins, T., Clark, J., Petersen, L. & Kressin, N. (2002) Racial differences in how patients perceive physician communication regarding cardiac testing. *Medical Care*, 40(1 Suppl), 27–34.

Connolly, S.L., Gifford, A.L., Miller, C.J., Bauer, M.S., Lehmann, L.S. & Charness, M.E. (2021) Provider perceptions of virtual care during the coronavirus disease 2019 pandemic: a multispecialty survey study. *Medical Care*, 59(7), 646.

Couchman G., Forjuoh S. & Rascoe T. (2001) E-mail communications in family practice: what do patients expect? *Journal of Family Practice*, 50, 414–418.

Delgreco, C. (2009) Wireless technology set to profoundly change the health industry. Available at http://www.businesswire.com/news/home/20090311006208/en/Wireless-Technology-Set-Profoundly-ChangeHealth-Industry (accessed November 17, 2023).

Donohew, L., Palmgreen, P. & Duncan, J. (1980) An activation model of information exposure. *Communication Monographs*, 47(4), 295–303.

Donohew, L., Lorch, E.P. & Palmgreen, P. (1998) Applications of a theoretic model of information exposure to health interventions. *Human Communication Research*, 24(3), 454–468.

Elliott, S.A., Dyson, M.P., Wilkes, G.V., Zimmermann, G.L., Chambers, C.T., Wittmeier, K.D., Russell, D.J., Scott, S.D., Thomson, D. & Hartling, L. (2020) Considerations for health researchers using social media for knowledge translation: multiple case study. *Journal of Medical Internet Research*, 22(7), e15121.

Finney Rutten, L.J., Blake, K.D., Greenberg-Worisek, A.J., Allen, S.V., Moser, R.P. & Hesse, B.W. (2019) Online health information seeking among US adults: measuring progress toward a healthy people 2020 objective. *Public Health Reports*, 134(6), 617–625.

Gottlieb, M. & Dyer, S. (2020) Information and disinformation: social media in the COVID-19 crisis. *Academic Emergency Medicine*, 27(7), 640.

Haean, O., Ray, M. & Allegrante, J. (2008) Perceptions of health care provider communication activity among American cancer survivors and adults without cancer histories: an analysis of the 2003 health information trends survey (HINTS) data. *Journal of Health Communication*, 13(7), 637–653.

Hawn, C. (2009) Take two aspirin and tweet me in the morning: how Twitter, Facebook, and other social media are reshaping health care. *Health Affairs*, 28(2), 361–368.

Henderson, A. (2023) 5 Mental health campaigns that are making a difference. *GWI*. Available at https://blog.gwi.com/marketing/mental-health.

Hiatt, E. (2013) Mayo Clinic announces video storytelling campaign with Hispanic patients and doctors. Available at http://www.diversityinc.com/diversity-press-releases/mayo-clinic-announces-video-storytelling-campaignwith-hispanic-patients-and-doctors (accessed November 17, 2023).

Hochbaum, G., Rosenstock, I. & Kegels, S. (1952) Health belief model. *United States Public Health Service*. Available at http://www.infosihat.gov.my/infosihat/artikelHP/bahanrujukan/HE_DAN_TEORI/DOC/Health%20Belief%20Model.doc (accessed November 17, 2023).

Intlekofer, K., Cunningham, M. & Caplan, A. (2012) The HPV vaccine controversy. *Medicine and Society*, 14(1), 39–49.

Istepanian, R.S.H., Laxminarayan, S. & Pattichis, C.S. (2006) *M-health: Emerging Mobile Health Systems*. Berlin: Springer.

Janz, N.K. & Becker, M.H. (1984) The health belief model: a decade later. *Health Education and Behavior*, 11(1), 1–47.

Kelly, J.T., Campbell, K.L., Gong, E. & Scuffham, P. (2020) The Internet of Things: impact and implications for health care delivery. *Journal of Medical Internet Research*, 22(11), e20135.

Kirk, R. (2022) Campaign showcase. Available at https://gcs.civilservice.gov.uk/blog/campaign-showcase-rethinking-social-media-to-outpace-the-spread-of-covid-19/ (accessed November 17, 2023).

Kostygina, G., Tran, H., Binns, S., Szczypka, G., Emery, S., Vallone, D. & Hair, E. (2020) Boosting health campaign reach and engagement through use of social media influencers and memes *Social Media + Society*, 6(2), 2056305120912475.

Ling, R. (2005) The sociolinguistics of SMS: an analysis of SMS use by a random sample of Norwegians. In: R. Ling & P.E. Pedersen (eds) *Mobile Communications: Renegotiation of the Social Sphere*, pp. 335–349. London: Springer.

McMillan, S. & Macias, W. (2008) Strengthening the safety net for online seniors: factors influencing differences in health information seeking among older Internet users. *Journal of Health Communication*, 13(8), 778–792.

Morahan-Martin, J. & Anderson, C.D. (2000) Information and misinformation online: recommendations for facilitating accurate mental health information retrieval and evaluation. *CyberPsychology and Behavior*, 3(5), 731–746.

National Cancer Institute (2001) *Making Health Communication Programs Work*. Bethesda, MD: NCI.

NCH (2023) NCH News. Available at https://nchmd.org/press-releases/household-disinfection-coronavirus-on-surfaces/#:~:text=Do%20I%20Need%20to%20Disinfectdown%20each%20and%20every%20item (accessed November 17, 2023).

Noon (2023) A healthier you, wherever you are. Available at www.noom.com.

Orr, M.F., Burduli, E., Hirchak, K.A., Dotson, J.A.W., Young, S.L., Nelson, L., Lennstrom, E., Slaney, T., Bush, T., Gillaspy, S.R., Roll, J.M., Buchwald, D. & McPherson, S.M. (2019) Culturally-tailored text-messaging intervention for smoking cessation in rural American Indian communities: rationale, design, and methods. *Contemporary Clinical Trials Communications*, 15, 100363.

Ortíz Soto, D.S. (2020) Características clínicas y epidemiológicas de pacientes fallecidos por COVID-19 en el Centro Médico Naval, de marzo a mayo del 2020.

Ratzan, S., Stearns, N., Payne, J., Amato, P., Liebergott, J. & Madoff, M. (1994) Education for the health communication professional: a collaborative curricular partnership. *American Behavioral Scientist*, 38(2), 361–380.

Roter, D. & Hall, J. (2006) *Doctors Talking with Patients/Patients Talking with Doctors: Improving Communication in Medical Visits*. Westport, CT: Praeger.

Say, R., Murtagh, M. & Thomson, R. (2006) Patients' preference for involvement in medical decision making: a narrative review. *Patient Education and Counseling*, 60(2), 102–114.

Stellefson, M., Paige, S.R., Chaney, B.H. & Chaney, J.D. (2020) Evolving role of social media in health promotion: updated responsibilities for health education specialists. *International Journal of Environmental Research and Public Health*, 17(4), 1153.

Suarez-Lledo, V. & Alvarez-Galvez, J. (2021) Prevalence of health misinformation on social media: systematic review. *Journal of Medical Internet Research*, 23(1), e17187.

Textspot (2023) Birth control text message reminders. Available at https://textspot.io/resources/birth-control-text-message-reminder/ (accessed November 17, 2023).

University of Kentucky (2001) Communication capstone theory workbook. Available at http://www.uky.edu/~drlane/capstone/health/act.html (accessed November 17, 2023).

US Department of Health and Human Services (2000) Healthy people. Available at http://www.healthypeople.gov/2020/default.apx (accessed November 17, 2023).

WHO (2021) WHO-convened global study of origins of SARS-CoV-2. Available at https://www.who.int/publications/i/item/who-convened-global-study-of-origins-of-sars-cov-2-china-part (accessed November 17, 2023).

15

Social Media and Civic Engagement

Introduction

Effective and regular communication with official health channels is just one step toward a positive and healthy lifestyle. Chapter 14 explained how social media helps increase the frequency of health communication and aids positive personal health management. However, there is much more to happy citizens than achieving good health. Research demonstrates how an increase in civic engagement and volunteering leads to better physical and mental health (Batista & Cruz-Ledón, 2013; Lum & Lightfoot, 2005). *Civic engagement*, or membership in formal community groups and participation in social activities (Shah, 1998), is an easy way to bolster your own sense of belonging and accomplishment within a culture. Chapter 3 demonstrated the importance of community in our lives. People feel better about

Strategic Social Media: From Marketing to Social Change, Second Edition. L. Meghan Mahoney and Tang Tang.
© 2024 John Wiley & Sons, Inc. Published 2024 by John Wiley & Sons, Inc.

themselves whenever they are making a positive impact on society. Social media makes it easier than ever for individuals to get involved in organizations and join causes that they care about.

The benefits of civic engagement do not stop at individual needs. Social connectedness leads to better schools, faster economic development, lower crime rates, and more effective government in society (Putnam, 1995). The greatest advantage of becoming a civically engaged citizen is that you can help others while also helping yourself. Chapter 14 urged you to consider strengthening health communication between physicians and patients at the community level for better self-care. The remaining chapters in this part encourage you to consider individualized behavior change to positively influence the lives of a larger community. Small steps can make a big difference to others.

Remember from Chapter 3 our discussion of why community is so important to the behavior change process? Humans actively seek communities, whether they are based on proximity, mutual interests, health concerns, or family. These social networks play the strongest role in how we behave and construct the world around us. The building blocks of community – membership, shared emotional connection, influence, and needs fulfillment (McMillan & Chavis, 1986) – allow individuals to share in an identity and engage in dialogue with members (Campbell & Jovchelovitch, 2000). Many of these dimensions have now shifted and are being fulfilled in the virtual realm. Social media provides resources for maximizing our own personal identity, as well as our collective identity.

Collective identity is a social psychological concept that helps to explain the human need to be part of a larger group, especially when tackling larger social issues. With a strong collective identity, movements can garner more support and power because individuals feel as though they are all working toward common goals. There is more power in larger groups. If the larger group has clearly defined objectives, opponents, and an integrated sense of being that is incorporated into the movement ideologies, they can become a strong force in society (McCaughey & Ayer, 2003). In a world with unlimited information at your fingertips, it has become nearly impossible to live in isolation from the world around you. It is only natural to find a community with others who share in your vision.

Traditional top-down diffusion media made it easy to receive information and messages. Many utilized this opportunity to share crisis information from around the globe. You may remember seeing TV commercials that call for individuals to send in money to help feed a child in a different part of the world. But what if you didn't have any expendable income? Does that mean you were unable to contribute to the cause? Often, the solutions offered were based on predetermined objectives and targeted toward a mass audience. Social media allows individuals to seek out information, engage in dialogue, and come up with collective solutions and action plans that work best within their lifestyle. Perhaps a group of similarly minded individuals can put their resources together to help coordinate a fundraiser or event.

Social media makes it easier than ever to make a positive difference in the world. Technology has connected the world on a smaller, more tightly bound scale. Stiglitz (2002) explains how *globalization* has integrated the countries and people of the world through an increase in transportation and communication. This has resulted in a breakdown of barriers between the flow of goods, services, and knowledge across borders. Think of your own social network: you have likely been able to stay in touch with individuals from many parts of your life that you otherwise would have lost touch with if not for social media. Maybe you have friends that you met from a summer camp, a study trip abroad, or even just a single connection that you made with a meaningful person. These connections are difficult to maintain without regular contact, but social media allows the opportunity with little effort from either party. Our sense of connection and network has completely transformed.

The purpose of this chapter is to explore the influence of social media on the nature and shape of civic engagement, and how it proves different from any other era. There is much ongoing debate in the field of communication about whether technologies are eroding our sense of civic responsibility (Dahlgren, 2009; Putnam, 2000; Stoll, 1995) or making it easier to get involved in our communities (Lévy, 1997; Rheingold, 2008). To better answer these questions, this chapter explores the historical trends of civic engagement, the influence of civic engagement on individuals, and the impact technology has on political communication and behavior change.

Historical Shifts of Civic Engagement

It would prove impossible to generalize levels of civic engagement across the world throughout history. While one country may experience record high levels, others may be in the process of disengaging. Civic engagement is a complex and dynamic process. While we often consider high levels of civic engagement as a positive phenomenon, spikes in levels may indicate problems within a culture, rather than a fluid functioning society.

In Chapter 4, we discussed many instances of collective action and civic engagement for social change, including the Ukraine refugee crisis. Social media played an intricate role in connecting and organizing individuals beyond their own social networks to provide transportation and shelter to those in need. We have discussed the many benefits of a civically engaged society, but lower levels of activism may indicate complacency with the status quo. How do you keep citizens from staying involved when they are happy with the way things are going?

In the United States alone, there have been many changes over time in the extent and purpose for which individuals got involved in their community (Figure 15.1). In the 1950s, civic engagement was high, especially through union membership, volunteering at schools and religious organizations following World War II. In the 1960s, this engagement shifted toward public demonstrations against oppression and gender rights, signifying an increase in citizens' sense of empowerment and dissatisfaction with government. This generation produced the National Organization of Women, Peace Corps, and Martin Luther King's "I Have a Dream" speech. The 1970s continued these fights, as well as held protests surrounding the Vietnam War and increased awareness for

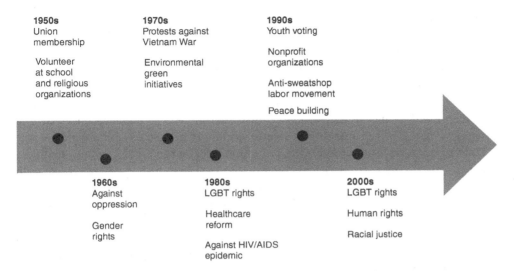

1950s
Union
membership

Volunteer
at school
and religious
organizations

1970s
Protests against
Vietnam War

Environmental
green
initiatives

1990s
Youth voting

Nonprofit
organizations

Anti-sweatshop
labor movement

Peace building

1960s
Against
oppression

Gender
rights

1980s
LGBT rights

Healthcare
reform

Against HIV/AIDS
epidemic

2000s
LGBT rights

Human rights

Racial justice

Figure 15.1   Civic engagement timeline.

environmental green initiatives. The 1980s were characterized as the "Me decade" due to low levels of individual volunteering at the community level. Parents were not as involved in local parent–teacher associations or the Red Cross. However, LGBT rights and healthcare reform were huge issues in the fight against the HIV/AIDS epidemic. In the 1990s, youth was seen as apathetic and irony-obsessed slackers. The 1992 Presidential election was the first time in twenty years that demonstrated an increase in youth voting, partially due to MTV's "Rock the Vote" campaign. There was also an increase in volunteering at nonprofit organizations, anti-sweatshop labor movements, and peace building work. The millennium drastically changed how individuals communicate with one another through social media platforms. Social media has emerged as a primary tool for communicating with personal communities, political organizing, and aiding disaster relief efforts. Since 2000s, young people are being seen as more socially, politically, and civically engaged than ever before, especially regarding human rights and LGBT issues, as well as racial justice rights in America (Jackson, 2021).

This timeline demonstrates just one country's flux in civic engagement levels. Here, you can see how complex and interconnected involvement is with issues of freedom, politics, public health, and technology. Every society, culture, and subculture have their own dynamic process for when levels increase and decrease. There are also many different types of civic engagement, making it difficult to monitor and evaluate.

Researchers suggest that one of the most difficult problems facing Western democracy today is the overall decline in citizens' political engagement (Dahlgren, 2009; Grasso *et al.*, 2019; Shah, 1998). They worry that the industrial and information revolution has led to the decline of community. This includes: the weaken private community, such as contact with neighbors and friends; the decline of public community, such as voluntary organizations and civic concerns; and disengagement from community, such as willingness to contribute to the well-being of the community (Quan-Haase *et al.*, 2002). Many believe that technology is making individuals more and more individualistic and less concerned about how their behaviors impact the group.

There are many reasons for this decline in community, including increased television watching, more women in the workplace, increased mobility of families, and changing dynamics (Shah, 1998). People criticize technology for playing a role in this process because it takes people away from their in-person communities and replaces it with virtual ones (Stoll, 1995). However, these virtual communities could be utilized as public spaces to discuss cultural issues and mobilize civic action.

In Chapter 3, we discussed Putnam's (2000) book *Bowling Alone*. This text portrayed today's generation as having the lowest trends of civic engagement and social capital in history, illustrating how there are higher instances of bowling, but fewer leagues than ever in the nation's history. Putnam (2000) believes that electronic entertainment is the cause of decreased civic engagement due to its ability to transform people into a society of watchers rather than doers. Other researchers believe that information technologies positively impact social capital, as well as online and offline civic and political participatory behaviors (Gil de Zúñiga *et al.*, 2012).

While our levels of civic engagement may not have changed significantly, they are becoming augmented and more geographically dispersed (Quan-Haase *et al.*, 2002). The Internet is providing new ways of finding information and engaging in community (Lévy, 1997). This process is more genuine, because it allows people to interact with others without their voices, faces, and bodies serving as a distraction to their messages (McCaughey & Ayer, 2003). Here, media users are active information seekers and are driving the engagement process, rather than being forced to participate in something that is not as relevant to their gratifications and needs.

Quan-Haase *et al.* (2002) explained how individuals who spend more time online value the technology for its positive social virtues and use it as a space for collective interactions. Technology provides a complementary and alternative way to find community in addition to those available offline. It allows us the ability to seek out those activities that fit to our interests and values, even if they are not directly in our own community.

Regardless of the influence new technologies have on levels of civic engagement, it is safe to say that they are not going anywhere. Younger generations are increasingly using social media to express themselves, explore their identities, and connect with peers as active creators and consumers of the culture (Rheingold, 2008). Today, you can share information just as quickly with your next-door neighbor as you are with individuals across the globe. Social media makes civic participation easy and free and increases the types of advocacy efforts with which you can engage (McAllister, 2013). Hyperlocal social media platforms, such as Nextdoor, have emerged as networking services for neighborhoods. These connection tools make civic engagement easier than ever.

The appeal of civic engagement through social media has much to do with the many benefits of participatory strategy discussed in Chapter 4. It allows users the ability to control conversation through blogs, wikis, RSS, tagging, social bookmarking, music/photo/video sharing, mashups, podcasts, digital storytelling, virtual communities, social network services, virtual environments, and videoblogs (Rheingold, 2008). Just as in the marketing realm, participatory media leads to more educated, empowered, and motivated citizens (Boulos & Wheeler, 2007). There is something more inherently satisfying about deciding that you want to make a change and organizing action to do so, rather than being told what to do by someone in a position of higher power.

Technology is the future of civic engagement. While previous generations may have had to physically travel to Congress to march on the front lawn to protest, today's Internet users are able to voice concerns from their living room. The challenge becomes making their voice heard when everyone else is doing the same thing. Thus, let's now explore the potential of social media and the impact of involvement on voicing the individual self.

Civic Engagement and the Individual Self

Mass media has traditionally been used to voice public sphere issues. Chapter 3 discussed key differences between private and public sphere issues of communication. Private sphere involves issues such as family, relationship, goals, values, and health. Public sphere topics include issues of civic activity, news, politics, weather, and sports. Habermas (1992) imagined the public sphere as a place for citizens to engage the political process through critical and rational deliberation. This was the space for civic engagement. Mass media has traditionally been an outlet for the public sphere; a place to go when you are interested in consuming "water cooler talk." Think of television and radio as the replacement for individuals standing in the middle of crowded streets screaming to the masses on a soapbox. Today, social media has transformed this public space into a convergence of both private and public forms. The blurring sphere has interesting implications when it comes to civic engagement.

The importance of our personal social network cannot be understated. Putnam (1993) describes the function and social elements of network, norms, and trust of our private sphere as our social capital. *Social capital* enables citizens to work together more effectively to resolve collective action problems. Social capital is also a public good because it benefits a wider community than just the self. There is power in numbers and individuals can accomplish more if they are part of a larger group with tangible goals.

You may have heard the saying that "It is not what you know, but who you know." Perhaps you were encouraged to take more internship opportunities in college with hopes that the experience and relationships formed would lead to your first job out of college.

We like to believe that we live in a society where with enough hard work anyone can achieve anything. However, the truth is that a larger social structure has much to do with who succeeds and who does not.

Your social capital of where you live and who you know helps define who you are and thus determine your fate (Putnam, 1993). For centuries, social groups were bound by proxemics to make connections and had to rely on local social capital. Many minority groups lack connections that allow them to get their feet in the door of the workforce. Nonetheless, social media today can minimize these inconsistencies, though not equalize them, by allowing individuals to connect through mutual causes, interests, and collective actions. 100% of US Congress members have an official Facebook page (Statista, 2023). Social media is the new face of community engagement and allows anyone to communicate directly with decision-makers (McAllister, 2013).

Social capital is seen as one of the most vital ingredients to economic development around the world. Everyone must find his or her own voice, or unique style of expression that distinguishes their communication from those of another (Rheingold, 2008). Once you can identify your voice, you are better able to engage with society as a citizen, moving from a private to a public voice. When aggregated with dialogue of the voices of other individuals, your voice becomes *public opinion*.

Remember from Chapter 3 the importance of authenticity, or recognizing and harnessing what you uniquely bring to the table. The same is true of your social media public voice. It should encompass your experiences, identity construction, and confirmation. What if someone were to give you $100 to donate to any organization or cause of your choice? Where would you choose to donate? Perhaps you have received a scholarship that allowed you to attend college. You know how important this was in your own life, so you choose to donate your money to a similar scholarship fund. Maybe your family has a history of breast cancer, so you choose to donate the money toward a cancer research organization. Animal lovers may choose to donate the money to their local animal shelter or the World Wildlife Fund.

We decide what issues are important to us based on our own lived experiences. If someone were to give you that money 100 years ago, chances are you would not have donated to the same organization. Without digital media, you may not have known about that scholarship or ever heard of the World Wildlife Fund. You were bound by the experiences of your local community. Most likely, the money would have gone to a local church or nonprofit organization within your own community, within walking distance from your home.

Today, you receive millions of messages from all over the world about causes, concerns, and organizations that need help. Some of these organizations are consistent with your own values and life experiences, but most of them are not. The only way to truly make a difference and find your authentic voice is to seek a community that shares in your values and passions. When utilizing social media to choose a civic engagement platform, it is important to have a strong action plan in place.

Civic Engagement Action Plan

1   Determine your own passions and values. What makes you excited about becoming civically engaged?
2   Seek out organizations that share in this vision. Don't become distracted by all other "virtual noises."
3   Research the authenticity and transparency of various organizations working toward this cause.
4   Determine whether you can make a tangible difference and mobilize for the organization, or whether you are just involved to improve your own virtual identity.
5   Spread awareness through your own social capital and network to recruit strong mobilized advocates with the same goals.

There is no reason to get involved with every organization or cause that asks you to connect through social media. There is something appealing about having your social network see that you relate to the local animal shelter. However, if you secretly have no interest in pets or animals, you should not feel pressured to connect with an organization just because it is a good cause. Their initiatives may be someone else's cause; you should only connect with those organizations that share in your voice and values.

When it comes to online activism, significant money and resources can be invested into social media with little return. Without a strong voice and little authenticity, efforts may result in "*slacktivism*" or half-hearted online activity that has no real effect on real-life outcomes (Morozov, 2009). One reason that this phenomenon may be so common is because social media makes it easy to virtually connect. With just a click of a mouse, an individual can say that they would like to receive more information and updates about an organization, even if they have no real interest in the mission. You may feel bad about turning down an organization that is trying to establish safe mining conditions and fair wages for diamond miners all over the world. It is okay to say no and be happy that someone else is interested in fighting for that cause. That person is just not you.

Social media is the communication tool that drives 57% of traffic to fundraising campaign pages (Matthews, 2023). However, there is often a disconnect between social media user's online self and offline charitable behavior (Wallace *et al.*, 2017). Users connect with various philanthropy social networks, because they want their friends to positively associate them with good causes. However, if a charity posts messages too frequently, or doesn't produce interesting content, it is easy for users to unfollow or ignore its messages. Users expect philanthropic organizations to be just as engaging and interesting as other connections.

What happens when you connect with a cause or organization that you feel as though shares in your voice and interests? Perhaps it is the same charity you decided would receive your $100 donation. You have decided that you want to increase your own life and the lives around you and have actively sought out a connection with the charity of your choice. However, you may not actually have the expendable money to donate. Maybe the charity is too far away to actively volunteer and get involved with, or maybe you just do not have the time right now. Is connecting through social media really going to make a difference?

One problem with virtual civic engagement is that you may feel as though you are helping without doing anything for the cause. While this satisfies the natural human desire to help others, not much is done toward the objectives of the organization (Morozov, 2009), which is especially true with organizations that only ask people to connect or follow them on social media.

Thus, it is important for you to make an active effort to do more than just connect with the organization. Be a participatory user. Share your opinions and contribute your voice to the ongoing discussions. Even if there is little you can do financially or through volunteer work, you are contributing to the organization's public opinion and that is a huge step toward becoming a campaign advocate. Spread awareness through your own social capital and network. It's a great first step toward becoming actively involved, even if most of your tangible participation is in the future.

If you oversee communication for a nonprofit or charity organization, be sure that you are not spending all your efforts toward gaining additional social media members. While it is important to spread awareness about your organization's efforts, you do not want to connect with hundreds of users who do not want to receive your messages and do not share in your passion. Just as true in marketing, a few highly participatory and active connections will do more for your return on investment than a surplus of passive connections. Also, remember to give those users who do want to participate clear and tangible direction. This should include monetary contributions, volunteering opportunities, and active dialogue centered around core issues in the area. Such tangible direction will allow everyone the ability to participate in areas that they feel comfortable with given their personal circumstances. Remember that your call to action likely falls under your mobilization strategy. As such, it should be clear, easy, and timely.

This section illustrates how to successfully connect causes with individual voice and passion. These recommendations will result in relationships that endure across a lifetime of advocacy. However, some acts of civic engagement require one-time real-life mobilization efforts. The field of political communication has explored how to prompt citizens to not only support a candidate on social media, but what it takes to transform that support into real-life votes on election day.

Technology and Political Communication

While civic participation includes activities such as volunteering for charities, attending political rallies, and forwarding online messages for social action, researchers generally equate civic participation with electoral activity (Gil de Zúñiga *et al.*, 2012).

Everyone has her or his own feelings about democratic elections. Many are excited to participate in the privilege of voting. Others begrudgingly deal with the onslaught of political advertisement campaigns in the months leading in. Yet others remain apathetic to the entire process.

American rhetoric teaches children that voting is the duty of citizenry (Jones & Hudson, 2000). However, with over $6.4 billion spent on campaign advertisements, only 66.8% of eligible voters participated in the 2020 American Presidential election (Census, 2021). Much research has been carried out into increasing these numbers and prompting voters, particularly first-time voters, to engage in the electoral process.

Voter turnout and decision-making over the past three decades have been a dynamic and complicated field of research. Social media has drastically changed the way people receive and disseminate political news. Today's Americans are the first generation who grew into voting age with unlimited information (and misinformation) at their fingertips. It is their right and freedom to express their beliefs, views, and values. Social media provides a public sphere for everyday citizens to debate and engage in dialogue about politics including Presidential elections (Burgess *et al.*, 2006).

Political discussion is difficult, and some people feel as though there is no place for it on social media. Some may advise you that it is best not to discuss alcohol use, religion, or politics on social networking sites. While there is some truth to these recommendations, especially regarding alcohol use, this section argues that healthy public dialogue is essential to an informed citizenry.

Before engaging a political discussion on an online forum, be sure that you take extra efforts to demonstrate that you are contributing to the social media conversation in a respectful manner. Tell others when you agree with them, and if you do not, point out that you respect where they are coming from and then explain why your life experience has made you feel differently. Encourage them to share their opinion because you should want to hear more. Even if you are not interested in changing your opinion, it helps to understand why other people feel differently from you. If you are not interested in hearing what others say, chances are you are not in a place to contribute to the discussion.

Social media has become the space where young adults go to read and share political information. According to Pew Research Center, 18% of adults in the United States, use social media as their most common way to get political information (Mitchell *et al.*, 2021). Just as television changed the election process by allowing voters to see candidates rather than simply hear them through radio, social media has been the most politically significant technological innovation of the twentieth century (Hong & Nadler, 2012), by providing candidates the opportunity to talk directly to voters and, more importantly, by granting voters access to talk directly with candidates. This holds a great opportunity for creating a culture of openness, transparency, and more egalitarian relationships.

Barack Obama has been applauded for being one of the first politicians to successfully incorporate social media into his 2008 Presidential campaign. He successfully harnessed 13 million individuals on his email list, 3 million on his text messaging programs, and

5 million connections on more than 15 social media sites. In addition, 8.5 million people visited his website (MyBarackObama.com) monthly, and 3 million personal phone calls were placed in the last four days of the campaign (Lutz, 2009). This multiplatform social media strategy mobilized people to utilize grassroots measures to spread campaign messages to their individual networks and transformed support into money and tangible votes.

While many candidates before Barack Obama also utilized social media in their campaigns, they were not as successful at transforming online connections into message advocacy. These efforts have continued to grow. During the 2020 Presidential election, Donald Trump's Facebook page had 30.6 million followers and Joe Biden averaged 148,600 engagements per social media post (D'Ercole, 2020). As discussed with any social media strategy, sending messages on social media platforms does not mean that the information process is participatory. Harnessing engaged and active participants is the strongest path to real-life advocacy efforts.

Despite the success of Barack Obama's campaign, many politicians continue to use social media outlets in the same top-down manner as traditional mass media platforms. Few politicians use their accounts to engage or answer voters. In fact, it was not until Father's Day 2011 that Barack Obama (@BarackObama) sent a tweet himself (Thomson, 2012). In 2015, Obama opened his own Twitter account (@POTUS) and was able to directly communicate with social media users, leading him to break social media records. He was the fastest user to reach 1 million followers, hitting the milestone in under five hours (Molina, 2015).

Every politician holds different comfort levels and norms when it comes to direct social media communication. Donald Trump was an avid Twitter user during his presidency, tweeting an average of 5.7 times per day during his first half of his term in the White House and an average of 34.8 times a day during the second half (McCarthy, 2021). Eventually, his tweets included a warning label, and his entire account was shut down to minimize the spread of misinformation on the platform. His successor Joe Biden relies on mostly communication staff to run official social media channels but utilizes social media influencers for more personal engagement (Cai, 2023).

One reason politicians may not be eager to utilize social media in a participatory manner is due to the control-participation balance that we discussed in Chapter 4. To allow users to participate, a politician must give up some control over what appears on his or her social media site. It does not matter what Barack Obama posts on his official Facebook account, users will respond in both positive and inflammatory ways. For instance, on May 7, 2022, the Obama's Twitter account (@POTUS) posted a video of their family dog, Commander, exploring the White House. While this is not a very politically divisive message, users commented on the picture to express their dissatisfaction with high gas prices, student loan debt and unemployment rates. Politicians have the option of leaving the comment function open and allowing these comments to appear, or to turn off the comment function and have more control over what appears on their site. Most choose not to censor their users completely, but do not respond to them either.

In addition to understanding how politicians are communicating with voters through social media, one of the most interesting takeaways of current voter research is the influence social media has on voter turnout. In one research study, a message was posted on various Facebook pages for users who were at least 18 years of age in the United States on Election Day, November 2, 2010. Users who received this message were shown a statement on top of their news feed that encouraged them to vote, providing a link to a local polling place and a clickable button where they could self-report that "I voted." This message would then be shared with their social network and displayed a counter of other users that had reported voting, including the names and faces of those that they know. Another group of Facebook users received the voting information but were not shown the names and faces of friends. A third group received no message on their timeline. Results from the study demonstrate that users who received the message with the names and faces of friends from their social network were significantly more likely to vote than users who received no message at all. Turnout among individuals who received the diffusion-only message, with no names or images from social network, proved identical to those with no message at all. This demonstrates the ineffectiveness of diffusion-only approaches in mobilizing voters into behavior change (Bond *et al.*, 2012). Community approaches proved to be a significant game changer for voting behaviors.

Based on what we know about behavior change research, it makes sense that individuals would be influenced to follow through with a requested behavior change if they know that their social network is also participating. Humans model the behaviors of those who they identify with. Moreover, we seek community and believe that issues that are important to our friends and family have importance to us as well.

Now we understand the importance that our private sphere relationships have on our political attitudes, a public sphere topic. Social media is the only media platform, thus far, that can converge these two spheres to encourage active voter participation. Each election cycle, we learn more about what works and what does not. However, it is important that human behavior change theory is not forgotten as new technologies emerge. Humans want to participate and share with their network. It is important to investigate how other types of organizations encourage users to do so through social media.

This chapter has explored the process of civic engagement and the influence technology has had on individual willingness to participate, sense of self, and political engagement. Social media plays an increasingly critical role in how individuals find community and mobilize online efforts into collective action. In this chapter, we've also discussed the importance of finding your personal voice and seeking causes and organizations that share in your passions and interests. Let's now focus on how the hyperlocal social media platform, Nextdoor, has emerged as a networking service for community engagement.

Case Study: Nextdoor #LoveYourNeighborhood Campaign

Civic engagement includes membership in formal community groups and participation in social activities. Getting involved with like-minded individuals is an easy way to bolster your own sense of belonging within a culture. One benefit of social media is that citizens no longer need to rely on those who live within close proximity to make these connections. Social media makes it possible for users to connect on any topic, with any person in the world. This social connectedness is important for promoting positive change. The more niche the community is, the easier it is to create tangible call-to-action toward change.

While a great benefit of social media is to connect individuals who do not live near each other, the tools of social media can also be used to unite neighbors. Nextdoor is a social media site used by nearly 1 in 3 households in the United States and more than 290,000 neighborhoods worldwide (Nextdoor, 2023). The intention of the platform is for neighbors to connect through shared interests, discover new places nearby, and get recommendations for local businesses. The social platform's mission statement is to use Nextdoor to cultivate a kinder world where everyone has a neighborhood to rely on.

Kindness is the authenticity of Nextdoor. Its branding aims to distinguish itself from other social media platforms, such as Instagram and Facebook, as being a friendlier, down-to-earth platform that fosters connections between real neighbors, not anonymous trolls, and scummy bots (Holder & Akinnibi, 2022). Within the platform, users can join communities based on interests, or simply ask questions or make a service recommendation. Despite all the efforts that aim to promote civic engagement among users, Nextdoor faced a challenge to their brand. For example, people began using Nextdoor as primarily a crime-spotting tool. They would warn others via the app when suspicious activity was going on in their neighborhood. Such a use often led to problematic and racially charged content (Holder & Akinnibi, 2022). Over time, some users did not feel safe or as though they belonged to the community.

In response, Nextdoor took steps to actively remove toxic content from the platform. In 2019, Nextdoor added a "kindness reminder" that prompts users to follow the network's guidelines and kindness standards (see Figure 15.2). These reminders were successful at removing 34% of divisive content (Holder & Akinnibi, 2022). Additionally, the platform created a mobilization campaign to entice users to share positive social media content to help bolster their sense of belonging within the community to promote civic engagement.

In 2022, Nextdoor launched the #LoveYourNeighborhoodphotography contest, a special initiative inviting neighbors to share the local flavor, faces, and beauty of their neighborhoods. The mobilization campaign received over 24,000 entries in the year showcasing what made users' neighborhood special. The mobilization campaign was effective in transitioning the conversation away from controversy, and onto the beauty of neighbors coming together for something positive.

Figure 15.2   Screenshot of Kindness Reminder from Nextdoor.com

Discussion questions

1   Reflect on your personal experience. How do social media sites, such as Nextdoor, make it easier for neighbors to connect?
2   Identify possible participatory structures of Nextdoor that could cause the platform to lose control of their mission to promote kindness. How could the platform use a mobilization strategy to regain control over their mission?
3   In your opinion, does sharing positive content via a social media platform like Nextdoor promote civic engagement? Why or why not?

Summary

This chapter illustrates the impact of social media on civic engagement. While we are still not certain whether this change is inherently good or bad, we do know that it is here to stay and holds great potential for breaking some traditional power structures, such as the oppression of minority networks and the relationship between political candidates and citizens.

We have learned that levels of civic engagement are constantly in flux, and today's digital climate allows us the opportunity to find causes and goals that match our own voice, experiences, and passions. The opportunity for connecting with individuals around the world is unprecedented, and it is important to capitalize on the many benefits of getting involved.

Social media has changed the ways individuals make decisions about their community, the world, and the people in charge. The tools and functions of social media make it possible to engage everyday citizens with political candidates. People's expectations of the political process have thus changed, as the community has grown beyond proximity boundaries. The issues and people we care about are bigger than ever before.

Social media is undoubtedly a game changer in the civic engagement arena. The technology is designed to allow society and groups within it to interact for their own needs and objectives. With enough virality, an invisible social media campaign can transform into public opinion. Nonetheless, while social media opportunity means great things for social change, it takes transparent and authentic voices as well as organized mobilization.

To maximize the amount of possible social change, people must feel as though they have control over their content. Social media brings opportunities for individuals to express their opinions, join causes, and interweave the private world of family and friends with their public interests (Valenzuela, 2013). The field of communication for development also believes that social media can be used for positive social change. Let's now explore this area in greater detail and explain how to best incorporate social media into development initiatives in Chapter 16.

Key Takeaways

1   Civic engagement allows individuals to meet in community groups and participate in social activities, leading to better health, sense of belonging, accomplishment, economic development, and more effective government within a society.
2   Globalization has integrated people around the world by breaking down many traditional barriers and transforming civic engagement to more augmented and geographically dispersed initiatives.
3   Groups with tangible goals and a clear voice can accomplish more than individuals alone. As individual voices become aggregated, they come together to form public opinion.
4   There is a danger that online activism has little authenticity and no real effect on real-life outcomes. It is important to seek out civic engagement that speaks to your experiences and passions, because half-hearted engagement may satisfy your desire to help others but have little impact on society.
5   Social media has become a key source for political information and significantly changed the election process by granting candidates and citizens the opportunity to communicate with greater openness and transparency, though few are using the technology to its full potential.
6   Social media campaigns should move beyond the awareness stage of advocacy, encouraging supporters to share in the narrative.

References

Batista, L.C. & Cruz-Ledón, A.M. (2013) The relationship between civic engagement and health among older adults. Available at http://digitalcommons.fiu.edu/cgi/viewcontent.cgi?article=1113&context=sferc (accessed November 17, 2023).

Bond, R., Fariss, C., Jones, J., Kramer, A.D.I., Marlow, C., Settle, J.E. & Fowler, J.H. (2012) A 61-millionperson experiment in social influence and political mobilization. *Nature*, 489(7415), 295–298.

Boulos, K. & Wheeler, S. (2007) The emerging web 2.0 social software: an enabling suite of sociable technologies in health and health care education. *Health Information and Libraries Journal*, 24, 2–23.

Burgess, J., Foth, M. & Klaebe, H. (2006) Everyday creativity as civic engagement: a cultural citizenship view of new media. Available at http://eprints.qut.edu.au/5056/.

Cai, S. (2023) Bidens digital strategy: An army of influencers. Available at https://www.axios.com/2023/04/09/bidens-digital-strategy-an-army-of-influencers (accessed November 17, 2023).

Campbell, C. & Jovchelovitch, S. (2000) Health, community and development: towards a social psychology of participation. *Journal of Community and Applied Social Psychology*, 10(4), 255–270.

Census (2021) 2020 presidential election voting and registration tables now available. Available at https://www.census.gov/newsroom/press-releases/2021/2020-presidential-election-voting-and-registration-tables-now-available.html#:~:text=APRIL%2029%2C%202021%20—%20The%202020by%20the%20U.S.%20Census%20Bureau (accessed November 17, 2023).

D'Ercole, A. (2020) U.S. election. Trump vs. Biden. *Pew Research Center*. Available at https://www.pewresearch.org/journalism/2020/07/30/demographics-of-americans-who-get-most-of-their-political-news-from-social-media (accessed November 17, 2023).

Dahlgren, P. (2009) *Media and Political Engagement*. New York: Cambridge University Press.

Gil de Zúñiga, H., Jung, N. & Valenzuela, S. (2012) Social media use for news and individuals' social capital, civic engagement and political participation. *Journal of Computer-Mediated Communication*, 17(3), 319–336.

Grasso, M.T., Farrall, S., Gray, E., Hay, C. & Jennings, W. (2019) Socialization and generational political trajectories: an age, period and cohort analysis of political participation in Britain. *Journal of Elections, Public Opinion and Parties*, 29(2), 199–221.

Habermas, J. (1992) *The Structural Transformation of the Public Sphere: An Inquiry into a Category of Bourgeois Society*. Cambridge, MA: Polity Press.

Holder, S. & Akinnibi, F. (2022) Nextdoor's quest to beat toxic content and make money. *Bloomberg*. Available at https://www.bloomberg.com/news/features/2022-06-09/nextdoor-s-quest-to-beat-toxic-content-and-make-money (accessed November 17, 2023).

Hong, S. & Nadler, D. (2012) Which candidates do the public discuss online in an election campaign: the use of social media by 2012 Presidential candidates and its impact on candidate salience. *Government Information Quarterly*, 29(4), 455–461.

Jackson, S.J. (2021) Making# BlackLivesMatter in the shadow of Selma: collective memory and racial justice activism in US news. *Communication, Culture and Critique*, 14(3), 385–404.

Jones, P. & Hudson, J. (2000) Civic duty and expressive voting: Is virtue its own reward? *Kyklos*, 53(1), 3–16.

Lévy, P. (1997) *Collective Intelligence*. New York: Plenum.

Lum, T.Y. & Lightfoot, E. (2005) The effects of volunteering on the physical and mental health of older people. *Research on Aging*, 27(1), 31–55.

Lutz, M. (2009) The Social pulpit: Barack Obama's social media toolkit. *Harvard University*. Available at http://cyber.law.harvard.edu/sites/cyber.law.harvard.edu/files/Social%20Pulpit%20-%20Barack%20Obamas%20Social%20Media%20Toolkit%201.09.pdf (accessed November 17, 2023).

Matthews, B. (2023) Social media stats for charities and nonprofits. Available at https://empower.agency/social-media-stats-charities-nonprofits/ (accessed November 17, 2023).

McAllister, A. (2013) New media and new voices. *The Philanthropist*, 25(2), 93–98.

McCarthy, N. (2021) End of the road for Trump's Twitter account. *Statista*. Available at https://www.statista.com/chart/19561/total-number-of-tweets-from-donald-trump/#:~:text=Trump%20tweeted%205.7%20times%20perdoes%20Trump%20go%20from%20here%3F (accessed November 17, 2023).

McCaughey, M. & Ayer, M. (2003) *Cyberactivism: Online Activism in Theory and Practice*. New York: Routledge.

McMillan, D.W. & Chavis, D.M. (1986) Sense of community: a definition and theory. *Journal of Community Psychology*, 14(1), 6–23.

Mitchell, A., Jurkowitz, M., Oliphant, B. & Shearer, E. (2021) Social Media and the News. *Pew Research Center*. Available at https://www.pewresearch.org/journalism/2020/07/30/demographics-of-americans-who-get-most-of-their-political-news-from-social-media/ (accessed November 17, 2023).

Molina, B. (2015) Obama's Twitter account breaks world record. *USA Today*. Available at http://www.usatoday.com/story/tech/2015/05/20/obama-world-record/27640321/ (accessed November 17, 2023).

Morozov, E. (2009) The Brave New World of slacktivism. *NPR*. Available at http://www.npr.org/templates/story/story.php?storyId=104302141 (accessed November 17, 2023).

Nextdoor (2023) Discover your neighborhood. Available at https://nextdoor.com (accessed November 17, 2023).

Putnam, R. (1993) The prosperous community: social capital and public life. *The American Prospect*, 13, 35–42.

Putnam, R. (1995) Bowling alone: America's declining social capital. *Journal of Democracy*, 6(1), 65–78.

Putnam, R. (2000) *Bowling Alone: The Collapse and Revival of American Community*. New York: Simon & Schuster.

Quan-Haase, A., Wellman, B., Witte, J. & Hampton, K. (2002) Capitalizing on the net: social contact, civic engagement, and sense of community. In: B. Wellman & C. Haythornthwaite (eds) *The Internet in Everyday Life*, pp. 289–324. Oxford: Blackwell Publishers Ltd.

Rheingold, H. (2008) Using participatory media and public voice to encourage civic engagement. In: W.L. Bennett (ed) *Civic Life Online: Learning How Digital Media Can Engage Youth*, pp. 97–118. Cambridge, MA: MIT Press.

Shah, D. (1998) Civic engagement, interpersonal trust, and television use: an individual-level assessment of social capital. *Political Psychology*, 19(3), 469–496.

Statista (2023) Percentage of U.S. Congress Members who posted on official social media accounts in 2020. Available at https://www.statista.com/statistics/958794/congress-members-posted-official-social-media-accounts-usa/ (accessed November 17, 2023).

Stiglitz, J. (2002) *Globalization and Its Discontents*. New York: Norton & Company.

Stoll, C. (1995) *Silicon Snake Oil: Second Thoughts on the Information Highway*. New York: Doubleday.

Thomson, S. (2012) Political organizations and social media. Available at http://digitalcommons.olin.edu/cgi/viewcontent.cgi?article=1000&context=ahs_capstone_2012 (accessed November 17, 2023).

Valenzuela, S. (2013) Unpacking the use of social media for protest behavior: the roles of information, opinion expression, and activism. *American Behavioral Scientist*, 57(7), 920–942.

Wallace, E., Buil, I. & De Chernatony, L. (2017) When does "liking" a charity lead to donation behaviour? Exploring conspicuous donation behaviour on social media platforms. *European Journal of Marketing*, 51(11/12), 2002–2029.

16

Communication for Development

Learning Objectives

After reading this chapter, you should be able to:
1 Understand and apply communication for development theories to your social media strategy.
2 Examine the differences between modernization, dependency, and participatory approaches to behavior change.
3 Navigate the social media opportunities and challenges provided by communication for development literature.

Introduction

Communication scholars have long been interested in the way popular culture is reflected in everyday life. Many believe that by looking at the media products that a society consumes, much can be understood about the society itself. With the advent of social media, it becomes more and more feasible to look at the media content that everyday citizens produce. What does it say about our world that over 2.9 billion active users log into Facebook each month (Kemp, 2023)? Does this mean that we are a highly connected society? Or does it mean that

Strategic Social Media: From Marketing to Social Change, Second Edition. L. Meghan Mahoney and Tang Tang.
© 2024 John Wiley & Sons, Inc. Published 2024 by John Wiley & Sons, Inc.

we are a society of deep isolation? Drawing conclusions about a society based on media consumption habits is a difficult and complex process that should not be taken lightly.

In previous chapters, we discussed the complicated process of how media influences user behavior. People negotiate media artifacts and engage in a sense-making process that contributes to the way in which they see the world. If nothing else, those 2.9 billion Facebook users can tell us who has access to the Internet around the globe and how willing those people are to use that technology to voice "what's on their mind." Clearly, media context influences the way cultures, ideologies, and societies evolve. Thus, it naturally lends itself as a resource in positive social change and is often utilized in development contexts for social advancement. Oftentimes, these interventions are done through communication for development initiatives.

The past few years have made it very clear that social media is able to spark human rights organization, such as the Ukraine refugee crisis, in ways previously unheard of. If we look back at all the lessons learned from communication for development literature, it becomes much clearer why digital media, specifically social media, has proven an innovative tool for permanent human behavior change. There have been many historical transformations that researchers interested in behavior change have studied over the past century. Despite these transformations, behavior change researchers suggest that media is a tool, and ultimately, we should be interested in the way everyday citizens make decisions regarding their own lives. Through a theoretical understanding of human behavior, communication specialists can attract, persuade, and entice users with media messages. Your goal as a social media practitioner is to best understand these theories so that you can navigate media consumers toward desired behavior change initiatives.

Thus, this chapter aims to look at three strands of communication for development theories: modernization, dependency and participatory theories, and the opportunities and challenges of each. It then examines the positive deviance approach to behavior change and demonstrates how this approach can be applied to social media campaigns. This understanding helps to better conceptualize the concepts of diffusion, community, and mobilization toward socially positive initiatives.

Exploring Communication for Development

Communication for development refers to the application of communication strategies and principles in the developing world toward political democracy, rising levels of productivity and industrialization, high literacy rates, and longer life expectancy (Waisbord, 2001). Specifically, these initiatives promote political, economic, and educational growth (Inkeles & Smith, 1974).

Communication for development practitioners are interested in establishing permanent behavior change among large audiences. *Behavior change* is defined as a research-based process for addressing knowledge, attitudes, and practices that are intrinsically linked to program goals (UNICEF, 2013). Here, participants are provided information through well-defined strategies, using a user-appropriate mix of interpersonal, group and mass media channels, and participatory approaches. When interested in social change, UNICEF (2013) argues that one must be concerned with the way society is organized, including the distribution of power among institutions. For human behavior to change on a large scale, societal norms and structural inequalities must be taken into consideration, and the focus is on the community as the unit of change. Thus, it is important for strategists to view their organization through a broader lens.

Permanent behavior and social change is a lofty and near-impossible goal. Often, communication practitioners fight against centuries of habit and fallacies. How do you get a community to start living their everyday lives differently, especially if the message is counter-intuitive to many of the society's most habitual practices? Some communication for development initiatives tackle enrollment, retention, and completion of education by female children in cultures where parents refuse to send girls to school because they are needed for household work (KCCI, 2013). Other initiatives promote safe-sex communication between parents and children in cultures where sexual conversation is considered taboo (Guijarro *et al.*, 1999). There are also broader media development initiatives that examine international immunization inequity due to different perceptions regarding immunization (Shrimp, 2023). Hopefully you can see why communication for development strategists need to inspire behavior change through more culturally nuanced approaches.

Communication for development interventions take the perspective that mass media is best suited for organization and efficiency through staffing and funding (Hornik, 1993), which is a fundamentally different approach than using media to sell. If you are looking to organize individuals with a limited number of finances and manpower, perhaps from your own living room, there is much to learn from the field of communication for development. This work has focused on effective message development, collaboration across various fields, and global implications. These are all imperative steps toward a successful marketing campaign.

Modernization, Dependency, and Participatory Approaches to Behavior Change

Chapter 2 explained how Rogers' diffusion of innovations theory helps spread new ideas through media outlets over time among members of a targeted community (Haider & Kreps, 2004). Behavior change occurs because of this complicated process of diffusion, adoption, and/or rejection of new ideas. This process involves four main interacting factors: an innovation, communication channels, social systems, and time (Haider & Kreps, 2004). However, we also learned that this process is difficult, often too top-down, and does not have a high return rate of permanent behavior change.

Think about how much you learn in a classroom where teachers only lecture at you, rather than allowing you to participate and engage in the process. It is probably not the most ideal learning environment. Without participation, individuals are much more likely to get sidetracked with their own thoughts or distractions, or even fall asleep due to boredom. The same is true in behavior change initiatives. Luckily, social media provides great opportunity for participation and engagement.

The hope with diffusion-centric messages is that, over time, people will pass through various stages and eventually adopt, implement, and confirm recommended messages (Svenkerud & Singhal, 1998). If adoption is successful, individuals could initiate new desired behavior through commencement or end undesirable behaviors through cessation (Haider & Kreps, 2004). However, the diffusion process is difficult to account for, and there is not much message producers can do to guide users along the way to ensure completion.

This top-down communication approach was apparent in every discipline, not just the field of development communication. We call this period the modernization era of communication. *Modernization theory* tends to be simple, ideal, and mechanical. This approach portrays development as an extremely linear process where media transmits an idealized lifestyle to audiences (Tufte, 2000). Here, the aim is to produce fully developed societies of mass consumption, much like the cultures of the Western World.

The assumption of modernization is that after an innovation is developed, wide adoption will follow in a highly predictable and systematic process. This era of communication for development research lasted for many years, and the same assumption has been mirrored in the way we started social media messages in marketing.

Consider the evolution of the modernization era like the inception of X (formerly Twitter). In 2006, Twitter's co-founder Jack Dorsey (@Jack) developed an SMS-based communication platform so that uses could update each other on their progress at work (MacArthur, 2013). At that time, text message plans were expensive, and Twitter allowed the opportunity for users to communicate without racking up their mobile phone bills. The goal of this social media was to increase production and efficiency and essentially make money. However, during its debut, this technology provided users with no way of replying or engaging with one another. Users did not like this (and who could blame them; no one wants to keep up with constant updates intended for no particular users), so they began including an @ symbol before their username to identify which user they were communicating with in their tweet. Eventually, the Twitter team added this structure, as well as other interactive features such as hashtags and retweets.

We see this top-down, one-way communication messages all the time on social media: "Buy our product!"; "Check out our new program"; "Visit our store." The dissatisfaction with these top-down modernization approaches was apparent. Users find constant selling with limited engagement patronizing and annoying. Our society is filled with this type of noise, through billboards, television commercials, and flyers on our car windshields. This type of marketing tells consumers that you don't care who they are or what they have to say. You are telling them that you find yourself more knowledgeable than they are. In essence, you are giving users information that is important to you, but not necessarily to them. This one-way communication process, where opinion leaders mediate the impact of mass media communications, is not an effective way to mobilize users.

In the 1960s, a new approach to communication for development began to emerge, as communication for development practitioners found that the early adopters of desired behavioral goals tended to be those individuals who were more involved in local organizations, better educated, and held community leadership roles (Glanz *et al.*, 1997; Melkote, 2001). This approach, *dependency theory*, served as a critique of the modernization process. Researchers from this paradigm did not believe that the problems of the Third World countries would simply disappear as soon as development occurred in the form of economic growth and industrialization (Sood & Rogers, 2000; Tufte, 2000). In fact, they argued that quite the opposite would occur, and that international capitalism was the root of developmental problem, not the solution. Developed nations profit from commerce while peripheral nations suffer from unequal exchange processes. In this theory, media promotes cultural imperialism and strengthens dependency on consumerism.

This peripheral process can be a complicated and difficult process to understand. Influenced by Marxist and other critical theorists, dependency theorists believe that the problems of the Third World reflect unequal distribution of resources created by the global expansion of Western capitalism (Waisbord, 2001). These challenges are due to a larger social structure, rather than a lack of information.

Let's take one community's challenge of drinking dirty water as an example. Yes, you can go in and teach a community through mass media the importance of boiling water before drinking it, but dependency theorists suggest that this transfer of information does not actually solve the problem. This disparity of resources is due to a broader social structure and inequity. In fact, by turning to mass media as the single resource in fighting these problems, fundamental problems of media access and content are often ignored. Media campaigns can reach millions through public service announcements on television. This can prove an effective and efficient way to spread information about boiling water before drinking. However, the uneducated and the poor often do not have access to the technology. Moreover, the most powerful and rich often own broadcast services. Thus, the cycle of haves and have-nots continues.

This cycle of economic disparity is strongly linked to media access. *Digital divide* explains the inequity between those who have access to the latest information technologies and those who do not (Compaine, 2001). If an individual has limited access to new media, it leads to economic and social handicap. Today, our concept of the digital divide is changing. Internet non-adoption is narrowing, with less than 7% of US adults self-reported that they had never gone online (Pew Research Center, 2021). Though new media (specifically mobile technology) is allowing more diversity among users than other mass media technologies, access is still influenced by factors such as age, education, income, race, and ethnicity.

The dependency approach to communication for development explained why the modernization approach didn't yield high levels of behavior change. It suggested that individuals do not like being talked down to. Individuals learn most when they can participate and engage in the information process. Unfortunately, this dependency era did not offer a lot of solutions. At that time, diffusion messages were still the most cost-effective way to reach a mass audience in a short amount of time. For many years, communication for development practitioners had little solution.

In the 1980s, an era of participatory approaches began to emerge. *Participatory theory* criticizes many of the underlying assumptions of modernization theory. However, unlike dependency theorists, the focus of participatory theory not only criticized media power structures and consumerism but also shifted efforts toward more of a facilitation role. Here, the goal becomes individual and collective empowerment of the people through community participation.

The role of media users is much different in this participatory approach. Like what we discussed in Chapter 5, participatory approaches view media users as playing an active role, rather than serving as receivers of information. This approach can be seen as a form of cultural studies, as it looks at popular culture as an outlet of everyday life and popular sectors of society. It examines the needs, histories, trajectories, and distinct sociocultural profiles (Tufte, 2000). Through participatory measures, the goal of communication moves toward sparking interpersonal dialogue to promote cultural identity, trust, and commitment (Waisbord, 2001). Rather than disseminating information from the top to the bottom, it is a process where everyone discusses possibilities together. This more human-centered approach believes that the role of media and technologies should be used to supplement, rather than dominate, interpersonal methods (Gray-Felder & Deane, 1999; Waisbord, 2001). Only through sharing and reconstructing experiences, can communication provide a sense of ownership to community members.

Let's go back to our earlier classroom example. Think about how much more you learn in a classroom when you were able to exchange ideas, ask questions, and take part in the creation of lectures. The role of the "expert" in this model is simply a facilitator. Communities do not need to be injected with expert knowledge. Rather, communication technologies should be used as a resource in facilitating ideas that are already within the community. Even though the solutions of one culture may be different from those of another (or from Western ideals), they still hold value. In fact, social media technology allows a space for every culture to have a voice.

The participatory approach is based on one of the concepts widely used by social media: collective intelligence. *Collective intelligence* is defined as the ability of a group to solve more problems than its individual members (Heylighen, 1999). There is wisdom in crowds, and everyone is essentially an expert in something. This phenomenon has been dubbed crowdsourcing, peer production and Wikinomics and is based very broadly on the premise that groups of individuals do things collectively that seem intelligent (Malone, 2011).

Wikipedia is a great example of how contributors from all over the world have collectively created a space for high-quality information with no centralized control; anyone can contribute and change anything at any time. Social media has provided a space where organizing and sharing is easier than ever, while traditional mass media technologies do not allow for this type of participation.

Today, most communication for development interventions fall along two conceptual continuums: diffusion and participation. The *diffusion model* is based on Rogers' diffusion of innovations theory and is central to the modernization approach of the 1950s and 1960s (Morris, 2003). Here, behavior change is achieved by educating individuals. By providing knowledge, individuals begin to experience a shift in attitudes, which then influences how they practice. These types of campaigns are generally completed through mass media.

The *participation model* suggests that behavior change is a horizontal not vertical process (Gray-Felder & Deane, 1999; Morris, 2003). It stresses the importance of community dialogue for empowerment (Gray-Felder & Deane, 1999). By using participatory approaches to media design, one is better able to include and reach the voices of the targeted and hard-to-reach media users (Pant *et al.*, 2002).

Paulo Freire, an influential thinker in the field, suggests that individuals can intervene actively in their own process of becoming aware and conscious of their own reality. The dialogue of the social commitment and the constant dialectic among action–reflection–action are core elements in what has become to be known as the *Paulo Freire method* (Freire, 1969; Tufte, 2000). This approach is based on horizontal dialogue between individuals, something that traditional media does not provide.

Researchers further found that most communication interventions fail because technocrats design them based on their own personal view of reality (Singhal & Rogers, 2003). They demonstrate that true participation does not involve a subject–object relationship, only a subject–subject relationship. Media users do not need to be provided with expert knowledge:

> Once the oppressed, both individually and collectively, begin to critically reflect on their social situation, possibilities arise for them to break the "culture of silence" through the articulation of discontent and action (Singhal & Rogers, 2003, p. 232).

This diffusion–participation continuum (Figure 16.1) is something that behavior change theorists still struggle with today. Mass media tends to lend itself more toward a diffusion approach. It is a great way to get your message to the mass audience. However, we know the benefits of allowing media users greater participation in the behavior change process. Social media has been able to bridge this gap by making it easier for thousands of individuals to engage and participate with media messages in a more egalitarian landscape. It is not always in your best interest to give the mass control and participation over your messages. However, a strict diffusion strategy will not get you far in today's digital climate. As a social media practitioner, it is important that you know the opportunities and challenges for each approach.

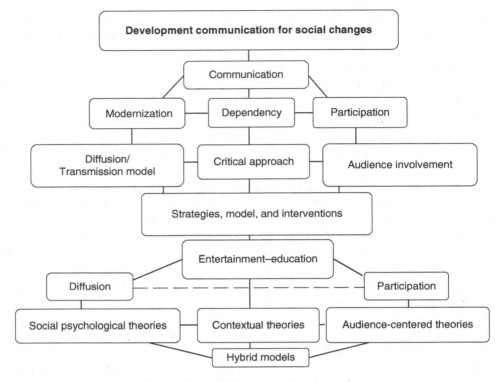

Figure 16.1   Diffusion–participation scale.

Opportunities and Challenges of Communication for Development Approaches

All three communication for development approaches continue to help guide various strategies, models, and interventions for social and behavior change in the field today. It is important to note that all types of communication for development interventions fall along the diffusion–participation continuum based on the objective and type of resources available. There has yet to be a magical formula developed where individuals interested in behavior change can plug into any initiative regardless of the circumstances. Each approach has its own strengths and weaknesses (Figure 16.2).

We have already discussed the many challenges of a diffusion-centric model. Media users are approached as the mass, which is not very effective in terms of behavior change. The likelihood of achieving permanent behavior change in many users is small. The process is also complicated and top-down in nature, which many users may find patronizing and annoying. It is also important to understand that the most problematic behaviors are cultural and habitual, not because of a lack of information. Diffusion-centric strategies are not the best at prompting permanent behavior change.

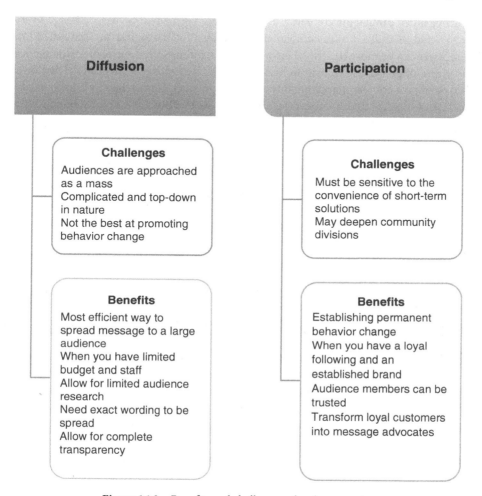

Diffusion

Challenges
Audiences are approached
as a mass
Complicated and top-down
in nature
Not the best at promoting
behavior change

Benefits
Most efficient way to
spread message to a large
audience
When you have limited
budget and staff
Allow for limited audience
research
Need exact wording to be
spread
Allow for complete
transparency

Participation

Challenges
Must be sensitive to the
convenience of short-term
solutions
May deepen community
divisions

Benefits
Establishing permanent
behavior change
When you have a loyal
following and an
established brand
Audience members can be
trusted
Transform loyal customers
into message advocates

Figure 16.2 Benefits and challenges of each approach.

However, it is important not to forget the many benefits of a diffusion approach. This approach is the most efficient way to quickly spread your message to a large audience. If you have a limited budget and staff, this approach may make the most sense. It allows you to reach many individuals and gain a mass following with limited audience research. Also, diffusion allows you to have strict control over your message. This may be the best strategy if you have very clear, tangible objectives and it is important that the exact wording (such as event time or date) is spread to your consumers. Diffusion also allows complete transparency for your product and/or organization. Though we often talk about strict diffusion as a negative marketing tool, every product needs one place for strict diffusion. Often, this is your company's website. Most social media messages should link users back to this diffusion landing page.

Participatory campaigns are better at establishing permanent behavior change in users. They should be utilized once companies have a loyal following and an established brand. These users can be more trusted when it comes to handing over control of media messages. The release of power will transform loyal customers into message advocates. The power of this type of peer-to-peer marketing through social media is unmatched by traditional diffusion. If your organization and messages are well trusted within a community, be confident in giving up control and provide as many opportunities as possible for users to create, share, and transform the media messages to their individual networks through social media.

Participatory communication for social change includes any process through which people define themselves what they need and how to get there, through dialogue (Byrne *et al.*, 2005, p. 3): "It utilizes dialogue that leads to collective problem identification of solutions to development issues." Participation makes content provider–consumer relationships more egalitarian (Dutta, 2006). However, not everyone is interested in having more equal relationships among producers and consumers.

There are several criticisms of an entirely participatory model. According to Waisbord (2001), participatory approaches must be sensitive to the convenience of short-term solutions, recognize the implications of outside manipulation, translate participatory ideas into actual programs, take note of uninterested communities, and understand that participation may deepen community divisions. Most of these challenges could be avoided if they were carried out in communities where participants already hold strong linkages.

It should also be noted that these two models are not completely antagonistic to one another. It is more impactful to draw components from both approaches based on cultural nuances, as even participatory projects require some sort of information transfer (Morris, 2003). It is imperative that practitioners consistently monitor and evaluate how consumers are responding to campaign messaging. Social media practitioners must utilize audience research to develop a clear strategy that links to goals on how and when to utilize each approach.

The following action plan can be used as a guide when you design your own media messages.

Diffusion/Participation Action Plan

1　Use more diffusion-centric techniques if tight control over your media message is needed, you have a limited budget, or attempt to build a large mass media audience.
2　Use more participatory techniques if you know your consumers well, are more interested in transforming existing consumers into loyal advocates and hold trust within the target community.
3　Complete frequent monitoring and audience evaluation of your communication strategy to determine where on the diffusion-participation continuum your message should fall.

Though many of these approaches have incredible points of difference along the communication for development continuum, there are many points of convergence that have been achieved in the past decades. These include the need for political will and empowerment, a "toolkit" conception of strategies that provide different diagnoses for different contexts, an integration of "top-down" and "bottom-up" approaches, a combination of multimedia and interpersonal communication, and an inclusion of both personal and environmental approaches (Waisbord, 2001). You may want to use mass media for the diffusion portion of a campaign, but then send interpersonal community reinforcement via social media to promote the participatory portion of the campaign.

One such example of a mixed methods "toolkit" strategy is a science-art social media initiative in India to promote vaccination. India-based filmmakers worked with various communication development teams to foster community leaders as script writers and film makers in their own communities (Burleson *et al.*, 2023). This intervention integrates diffusion and participatory approaches by utilizing mass media and interpersonal communication. Communities were provided with communication technologies and resources for post-production editing and were asked to make 8 short films that encourage citizens to get their second COVID-19 vaccination. These videos were broadcast through the Wasthya Plus Network Odia website; Facebook page with 513,000 subscribers; YouTube channel with 248,000 subscribers; and local WhatsApp groups. This intervention also includes a community-based interpersonal communication component. Such an "on-the-ground" community approach is a great way to get specific users involved in a culturally specific manner toward an overall campaign goal.

As mentioned previously in this chapter, the goal of communication for development is to promote political, economic, and educational growth through the application of communication strategies. These strategies range on a continuum of diffusion and participatory approaches to behavior change. The final widely shared media products combined both strategies. They were culturally specific and research-based that resonated with the target population. "Engaging local filmmakers in both the planning and implementation stages helps foster ownership of the content and creates appealing media for society that aims to nudge them toward healthy behaviors" (Burleson *et al.*, 2023). These localized media campaigns prove much more influential than top-down government PSAs.

Regardless of where you stand on the continuum in your own approach to creating social media messages, the end goal is likely the same – to pass information to a group of target users. Some messages are more successful than others (often, the most successful messages are those that have conducted the best audience research prior to content creation). Sometimes, a communication strategist follows every theoretical rule for prompting behavior change and audiences still do not react.

Faced with this challenge, a new trend in communication for development interventions begins to look through the positive deviance approach to behavior change. Rather than focusing on the best way to promote behavior change in a target audience, positive deviance "enables communities to discover the wisdom they already have and then to act on it"

(Singhal, 2010, p. 2). This approach changes the role of media users from passive receivers of information to a more empowered and participatory role. Media users are problem solvers that play an intricate role in message design and campaign goals.

In one famous positive deviance case study in Vietnam, childhood malnutrition across a village was reduced by 75% (Bradley *et al.*, 2009). Here, researchers examined community children that were thriving despite high rates of malnutrition and stunting in their rural village and found that these mothers were feeding their children shrimp and crabs that they found on rice paddies. These fish were not traditionally used by the mass because they were thought to be inappropriate for young children. However, once this information was disseminated across the rural village, nutrition rates dramatically increased. Rather than an expert arriving and informing the population of solutions that work in an outside culture, communication for development practitioners identified deviants within the culture to find viable solutions.

This positive deviance approach demonstrates our changing perception of power and media users. Rather than viewing your consumers as passive receivers of information, consider how valuable their experiences and contributions would make to message design and product creation. After all, they know their lifestyle better than anyone.

While most social media practitioners do preliminary research to determine who is most likely to be interested in their organization and then construct a message according to their ideals and values, the positive deviance approach challenges you to think differently. Rather than focusing on what is wrong with a community (e.g., "Why isn't anyone donating to my cause?"), the positive deviance approach seeks out those few key community members who are in less-than-ideal situations but who, despite their circumstances, are engaging the desired behavior anyway. Instead of focusing on the most likely mass, it encourages you to give attention to outliers. Gladwell's (2008) best-selling book *Outliers* explains how outliers play a part in our intelligence and decision-making processes. It makes sense to examine these outliers, who have taken purposeful steps toward individual decision-making when interested in behavior change.

As a social media practitioner, you would examine your network to see who is most likely *not* in a life situation to participate in the campaign but has gone ahead and done so anyway. This analysis allows you to highlight secondary communities that are likely to follow through with your projected goal, but which are not always apparent in a traditional audience analysis.

It should be noted that it takes time to learn how and why these individuals follow through with the desired behavior change and then mirror their suggestions with other members of the community. The positive deviance approach is a behavior change strategy that requires message creators to give up a lot of control. It takes time to begin thinking about your consumers differently and consider how much there is to learn from them.

In summary, communication development research has gone beyond individual-level behavior change to looking at interventions and processes at the community level. The most important takeaway from this theoretical research is that behavior change interventions based on theory hold a better chance of success than those that are not (King, 1999). Theory makes it easier to understand why or why not an intervention proves successful. This is one area that will set you apart from other individuals on the social media job market. Having a clear understanding of theoretical approaches to behavior change makes you much more valuable than a professional who is only familiar with the various tools of social media technology. Let's now examine how one communication for development project, Social Media 4 Peace, uses a hybrid approach to ignite social change.

Case Study: Social Media 4 Peace

With rapid dissemination of misinformation, media literacy becomes an important global concept. The Social Media 4 Peace project (see Figure 16.3) aims to tackle online information that incites violence and hatred in conflict-prone communities, while protecting freedom of expression and enhancing messages of peace (Hulin, 2023). To date, over 50 partners from four countries have formed a coalition to tackle online misinformation and hatred through a combination of structural policy changes, as well as localized community interventions.

The first step of the project is to conduct research in each of the cultures to determine root causes, scale, and impact of the harmful online content (Hulin, 2023). Though many of the media literacy challenges are the same globally, each culture's power structures and norms influence the way misinformation spreads. These cultural nuances are

Figure 16.3   Screenshot of UNESCO's Social Media 4 Peace Project.

important for tackling changes. Thus, to create policy change, Social Media 4 Peace need to identify effective leaders and agents of change in these communities.

At the structural level, the Social Media 4 Peace project works with tech companies to interpret global policies to help with platform regulation. These stakeholders work together to improve the content moderation process. These revised legal frameworks keep various stakeholders accountable in the mission, as well as provide media professionals training necessary for conflict-sensitive reporting. While these top-down efforts are commendable, they don't do much to stop the root of the problem, instead they only regulate problematic content.

Using communication for development strategies, the Social Media 4 Peace project tackled the problem from a community level as well. They provided media and information literacy training to empower youth to detect and be more resilient to harmful content. They selected youth champions to train and share peace-building narratives that were culturally appropriate and engaging for other youth. Additionally, 50 girls were trained for coding skills to provide more equitable opportunities for online content creation.

The Social Media 4 Peace project "takes into account social, cultural, and linguistic nuances to develop and review content moderation and curation rules and tools in a localized manner" (Hulin, 2023). Had the project solely utilized a top-down approach, less would be done to combat the root of the problem. Additionally, had the project solely utilized a participatory bottom-up approach, the policy and structures needed to regulate would not exist. The integrated hybrid approach considers the structural complexities of information dissemination. Various organizations that already worked within high-risk communities were given support to help train individuals they were serving. The training took place on an interpersonal face-to-face level. Media is used simply as a resource, and *people* are the change makers and storytellers of the movement. Organizations do whatever they can to ensure that individuals are able to tell the story that they choose to tell and do not become a burden to the process. Officials are used as a resource to facilitate technology, law, or policy challenges. However, they strive to make the actual stories as participatory and bottom-up as possible. This shift from an agent of change to a facilitator of change has proven highly effective.

Discussion questions

1   In your opinion, how technology plays a role in the Social Media 4 Peace Project?
2   What role did community-level initiatives play in the Social Media 4 Peace mission? Why is this hybrid approach necessary to entice change?
3   Reflect on your own experiences. What advantages did communities gain when official policies were created to combat the spread of misinformation? What challenges could remain?

Summary

The field of communication for development has clearly evolved toward two very different positions. The first position argues that development problems stem from a lack of information among population. The second position believes that power inequality proves the underlying problem of development challenges (Waisbord, 2001). These dyadic paradigms have informed diagnoses, recommendations, and intervention implementations differently at every level. Arguably, the aim of both camps is to remove constraints for a more equal and participatory society (Waisbord, 2001). However, how each paradigm attempts to achieve such change is very different.

There is no right or wrong way to create behavior change messages. The goal of this chapter is to provide you with the knowledge and theory behind when to use each approach. If you are marketing a new product that needs tight control over your message and you are interested in short-term minimal behavior change across a mass audience, a primarily diffusion-centric approach may be right for you. If you have a strong understanding and faith in your consumers and are ready to ask them for bigger, more permanent behavior change, a participatory approach is necessary. However, regardless of where you sit on this continuum, it is wise to include some elements of both paradigms.

In fact, many communication for development interventions combine elements of both diffusion and participation. A hybrid model proves the most effective. In addition, communication for behavior change efforts also stress the need for monitoring and evaluating efforts through community dialogue and feedback at all stages (Waisbord, 2001), not just at the production level. Ultimately, behavior change is a process of public and private dialogue through which people define who they are, what they want, and how they can get it (Gray-Felder & Deane, 1999). Hopefully, this chapter has demonstrated the need for including theory in your social media strategy. One might even argue that this theoretical understanding of human behavior is more important to social media marketers than mastering business models and technological tools. We now know how users negotiate media messages in accordance with their own experiences and lived reality. Just as media contexts influence the way cultures, ideologies, and societies evolve, they also change these perceptions.

Chapter 17 will focus on a particular communication for development intervention, entertainment–education (E-E). This media strategy illustrates our need for oral storytelling and culture as we make decisions about our daily lives. As the world around us becomes more and more globalized, it is easy to ignore the nuances from one culture to another. We begin to make consumer decisions based on these conceptualizations. E-E research demonstrates how imperative narrative constructions shape how we identify ourselves with the world around us. Through a thorough understanding of E-E, more can be done to ensure that consumers are not only interested in receiving your brand narrative but also want to contribute and share it with their own personal networks. Let's talk more in Chapter 17.

Key Takeaways

1 Communication for development is the application of communication strategies to promote political, economic, and educational growth around the world.
2 Communication for development interventions have transitioned through three eras of approaches to behavior change: modernization, dependency, and participation. There are challenges and opportunities with each approach, and communication professionals should know where and why their message falls on the diffusion–participation continuum.
3 The positive deviance approach to behavior change does not focus on the best way to establish behavior change in a target audience, but instead enables communities to discover the wisdom they already have and then to act on it. This makes it a great strategy for gaining potential secondary consumers.
4 Theory makes it easier to understand why or why not an intervention proves successful. This is one area that will set you apart from other individuals on the social media job market. Having a clear understanding of theoretical approaches to behavior change makes you much more valuable than a professional who is only familiar with the various tools of social media technology.

References

Bradley, E.H., Curry, L.A., Ramanadhan, S., Rowe, L., Nembhard, I.M. & Krumholz, H.M. (2009) Research in action: using positive deviance to improve quality of health care. *Implementation Science*, 4(1), 25.

Burleson, J., Ganjoo, R., Rath, S., Rath, N., Bhaktaram, A., Jamison, A.M., Alperstein, N., Pascual-Ferra, P., Barnett, D.J., Mohanty, S., Parida, M., Orton, P., Kluegel, E. & Rimal, R. (2023) Production of vaccination videos in India: learnings from a science-art Partnership. *BMC Public Health*, 23, 736.

Byrne, A. with Gray-Felder, D., Hunt, J. & Parks, W. (2005) Measuring change: a guide to participatory monitoring and evaluation of communication for social change. Available at http://www.communicationforsocialchange.org/pdf/measuring_change.pdf (accessed November 17, 2023).

Compaine, B. (2001) *The Digital Divide: Facing a Crisis or Creating a Myth?* Cambridge, MA: MIT Press.

Dutta, M. (2006) Theoretical approaches to entertainment education campaigns: a subaltern critique. *Health Communication*, 20(3), 221–231.

Freire, P. (1969) *Education for Critical Consciousness*. New York: Continuum.

Gladwell, M. (2008) *Outliers: The Story of Success*. New York: Little, Brown and Co.

Glanz, K., Lewis, M. & Rimer, B. (1997) *Health Behavior and Health Education: Theory, Research, and Practice*. San Francisco, CA: Jossey-Bass.

Gray-Felder, D. & Deane, J. (1999) Communication and social change: a position paper and conference report. New York: The Rockefeller Foundation. Available at http://www.communicationforsocialchange.org/publications-resources?itemid=14 (accessed November 17, 2023).

Guijarro, S., Naranjo, J., Padilla, M., Gutiérez, R., Lammers, C. & Blum, R.W. (1999) Family risk factors associated with adolescent pregnancy: study of a group of adolescent girls and their families in Ecuador. *Journal of Adolescent Health*, 25(2), 166–172.

Haider, M. & Kreps, G. (2004) Forty years of diffusion of innovations: utility and value in public health. *Journal of Health Communication*, 9, 3–11.

Heylighen, F. (1999) Collective intelligence and its implementation on the Web: algorithms to develop a collective mental map. *Computational and Mathematical Organization Theory*, 5(3), 253–280.

Hornik, R.C. (1993) *Development Communication: Information, Agriculture, and Nutrition in the Third World*. Lanham, MD: University Press of America.

Hulin, A. (2023) Social media 4 peace project. Available at https://www.comminit.com/global/content/social-media-4-peace-project (accessed November 17, 2023).

Inkeles A. & Smith D. (1974) *Becoming Modern*. Cambridge, MA: Harvard University Press.

KCCI (2013) Meena ki Duniya: an entertainment–education radio programme. Available at http://www.kcci.org.in/Document%20Repository/13.%20Meena%20Radio.pdf (accessed November 17, 2023).

Kemp, S. (2023) Facebook statistics and trends. Available at http://datareportal.com/essential-facebook-stats.

King, R. (1999) *Sexual Behavioral Change for HIV: Where Have Theories Taken Us?* Geneva: UNAIDS. Available at http://www.who.int/hiv/strategic/surveillance/en/unaids_99_27.pdf.

MacArthur, A. (2013) The real history of Twitter, in brief. *Twitter*. Available at http://twitter.about.com/od/Twitter-Basics/a/The-Real-History-Of-Twitter-In-Brief.htm.

Malone, C. (2011) Can you hear me now? Web-enabled brand experiences that cut through the clutter. *Forbes*. Available at http://www.forbes.com/sites/onmarketing/2011/11/03/can-you-hear-me-now-web-enabled-brand-experiences-that-cut-through-the-clutter/#563d12b8214f (accessed November 17, 2023).

Melkote, S.R. (2001) Theories of communication for development. In: W.B. Gudykunst & B. Mody (eds) *Handbook of International and Intercultural Communication*, p. 419. Newbury Park, CA: Sage Publications.

Morris, N. (2003) A comparative analysis of the diffusion and participatory models in communication for development. *Communication Theory*, 13(2), 225–248.

Pant, S., Singhal, E. & Bhasin, U. (2002) Using radio drama to entertain and education: India's experience with the production, reception and transcreation of "Dehleez." *Journal of Communication for Development*, 13(2), 52–66.

Pew Research Center (2021) 7% of U.S. adults don't go online. Who are they? Available at https://www.pewresearch.org/short-reads/2021/04/02/7-of-americans-dont-use-the-internet-who-are-they/ (accessed November 17, 2023).

Shrimp, L. (2023) Addressing immunization inequity. Available at https://www.comminit.com/global/content/addressing-immunization-inequity-what-have-international-community-and-india-learned-ove (accessed November 17, 2023).

Singhal, A. (2010) Positive deviance and social change. Available at http://www.communicationforsocialchange.org/pdfs/singhal_arvind_positive%20deviance%20and%20social%20change_mazi%20june%202010.pdf (accessed November 17, 2023).

Singhal, A. & Rogers, E. (2003) *Combating AIDS: Communication Strategies in Action*. Thousand Oaks, CA: Sage Publications.

Sood, S. & Rogers, E. (2000) Dimensions of parasocial interaction by letter-writers to a popular entertainment-education soap in India. *Journal of Broadcasting and Electronic Media*, 44, 386–414.

Svenkerud, P. & Singhal, A. (1998) Enhancing the effectiveness of HIV/AIDS prevention programs targeted to unique population groups in Thailand: lessons learned from applying concepts of diffusion of innovation and social marketing. *Journal of Health Communication*, 3, 193–216.

Tufte, T. (2000) *Living with the Rubbish Queen: Telenovelas, Culture and Modernity in Brazil*. Bedfordshire, UK: University of Luton Press.

UNICEF (2013) Communication for development. Available at http://www.unicef.org/cbsc/index_42352.html (accessed November 17, 2023).

Waisbord, S. (2001) Family tree of theories, methodologies and strategies in communication for development. Available at http://www.communicationforsocialchange.org/pdf/familytree.pdf (accessed November 17, 2023).

17

Social Media and Entertainment–Education

Learning Objectives

After reading this chapter, you should be able to:
1 Understand the theoretical underpinnings of entertainment–education strategies.
2 Apply entertainment–education to social media campaign initiatives.
3 Examine the role of culturally appropriate narratives in behavior change models.

Introduction

Stories are an important piece to any culture. We teach children lessons, entertain ourselves, and share experiences through narratives. How many different stories have you been exposed to in just this week alone? Do you have a favorite television program that you just can't miss? Perhaps you shared a heartwarming story that you found online with your social network. Though storytelling has roots as an oral tradition, most of the stories that you encounter are broadcast through mass media. Mass media provides opportunities to disseminate stories to a large audience and incorporate more visual stimulation through media content.

As discussed in Chapter 16, it is a very complicated process for media messages alone to spark permanent behavior change in individuals. The field of development communication

Strategic Social Media: From Marketing to Social Change, Second Edition. L. Meghan Mahoney and Tang Tang.
© 2024 John Wiley & Sons, Inc. Published 2024 by John Wiley & Sons, Inc.

has long been interested in applying communication strategies in the developing world toward political democracy, rising levels of productivity, industrialization, high literacy rates, and longer life expectancy (Waisbord, 2001). This has been done through various interventions along the diffusion–participation continuum. The behavior change intervention most often associated with mass media is through entertainment–education (E-E) initiatives.

One of the most successful and well-known examples of an E-E campaign sparking social and behavior change in a community is *Soul City*. This South African television series aimed to tackle the public health crisis of domestic violence. Producers used the drama to illustrate beloved characters of the show engaging in a new collective behavior that demonstrates how neighbors could intervene in a domestic violence situation, as domestic abuse is a substantial problem in South Africa that traditionally most citizens do not wish to discuss. Thus, a holistic E-E campaign provides a behavior for media users to model through traditional and new media stories if they find themselves in a similar situation.

The *Soul City* television series (Figure 17.1) aimed to intervene with this problem by developing a storyline in which its characters gathered around an abuser's residence, banging pots and pans to bring awareness and stop the violence (Singhal & Rogers, 2003). This storyline showed viewers that domestic violence is unacceptable, and it is a citizen's duty to bring attention to abuse in their neighborhood. Furthermore, this action lets abusers know that it is not okay and will not be tolerated within the community. This entertainment program sparked subsequent real-life action in its users. Numerous media reports showed instances where community members intervened in domestic abuse situations in their own neighborhood following the program's broadcast. Here, you see how a media intervention can spark real-life behavior change. Social media can reinforce the traditional media message and provide more engaging and bottom-up communication surrounding the issue.

Figure 17.1   Scene from *Soul City*. Source: Soul City Institute. Reproduced with permission of Leah Marais.

In this context, it is important to understand how E-E, though formerly believed to be a diffusion-centric development tool, has transformed over time toward a more communication for social change approach (Waisbord, 2001). This chapter explores the theoretical underpinnings of E-E interventions, and how to apply E-E to many social change initiatives, including domestic abuse, HIV, and everyday practices such as proper hand washing campaigns. Indeed, this approach can be applied to any social media message hoping to inspire behavior change. Finally, we will take a deeper look into a specific E-E model, the MARCH model, to gain a better understanding of how to integrate a diffusion approach with more participatory, community-based reinforcement.

Theoretical Underpinnings of Entertainment–Education

Have you ever been influenced to change behavior because of something you have watched on television? Perhaps a food documentary has taught you to make heathier choices at mealtime. Most often, people talk about the negative effects of television. There are fears of excessive television viewing causing violence, promiscuous behavior, and obesity. This chapter suggests that storytelling media, such as television, can teach people to be more socially responsible citizens through E-E.

Many communication theories provide the foundation for the E-E strategy, as it is one of the most interdisciplinary approaches to behavior change. *Entertainment–education* "seeks to capitalize on the popular appeal of entertainment media in order to show individuals how they can live safer, healthier and happier lives" (Pant et al., 2002, p. 53). It involves a process of purposely designing and implementing a media message that both entertains and educates users, with the aim of increasing knowledge about an educational issue (Singhal et al., 2004). E-E programs can hit on people's emotions and retell narratives until the stories become popular narratives of a culture. It is important to note that E-E is not a theory of communication, but rather a communication strategy that is informed by several theories to bring behavioral and social change (Singhal et al., 2004).

E-E programs generally have two central components: a broad multidisciplinary theoretical framework and a developed media production system (Singhal et al., 2004). Many communication theories have been applied to E-E interventions. These include social learning theory, Shannon and Weaver's communication model, dramatic theory, theory of archetypes and stereotypes, elaboration likelihood model, user involvement, dramatic theories, social constructivism, uses and gratifications, agenda-setting, knowledge-gap, cultivation analysis, diffusion of innovations, and Habermas' theory of communicative action (Barker, 2007; Singhal et al., 2004; Sood, 2006). Clearly, the strategy is well-researched and far reaching across many disciplines. One of the reasons that E-E is such a powerful behavior change strategy is due to its multidisciplinary approach.

The purpose of this chapter is not to explain each of these theories in detail but rather to provide a more conceptual understanding of how to best engage users through media narratives (Sood et al., 2003), a task that social media practitioners are familiar with today. These lessons can be applied to many public health and marketing social media campaigns. Chapter 3 explains how powerful narratives are in the human decision-making process. Humans think in narrative patterns by nature. That is what makes E-E one of the most powerful ways to prompt behavior change in users. Fiske (1987) explains how consumers of media narratives go through a constant and subtle negotiation and renegotiation of the relationships between the text and the real life to make pertinent and pleasurable meanings from a story. Stories are part of a long trajectory of culture historical process (Degh, 1994).

Most children's programming is built on the principles of E-E. One of the most popular preschool programs around the world is *Sesame Street*. The purpose of the program is to utilize colorful Muppets, music, and celebrity visits to increase cognitive learning skills. It teaches young children letters, numbers, geometric forms, and prosocial qualities such as kindness and cooperation (Singhal & Rogers, 1999). Findings from research across all countries and cultures where *Sesame Street* is broadcast demonstrate its effectiveness in preparing preschool children for primary education (Fisch et al., 1999). One reason that the program is such a great success is that the production is grounded in traditional behavior change E-E literature.

Two organizations drove the beginnings of E-E projects worldwide: Population Communications International (PCI), a nongovernmental organization from New York City, and Johns Hopkins University's Center for Communication Programs (JHU/CCP). *The Sabido Dramas*, named after the Vice President for Research and Scriptwriter at Televisa in Mexico, Miguel Sabido, were the pioneers of E-E in the 1970s (Refera, 2004). Audiences of these programs can enjoy conflict-filled suspense dramas while simultaneously receiving education. The success of these dramas led to the formulation of the *Sabido methodology*, which is based on character development and plot lines that provide individuals with positive, negative, and transitional characters that impart messages and values.

Programs that represent similar structure and content of human behavior become a very telling depiction of the way a culture lives. These archetype stories are even more meaningful today because there are so many opportunities for media content creation and distribution. At almost every level, individuals can share stories of their lived reality. Through a complex identification process, media users can negotiate these stories and understand the role that they play in society. Identification with characters is crucial to the success of E-E narratives. As such, programming like *Sesame Street* often introduces new characters when tackling new public health issues. For example, in 2017, the children's program introduced Julia, a 4-year-old Muppet with autism. The E-E storyline aimed to teach children how to interact with friends diagnosed with autism (Pasha et al., 2017). Modeling of characters has huge implications for everyday decision-making and long-term behavior change.

Today, E-E initiatives are used to tackle many social and public health crises across various media outlets. Introducing new characters doesn't always prove the most effective method for inciting behavior change. In fact, one demonstrates how incorporating a long-standing protagonist that undergoes an attitudinal transformation stimulates deeper cognitive processing (Igartua *et al.*, 2022). To tackle prejudice toward immigrants, three E-E initiatives in Spain, Italy, and Greece had beloved soap characters transition from harboring negative attitudes toward immigrants into a positive position. This storyline proved more influential than introducing a new immigrant character for audiences to identify and model. Effective storytelling is the pillar of the behavior change process.

Conceptualizations of E-E argue that it contributes to behavior change in different ways. First, it influences members' awareness, attitudes, and behaviors toward a socially desirable end. It influences the user's external environment to help create the necessary conditions for change at a system level (Singhal et al., 2004). In addition, it triggers and facilitates public debate and discussion about difficult issues and helps mobilize social groups toward individual, community, and policy action (Tufte, 2005; Usdin et al., 2003). You can see from this description how diffusion, community, and mobilization are all essential to a successful E-E strategy.

One of the earliest examples of E-E is the world's longest-running radio soap opera, *The Archers* (Singhal et al., 2004). This British soap has long been regarded as representing realistic depictions of working-class individuals and their problems. It also demonstrates a formula of drama, humor, and education that was a balance of 40% education and 60% entertainment.

The success of this program paved the way for future British soaps, such as *EastEnders*, which produced "slice of life" stories that focused on issues of homosexuality, rape, unemployment, racial prejudice, single-parent families, teenage pregnancy, prostitution, arranged marriages, attempted suicide, drug dissolution, sexism, urban deprivation, problems with pregnancies, breast-feeding, domestic abuse, safety hazards, and mental health (Singhal et al., 2004). Clearly, E-E strategies can incite behavior change in media users older than preschool-aged children.

Now that we have a better sense of the theoretical underpinning of E-E, it is important to turn our attention toward the modern complexities of designing and implementing an E-E strategy to promote behavior change. One of the greatest attributes of social media is that users no longer take the role of passive receivers of narrative content. While there has been great success in traditional E-E transmission broadcasting, such as *Sesame Street* and *EastEnders*, we are finding even greater advancements when individuals are able to participate and produce the content on their own.

Entertainment–Education and Public Health

As we know, people negotiate media messages in different ways from one another. What prompts behavior change in one person may turn someone else off altogether. Regardless of how much effort producers put into content creation; message reception is an incredibly critical component to the E-E strategy. Producers can never be certain how media consumers will decode a message. Your job as a social media professional is to understand the best ways to ensure individuals identify with your product narrative.

One of the best-known examples of media users resisting an E-E initiative has been dubbed the *Archie Bunker effect*. Vidmar and Rokeach (1974) explained how the main character of *All in the Family*, Archie Bunker, was created as a negative role model that perpetuated sentiments of bigotry, racism, and prejudice. Producers were hoping that audiences would dislike this antagonist and the way he behaved. However, rather than seeing this character as a negative role model, audiences identified with him and subsequently emulated his behavior (Singhal et al., 2004). This case demonstrates the challenge in the use of media narratives to educate and promote behavior change: content creators can never account for how audiences will identify with a story. A stronger understanding of what makes a successful E-E intervention is needed.

A 25-year meta-analysis shows that the most successful E-E campaigns are those in which cultural values hold a strong foundation in national and cultural artifacts. Because individuals within a cultural group may be at different stages of readiness, media messages must be modified to incorporate cultural settings (King & Howard-Hamilton, 2003). The best way to ensure this is to have members of the actual culture where the program will be consumed assist with the production.

Let's take the public health crisis of HIV/AIDS as an example. This initiative comes with four distinct challenges: transmission challenges, behavioral challenges, response challenges, and targeting challenges (Singhal & Rogers, 2003). Transmission challenges are due to the nature of HIV/AIDS as an invisible, yet infectious disease. Behavioral challenges deal with human behaviors that involve interaction between unequal parties, as in a patriarchal society. Response challenges exist because efficacious response to the disease involves adoption of behaviors that depend on the compliance of more than one party. For example, if a husband is being secretly unfaithful to his wife with someone who is HIV positive, then she may still be at risk without engaging in any risky behavior herself. Targeting challenges deal with populations that are often hard to reach by means of conventional media channels. Some of the most infected regions are rural and exclusive in nature, especially in countries such as Botswana, Namibia, Swaziland, and Zimbabwe, where many urban dwellers and migrant laborers return to their village of origin when they fall ill (FAO, 2011). While your own campaign may not have challenges quite this complex, it is important to see how utilizing E-E strategies helps tackle such a complicated public health crisis through culturally integrated means.

At first glance, it seems reasonable to utilize media to promote individual behavior change requests: "Go get tested!" "Use a condom!" "Don't share needles!" These are solutions to the HIV/AIDS crisis for any culture. However, it is also a very top-down message that asks individuals to change their behavior to reach a goal. Narratives must go beyond this individual behavior change initiative and portray stories of how to participate in advocacy, policy change and facilitate public dialogue. This dialogue has been identified as critical, particularly through UNAIDS, the Joint United Nations program on HIV/AIDS (UNAIDS, 1999).

In addition, rather than searching for a universal approach to E-E, it is more important to individualize each campaign based on the cultural context (Airhihenbuwa & Obregon, 2000). Media messages should never be identical in different countries, as culture is one of the most important components in production (Singhal & Rogers, 2003). While Western practitioners may feel as though an individual approach to HIV/AIDS messages is appropriate, other cultures, such as those in Africa, Asia, and Latin America, are more influenced by collective sentiments and stories (Airhihenbuwa & Obregon, 2000).

South Africa's Sesame Street program, *Takalani Sesame*, utilized this individualized E-E approach in 2002 when they introduced an HIV-infected Muppet, Kami, into the program. The purpose of the narrative was to teach kids how to interact with an infected playmate, stressing positive attitudes and inclusion. This was the result of the AIDS epidemic, with over 250,000 South African children infected with HIV under the age of 15 facing isolation, rejection, and grief from their community (Lim, 2002). While *Sesame Street* storylines produced in other cultures may have also taught positive prosocial behaviors, this narrative was unique to a specific localized crisis.

Social media is a much more accessible distribution for public health storytelling. A public health intervention was developed through video storytelling during the COVID-19 pandemic with the aim of incorporating culturally nuanced animation and humor storytelling approaches. These social media videos aimed to reduce vaccine hesitancy in key demographic populations, increase behavioral intent to get vaccinated, and increase hope during a time of public health crisis (Chen et al., 2022).

This is one of the biggest strengths of utilizing social media in E-E initiatives. Social media content is inexpensive, fast, and easy to produce. There is no reason why in today's media landscape, one narrative should be pushed out repeatedly across different people. Conduct strong audience analyses and bring cultural social norms and policies into your narratives. Ensure that media users can see their lived reality through your media message. The easiest way to do this is to allow others to use social media to share their own story.

E-E interventions only begin to demonstrate the complexities of initiating a media strategy for positive social change. Despite these complications, because of the powerful nature of storytelling, E-E has evolved into one of the most utilized components of public health campaigns in developing countries. Let's now turn our attention toward an E-E strategy that focuses on moving beyond transmission narratives to prompt media users to make positive behavior change.

MARCH Model of Behavior Change

Many food documentaries have been produced that focus on the meat industry crisis. They often contain horrific images of animal torture and unsanitary packaging practices. For some, these images are powerful enough to change the type of meals eaten in their everyday life permanently. They forswear meat altogether and become vegetarians. These individuals have followed the diffusion process by becoming aware of the problem (knowledge), agreeing with the documentary's concerns (approval), and deciding that they are no longer going to participate as a carnivore (intention to act practice).

Traditional E-E initiatives define success as an individual's willingness and ability to take appropriate preventive measures and adhere to recommended treatment regimens (Centers for Disease Control, 2009). It can be difficult to transition into a vegetarian diet, especially for individuals who use meat products as the staple of all their favorite meals. To permanently change behavior is hard, no matter how powerful the documentary proves. However, the ability to connect with other vegetarians helps to make this transition less likely to fail. Social media allows a space to connect with networks of likeminded individuals that makes the process less scary and isolating. Eventually, this new diet became second nature and they become the advice-giver, rather than receiver. Perhaps most importantly, social media provides information about how this community can help change laws and regulations of the meat industry, beyond just their own individual lifestyle.

In Chapter 2, we learned that the five steps toward effective behavior change from a diffusion-centric message include knowledge, approval, intention to act, practice, and advocacy (De Fossard, 1996). The component of advocacy is incredibly important to establishing permanent behavior change, as people must engage with the message and take a participatory role in a larger movement. Participants solidify their decision to act in a particular way and permanently change their own personal behaviors.

It must be noted that not everyone who watches the food documentary will be influenced to become a vegetarian. Maybe a media user does not recognize his or her everyday life in what is being portrayed on screen. This is often the case when characters in a film only represent one niche demographic. Behavior change interventions must understand contextual differences, including social and cultural context, that are incorporated into E-E narratives (Airhihenbuwa & Obregon, 2000; Dutta-Bergman, 2004). Maybe the user grew up in a culture where animals are not as highly valued as they are in the first viewer's life. Perhaps the individual just enjoys the taste of meat too much to ever become a vegetarian. E-E programs must understand their audiences' willingness to engage and speak to their cultural norms to influence.

It may be easier to change the behavior through interpersonal reinforcement than it is through mass media. If personal vegetarian friends forward emails, ask to sign petitions, and cook tasty meatless meals, the result may be stronger. This type of community-level reinforcement may eventually be able to change a meat-lover's perception of the industry.

But wait! How can producers reach large numbers of individuals and get them to agree with a cause if the intervention must be conducted through an interpersonal community level? Practitioners cannot possibly go door to door around the world and find everyone who may be interested in their message. This is where the principles of true user participation begin to take shape.

The E-E approach demonstrates the need for you to take the issue away from yourself and turn attention toward relevant cultures, characters, and situations that your target consumers can identify with. Let's pretend you are dedicated to the cause of stopping the consumption of plastic water bottles. You feel as though they are wasteful, unnecessary, and harmful to the environment. Rather than explaining to your social network why the plastic water bottle crisis is important to you, bring the issue to a community level.

BantheBottle.net is a social media campaign designed to advocate bans on one-time-use plastic water bottles. Their approach to this social change is to ask individuals to organize screenings of the documentary *Tapped* in their own local neighborhoods and communities. This documentary focuses on the commodification of the water bottle industry and its impact on the environment. The campaign stresses the need for these screenings to be subsidized with support from community leaders, including office and school administrators. The website includes an interactive map where you can see the progress that each individual community initiative has made. Dozens of communities around the world have effectively banned the sale of water bottles through this initiative.

One of the reasons that this campaign has proved successful is that it subsidizes a mass media intervention with community reinforcement. In addition to the documentary screening, the campaign asks clear tangible actions from media consumers. Their social media links directly to a declaration page, where individuals can commit their efforts, and a page where individuals can find local government addresses to send letters and emails asking for regulatory legislation.

These same communication strategies could be used in a holistic social media campaign. Rather than just using social media to rant about how much you dislike plastic water bottles (diffusion), you could use the space to network with other environmentalists with the same goal (community). Through these efforts you could start a mobilization campaign initiative asking people to create videos of all the plastic water bottles they use in a week and upload it on YouTube. That lived experience is much more powerful than anything that happens in a virtual setting. It empowers media users and gives them complete control of the message. You have just transformed everyday social media users into empowered advocates for your cause.

True participation would take this campaign one step further. If you are truly looking for meaningful mass behavior change through a participatory process, you must discard your message's predetermined objectives. Though *you* may be interested in decreasing the amount of plastic water bottle use, that cause may not be relevant to your audience. Facilitate discussion through social media of what is important (in this case, the environment), participate in the discussion by mentioning how you have cut back on plastic water bottle purchases, and ask for others to come up with their own solutions. This is how you achieve true participation. Such a campaign allows you to prompt interaction and dialogue, gives users ownership of their own ideas, and diminishes power differentials.

Participatory social media platforms such as TikTok are emerging as huge resources for E-E initiatives. Identifying influencers within a community and asking them to develop more nuanced messages and stories that make sense and are believable within the local context may be more impactful than more professionally produced videos (Frank, 2021). Creating a social media challenge where other users are prompted to create their own short form videos around the same narrative would invite true participation into the campaign.

The Indonesian government launched a continuing education campaign to invite the public to create educational TikTok videos that promote a positive image of the government. The campaign asked users to tell their own story and tag videos using the hashtag #samasamabelajar. The mobilization campaign lasted just over four weeks and had more than 974 videos created. Here, the government provides space for the public to play an active role in producing educational social media content (Rachmawati *et al.*, 2022), User-generated content campaigns allow social media users to consider the initiative and tell their own stories. Each content creator has their own personalities, storytelling styles, and brand. Media consumers voluntarily follow these content creators because they identify or, at the very least, are interested in what they have to say. As such, the messages provide more power in the modeling process. These loyal consumers already hold trust in what the producer has to say.

The power of interpersonal community measures has been applied to behavior change initiatives. Most notably, behavioral scientists from the Centers for Disease Control and the International Partnership Against AIDS in Africa launched the Leadership and Investment in Fighting an Epidemic (LIFE) and developed a new E-E strategy called the MARCH model (Galavotti et al., 2001). This strategy sets to influence consumer behavior through a combination of mass media transmission, as well as community reinforcement and participation.

There are four key elements of the *MARCH model*: progression of change over time, the use of E-E as a vehicle of modeling, use of modeling in program content, and the creation of character models like the target audience (Pappas-DeLuca et al., 2008). These interventions are not intended to result in quick behavior change but are designed for setting up long-term models lasting for months.

Perhaps most importantly, behavior change in the MARCH model is built on two principles: modeling and reinforcement. Modeling shows people how to change, and reinforcement supports them in these efforts (Centers for Disease Control, 2009). The strategy also utilizes two main components: broadcast media and interpersonal community mobilization.

The broadcast media is used in line with early approaches of the Sabido methodology for E-E and is established through a positive, negative, and transitional character development strategy. MARCH narratives always include a positive role model who consistently makes responsible decisions, and a negative character that consistently engages in risky behavior.

Think of *Takalani Sesame*, the South Africa's Sesame Street program that we discussed earlier. Kami is the positive role model for children based on the narrative centered around inclusion of HIV-infected community members. She is the center protagonist for most stories and behaves in a positive, identifiable manner. Storylines also include negative characters that tease and exclude Kami from games. These are antagonists in the story that media users are not to identify with.

Transitional characters who may start by making negative decisions, but evolve over the series into empowered, knowledgeable, and positive characters are also included in MARCH narratives. For *Takalani Sesame*, these characters may start the program by having negative preconceptions regarding HIV-infected individuals. However, through the storyline, they learn to include Kami in the fun. These dynamic transitional characters serve as the most identifiable role models for media users, as they are neither consistently positive nor consistently negative.

Then, through the reinforcement state, media users are encouraged and given the necessary skills to achieve behavior change. Ideally, these reinforcements support the messages verbatim that the modeling characters are facing. Media users can internalize these challenges, apply them to their own lives, and come up with solutions through interpersonal interactions.

Still, this three-pronged approach to storytelling narratives may not be enough to prompt permanent behavior change. Remember that media users are influenced differently from one another. *Sesame Street* tries to move beyond a one-way transmission model of broadcasting by having the Muppets look directly into the camera and ask questions to the audience throughout the storyline (i.e., "Our letter of the day is Z. Can you think of an animal that begins with the letter Z?"). These questions are followed by a brief silence where viewers at home can interact with what is going on in the program. The Muppet will then congratulate audience members for participating. For many years, this is as interactive as traditional media allowed for E-E programs. However, there are many more opportunities today for participation through social media.

A unique feature of the MARCH model is an interpersonal community mobilization component. The idea of interpersonal reinforcement is that programs train key leaders in the target community about the initiative. This could be a preschool teacher using the storyline of Kami and *Takalani Sesame* in their own lessons. Generally, the MARCH model provides subsequent media materials to use as well, such as workbooks, brief videos, or magazines. Reinforcement activities may also include holding listening and discussion groups, as well as community activities such as meetings or road shows. Some of the most effective community reinforcement activities are those in which individuals are asked to produce theater or stories that carry out these educational messages. This gives media users a chance to ask questions and receive immediate feedback. It also provides a takeaway for them to bring home.

Consider how much more fun it is to watch favorite characters in person compared to on television. Children become so excited when they see characters walking around in amusement parks and adults pay large amounts of money to attend live events. Interpersonal experiences are much more powerful and provide a much greater catalyst for behavior change than transmission media messages. Nevertheless, E-E research demonstrates that a combination of both can be effective.

Social media provides a great opportunity to bridge the gap between transmission E-E models and interpersonal reinforcement. *Sesame Street* has many online resources where children can talk to characters through smartphone applications, download educational games, and even create their own versions of Muppet characters (SesameStreet.org, 2014). This type of user-generated content is a great way to incorporate the principles of the MARCH model into positive behavior change.

When creating an E-E intervention that models the MARCH strategy, it is important to follow the reinforcement action plan below.

Reinforcement Action Plan

1   Conduct an audience analysis to determine the cultural norms of your target audience.
2   Create positive characters that make decisions in accordance with the desired behavior change.
3   Create negative characters that make decisions antagonistic to the desired behavior change.
4   Include transitional characters that start out as either a positive or negative character but transform over time.
5   Create an interpersonal community-based mobilization effort to reinforce the message.

There is still much to learn regarding behavior change through social media messages. Practitioners and researchers are now beginning to understand that the most critical factor of behavior change has nothing to do with using an appropriate communication strategy or model but does allow for the culture and traditions of the intended campaign audiences to be integrated within the narrative. It is impossible for a campaign that proved successful in South Africa to be mirrored in India and work in the same capacity. Every culture requires its own adaptation of these recommendations. Furthermore, it is important that E-E campaigns have community support that reinforces their messages. Community members should be involved in the inception, production, distribution, and evaluation of the messages. This in-house participation is key to a successful intervention and is most often left out of traditional marketing strategies.

This chapter has discussed the importance of including culturally appropriate narratives and community reinforcement in behavior change strategies. One such example is Botswana's *Makgabaneng*.

Case Study: *Makgabaneng*

Makgabaneng is an E-E radio serial drama in Botswana that was designed using the MARCH model. The name means "Rocky Road" as its motto is "Life is a journey on a rocky path. The hope is, with every fall, there is a rise" (Peirce, 2011). It first aired on August 20, 2001, to address critical HIV/AIDS awareness messages among citizens aged 10–49 years old across Botswana (Republic of Botswana Popular Report, 2005).

The *Makgabaneng* drama is the only Botswana-produced serial drama of its kind. Therefore, it is one of the only forms of media entertainment that citizens can turn to and see their culture played out in narratives. Many culturally specific issues are tackled, including infidelity, intergenerational relationships, and alcohol abuse. The program began as a radio drama that broadcast the same 15-minute episode twice weekly, on two different national broadcast stations.

It is important to note that *Makgabaneng* is more than a transmission media; it is an interactive, holistic, behavior change initiative. The program incorporates both the broadcast and interpersonal, community, and mobilization components of the MARCH model. One of the elements that make this E-E initiative successful is that is written, acted, and produced by local talents within the urban center of the country, Gaborone.

The efforts for culturally specific content go beyond this in-house production. Producers of *Makgabaneng* recognize how various communities across Botswana have very distinct ideologies, values, and even language from one another. A separate department has been created to monitor and evaluate the reinforcement initiatives. The reinforcement department engages in many activities such as organizing health fairs and disseminating promotional materials, writing a teen magazine, managing field partners who host rallies at schools, overseeing and transcribing guides for field partners, and contracting special project coordinators who develop campaign materials with similar messages for other stakeholders. These efforts ensure that audiences can engage with the characters and storylines long after the program is over. Moreover, trained officers within local communities began to host interpersonal listener discussion groups (LDGs) to reinforce the messages of the drama in 2002. LDGs serve as one of the greatest reinforcement activities aimed to encourage safer HIV-related behaviors.

Because of these, *Makgabaneng* is successful in reaching and sustaining listenership among demographics aged 15–24 years. Audiences of *Makgabaneng* have higher levels of HIV knowledge and less stigmatizing attitudes toward those affected by HIV. Listeners also report increased intentions to get tested for HIV and greater preventive behaviors such as continued discussion with partners about HIV testing, and HIV testing during pregnancy (Republic of Botswana Popular Report, 2005). Due to the overwhemlingly positive reaction, *Makgabaneng* became an official NGO in 2006 and launched a television version of the series in 2013.

In addition to the newly launched television series, producers have also begun utilizing social media in their strategy. At the end of every episode, fans respond and interact on the show's Facebook page (Facebook.com/Makgabaneng). There, they are encouraged to ask questions and share their own stories. Pictures from various road shows and discussion groups are uploaded on the *Makgabaneng* website for participants to check out. There is also a X (formerly Twitter) feed (@Makgabanen) that reinforces key messages from the program, as well as promoting casting and production announcements. Hashtags centered on the program are encouraged for users to promote live feedback as the series airs. These are all ways in which *Makgabaneng* is bridging the gap between one-way transmission broadcasting and interpersonal community reinforcement.

Today, *Makgabaneng* continues to grow its community participation framework. What was once a diffusion-centric radio drama has grown into a multifaceted community resource. The initiative recently launched an annual creative arts festival designed to bring together various creative industry professionals to network, share knowledge, and help community members grow their businesses for the local and international markets (Mlilo, 2022). Instead of merely disseminating health information through entertainment storylines, the organization invites community members together to learn from each other and build skills that could change life situations. The community event provides many resources, including women in business networking, assistance for creative issues of copyright, and other panels designed to use media as a launching point for diversifying economic development in the region.

This holistic E-E initiative encourages media users to acquire the necessary skills and attitudes to achieve behavior change and provides resources and tools that help media users reach their goals. Through community reinforcement and use of social media, *Makgabaneng* can engage users to stimulate applicable, individualized, relevant health conversations. As Byrne and colleagues suggest (2005), evaluations of behavior change initiatives must move away from people as the objects of change and focus on more participatory methods, such as community dialogue, local decision-making processes, and cultural identity. *Makgabaneng* proves a successful case for this kind of participatory behavior change initiative.

Discussion questions

1   Consider advantages to utilizing an E-E approach to behavior change, like the production of *Makgabaneng*. How does the likelihood for behavior change transition when media is not produced solely for the sake of profit?
2   How does the Makgabaneng Creative Arts Festival meet the goals of true participation within a community and go beyond diffusion techniques? Can you think of any community reinforcement that you have attended from your own life?
3   *Makgabaneng* combines a broadcast narrative and community reinforcement in a behavior change initiative. How is social media able to speak to both needs better than traditional media?

Summary

This chapter focuses on the importance of utilizing culturally specific narratives and community reinforcement in behavior change initiatives. This method has been applied to E-E interventions across the world and has yielded great results.

Fiske (1987) explains how individuals are likely to use media for their own purposes, rather than the goals of others. We know that media users are very different from one another. They have unique emotions, relationships, passions, goals, and stressors. They do not even need to misunderstand or disagree with a message to disregard it. Clearly, sparking behavior change through media messages is hard. One way to overcome these challenges is through narrative structures and community reinforcement strategies found in E-E interventions.

There are many ways to apply the lessons learned from communication for development and E-E research to develop your own social media messages. The most important lesson is that your social media message is not all about you and your organization. Resist the temptation to use the media for your own objectives, rather than the goals of others. Participatory social media platforms such as TikTok create strong spaces for users to share their own stories. Listen to your consumers and allow them to participate with your campaign at all levels. Provide resources that help them reach their own goals. The aim of social media marketing should shift from selling products toward empowering users to contribute to positive behavior change. This section of the book has discussed ways in which social media can be used for social good. Part V will explore the future social media landscape and how to incorporate the old with the new.

Key Takeaways

1   Development communication interventions take advantage of strong storytelling to inspire behavior change in media users. Entertainment–education is one approach.
2   The MARCH model is an E-E approach that uses media interventions in a more participatory manner through community-centered initiatives. The interpersonal component has proven a more successful way to promote behavior change.
3   Social media holds a great potential in bridging the gap between diffusion-centric mass media approaches and more participatory interventions for behavior change. E-E initiatives stress the importance of participatory components throughout all stages of the production process.
4   It is important that members of the culture that you are trying to reach assist with the production of media content. This will ensure that it is influential and appropriate for their lived reality.

References

Airhihenbuwa, C. & Obregon, R. (2000) A critical assessment of theories/models used in health communication for HIV/AIDS. *Journal of Health Communication*, 5, 5–15.

Barker, K. (2007) Sex, soap and social change: the Sabido methodology. *Population Media Center*. Available at https://www.populationmedia.org/2007/08/09/sex-soap-social-change-the-sabido-methodology/.

Byrne, A., Gray-Felder, D., Hunt, J. & Parks, W. (2005) Measuring change: a guide to participatory monitoring and evaluation of communication for social change. Available at http://www.communicationforsocialcha nge.org/pdf/measuring_change.pdf (accessed November 18, 2023).

Centers for Disease Control (2009) Global reproductive health: modeling and reinforcement to combat HIV/AIDS (MARCH). Available at http://www.cdc.gov/globalhealth/programs/reproductive.htm (accessed November 18, 2023).

Chen, S., Forster, S., Yang, J., Yu, F., Jiao, L., Gates, J., Wang, Z., Liu, H., Chen, Q., Geldsetzer, P., Wu, P., Wang, C., McMahon, S., Barnighausen, T. & Adam, M. (2022) Animated, video entertainment–education to improve vaccine confidence globally during the COVID-19 pandemic: an online randomized controlled experiment with 24,000 participants. *Trials*, 23(1), 1–10.

De Fossard, E. (1996) *How to Write a Radio Serial Drama for Social Development: A Program Manager's Guide.* Baltimore, MD: Johns Hopkins School of Public Health, Center for Communication Programs.

Degh, L. (1994) *American Folklore and the Mass Media.* Bloomington, IN: Indiana University Press.

Dutta-Bergman, M.J. (2004) Health attitudes, health cognitions, and health behaviors among Internet health information seekers: Population-based survey. *Journal of Medical Internet Research*, 6(2), e15.

FAO (2011) HIV/AIDS: A rural issue. Available at http://www.fao.org/FOCUS/E/aids/aids1-e.htm (accessed November 18, 2023).

Fisch, S., Truglio, R. & Cole, C. (1999) The impact of *Sesame Street* on preschool children: a review and synthesis of 30 years' research. *Media Psychology*, 1(2), 165–190.

Fiske, J. (1987) *Television Culture.* London: Routledge.

Frank, L. (2021) Entertainment–education behind the scenes. *The Communication Initiative Network.* Available at https://www.comminit.com/global/content/entertainment-education-behind-scenes (accessed November 18, 2023).

Galavotti, C., Pappas-DeLuca, M. & Lansky, A. (2001) Modeling and reinforcement to combat HIV: the MARCH approach to behavior change. *American Journal of Public Health*, 91(10), 1602–1607.

Igartua, J.J., González-Vázquez, A., & Arcila-Calderón, C. (2022) The effect of similarity with a transitional role model of an entertainment–education narrative designed to reduce Xenophobia: evidence from three European countries. *The International Communication Association 72nd Annual Conference.*

King, P. & Howard-Hamilton, M. (2003) An assessment of multicultural competence. *Journal of Student Affairs Research and Practice*, 40(2), 119–133.

Lim, M. (2002) A-B-C, 1-2-3, H-I-V: *Sesame Street* tackles AIDS. *Virtual Mentor*, 4(9), ii.

Mlilo, P. (2022) Makgabaneng to host three-day arts festival. *The Voice.* Available at https://www.pressreader.com/botswana/the-voice-botswana/20220722/281960316486818 (accessed November 18, 2023).

Pant, S., Singhal, A. & Bhasin, U. (2002) Using radio drama to entertain and educate: India's experience with the production, reception, and transcreation of "Dehleez". *Journal of Development Communication*, 13(2), 52–66.

Pappas-DeLuca, K., Kraft, J., Galavotti, C., Warner, L., Mooki, M., Hastings, P., Koppenhaver, T., Roels, T.H., & Kilmarx, P.H. (2008) Entertainment–education radio serial drama and outcomes related to HIV testing in Botswana. *Global Health Sciences Literature Digest*, 20(6), 486–503.

Pasha, S.B., Qadir, T.F., Fatima, H., & Hussain, S.A. (2017) Sesame Street's recognition of autism. *The Lancet Psychiatry*, 4(7), 520–521.

Peirce, L.M. (2011) *Botswana's Makgabaneng: An Audience Reception Study of an Edutainment Drama.* Doctoral dissertation, Ohio University.

Rachmawati, F., Wibowo, A.A. & Arianto, I.D. (2022 November) Sentiment Analysis# samasamabelajar Public Relations Campaign Based on Big Data on TikTok. *Proceeding of The International Conference on Economics and Business*, 377–388.

Refera, T. (2004) The role of Sabido entertainment–education radio serial dramas in the struggle for the prevention of HIV/AIDS: with specific reference to "Yeken Kingit" and "Dhimbiba". Available at http://www.comminit.com/hiv-aids/content/role-sabido-entertainment-education-radio-serial-dramas-struggle-prevention-hivaids-spec (accessed June 8, 2016).

Republic of Botswana Popular Report (2005) *Botswana AIDS Impact Survey III*. NACA in Collaboration with CSO and Other Development Partners.

SesameStreet.org (2014) Available at http://www.sesame street.org (accessed November 18, 2023).

Singhal, A. & Rogers, E. (1999) *Entertainment–Education: A Communication Strategy for Social Change*. London: Routledge.

Singhal, A. & Rogers, E. (2003) *Combating AIDS: Communication Strategies in Action*. Thousand Oaks, CA: Sage Publications.

Singhal, A., Cody, M., Rogers, E. & Sabido, M. (2004) *Entertainment–Education and Social Change*. Mahwah, NJ: Lawrence Erlbaum Associates.

Sood, S. (2006) Audience involvement and entertainment education. *Communication Theory*, 12(2), 153–172.

Sood, S., Witte, K. & Menard, T. (2003) The theory behind entertainment education. In: M.J. Cody, A. Singhal, M. Sabido & E.M. Rogers (eds) *Entertainment–Education Worldwide: History, Research, and Practice*, pp. 117–149. Mahwah, NJ: Lawrence Erlbaum.

Tufte, T. (2005) Entertainment–education in development communication: between marketing behaviors and empowering people. In: O. Hemer & T. Tufte (eds) *Media and Global Change: Rethinking Communication for Development*, pp. 159–174. Buenos Aires: CLACSO.

UNAIDS (1999) Communications framework for HIV/ AIDS. Available at http://www.unaids.org/sites/default/ files/media_asset/jc335-commframew_en_1.pdf (accessed November 18, 2023).

Usdin, S., Scheepers, E., Goldstein, S. & Japhet, G. (2003) Achieving social change on gender-based violence: a report on the impact evaluation of *Soul City's* fourth series. *Social Science and Medicine*, 61(11), 2434–2445.

Vidmar, N. & Rokeach, M. (1974) Archie Bunker's bigotry: a study in selective perception and exposure. *Journal of Communication*, 24(1), 36–47.

Waisbord, S. (2001) *Family Tree of Theories, Methodologies and Strategies in Communication for Development*. The Rockefeller Foundation.

Part V

Social Media for Social and Behavior Change

18

Social Media in a Post-convergence Era

Learning Objectives

After reading this chapter, you should be able to:

1   Identify the impact of convergence culture on society.
2   Explain remediation theory and apply it to a social media marketing strategy.
3   Integrate social media and traditional media into a campaign in a post-convergence era.

Introduction

One of the greatest advances in society brought by social media is our ability to connect easily with individuals around the world. This insight into how other people live creates a greater sense of empathy toward others, a characteristic that allows us to emotionally participate, understand, relate, and value the core elements that make us all members of the human race (Frenk & Gómez-Dantés, 2002). Hopefully, you have learned how creating social media messages for positive social change is not so different from creating messages for marketing and business goals.

Strategic Social Media: From Marketing to Social Change, Second Edition. L. Meghan Mahoney and Tang Tang.
© 2024 John Wiley & Sons, Inc. Published 2024 by John Wiley & Sons, Inc.

This book has taken you through foundational principles of behavior change theory, the role of users and messages in the communication exchange process, and strategies for marketing and social good. These are all important elements in creating social media messages for your own objectives and goals. We will now turn attention toward the future social media landscape to explain why today's globalized world requires that all social media messages are communicated in a context that accounts for each of these areas.

While this book is unable to teach you everything about the future of social media practices, we can advise how to integrate new technological advancements, whatever they may be, into an existing marketing strategy. This chapter explores how to ensure that your social media strategy stays relevant in an ever-changing and unpredictable media landscape. In Chapter 19, we will argue for a general framework for social media scholarship. Finally, Chapter 20 will provide general conclusions and recommendations for creating social media strategies for increased social participation.

Today, there are more than 3.7 billion social media users worldwide, and 97% of all Fortune 500 companies use social media to foster communication with their stakeholders (Porteous, 2021). The power of social media in reaching and communicating with customers cannot be ignored. However, too many view social media platforms as stand-alone elements, rather than an "ecosystem whereby all elements work together toward a common objective – whether to launch and promote a new product or service; to communicate a new company initiative; or to simply further engage customers in a rich, meaningful, and interactive dialogue" (Hanna *et al.*, 2011, p. 273). These principles of integration are critical to success and require a long-term view of media marketing. Getting the correct balance of traditional and new media elements is important.

You do not want to set the technological bar too high that customers find it overly different and demanding from what they are used to. You also do not want your brand to seem outdated from the technology that your competitor is embracing. Today's marketing and communication professionals must be able to purposefully integrate traditional technologies with the new ones and have a sense of what advances are ahead.

To better understand how to synthesize a social media strategy, let's first examine the transition from Web 1.0 to a convergence culture, a time in society where companies were forced to create strategy for an unimaginable media landscape that was changing at a rapid pace. We will then turn our attention toward the many challenges that we must consider in a post-convergence era. This knowledge will help you create your own marketing strategy for any media environment.

The Culture of Convergence

If you were interested in listening to music, which technological tool would you use? Perhaps you would turn on the radio and listen to your favorite local DJ during the morning drive. Maybe you would open iTunes and listen to your personal music collection. Or, if you wanted to be surprised by the playlist, maybe you would open the TikTok app on your phone and let the social media determine your playlist. It is difficult to remember a time when we didn't have so many choices in media platforms and content. Your choice of media device is dependent on several factors, including access, competence, and connection. It could also depend on what other tasks you are attempting to accomplish simultaneously. Maybe you are working on a research report, so your personal computer is already open. Though you may not have purchased your personal computer with the intention of using it as a music player, it is a convenient function of the device. The ways in which distinct tools or technologies combine from several different products is called *convergence* (DeVoss & Webb, 2008; Griffiths & Light, 2008).

The term *media convergence* extends beyond just the merging of technological devices. It includes the flow of content across multiple media platforms, the cooperation between multiple media industries, and the migratory behavior of media users who will go almost anywhere in search of the kinds of entertainment experiences they want (Jenkins, 2006). In this definition, you can see the impacts that convergence has on user behavior and expectations. Convergence is a process of industry changes that combine markets and products to meet various consumer needs (Thielmann & Dowling, 1999). It is likely that your expectations regarding music choice have changed over the course of your lifetime. You may expect that you should be able to hear any song, anywhere, at any time. This expectation could only be fulfilled if various industries work together.

Media convergence creates many technological, industrial, cultural, and social changes. Media devices are becoming increasingly less expensive and easier to use. More media users have access and can accomplish their own goals and gratifications when they wish. This puts pressure on businesses to push toward stronger customer relationships, especially in a culture that privileges an active user (Deuze, 2007). The effect of multiple entry points into the consumption process enables consumers to participate in a prolonged relationship with a brand's narrative, encouraging businesses to be more attentive to consumer interests and directly solicit feedback to their products (Jenkins, 2003). Here, you can see the shift in power from top-down corporate control to one where customers are able to actively engage in the process.

Media convergence is heavily dependent on consumers' active participation (Jenkins, 2006). TikTok is only successful because users were willing to engage in the consumption and production process. Rather than thinking of convergence as simply a merging of technological devices and media content, it should be seen as a cultural shift that alters the relationship between existing technologies, industries, markets, genres, and consumers (Jenkins, 2004). This has created a new culture of expectations.

Convergence culture emphasizes the changing patterns in the way narrative, informational, and visual content circulates, resulting in a cultural shift where consumers are encouraged to seek out new information and make connections among dispersed media content (Trigg, 2008). This process has merged the roles of the producer and consumer in an interactive environment, representing an entirely new way of perceiving media users, as it can be difficult to tell who is producing content for whom (Bird, 2011). The shift toward multimedia integration of consumer inclusion in the production and product-innovation process of media companies has resulted in many changes in society (Deuze, 2008). As Jenkins (2004, p. 37) suggested:

> Consumers are learning how to use these different media technologies to bring the flow of media more fully under their control and to interact with other users. They are fighting for the right to participate more fully in their culture, to control the flow of media in their lives and to talk back to mass market content. Sometimes, these two forces reinforce each other, creating closer, more rewarding relations between media producers and consumers.

As such, it is important to consider the action plan below when a social media practitioner is struggling to see the benefits of embracing the opportunities of a convergence culture. The action plan consists of seven steps: communication, commitment, cooperation, compensation, culture, competition, and customer (Appelgren, 2004).

Convergence Culture Action Plan

1   *Communication*: Social media is defined by the ability to facilitate dialogue between users. Media convergence makes it easier than ever for businesses to facilitate dialogue between content consumers and producers. However, it is important for businesses to understand the types of communication that works best with their individual company goals. Part I of this book discusses how the amount of participation users are given influences the amount of control producers have over content. Decisions regarding communication should be made carefully with long-term strategy in mind.

2   *Commitment*: Media convergence provides opportunities for consumers to take part in the narrative of your brand. Therefore, it is important to consider how every individual associated with your product, both internal employees and external customers, are familiar with and committed to your goals. The importance of audience research may help you determine the level of commitment from each sector.

3   *Cooperation*: Convergence requires multiple industries to work together to fulfill new user expectations. There are many available options for content delivery, and it is imperative that your business is willing to take risks and cooperate with other organizations that have similar goals. This requires a heightened sense of a product's brand and authenticity, as different sectors must share stories and ideas in a unified fashion that meets the goals of the organization.

4   *Compensation*: Though not a factor that many communication strategists consider immediately, compensation is a growing concern for individuals in a convergence culture. Access, devices, and production costs are all decreasing, yet social media has brought greater transparency than ever before regarding compensation and profit margins. Consider both employee wages and the gap between the top and the bottom. Would you be comfortable if this information became public? Compensation considerations should also consider the external benefits to customers and society.

5   *Culture* involves the language, methods, and environment of an organization (Appelgren, 2004). Because convergence culture changes patterns in the way narrative, informational, and visual content circulates, your brand message can easily change or become diluted through multiple channels of distribution. Great care must be taken in fostering a unique culture for your product. Transforming your brand into a lifestyle is one way to ensure cohesiveness.

6   *Competition*: The Internet has made virtually everyone with an Internet connection your competitor, as every market now faces national and global competition. This can either be seen as a disadvantage or motivator for success. Companies that excel are those with a strong sense of authenticity, brand name, and credibility. If you are your authentic self, you have no competition (Stratten, 2012). Thus, find your niche in the marketplace and foster an engaged and like-minded community.

7   *Customer*: Finally, customers are central to the principles of convergence. Be sure that you are not considering them as passive receivers of your content, but rather active users that play a central role in your narrative. The more power that they have, the more invested they will feel in your brand. Remember that in a convergence culture, it is better to have a few invested brand advocates than it is to have high numbers of passive message receivers. Empower the customers and keep them at the center of every decision that you make.

This action plan should help you as you consider the many ways in which media convergence could impact your organization's business and marketing strategies. These overall considerations illustrate the shift in power from content producers to content consumers. Additionally, there are practical rules that can further guide you in the strategic process.

Remember that consumers need to see, hear, and/or interact with your message three to five times before they start to believe what you are saying (Brito, 2013). Use converged media to distribute messages where your consumers are most likely already visiting in their daily media routine, such as Instagram or Snapchat. Be sure to integrate traditional paid media with free social media platforms in your brand strategy. Converged media allows a space where users are not being sold to in a manner that is as obvious as a pop-up banner ad. By taking advantage of paid media in your marketing strategy, your content can reach a large number of people who are likely interested in your message based on filters that you set. Your marketing strategy should not end there though. Integrate branded stories on social media as well. Use a cross-platform strategy to share voice (Busick, 2022). While your Instagram stories can reach up to 996 million people, it is important to note that only 0.1% of Instagram users solely use Instagram (Newberry, 2023). It's likely your Instagram users also use TikTok, watch ESPN, and listen to WKDD FM radio. In a convergent media environment, you want to constantly integrate different platforms (social media and traditional media) to reach a higher percentage of your target consumers.

Hopefully, these suggestions will help guide you as you develop social media content and strategy. Remember that media landscapes are constantly changing, and some of the principles of media convergence may not remain true across your career as a social media practitioner. You will never be certain of what technological advances lie ahead. Instead, be sure that communication, media, and behavior change theories guide your strategy, especially when the media environment is uncertain. One such theory that explores the integration of traditional and new media content is Bolter and Grusin's (2002) remediation theory.

Remediation Theory

Media convergence is often turned to when individuals are interested in how new media has impacted traditional media marketing and business models (Cooper & Tang, 2009; Picard, 2000). In this chapter, we have learned how media convergence impacts the flow of content across platforms, the cooperation between industries, and the migratory behavior of media users (Jenkins, 2006). The implication is that media convergence is better for users, producers, and content managers alike. Remediation theory attempts to provide further guidelines for developing and understanding convergent media products.

Remediation theory is the idea that new visual media are best able to achieve their cultural significance by integrating and refashioning more traditional media forms (Bolter & Grusin, 2002). This theory refers to the blending of traditional and new media and was one of the first to explain why incorporating new media structures is not always the best decision as a media practitioner. Traditional media can refashion new media just as well as new media changes existing forms. Rather than drastically changing the existing media landscape, media convergence simply alters traditional forms.

Remediation theory suggests that media can be divided into two principal styles: hypermediacy and transparent immediacy (Bolter & Grusin, 2002). *Hypermediacy* privileges fragmentation, indeterminacy, and heterogeneity, emphasizing process and performance, much like Pinterest boards, rather than the finished product (Bolter & Grusin, 2002). It offers random access, with no physical beginning, middle, or end, serving much less as a story and more as immediate clips of information.

Hypermediacy requires interactivity as an "immutable law" of the medium (Bolter & Grusin, 2002; Lin & Cho, 2010). This is key to practitioners, as interactivity creates brand identity, enables greater control over media choice, and encourages direct communication between content producers and consumers (Lin & Cho, 2010; McMillan *et al.*, 2008). Hypermediation calls attention to the medium it deploys by encouraging users to look at it (McKain, 2005). These are all functions of media convergence as well.

Transparent immediacy does not rely on interactivity. Instead, it includes two- and three-dimensional images projected onto traditional computer, film, or television screens (Bolter & Grusin, 2002). Media users of transparent immediacy have an immediate relationship with the content of what they are viewing, as it is produced with a clear fourth wall. Content is more linear in nature, with a finished narrative structure, complete with a beginning, middle, and end (Bolter & Grusin, 2002). Transparent immediacy encourages users to look through the platform to view content (McKain, 2005).

When a form of new media comes along, as a marketing practitioner, you will be forced to decide how to refashion your existing marketing strategy. While the inclination may be that newer is always better, remediation theory cautions against this. It suggests that you should include elements of both hypermediacy and transparent immediacy in your communication strategy (Bolter & Grusin, 2002; Peirce, 2011). Adapting new media forms too quickly will turn users away. They may not feel competent enough to engage with your strategy, or the result may seem too unfamiliar. However, the inability to incorporate new media elements will make your brand seem outdated.

Remediation theory is especially important in a convergence culture, as no media exists in isolation from other media, or from other social and economic forces (Rajewsky, 2005). It is important to make purposeful decisions about which technologies to embrace into your strategy. Many organizations are still transitioning toward a convergence culture under the assumption that new media is always better. The smartest practitioners are those that are looking forward to finding a balance as we enter a post-convergence era.

Integrating Social Media in a Post-convergence Era

The convergence era brought many exciting changes to society. As we step toward a time when these advances are the expected norm for consumers, there are questions about the future of marketing. Some believe that the concept of convergence has been stretched beyond what is meaningful (Fagerjord, 2010), and many of the same industry concerns and power structures that existed prior to the convergence culture are surfacing again.

Convergence culture is often talked about in very ideal terms, where media producers are catering to consumers. While this era certainly marks a shift in thinking about the relationship between media producers and consumers, the impact should not overshadow the need to consider the process of sociocultural stratification (Apperley, 2007). For example, convergence has created a shared space where different genres in different media may be combined in new ways. Individuals can produce, add to, or change media texts. This has resulted in a remix of culture. *Remix* is the process of creating an alternative version of a media text by altering or introducing new elements to the existing form (Fagerjord, 2010).

Remix is a great way for individuals from different cultures to work together, collaborate on projects, and even create new cultural forms of media. However, this blending of cultures can have other implications. Often, the dominant culture will take over subcultures. Today, we can see how people live around the world, and many adopt the cultural depiction of those with whom they identify most, rather than those they live. While this has many benefits to individuals who may feel out of place in their immediate community, it can also erode cultural borders and small nuances between regions. One must consider the importance of culture preservation in a post-convergence era.

Media convergence also raises many questions about communication policy. In a world where everyone is contributing to the production process, it is difficult to determine who owns and has rights to what content. In a globalized era, it is also difficult to determine who can regulate or govern virtual spaces. Each platform could potentially require a different rule or government agency (Bar & Sandvig, 2008). For example, in 2023, many vocal artists including Michelle Clarke found that their voices have been re-generated by AI Voice for various uses without the artists' permission or even awareness. While the artists tried to protect their rights via lawsuits, the current copyright law could not decide what happens when a person's voice is copied for profit (Verma, 2023). These policy and ownership issues are just starting to surface, and the implications are unclear.

Furthermore, much rhetoric surrounding media convergence examines the new opportunities for everyday consumers, especially regarding media production. Anyone can become the next viral hit in a converged media environment. However, it is important to note that media structures still play a role in how users access and produce online information. While media users do have unlimited access to information online, most of their uses are filtered by the results of structures such as search, recommendations, hashtags, and advertising. The AI powered algorithms take many factors (e.g., the popularity of the content producer) into consideration when creating customized content for each user. The customized content very much guides (or constrains) people's attention. Unconventional and less mainstream sources are still not easy to be found. Some of the same power differentials remain.

These concerns show us that in an environment where everything seems new, there are still many of the same challenges of media production that content creators have faced since the beginning of time. Overall, a strong consumer analysis is the foundation of any convergence marketing strategy. Specifically, there are eight items that practitioners should consider when creating content in a post-convergence world: transmedia, environments, narratives, rituals, community, consumers, identity, and devices (Laurel, 2000).

1   *Transmedia* is the ability to create media texts across multiple media platforms. Rather than producing text for one particular medium, it is time to start thinking about how it will be distributed across multiple platforms from the beginning. This new approach places the emphasis on developing materials that can be selected and arranged to

produce many different forms (Laurel, 2000). It also gives users more control and ensures that the same message produced for one social media platform is not identical to a message produced for another.

2   *Environment*: Every product needs a strong narrative. This narrative exists within an overarching brand environment. Rather than retelling the same story over and over, focusing on a brand environment allows your product to support many stories, characters, and play patterns. This will help your social media messages focus on a lifestyle, rather than a product.

3   *Narratives*: Once you have established your brand environment, you can begin considering its narrative. The importance of brand narratives was discussed in Chapter 3, but this advice focused on the brand's authentic story. In a post-convergence world, it is imperative to allow a space where users can share their narratives in a structure that can fit in with the overall brand story.

4   *Ritual* is a kind of social form in which a designed narrative can unfold harmoniously (and simultaneously) within the larger context of an interactive environment in which most action is improvisational (Laurel, 2000). These unique patterns of behavior, such as an inside joke between your consumers and you, help individuals feel a deeper connection to the community, as it is something that they are unable to share on other online forums.

5   *Community*: Media structures must promote dialogue and interaction among members. While this communication can be facilitated, you want to ensure that your consumers feel as though the space is shared. This requires a high level of trust, where consumers feel confident that their input matters, and you feel confident that they will stay true to the brand. A strong balance between control and participation must be maintained.

6   *Consumers* are central to marketing practices in a post-convergence era. Without them, your message does not spread. Therefore, user engagement and consumer research must be the priority of any social media marketing strategy. User participation must be supported and integrated into your product's foundational narrative, not just an evaluation once the marketing strategy has been deployed.

7   *Identity*: It can be difficult to transition from your product to your consumers being central to your brand narrative, but participation is essential to success. Remember that individuals are more likely to engage in a process that speaks to their own lived identity. Focus on an idealized lifestyle, allow collaboration with influencers, or create characters with functional identities (Laurel, 2000). You can even enable technologies where users are able to create virtual identities on their own, even if they are different from their real-life personas. The more people can customize their experience, the better.

8   *Devices*: Media will take many different forms in a post-convergence world. Be sure to test content in different situations across various devices to ensure that it is working properly. Pay specific attention to the technologies that your consumers are most likely utilizing, not what is most convenient or critical for you to produce. Remember that not everyone has the most up-to-date device or software. Ensure that you are not losing users because your content is not compatible.

These guidelines should help you determine how well your marketing strategy fits in a post-convergence world. In the era of convergent media, it can be difficult for marketers to determine the content, timing, and frequency of social media messages about their product (Mangold & Faulds, 2009). Rather than adapting a business strategy around social media, it is better to let social media integrate into your business (Bond, 2011). After all, conversations about your product are happening whether you facilitate them or not.

To guide strategic decisions regarding monitoring, understanding, and responding to different social media activities, it is recommended that four Cs are followed (Kietzmann et al., 2011): (1) *cognize*, where practitioners have a strong understanding of the social media landscape and the unique functions of various platforms; (2) *congruity*, which determines how social media functions align with the goals of your organization; (3) *curate*, where practitioners determine who, how often, and when they engage in conversation on a social media platform; and (4) *chase*, where practitioners scan the Internet to find information that influences the company's current or future position on the market.

It is important that you trust the information that you find about your product on social media platforms. Social media provides brands with one of the most personal, trusted, and direct points of access to their customers (Drury, 2008). Take time to read these online conversations and get to know your competitors, consumers, prospects, peers, critics, influencers, and supporters (Bond, 2011). Remember that the best social media strategies consist of 90% listening and 10% activation (Bond, 2011). Most of your marketing strategy should consist of not saying anything at all. Rather, stay up to date on what the public sphere has to say about your product. Information about products and services is now based on the experiences of users, rather than predetermined marketing messages. The focus of social media specialists should not always be on the creation of online content. A strong practitioner will spend most of their time gathering and reading online content.

While the focus of a convergence culture was on the opportunities brought by increased user dialogue, it is interesting that the focus of a post-convergence era is on not saying anything at all. Integrating social media into a marketing strategy requires a long view of an entire ecosystem, where all elements of traditional and new media work together (Hanna et al., 2011). The focus of this type of strategy must remain on the users. Let's now turn our attention toward a case study to see how a university builds an integrated multimedia communication plan that focuses on its volatile and diverse stakeholders (e.g., students, parents, alumni, residents in the community, donors).

Case Study: Case Western Reserve University's Multimedia Wall

Media convergence has substantially changed the ways in which individuals engage content. Universities have employed various platforms (e.g., glossy brochures, campus tours, billboards, social media) for their communication and marketing efforts (Tang, 2011). As university audiences (i.e., mainly students) tend to adapt to convergence and technologies quickly, the communication efforts need to suit their expectations.

However, many universities have struggled with giving voices to their audiences and integrating traditional and new media elements in their communication and marketing plan.

To keep students, alumni, and other stakeholders engaged, Case Western Reserve University (CWRU), a private university in the United States, set up a large-scale social wall. The social wall is a two-story LED media wall, with 32 LED panels and 60 micro tiles that display an aggregation of social media content created by users (Katschthaler, 2023; Turcanu, 2023). The social wall is launched to connect with different stakeholders (e.g., students, faculty and staff, alumni), foster on-campus interaction, and increase engagement for university events (McCrary, 2022).

During the graduation season, Case Western Reserve University has invited students and their families to use hashtag #CWRUGrad2023 in their social media posts. The University's communication and marketing staffs then curated the content that goes on the social wall to showcase images, tweets, stories of students, to celebrate this significant milestone with the university community together (Katschthaler, 2023). Parents and students were enthusiastic about sharing graduation pictures and videos on social media and seeing them pop up on the gigantic digital wall (see Figure 18.1). By using such an innovative way to give voices to audiences, the University successfully made the campus community connected and engaged. The social wall has also been used for special events and/or issues. For example, during the protests around racial injustice in 2020, the social wall encouraged students and other stakeholders to express their opinions/concerns on social issues (Banerjee, 2022; McCrary, 2022).

Case Western Reserve University's communication and marketing plan is not solely focused on social media (CWRU, 2023a), but includes campaigns via broadcast, mobile, sponsorship, merchandise, and more. Indeed, to supplement the social wall, there are two physical walls on CWRU campus – advocacy wall and spirit wall – for the university community to exchange ideas and express opinions. The spirit wall provides a space for CWRU students to post advertisements, event information, and exchange ideas. The advocacy wall was created in 2021 along with the "Black Lives Matter" event, giving students a space for social and political expression (Banerjee, 2022). These traditional walls give voices to students and engage the university members. As "free exchange of ideas" is a central branding of the University (Banerjee, 2022), allowing a space where students can share their narratives and opinions creates a stronger campus community.

Here you can see many of the elements of a convergence culture at play. Not only is there a merging of traditional and new platforms, but there are cultural equalizers as well. Users are given more power in creating and distributing messages. They are encouraged to create, share the content they created, follow along and interact with other members in the community, as well as see each other' reactions through one centralized hub (e.g., social wall or traditional wall). The key to a successful communication plan in a convergent environment is to optimize user participation. The CWRU's social media guideline specifically asks practitioners not to censor but

Figure 18.1   Case Western Reserve University's Social Wall.

allow open discourse and encourage a conversation (CWRU, 2023b). All in all, media convergence provides communication and marketing practitioners unique opportunities to interact with your users and build connections. Case Western Reserve University shows you one of the many ways in which you engage your social media users in this changing media landscape.

Discussion questions

1   Have you seen a social wall before? How do social walls like the CWRU one change many of the transparent immediacy norms of traditional marketing messages?
2   In your opinion, how does CWRU's integrated communication and marketing plan go beyond just the merging of technological devices but encouraging the cooperation between various stakeholders?

3   The post-convergence era will bring challenges and issues related to culture, policy, and media structure. If you oversaw your university/organization's communication and marketing plan, what advice would you give?

Summary

This chapter discusses the many ways in which media convergence has influenced society. Beyond just the blending of traditional media and new media platforms, convergence has changed assumptions and powers associated with today and tomorrow's media users. Many media practitioners have approached the convergence era as an opportunity to reach a diverse consumer base across various media platforms. This still designates a push strategy, where strategies are developed based on predetermined marketing objectives. Instead, the convergence culture should focus on bringing consumers to the center of your production and product-innovation process.

Still, it can be confusing to navigate marketing strategies when new media landscapes are constantly changing. You must purposefully incorporate new technologies into existing business models. The principles of remediation theory should help guide your decisions. Remediation tells us that media users adapt gradually to change, and therefore it is best to slowly introduce elements of hypermediacy, rather than revamping all existing media content at once. Rather than focusing on how existing models can be reformatted to fit within the media landscape, let user behaviors and feedback guide these decisions. Remember that as a social media practitioner, it is almost always better to listen than speak.

There are many unknowns for the future of social media marketing. As we reach a post-convergence era, it is important to look ahead at many of the challenges future practitioners will face. The move toward user-generated content has certainly brought many great opportunities for everyday consumers. However, many of the promises of a more democratic marketplace have fallen short. Issues of culture, policy and agenda-setting have yet to be sorted out, and without a careful watch we may lose the opportunity for substantial social change. It is important not to get lost in individual company goals. Take a long-term approach, as every decision impacts your future.

Overall, this chapter introduces principles that should help guide strategic social media marketing decisions in a changing media landscape. All decisions should be made with a focus on consumer expectations and brand authenticity. This becomes even more important as consumers expect an increased amount of transparency from your company. These new expectations will be the center of future technological changes. In fact, it is not just communication and marketing practitioners that prove interested in these changes. Nearly every field has been impacted by changes in consumer communication and expectations through social media. Let's explore some of these areas and argue for a general framework for social media scholarship in Chapter 19.

Key Takeaways

1 Media convergence is a process of technology changes that inspire the combination of markets and products to meet various consumer needs. Specifically, it is noted that media convergence goes beyond just the merging of technological devices but includes the flow of content across multiple media platforms, the cooperation between multiple media industries, and the migratory behavior of media users.

2 In a convergent media environment, consumers should be at the center of the product-innovation and content creation process and be given more control over the flow of media content, especially through social media platforms.

3 Decisions about how to integrate new and traditional media forms into a marketing strategy should be guided by the remediation theory. Strategies should include elements that favor both hypermediacy and transparent immediacy to ensure the best reception from users. Integrating new media elements too quickly or slowly could be detrimental to an organization.

4 While the convergence culture brought many positive opportunities to society, many important concerns are surfacing again in a post-convergence era, including issues of culture, policy, and structure. While these concerns have not yet been resolved, they should be considered as future marketing strategies are developed.

References

Appelgren, E. (2004) Convergence and divergence in media: different perspectives. Available at http://elpub.scix.net/data/works/att/237elpub2004.content.pdf (accessed November 18, 2023).

Apperley, T. (2007) Citizenship and consumption: convergence culture, transmedia narratives and the digital divide. In: *Proceedings of the 4th Australasian Conference on Interactive Entertainment*, article no. 2. Melbourne, Australia: RMIT University.

Banerjee, S. (2022) Advocacy wall built to facilitate social expression on campus. *The Case Western Reserve Observer*. Available at https://observer.case.edu/advocacy-wall-built-to-facilitate-social-expression-on-campus/ (accessed November 18, 2023).

Bar, F. & Sandvig, C. (2008) US communication policy after conference. *Media, Culture, & Society*, 30(4), 531–550.

Bird, S.E. (2011) Are we all producers now? Convergence and media audience practices. *Cultural Studies*, 25(4–5), 502–516.

Bolter, J. & Grusin, R. (2002) *Remediation: Understanding New Media*. Cambridge, MA: MIT Press.

Bond, M. (2011) Demystifying social media. Available at http://www.coastdigital.co.uk/files/publications/coast_digital/social-media-guide.pdf (accessed November 18, 2023).

Brito, M. (2013) Converged media is imperative to your content strategy. Available at http://blog.hootsuite.com/converged-media-brito-part-2/ (accessed June 8, 2016).

Busick, M. (2022) The state of social media. *Comscore*. Available at https://www.comscore.com/Insights/Presentations-and-Whitepapers/2022/The-State-of-Social-Media (accessed November 18, 2023).

Case Western Reserve University (2023a) Our social strategy. Available at https://case.edu/umc/marketing/social-media/our-social-strategy.

Case Western Reserve University (2023b) Best practice. Available at https://case.edu/umc/marketing/social-media/best-practices.

Cooper, R. & Tang, T. (2009) Predicting audience exposure to television in today's media environment: an empirical integration of active-audience and structural theories. *Journal of Broadcasting and Electronic Media*, 53(3), 400–418.

Deuze, M. (2007) Convergence culture in the creative industries. *International Journal of Cultural Studies*, 10(2), 243–263.

Deuze, M. (2008) The professional identity of journalists in the context of convergence culture. *Observatorio Journal*, 7, 103–117.

DeVoss, D.N. & Webb, S. (2008) Media convergence: *Grand Theft Audio*: negotiating copyright as composers. *Computers and Composition*, 25(1), 79–103.

Drury, G. (2008) Opinion piece: social media: should marketers engage and how can it be done effectively? *Journal of Direct, Data and Digital Marketing Practice*, 9(3), 274–277.

Fagerjord, A. (2010) After convergence: YouTube and remix culture. In: J. Hunsinger, L. Klastrup & M. Allen (eds) *International Handbook of Internet Research*, pp. 187–200. Dordrecht, Netherlands: Springer.

Frenk, J. & Gómez-Dantés, O. (2002) Globalization and the challenges to health systems. *Health Affairs*, 21(3), 160–165.

Griffiths, M. & Light, B. (2008) Social networking and digital gaming media convergence: classification and its consequences for appropriation. *Information Systems Frontiers*, 10(4), 447–459.

Hanna, R., Rohm, A. & Crittenden, V.L. (2011) We're all connected: the power of the social media ecosystem. *Business Horizons*, 54(3), 265–273.

Jenkins, H. (2003) Quentin Tarantino's Star Wars? Digital cinema, media convergence, and participatory culture. In: D. Thorburn & H. Jenkins (eds) *Rethinking Media Change: The Aesthetics of Transition*, pp. 281–312. Cambridge, MA: MIT Press.

Jenkins, H. (2004) The cultural logic of media convergence. *International Journal of Cultural Studies*, 7(1), 33–43.

Jenkins, H. (2006) *Convergence Culture: Where Old and New Media Collide*. New York: New York University Press.

Katschthaler, K.A. (2023) CWRU's multi-storey university social wall. *Walls.Io*. Available at https://blog.walls.io/showcases/case-western-reserve-university-large-social-media-wall-on-campus/ (accessed November 18, 2023).

Kietzmann, J., Hermkens, K., McCarthy, I. & Silvestre, B. (2011) Social media? Get serious! Understanding the functional building blocks of social media. *Business Horizons*, 54(3), 241–251.

Laurel, B. (2000) Creating core content in a post-convergence world. Available at http://tauzero.com/Brenda_Laurel/Recent_Talks/ContentPostConvergence (accessed November 18, 2023).

Lin, J. & Cho, C. (2010) Antecedents and consequences of cross-media usage: a study of a TV program's official web site. *Journal of Broadcasting and Electronic Media*, 54(2), 316–336.

Mangold, W. & Faulds, D. (2009) Social media: the new hybrid element of the promotion mix. *Business Horizons*, 52(4), 357–365.

McCrary, J. (2022) 5 Smart ways to use social walls in higher education. *Leadsquared*. Available at https://www.leadsquared.com/industries/education/social-walls-higher-education/ (accessed November 18, 2023).

McKain, A. (2005) Not necessarily not the news: gatekeeping, remediation, and *The Daily Show*. *Journal of American Culture*, 28(4), 415–430.

McMillan, S., Hoy, M., Kim, J. & McMahan, C. (2008) A multifaceted tool for a complex phenomenon: coding web-based interactivity as technologies for interaction evolve. *Journal of Computer-Mediated Communication*, 13, 794–826.

Newberry, C. (2023) 34 Instagram stats marketers need to know in 2023. *Hootsuite*. Available at https://blog.hootsuite.com/instagram-statistics/ (accessed November 18, 2023).

Peirce, L.M. (2011) Remediation theory: analyzing what made *Quarterlife* successful as an online series and not a television series. *Television and New Media*, 12(4), 314–325.

Picard, R.G. (2000) Changing business models of online content services. *International Journal of Media Management*, 2(2), 60–68.

Porteous, C. (2021). 97% of Fortune 500 companies rely on social media. Here's you should use it for maximum impact. *Entrepreneur*. Available at https://www.entrepreneur.com/science-technology/97-of-fortune-500-companies-rely-on-social-media-heres/366240 (accessed November 18, 2023).

Rajewsky, I. (2005) Intermediality, intertextuality, and remediation: a literary perspective on intermediality. *Intermédialités*, 6, 43–64.

Stratten, S. (2012) *UnMarketing. Stop Marketing. Start Engaging*. Hoboken, NJ: John Wiley & Sons, Inc.

Tang, T. (2011) Marketing higher education across borders: a cross-cultural analysis of university websites in the U.S. and China. *Chinese Journal of Communication*, 4, 417–429. doi: 10.1080/17544750.2011.616288.

Thielmann, B. & Dowling, M. (1999) Convergence and innovation strategy for service provision in emerging Web-TV markets. *International Journal on Media Management*, 1(1), 4–9.

Trigg, S. (2008) Medievalism and convergence culture: researching the Middle Ages for fiction and film. *Parergon*, 25(2), 99–118.

Turcanu, D. (2023) Social media case studies that will inspire you. *Walls.Io*. Available at https://blog.walls.io/socialmedia/social-media-case-studies/ (accessed November 18, 2023).

Verma, P. (2023) Their voices are their livelihood. Now AI could take it away. *The Washington Post*. Available at https://www.washingtonpost.com/technology/interactive/2023/ai-voice-generators/ (accessed November 18, 2023).

19

Arguing for a General Framework for Social Media Scholarship

Introduction

This book has examined the many ways in which media users utilize social media to meet their lifestyles and needs. It has identified ways in which marketers are able to craft social media messages and create strategies to incite behavior change. Chapter 18 discussed many of the challenges of media convergence. This consolidation of traditionally separated communication has substantially changed the way organizations reach and interact with audiences. Media convergence requires you to incorporate structural elements from both transparent immediacy and hypermediacy into a new communication strategy.

This knowledge is essential for any social media practitioner looking to make mindful communication decisions in today's convergent environment. This understanding should not emerge as a silo of information, disconnected from its historical trajectory. Social media

---

Strategic Social Media: From Marketing to Social Change, Second Edition. L. Meghan Mahoney and Tang Tang.
© 2024 John Wiley & Sons, Inc. Published 2024 by John Wiley & Sons, Inc.

practitioners must understand a macro view of the roots of social media scholarship and how it fits into the overall framework of communication and mass media scholarship.

This chapter examines social media scholarship through an inverse triangle of information by examining the six paradigms of general communication theory. This knowledge is crucial in the recognition of the various ways in which communication practitioners have come to understand the role of media users. Second, we look at mass media scholarship specifically, including a definition and conceptualization of the industry, message production, and its impact on society. Finally, we explore how social media scholarship is unique in the many ways it intersects each of these arenas.

Theory makes it easier to understand why a social media endeavor proves successful or not. A strong understanding of theory will set you apart from other individuals on the social media job market because it allows you the ability to make mindful decisions regarding your consumers and makes you much more valuable than a professional who is only familiar with social media marketing cases and the various tools of social media technology. Let's begin with a holistic examination of the communication discipline.

The Six Paradigms of Communication Theory

Six paradigms of communication theory are essential to our understanding of effective communication: social psychological theories, psychological models, drama theories, audience-centered theories, contextual theories, and hybrid models. Each of these paradigms posit theories based on their understanding of the role media users play in the communication transactional process, ranging from passive consumption to active involvement (Sood *et al.*, 2003). Once we understand the differences between them, a better understanding will be gained of the foundation of social media scholarship.

Social Psychological Theories

Social psychological theories address individuals' psychological beliefs and perceptions about their environment, whereby human behavior is the result of an interplay between the person, culture, and society. Perhaps the most prominent social psychological theory is *Bandura's social learning theory* (later developed to social cognitive theory). This theory explains how humans learn by modeling the behavior of others, even modeling behaviors we see through media. Here, people are viewed as self-developing, proactive, self-regulating, and self-reflecting, not just reactive in nature (Bandura, 2004). This is the foundation of most research and communication practices interested in using media for behavior change. Based on this understanding of media users, social learning theory posits individuals as the producers of social systems, rather than merely products. Individuals can comprehend and regulate their environment and make meanings regarding what they see (Bryant & Oliver, 2009). Through these experiences, people process symbols and "transform transient experiences into cognitive models that serve as guides for judgment and action" (Bryant & Oliver, 2009, p. 95). How influential experiences prove depends on personal determinants, behavioral determinants, and environmental determinants.

Social learning theory explains how we learn to communicate through modeling the behaviors around us. Most often, our first communication pattern models those of our primary caregivers. However, as we grow up and our world gets bigger, so do our schema for interpretations. We do not just learn to behave based on the behaviors of our parents and primary caregivers. Instead, friends, teachers, and even media role models begin to influence how we behave. As a future social media strategist, it is important for you to understand these schemata of interpretation, because it helps explain how difficult it is to persuade users through media messages alone.

Schema theory illustrates how individuals base their behavior on their existing life experiences. With each new experience, we organize our behavior according to similar events that will be used in subsequent interaction. For example, one of the first relationships most people form is with their mother. When she is happy, babies tend to be happy. One day, the baby may throw a cup onto the floor while the mother is feeding. She consequently gets upset and yells, causing the baby to become upset and cry. Based on the premise of schema theory, the next time the baby has the urge to throw a cup on the floor, they will remember the schema of the previous negative exchange and learn not to follow through with this disruptive behavior.

As we get older, our primary caregivers become a less and less important part of our schema. A mother may tell a young child never to touch a hot stove. This warning should be sufficient to influence a child's behavior during formative years, but eventually, children begin branching out, and peers become a stronger presence in their life. If peers begin urging the child to touch a hot stove and the mother is not around, the child may be tempted to touch the stove despite previous cautions. The content of the message and relational history remain the same, but the influence on child behavior changes. With this understanding of social learning theory and the concept of schema, we can see how difficult it is for a simple message to cause direct behavior change. The process is not linear, but transactional in nature.

Some parenting messages are strong enough to provide children with a schema that will overcome any amount of peer pressure. This is difficult to achieve because children do not always look up to their parents. The process of *symbolic role modeling*, where humans tend to model behaviors from those whom they admire most, is imperative to understanding the effects of communication. By viewing corrective adjustments of others during behavior production, we learn through modeling. Thus, we may not necessarily need to experience those same behaviors to make a change (Bandura, 2004). Instead, we see that someone who is like us had success when behaving in a certain manner, and those lessons then become a part of our own cognitive process. This is why influencer marketing has been a successful social media marketing practice.

Social psychological theories account for the premise that individuals with limited schema, such as children, or individuals with a dysfunctional upbringing may be more prone to model media messages than those with more positive schema to draw from. They suggest that people are more likely to model behavior if they identify with the character they are viewing and if society would value the outcomes (Bryant & Oliver, 2009). Here, you can see how everyone would interact with and respond to media messages very differently from one another. Social psychological theories help explain why one person can watch a violent TikTok video, and it has no effect, while someone else can watch the same video with great effect.

Psychological Models

Not all communication paradigms take into account individuals' psychological beliefs and perceptions about their environment. Psychological models are based on a cognitive processing model. Here, individuals are exposed to a mass communication program, and this exposure is used to predict subsequent behavior interactions. It is a much more direct media effects model. A prominent example of a psychological model is the *elaboration likelihood model* (ELM). ELM recognizes that media holds the power to sway users in identical manners. The extent to which media can persuade depends on whether the messages are effective in changing attitudes and whether these attitudes influence behaviors (Bryant & Oliver, 2009).

According to ELM, people are persuaded through central or peripheral routes of persuasion (Petty & Cacioppo, 1981). The *central route to persuasion* is when a person draws upon prior experience and knowledge counter to the messages that they are receiving. Once feelings regarding the message are determined, the final step involves integrating the new thoughts into their cognitive structure (Bryant & Oliver, 2009). The *peripheral route of persuasion* is when a person's ability to process a message is low or when they are being a more passive audience (Bryant & Oliver, 2009). Researchers found that people persuaded through peripheral routes are usually only persuaded for short periods of time. Attitude change through peripheral routes tends to be based more on passive acceptance or rejection of simple cues and has a less well-articulated foundation (Bryant & Oliver, 2009; Petty & Cacioppo, 1981). This process is generally referred to in propaganda research.

Herman and Chomsky (1988) developed a *propaganda model* that presents four factors that determine what is considered newsworthy in society:

- the size, concentrated ownership, owner wealth, and profit orientation of the dominant mass media firms.
- advertising as the primary source of income for mass media.
- the media's reliance on information provided by government, business, and experts, which is funded and approved by these primary sources and agents of power, who use flak as a means of disciplining the media.
- anticommunism as a national religion and control mechanism.

Clearly, this model is based on the notion that media has the potential to influence and possess great power over users. However, social media makes it possible for news stories that do not match these four factors to become viral. The notion of passive audience acceptance or rejection of media messages is outdated, yet there are still many benefits to considering the cognitive processes of media users through psychological models.

Drama Theories

Drama theories are based on a paradigm that examines the roles people play or the scripts they follow in their daily lives. The assumption of this paradigm is that media users have specific emotional reactions to different storylines, influencing the way they exchange ideas and opinions on real-life issues. The presentation of a message is intrinsically as important as its content. An example of a drama theory would be Bentley's dramatic theory.

Bentley's dramatic theory suggests that media producers should utilize structure as the framework for creating character archetypes in dramas. This theory breaks theater genres into five categories: tragedy, comedy, tragicomedy, farce, and melodrama (Bentley, 1967). Each of these categories has its own structure and effect on media users. This includes providing specific and easily recognizable tones, anecdotes, and characters (Singhal *et al.*, 2004). These patterns are like narrative media created all over the world, including books, theater, television programs, and movies. Tensions between protagonists and antagonists help guide media users through their own evolution toward the adoption of desired behavior change. Here, individuals follow patterns of behavior based on the role that they see played out in narratives, in media, and in their daily lives.

Audience-centered Theories

Audience-centered theories examine how users interact and react to media messages. This paradigm views media users as having a much more active role in the media selection and interpretation process. An early example of an audience-centered theory is the *uses and gratifications theory*, which explains why and how people seek out specific media to satisfy their specific needs.

As discussed in Chapter 5, the uses and gratifications theory has been a major mass communication perspective over the last decades due to its view of media users as active agents in the media consumption process, rather than passive consumers. This perspective stresses the impact of individual differences on media uses and effects by assuming that unique social and psychological circumstances help shape users' needs (Haridakis, 2006). While social media has transformed audiences into more active participants, technologies like artificial intelligence and customized recommendation could still guide or constrain people's content choices (Webster, 2014). In addition, environments and structures of time, access, and interactive features could influence people's media use.

As such, other audience theories, such as the active within structure approach, suggest that media users actively seek media content within internal and external structures

(Cooper & Tang, 2009). Webster's dynamic model of exposure also points out that media users are agents "who recursively draw upon structured media resources. As they do so, they both reproduce and change the media environment" (Webster, 2017, p. 357). Individual predispositions, such as needs, preferences, and moods, can be motivators for media use; however, media choices are also to some degree a result of media and social structures (Webster, 2014). These perspectives highlight the role of active choice in convergent media environments while acknowledging the continuing influences of habit and media structures. The takeaway is that you should consider the various kinds of media users with differing levels of participation and guide their attention accordingly.

Audience-centered theories are also critical precursors to audience reception research (discussed in Chapter 12). These are the basic foundations of *participatory audience research* that focuses more on audience dialogue, examines cultural identity, and looks at local and unique decision-making processes (Petraglia, 2007). Ultimately, achieving a comprehensive understanding of your consumers is the first step toward developing successful social media strategies, which should reflect an understanding of the interplay between active choice, habit, and structures.

Contextual Theories

Current contextual theories are those that take a social constructivist approach, where meaning is constructed through the interaction of media users and content, pointing to the sociocultural context. Rather than viewing media users as a self-selecting body, outside environments become critical to behavior change. An example of a contextual theory is the *theory of hegemony*, where dominant culture maintains a dominant position using institutions such as media (Sood *et al.*, 2003). The basis of contextual theories is that audience involvement is multidimensional and serves as a medium for prompting behavior change. The more involvement and active role users play in the media reception process, the greater the potential for behavior change (Sood, 2006).

Contextual theories examine humanistic and critical perspectives focused on power and dominance structures. One of the earliest examples of a contextual theory is the *agenda-setting theory*. Agenda-setting theory indicates the ability of a media source to influence its audiences to think about a particular issue. Media does not tell users what to think but rather what to think about.

Media agenda, public agenda, and corporate agenda are dominant structures often advanced through the agenda-setting process (Carroll & McCombs, 2003). This selection process is what makes agenda-setting potentially persuasive. The process of disseminating information from the press to the public gives an issue salience and is the core mechanism of the agenda-setting process (Kiousis, 2003). Studies have shown that the public's concerns over issues fluctuate greatly according to the amount of attention it is given by media outlets.

An example of agenda-setting theory was evident during the "Tide Pod Challenge" Hoax. In 2018, the Tide Pod Challenge, a viral challenge that originated through videos depicting people consuming laundry detergent pods on social media, received significant media coverage (Chokshi, 2018). The media's sensationalized reporting of the social media challenge and the dangers of consuming laundry detergent products created widespread panic and societal concerns. Even the American Association of Poison Control Centers and Procter & Gamble (the company that owns Tide products) issued warnings and statements discouraging the consumption of detergent products (Nedelman, 2018). The process of media outlets choosing to report on the Tide Pod Challenge over other incoming news stories is the process of agenda-setting. While the media was not relaying untruthful information or directly warning the public that detergent products were more dangerous than before (or the harm of social media), that was the message its users received due to the extra coverage.

Media users were exposed to an overwhelming amount of the Tide Pod Challenge stories, leading them to prioritize the challenge as an important issue. However, only a limited number of people ate Tide pods to create social media videos. The media did not provide its users with a viewpoint through which to examine the incoming messages. Simply by giving more attention to an issue, the public's concern rose. While generally, traditional media outlets have served as the gatekeepers of information, everyday users are beginning to have more power to set the agenda through social media. This has created many opportunities and challenges for social media marketers like you.

Hybrid Theories

Finally, hybrid theories of communication utilize a combination of elements from the other five paradigms. This approach tends to combine linear direct effects models of communication with more active audience participation assumptions and generally results in a communication intervention or campaign with a limited number of resources and challenges (Phillips, 2011). Chapter 17 introduced the entertainment–education approach to behavior change, a hybrid communication model. While hybrid theories are generally more difficult to monitor and evaluate for causation, they present a strong yield for behavior change when implemented appropriately. This requires a strong understanding of all the other five paradigms.

Each of these six paradigms of communication theory (social psychological theory, psychological models, drama theory, audience-centered theory, contextual theory, and hybrid models) has very different assumptions about how users interact with media texts. However, regardless of where you situate yourself as a social media practitioner, it is important to note that when communicating, regardless of the platform, messages must be constructed, disseminated, and consumed with the intended audience in mind. The more you can account for a media user's own individual experiences and preferences, the more powerful your message becomes.

A General Framework for Mass Media Scholarship

The field of media research covers vast areas through various and often-competing approaches. Potter (2013) identified 10 individual definitional elements of mass media. To be considered mass media, all 10 of these elements must be met. They are outlined in Table 19.1.

Traditional mass media research offers a medium-by-medium examination of print, electronic, and new media (Sterling, 2011), which makes the discipline seem disconnected, with little sense of who we are and what unites us, and does little to examine the deep and changing impact of media on society. Potter (2009) attempts to create a more unified approach to mass media research in his book *Arguing for a General Framework for Mass Media Scholarship*. Through an extensive examination of five decades of research in the field, he identifies patterns and synthesizes interconnections among scholarship. He argues that:

> all media research should focus on the ways media channels are used, how audiences choose certain media and media messages, and how they process meaning from those messages, and how those messages shape their knowledge, structures, attitudes, beliefs, emotional reactions, and behavioral patterns over time (Potter, 2009, p. 18).

We should look at media scholarship more broadly and build a general framework to guide our practice.

Potter's (2009) synthesis identifies four main facets of mass media scholarship: organizations, media users, messages, and effects. The *organization approach* examines the institutions and media organizations by defining the business, marketing, and employment strategies of media companies and services. This approach examines the structure of various media

Table 19.1 Synthesized working definition of mass media.

Sender of messages:
- is a complex organization or institution, not an individual.
- uses standardized practices to mass-produce the messages and disseminate them.
- has an awareness of specific niche audiences and actively promotes itself to attract as many audience members of that niche as possible.
- conditions audience members for habitual repeated exposures

Audience members:
- are widely dispersed geographically, i.e., not all in one place.
- are aware of the public character of what they are seeing or hearing.
- encounter messages in a variety of exposure states but most often in a state of automaticity.

Channels of message dissemination are technological devices that:
- make messages public, i.e., available to anyone.
- extend the availability of messages in time and space.
- can reach audiences within a relatively short time, even simultaneously.

Source: Potter (2013). Reproduced with permission of John Wiley & Sons.

channels and the relationships within the institution. The *audiences approach* examines audience behavior and the concept of what is an audience. This includes cognitive algorithms, filtering of media messages, and the changing meaning and construction of audience. The *media messages approach* reviews the formulas and conventions of media content. This includes the creation of marketing strategy and message design. The *effects approach* examines the multiple effects line of thinking, conceptualizes media effects, and discusses the design of media effects studies (Potter, 2009; Sterling, 2011).

This general framework provides an integrated explanation of mass media as an industry, the messages that are produced and marketed, the consumers for those messages, and the effects of those messages on individuals and larger social structures (Potter, 2009). It is through this lens that the social media concepts of this book have emerged.

Parts I and II of this book examined how individuals utilize various social media platforms, why they choose them, and how they interpret messages given their individual life experiences. We learned the complex process of user negotiation and the difficulty in inciting persuasion through social media messages. Concepts of diffusion, community, and mobilization were offered to help you balance your need for control with the possibility for behavior change given this knowledge.

Part III of this book focused on how social media practitioners are best able to create messages according to this knowledge to influence human behavior change. Through an understanding of social media business models and marketing strategies, you learned to incite behavior change in media users to meet the objectives of your organization. Part IV of this book discussed how to use this knowledge to create social good and aid behavior change in a globalized stage.

The future of scholarship and communication/marketing endeavors should cross boundaries between different media facets to produce more compelling results (Sterling, 2011). Thus, as a social media practitioner, you should be aware that it is important to understand where your assumptions fit within these frameworks and to keep your social media strategy in an integrated approach. Before completing your social media endeavor, consider the following action plan.

Media Scholarship Action Plan

1   Understand your assumptions about the role media users play in the communication process based on the six paradigms of communication theory.
2   Identify in which of the four main facets of the communication process your social media endeavors reside.
3   Seek out ways in which your work can cross boundaries between various media platforms, alternative facets, and different disciplines to produce more complete and compelling results.

Key Intersections of Social Media Scholarship

The previous sections have offered a critical assessment of communication and mass media research. This assessment illustrates that social media scholarship is a dynamic academic discipline. Despite the varying strands of communication research, there are many points for possible convergence. While mass media has traditionally been seen as its own area of focus, this section calls for social media scholarship to be seen as a more integrative area of study by offering ideas and directions for future social media research.

Each paradigm of communication scholarship has shown interest in the impact of social media technologies. Scholars from disparate fields have examined social media practices, implications, culture, the meaning of social media, and user engagement through various methodological techniques, theoretical traditions, and analytic approaches (Ellison, 2007).

For example, social psychological theories have examined an individual's perceptions about a particular social media platform (Miller & Morris, 2014; Ruckert *et al.*, 2014); psychological models have examined how exposure to social media could be used to predict subsequent behavior interaction (Nekmat *et al.*, 2019; Xie & Feng, 2023); drama theories have examined the way social media users are influenced in real life by online narratives (Ji & Raney, 2015; Penner, 2014); audience-centered theories have examined why people use social media messages (Bossetta & Schmokel, 2023; Stamps, 2022); and contextual theories have examined how people derive meaning through their interaction with social media content and other social media users (Johnson, 2013; Meraz, 2011).

Though these are ways in which each paradigm of communication scholarship has incorporated social media into their research, it is not the best strategy for advancing our understanding of its impact. Together as a discipline, we must challenge the current state of our divided assumptions. A more integrative and hybrid approach to social media scholarship will help us to understand its role more completely.

A strong social media scholarship framework should mirror Potter's (2009) approach and provide an integrated explanation of social media as an industry, the messages that are produced and marketed, the consumers for those messages, and the effects of those messages on individuals and larger social structures.

Much of social media research discusses the benefits of interactivity and participation. However, a reliable, valid, and empirically derived instrument of social participation has yet to be developed. Many of the instruments being used have been designed for traditional mass media. Social media proves different, and it is necessary that we have a valid and reliable way to examine audience use and preferences, social media structures, and the concepts of diffusion, community, and mobilization of social media messages.

It is also imperative for scholarship to embrace a one-to-one model of communication technology. Not all social media platforms are designed for the one-to-many mass audience. In fact, many of the newest social media applications, such as Snapchat and WeChat, are designed for more personal communication between friends rather than mass dissemination to a larger audience. This mirrors interpersonal communication structures more than mass media conceptualizations. Therefore, if appropriate, future research should integrate this area of communication research into social media scholarship.

Much more work also needs to be done to design an effective monitoring and evaluation system for social media endeavors. Chapter 12 discussed the importance of holistic measurement that includes both quantitative analysis and qualitative audience reception research. This triangulation approach will allow a much more nuanced understanding of users' social media experiences, including overall generalizations and distinct outlier behavior.

Additionally, the discipline needs more longitudinal scholarship. The long-term impacts of social media are unrealized, as the technology is still relatively new. We have a limited understanding of who is and who is not using these platforms and why (Solvoll & Larsson, 2020; Wakefield & Knighton, 2019). Future scholarship should include large-scale quantitative and qualitative research, with richer ethnographic research on populations more difficult to access, to help us better understand the long-term implications of these tools.

In the classroom, professors must consider the idea of social media scholarship and remain open to data sharing, the democratization of expertise, and alternative models of peer review and reputation management (Greenhow & Gleeson, 2014). Otherwise, social media will continue to be seen as something unscholarly. We must continue to highlight the relationship between scholarly work, industry practice, and society without pitting scholars who embrace innovative approaches against more traditional practices.

Finally, and perhaps most importantly, social media is the most fragmented experience of all the media technologies. It is important to understand that most individuals are accessing social media on the go while multitasking with many elements of their everyday lives. Controlled experimental settings and self-report surveys may not capture the true essence of this mobile and integrated experience. It is important for researchers to design more studies that use noninvasive tracking and observation methods. Online and offline behaviors are interconnected, and it is time that we study them accordingly.

For one researcher to incorporate all these assumptions and alternative designs in a single research agenda would be impossible. However, your role as a social media practitioner is to understand the various communication paradigms, identify where your assumptions regarding users and technology align, and actively seek out collaboration with those who think differently. As many mass media programs pair off from the communication discipline, we believe that the future of social media scholarship is strongest when we advance knowledge as a united front.

Case Study: CIRCLE

CIRCLE, or Center for Information and Research on Civic Learning and Engagement, conducts research on the civic and political engagement of young Americans (www.civicyouth.org). This initiative was established in 2001 to change public discourse on how young citizens engage in civic and political life with the goal of developing programs that foster civic learning and engagement in democracy.

Oftentimes, public discourse surrounding young citizens posits the demographic as apathetic toward public affairs, having a low sense of efficacy, and filled with negativism (Pinkleton & Austin, 2004). This initiative is interested in utilizing media messages to inspire more proactive and positive behavior change in young adults. Based on the transactional model of communication defined in Chapter 1, it is understood that media messages should be constructed not just on the producer's own goals but on the needs of the target consumers. Additionally, barriers such as competence, access, and relational history must be considered.

Due to the ongoing societal discourse about younger generations, the target audiences of CIRCLE prove interesting. They have been described as having the lowest trends of civic engagement and social capital in history (Putnam, 2001). CIRCLE aims to change such public discourses about young citizens and alter the way that people think about civic education and engagement (CIRCLE, 2023a). Its research found that younger generations are still participating in civic activities, just in a different manner through social media. Today's digital natives prefer to participate through interdisciplinary and community-based means.

For example, one of CIRCLE's projects, Rep Us, aims to explore and advance connections between youth media creation and more diverse youth representation in media, ultimately encourage more young adults to participate in civic life (CIRCLE, 2023b). The project asked young people to create their own podcasts and videos that express their political opinions and share them on social media (See Figure 19.1). As a result, the project led to several youth advisory groups, such as Youth and Government, a group that encourages young adults to take part in mock legislative sessions (CIRCLE, 2023b). By encouraging media users to become media producers and amplify their voices, CIRCLE highlights the potential of project-based, community-building initiatives that do not fit into the traditional model for social change.

Figure 19.1   Screenshot from CIRCLE *Rep Us* project.

Social media today provides the opportunity to share stories and pictures of initiatives close to the users' hearts. This is an example of how social media can transform social change programs for the better. Moreover, it illustrates how participatory community mobilization through hybrid approaches is the key to positive social change and is more possible than ever before due to social media.

Discussion questions

1   How might the target audience of CIRCLE (i.e., young adults) impact behavior change outcomes? How could producers use social media to better reach these consumers in their communication strategy?
2   It is argued that youth may feel a sense of gratification by engaging in civic activities through technology, rather than traditional means such as volunteering or voting. Which of the six paradigms of communication theories do you feel this selection process most closely aligns with? Why?
3   Much debate centers around how technology influences users in a positive or negative manner. Based on what we know about the communication models and paradigms, how can you explain the positive impacts of CIRCLE on society?

Summary

The field of communication is huge, with many points of distinction and intersection. Strong social media practitioners need to understand their place within the historical trajectory. By understanding the roots of social media scholarship, one can make more mindful decisions about message strategy.

This chapter presents the six paradigms of general communication theory, the definition and conceptualization of mass media scholarship, and the many ways in which social media scholarship intersects with each of these arenas to guide future practice and research. Though the field is still new to conduct a large-scale analysis such as Potter's (2009) framework for mass media scholarship, many of the patterns emerging are similar. This includes looking at social media as an industry, the messages that are produced and marketed, the consumers for those messages, and the effects of those messages on individuals and larger social structures.

Future social media scholarship should include a more integrative approach across communication paradigms, test new empirical theories and measurements, embrace more interpersonal communication research, design more effective and longitudinal monitoring and evaluation systems for social media endeavors, incorporate social media scholarship in the classroom, and study social media use in more natural, noninvasive, and fragmented settings. These changes will put us one step closer toward creating a general framework for social media scholarship.

Now that we have a more thorough understanding of the theories that guide social media strategy and practice, let us turn our attention to the future of social media. Chapter 20 focuses on how marketing strategy and social participation will change in the coming years. Many of the points of distinction outlined in this chapter will become blurred in future practice. Based on this understanding, recommendations for future social media practices will be offered.

Key Takeaways

1 Six different paradigms of communication theory – social psychological theory, psychological models, drama theory, audience-centered theory, contextual theory, and hybrid models – help explain how media users interact with and are influenced by media texts.
2 The strongest social media strategies integrate hybrid approaches into their campaigns.
3 There are four main facets of mass media: organizations, media users, messages, and effects. Practitioners should cross boundaries between each in today's convergent environment.
4 Integration requires putting media industries, social media messages produced, marketing strategies, users reached and societal effects all into consideration.

References

Bandura, A. (2004) Health promotion by social cognitive means. *Health Education and Behavior*, 31, 143–164.

Bentley, E. (1967) *The Life of the Drama*. New York: Atheneum.

Bossetta, M. & Schmokel, R. (2023) Cross-platform emotions and audience engagement in social media political campaigning: comparing candidates' Facebook and Instagram images in the 2020 US election. *Political Communication*, 40(1), 48–68. doi: 10.1080/10584609. 2022.2128949.

Bryant, J. & Oliver, M.B. (2009) *Media Effects: Advances in Theory and Research*, third edition. New York: Routledge.

Carroll, C. & McCombs, M. (2003) Agenda-setting effects of business news on the public's images and opinions about major corporations. *Corporate Reputation Review*, 6(1), 36–46.

Chokshi, N. (2018) Yes, people really are eating Tide pods. No, it's not safe *The New York Times*. Available at https://www.nytimes.com/2018/01/20/us/tide-pod-challenge.html (accessed November 18, 2023).

CIRCLE (2023a) About. Available at https://circle.tufts.edu/about.

CIRCLE (2023b) Rep Us project. Available at https://circle.tufts.edu/index.php/circle-action/rep-us-project#for-young-people (accessed November 18, 2023).

Cooper, R. & Tang, T. (2009) Predicting audience exposure to television in today's media environment: an empirical integration of active-audience and structural theories. *Journal of Broadcasting and Electronic Media*, 53(3), 1–19.

Ellison, N. (2007) Social network sites: definition, history, and scholarship. *Journal of Computer-Mediated Communication*, 13(1), 210–230.

Greenhow, C. & Gleeson, B. (2014) Social scholarship: reconsidering scholarly practices in the age of social media. *British Journal of Educational Technology*, 45(3), 392–402.

Haridakis, P. (2006) Men, women, and television violence: predicting viewer aggression in male and female television viewers. *Communication Quarterly*, 54(2), 227–255.

Herman, E. & Chomsky, N. (1988) *Manufacturing Consent: The Political Economy of the Mass Media*. New York: Pantheon Books.

Ji, Q. & Raney, A.A. (2015) Morally judging entertainment: a case study of live Tweeting during Downton Abbey. *Media Psychology*, 18(2), 221–242.

Johnson, T. (2013) *Agenda Setting in a 2.0 World: New Agendas in Communication*. New York: Routledge.

Kiousis, S. (2003) Job approval and favorability: the impact of media attention to the Monica Lewinsky scandal on public opinion of President Bill Clinton. *Mass Communication and Society*, 6(4), 435–451.

Meraz, S. (2011) Using time series analysis to measure intermedia agenda-setting influence in traditional media and political blog networks. *Journalism and Mass Communication Quarterly*, 88(1), 176–194.

Miller, B. & Morris, R.G. (2014) Virtual peer effects in social learning theory. *Crime and Delinquency*. doi: 10.1177/0011128714526499.

Nedelman, M. (2018) Poison control calls "spike" due to online laundry pod challenge. *CNN*. Available at https://www.cnn.com/2018/01/17/health/tide-laundry-pod-challenge-poison-control/index.html (accessed November 18, 2023).

Nekmat, E., Gower, K.K., Zhou, S., & Metzger, M. (2019) Connective-collective action on social media: moderated mediation of cognitive elaboration and perceived source credibility on personalness of source. *Communication Research*, 46(1), 62–87. doi: 10.1177/0093650215609676.

Penner, J. (2014) On Aggro performance: audience participation and the dystopian response to the living theatre's paradise now. *Comparative Drama*, 48(1), 75–92.

Petraglia, J. (2007) Narrative intervention in behavior and public health. *Journal of Health Communication*, 12(5), 493–505.

Petty, R. & Cacioppo, J. (1981) *Attitudes and Persuasion: Classic and Contemporary Approaches*. Dubuque, IA: Wm C. Brown.

Phillips, L. (2011) *The Promise of Dialogue: The Dialogic Turn in the Production and Communication of Knowledge*. Philadelphia: John Benjamins Publishing Company.

Pinkleton, B. & Austin, E. (2004) Media perceptions and public affairs apathy in the politically inexperienced. *Mass Communication and Society*, 7(3), 319–337.

Potter, W.J. (2009) *Arguing for a General Framework for Mass Media Scholarship*. Thousand Oaks, CA: Sage Publications.

Potter, W.J. (2013) Synthesizing a working definition of "mass" media. *Review of Communication Research*, 1, 1–30.

Putnam, R. (2001) *Bowling Alone: The Collapse and Revival of American Community*. New York: Simon & Schuster.

Ruckert, E., McDonald, P., Birkmeier, M., Walker, B., Cotton, L., Lyons, L.B., Straker, H.O. & Plack, M.M. (2014) Using technology to promote active and social learning experiences in health professions education. *Online Learning: Official Journal of the Online Learning Consortium*, 18(4). Available at http://olj.online-learningconsortium.org/index.php/olj/article/view/515 (accessed June 8, 2016).

Singhal, A., Cody, M., Rogers, E. & Sabido, M. (2004) *Entertainment-Education and Social Change*. Mahwah, NJ: Lawrence Erlbaum Associates.

Solvoll, M.K. & Larsson, A.O. (2020) The (non)use of likes, comments and shares of news in local online newspapers. *Newspaper Research Journal*, 41(2), 204–217. doi: 10.1177/0739532920919826.

Sood, S. (2006) Audience involvement and entertainment-education. *Communication Theory*, 12(2), 153–172.

Sood, S., Witte, K. & Menard, T. (2003) The theory behind entertainment education. In: M.J. Cody, A. Singhal, M. Sabido & E.M. Rogers (eds) *Entertainment-Education Worldwide: History, Research, and Practice*, pp. 117–149. Mahwah, NJ: Lawrence Erlbaum.

Stamps, D. (2022) Black audiences' identity-focused social media use, group vitality, and consideration of collective action. *Journalism & Mass Communication Quarterly*, 99(3), 660–675. doi: 10.1177/10776990221104153.

Sterling, C. (2011) Arguing for a general framework for mass media scholarship. *Journal of Broadcasting and Electronic Media*, 55(4), 615–616.

Wakefield, R. & Knighton, D. (2019) Distinguishing among publics, audiences, and stakeholders in the social media era of unanticipated publics. *Public Relations Review*, 45(5). doi: 10.1016/j.pubrev.2019.101821.

Webster, J.G. (2014) *The Marketplace of Attention: How Audiences Take Shape in a Digital Age*. Cambridge, MA: The MIT Press.

Webster, J.G. (2017) Three myths of digital media. *Convergence: The International Journal of Research into New Media Technologies*, 23, 352–361. doi: 10.1177/1354856517700385.

Xie, Q. & Feng, Y. (2023) How to strategically disclose sponsored content on Instagram?: the synergy effects of two types of sponsorship disclosures in influencer marketing. *International Journal of Advertising*, 42(2), 317–343. doi: 10.1080/02650487.2022.2071393.

20

The Future of Social Media

Learning Objectives

After reading this chapter, you should be able to:
1   Identify changes to the future social media landscape.
2   Integrate the Internet of Things into your social media strategy.
3   Explain the influence of Artificial Intelligence to social networking.

Introduction

The first edition of this book discussed mobile marketing, wearable technology (e.g., Apple Watch), and standalone applications as the future of social media. Each of these has influenced our everyday lives and how we connect with family and friends. Today, users are accustomed to these technology advancements. Smart appliances that we interact with each day are now easily controlled through mobile technology. We can use our mobile devices to activate robot vacuum cleaners, close garage doors, and more, all through standalone applications. The notifications generated by these apps can automatically be shared with all members connected to the household, allowing family members to keep

Strategic Social Media: From Marketing to Social Change, Second Edition. L. Meghan Mahoney and Tang Tang.
© 2024 John Wiley & Sons, Inc. Published 2024 by John Wiley & Sons, Inc.

each other in the loop regarding what is happening at home. As physical objects become increasingly embedded into our communication networks, it is important to examine how the Internet of Things (IoT) continues to influence social media.

This book argues that the focus of a marketing campaign should reside in the quality of connections with consumers, rather than the quantity of followers. Just as with social connections, companies cannot fake relationships online. Authenticity and trust are crucial to the user identification process. If the future of social media requires users to be connected to everyone, and increasingly everything, in their lives 24/7, there must be a tipping point. If the primary goal of most social media strategies is to build a stronger relationship with consumers, it is comforting to know that traditional machines have not been capable of making strong authentic connections. However, profound advancements in Artificial Intelligence (AI) technology are making that notion less and less true.

AI technology today is different than a decade ago. It is important to consider how AI will disrupt the social media landscape. Today, 42% of companies are implementing AI into their everyday operations, as it holds the potential to enhance customer service, boost productivity, and reduce human errors (Watters, 2023). As such, we must examine the role of AI in future social media. Remember that marketing campaigns exist as a part of an ever-changing social media landscape. What worked for one company last month is not likely to work again today. It is important for social media practitioners to always remain forward-thinking.

Chapter 19 argued for a general framework for current social media scholarship and practice. It is time to turn our attention toward the future of social media marketing. This chapter explores upcoming innovations in the social media landscape, including IoT and AI. We will also discuss the privacy and security concerns brought about by these technological advancements. Finally, we will talk about general conclusions and recommendations for future social media marketing practices. It is important to be cautious about overstepping the promises of social media. Just because the technology makes it easier than ever to form connections, it also makes it easier for users to ignore them. Social and behavior changes are difficult to establish, and the only thing worse than developing an unsuccessful marketing campaign is to miss out on the conversation altogether.

The Future Social Media Landscape

It would prove impossible to predict all the new media changes that we will see in our lifetime. You should be cautious with any reference that claims to have all the answers to what a future technological landscape will look like. This section aims to explore some emerging technology trends that today's practitioners should consider when developing business models and marketing strategies. These include the integration of the IoT and AI into our everyday lives. While there are many more important advancements over the past 5 years, these trends have already proven huge disruptors to the industry.

Remember from Chapter 2 the differences between a Web 1.0 and Web 2.0 environment. Web 1.0 views the media users as a large, anonymous, and heterogeneous audience and promotes communication across a one-to-many unidirectional model (Pearce, 2009). Web 2.0 brought much advancement for user interactivity and participation, including the ability for social networking, interaction, customization, and user-added possibilities (Cormode and Krishnamurthy 2008; Wirtz et al., 2010). We have discussed the shift in power from media producers to everyday users driven by these technological advancements. These changes have been significant, resulting in a globalized society where individuals are more connected than ever before. This interconnectedness brings new opportunities for online collaboration among users, And this trend will only be magnified as we look ahead to the future of social media marketing.

One key function of a Web 3.0 environment, identified by Markoff (2006), is the idea of a semantic web. The *semantic web* is a collaborative movement that provides a common framework for data to be shared and reused across applications and community boundaries. Although semantic technologies have been around since 2000, the World Wide Web Consortium is now developing proposed standards for the industry to follow. The function of a semantic web encourages users to find, share, and combine information more easily, while also being more easily interpreted by machines to advance more useful Internet structures (Hendler, 2008). It reorganizes and structures online content, enabling users anywhere in the world to collaborate on projects.

> Whereas Web 1.0 and 2.0 were embryonic, formative technologies, Web 3.0 promises to be a more mature web where better "pathways" for information retrieval will be created, and a greater capacity for cognitive processing of information will be built (Giustini, 2007, p. 1273).

These features allow users to share, produce, and expand upon content more easily than ever before, enabling more efficient and automated data integration, discovery, and reuse that will increase machine-to-machine communication. The integration of everyday objects into networks within the field of information technology has led to the emergence of the IoT.

Internet of Things (IoT)

IoT is defined as any consumer products, durable goods and other everyday objects combined with Internet connectivity and powerful data analytic capabilities (Rose et al. 2015). These utility sensors promise to transform the way we work, live, and play. While users expect computers and mobile devices to allow network connectivity, it is becoming common for other objects, such as cars, television, vacuum cleaners, light bulbs, speakers, sunglasses, or even golf balls, to carry and communicate individual surveillance data about our lives. This passive interaction with the Internet converges our "real-life" experiences with our online behaviors.

While everyday automation with products does not inherently seem like a social experience, there are countless ways in which IoT devices can influence the social media landscape. For example, users have long been sharing data from wearable devices, such as fitness watches tracking their running sessions or biking routes, on their social media feeds. These metrics keep users accountable with distance, time, and routes. Thus, users often trust that IoT data reports are accurate, while Instagram photos can be filtered. In general, IoT expands the availability of information along the production value chain by utilizing networked sensors (Rose *et al.*, 2015). There is strong authenticity and transparency in IoT data sharing.

Wearable IoT technology is the product of convergence between nanotechnology and an expectation of increased mobility from users that allows hands-free interaction worn as clothing or jewelry (De Freitas & Levene, 2003). Users of wearable IoTs do not have to pullout and log into a mobile device each time they wish to access content. Instead, the technology is integrated into something that they are already wearing. Messages disseminated through wearables are integrated into users' daily lives the same way as an individual speaking to them. Users can also add other people to their IoT devices to create a more social and shared experience between select users and machine information.

Consider the many benefits discussed in this book regarding the real-life mobilization of user experiences. Brands struggle to get users to share real-life experiences with their products on social media. IoT technology allows users to seamlessly share with their network what they are doing while they are doing it. Brand advocates now can constantly send out information about how they interact with your product in more positive and natural capacities.

The notion of what it means to be "on the Internet" has gone away. IoT devices mean that users are always connected, both to machines and to people. Organizations no longer need to conduct research to make educated guesses about our behavior patterns. IoT data provide real behavior data about how we spend our days. For example, if a person can download a supermarket application that includes their profile, preferred brands, and routine shopping times. This information allows more personalized coupons and incentives for the individual user. The car they drive can suggest alternative routes based on traffic patterns collected by sensors on the vehicle. The mobile application can also interact with the user's smart refrigerator to send alerts when products run low or make recommendations for recipes to cook given the availability of products. A smart shoe can sense body activities and reshape based on the movements of a person. This information can be combined with exercise IoT devices for a more comprehensive report of physical activity. The plethora of data from all consumers allows the company to make better-informed stocking and layout decisions of their store. Here, you can see how IoT creates smarter and more efficient systems for everyone.

While mobile technology allowed two-way or multi-way communication between an organization and its customers (Shankar & Balasubramanian, 2009), IoT technology allows communication between machines. IoT connectivity means that users are always connected with something. Thakkar (2023) presents a world where a user can use smart technology to engage with a virtual assistant based on the visiting patterns, interests, likes, and dislikes captured from social media in any public space. The virtual assistant can then guide the person through the space, informing her or him about the specialties, thus enhancing the user experience. This increases the culture-specific personalization, interactivity, and socialization of location-based marketing (Bauer *et al.*, 2005).

IoT technologies undoubtedly inform the future of marketing. It provides real-life metrics regarding how users interact with the Internet. Less time needs to be spent on consumer research, which traditionally involves tracking what time of day, through what devices, and for how long users utilize social media. IoT automates this research and presents practitioners with easily digestible reports.

IoT devices give the data and insights required to optimize workflows, visualize usage patterns, automate operations, and allow more effective competitions (Kundariya, 2021), but passive surveillance also raises important questions about what information we are showing with whom. What happens when your refrigerator and grocery app are also connected with your healthcare provider? What if your health insurance knew the products you were buying and the recipes you were cooking each meal? The plethora of IoT devices makes it impossible for users to track what data are being tracked and where they are being shared. Security and privacy concerns of IoT are discussed in greater detail in the next section.

As a social media marketer, you should know that not all customers wish to make every experience a connected experience. Research demonstrates that 50% of customers never connect their smart appliances (Purdy, 2023). Many have hesitations about giving this information away to companies. Because connecting to the Internet is generally a simple process, users do not always see the value of connecting IoTs to every device in their lives. If future marketers wish to integrate IoT devices into their strategy, they must focus on creating greater value for users rather than solely prioritizing the collection of surveillance information for their businesses. Your IoT content should be less interruptive but responsive to consumers' personalized needs. Ensure the usability and simplicity of your IoT marketing strategy. Provide instant gratification for what your consumers are seeking, as they will not engage with technology that is cumbersome and does not add inherent value.

Artificial Intelligence (AI)

Social media practitioners would be hard-pressed to attend a conference over the past 5 years that has not focused on the rapid advancements of AI technology in the field. AI is defined as the science and engineering of making intelligent machines (McCarthy *et al.*, 1955). AI relies on autonomous systems that improve the perception, knowledge, thinking, or actions based on data (Manning, 2020). Most AI machine learning relies on predictive statistics, where a computer learns from previous behavior data to predict future human behaviors through action sequences and algorithms. As such, marketers have started embracing AI capabilities in their practices to help enhance existing products and services, generate ideas for new products and services, and enhance customer relationships (Davenport et al. 2021). According to the American Marketing Association, 27% of chief marketing officers (CMOs) reported utilizing AI and machine learning in their company's marketing efforts (Steimer, 2019). In addition, the AI market in social media is expected to reach $3,714.89 million by 2026 (Watters, 2023).

Today's AI technology can help marketers with simple narrow tasks, including sending a welcome message to new customers and placing digital ads, as well as broader, more predictive efforts, such as providing sales forecast, anticipating customers' responses, and suggesting interventions by a human representative supervisor (Davenport *et al.*, 2021). AI offers advantages in enhancing processing speed, accuracy, and consistency (Babic *et al.*, 2020). Industry surveys indicated that the top uses for AI in marketing include customer service, content personalization, and predictive analytics for customer insights and targeting decisions (Davenport *et al.*, 2021; Steimer, 2019).

One of AI's strengths is its ability to assist humans with repetitive and time-consuming tasks. The technology is designed to follow a set of rules or structures to augment human efforts, such as identifying and collecting news relevant to your company (Babic *et al.*, 2020; Davenport *et al.*, 2021). AI applications, such as ChatGPT, can sort and analyze big data quickly and accurately, which allows marketing practitioners to focus more on making campaigns creative and engaging. The future of social media management lies in balancing monitoring and reading big data from AI systems and keeping strategy and messages creative. AI can help brands get data about their consumer behaviors, but only practitioners are able to understand why consumers do what they do. In the era of AI, asking good questions and committing to a creative and curious campaign process are important for social media marketers.

In addition, human-level AI provides much more context-aware capabilities and allows for speech or facial recognition. Here, human-robot interaction is possible through social chatbots. AI automation can monitor and synthesize conversations that are going on about your brand and products. This information can help streamline the customer service process. AI technologies, specifically ChatGPT, can understand natural language and generate human-like responses in a conversational way to tailor unique responses depending on the customers' needs. While your customers do hope to interact and engage with a human as part of their customer service experience, AI can provide first-point automatic responses to customer queries on a 24/7 basis. While Chatbots are not able, nor should they, to handle every customer situation, they can significantly save time and resources by handling simple and routine customer service inquiries, such as providing product information or tracking orders (Entrepreneur, 2023). AI can also be utilized to personalize user experiences by remembering previous purchasing behaviors. Moreover, customer service agents can use AI when there is a language or cultural barrier between the customer and the customer service agent. ChatGPT could serve as a multilingual customer representative for global businesses. As such, it is important to reconceptualize social media strategy about how organizations can tackle their customer service tasks. The key is to consider how to integrate human tasks and AI tasks into the workflow (Davenport *et al.*, 2021).

The use of AI technology today has extended beyond the handling of simple structured tasks to leveraging its predictive capabilities. With machine-learning and deep-learning programs, AI can predict a user's decision. Marketers can use the information to develop target ads at every stage of a customer journey (i.e., before, during, and after the purchase), suggest different responses to customers' requests, optimize the scheduling of social media posts, and create new products and services (Babic et al., 2020; Davenport *et al.*, 2021). For example, Wayfair, a furniture retailer, uses AI to determine which products to show to customers based on their browsing histories. Procter & Gamble's Olay Skin Advisor utilizes AI deep learning to analyze customers' selfies to assess their skin type and recommend products accordingly (Davenport *et al.*, 2021). Starbucks also tracks customer data, including where and when they made the orders, and then offers personalized marketing messages based on the predictive analytics offered by its AI tool. By utilizing AI technology to predict customer needs, Starbucks saw a year-over-year organic revenue increase of 21% (Wilson, 2018).

Marketers have pushed the use of AI into more creative spaces. AI and natural language processing (NLP) tools can create blog entries, social media posts, promotional video scripts, and even visual social media content that traditionally can be difficult and expensive to create (Sachs, 2023). For example, Lensa AI is a highly popular application that uses facial recognition and filter technology to allow users to reimagine their faces with various filters, turning themselves into highly stylized fairies, princesses, animals, or avatars. Utilizing AI photo generator, Photoleap, users can simply provide a prompt (e.g., *border collie skateboarding on the moon*), and the AI generator will then produce an original image (see Figure 20.1).

Figure 20.1   A.I. Generated image using Photoleap.

Heinz, a food processing company, launched the first ad campaign with entirely AI-generated images in 2022 (Kulp, 2022). Here, the company's marketing team fed DALL-E 2, an AI image generator, a series of prompts related to ketchup for random drawing. While the results vary, many adopted elements from Heinz ketchup bottles, such as their shape, letter style, and more. The team also invited Heinz fans to share their suggestions for ketchup image prompts. The best ones were selected for print ads and social media posts (Campaigns of the World, 2022). Coco-Cola launched its creative AI platform that allows customers to create their own digital artwork using the brand's contour bottle and script logo. The best user generated AI artworks were displayed on digital billboards in Time Square in New York and Piccadilly Circus in London (Norris, 2023).

As AI continues to explode in social media marketing, many have expressed concerns regarding AI image content generators. Lifelike AI reproductions that alter facial appearance may negatively impact body image and self-conceptualization (Shafer, 2023). Digital artists are concerned that AI generators co-opt their worth, as apps rely on existing artwork to make their images. However, real people are not credited or compensated for their work (Sottile, 2022). It is also impossible to compete with the instant gratification of AI content creation, as real-life digital artistry takes great skill and time to create.

It is also becoming more difficult for users to detect what is real and what is fake. For example, there was an image of Pope Francis wearing a gigantic white puffer coat that was widely shared on X (formerly Twitter). The image was entirely generated by AI prompts, but many users thought it was real. AI technology allows any image to be created using real names and faces of people engaging in activities that did not happen. It is possible that this plethora of fake information and images on social media will result in a call for more authentic and less filtered social media platforms, such as the concept behind BeReal (discussed in Chapter 4) – with synchronous, no editing, limited social network sharing.

Opportunities and Concerns

Marketing practitioners are eager to integrate the newest innovations into their business strategy. Today, this means the increased mobility, interactivity, customization, and consumer participation. IoT, AI, and social media technologies allow users to share their experiences while they are in the moment. While we always hope customers could engage with our product, it is important to note that even the greatest advances to the consumer experience can become overwhelming and cumbersome when they reach a certain point of saturation.

The tipping point of data sharing

Hyperconnectedness provides the ability to connect with consumers where and when you wish. As a marketer, you no longer have to wait for your customers to turn on television or radio to receive your messages. Consumers are now constantly engaging with digital media content, providing endless opportunities for you to connect with them. Mobile applications, IoT devices, and AI technology make it easier than ever to reach users because, generally, users have voluntarily sought out a media structure that makes it easier to receive notifications about brands they love.

Increased connectedness and surveillance come with increased interruption of our daily lives. For the most part, individuals do not like being disturbed when they are in the midst of doing something else. Mobile technology has already made it easy for one friend to interrupt your conversation with another friend through text messaging or app alerts. This disturbance will prove even more frustrating if it comes from a machine or marketer rather than a personal contact.

Users are increasingly bombarded with devices that interrupt. Even if content producers are just trying to be helpful, users can take purposeful actions to block these alerts (Picard & Liu, 2007). We may have initially thought that we would want to be alerted every time we are near our favorite coffee shop. However, these notifications become overwhelming when they are combined with alerts from our favorite clothing and shoe stores, car dealers and movie theaters, as well as through the shoes we wear and car we drive. There is a tipping point to the benefits of IoT and AI. The novelty and innovation of constant surveillance are beginning to fade, and users will soon regard interruptive mobile technologies in the same way they view traditional spam marketing.

Having companies know everything about our purchasing behaviors, preferences, and everyday lives is scary to most consumers. While it may have been easy at one time to dismiss privacy concerns of technology, today's consumers are becoming more conscious about the security of constant surveillance. It is important for marketing practitioners to begin taking issues of customer privacy more seriously when creating marketing content.

Privacy concerns

Generation Z is frequently criticized for being flippant about the amount and type of information that they share through social media. Growing up in an age of social media, they are used to sharing stories, photos, and videos of everyday interactions. However, research demonstrates that this generation has high concerns about the safety of their online data (Hiezl & Gyurácz-Németh, 2021). Users want the ability to control when, to what extent, and how information about their lives is communicated to others (Ellison et al., 2011). The power of social media and other new technologies provides consumers with a stronger voice when they do not like the privacy policy implemented by your organization.

Trust is a critical component of marketing, and you want to avoid situations where it seems like you are being deceptive or attempting to deceive your customers without their knowledge. Your consumers should always be your primary focus, and every decision you make should benefit them in some capacity.

Poorly secured IoT and AI technologies could serve as potential entry points for cyberattacks and user data theft (Rose et al., 2015). The interconnected nature of IoT devices means that each device is only as secure as the networks that it engages with. Even though a data breech may not come from your own connection, customers will not decipher which company is at fault. Ensuring security must be a fundamental priority for businesses. Once users lose trust in data related services, they will be slow to adopt them in the future. A collaborative approach to security is imperative for future IoT and AI marketing practitioners.

Privacy concerns may hold back adoption until users have confidence in their service. This includes the way personal data is collected, analyzed, used, and protected (Rose et al., 2015). You must respect individual privacy choices across a broad spectrum of expectations. One-size-fits-all service agreements no longer apply. Companies should resist selling customer information to third party organizations. If you do, it is important that you are upfront with users about your intention. Do not be surprised when they go somewhere else though. Ensure that your software is secure and that every measure is taken to protect customers against hackers. Be certain that your users are confident in the data security and privacy of your organization. As such, you may consider the following three-step action plan as you set up your privacy and security policies.

Privacy and Security Action Plan

1   Understand the value of human privacy and security. Make it a priority for your organization.
2   Measure the rewards and risks for users when it comes to user data collection. Just because a technology can gather data, it does not always create value for users.
3   Be transparent about privacy and security risks that users take when interacting with your technology.

The best strategy for ensuring strong security and data privacy resides in holistic and integrated media literacy programs. *Media literacy* is defined as the ability of users to critically access, analyze, evaluate, and create messages in a variety of forms (Livingstone, 2004). People must acquire the knowledge to utilize the Internet confidently, competently, and safely. Many school programs are beginning to integrate a media literacy curriculum into their lessons (Hobbs, 2010), suggesting that the next generation of digital media users will be even more concerned and knowledgeable about issues surrounding their privacy and security.

Conclusions in the Future Social Media Landscape

By effectively managing the influx of interruptive technology and addressing privacy concerns in your business strategies, you can better ensure that consumers associate your brand with feelings of trust, respect, and commitment. Opportunities will exist in products and services that can enhance data privacy, control, and transparency. In the next five years, we will see increasing demands for automate security and new security standards for cloud (Baig et al., 2023). Companies that uphold ethical data policies will earn consumer trust, leading to more business opportunities (Deshpande, 2020).

Social media marketing and businesses may also want to focus on content and strategy regarding family and home productivity. With 71% of working moms, there is a need for content, tools, and services that help manage consumers' home projects (Deshpande, 2020). Social media practitioners could utilize these concepts for their next marketing campaigns. The mindfulness culture also brings opportunities to social media practitioners. In 2019, Calm, an app for meditation and mental health, hit US$1 billion valuation (VentureBeat, 2019). Younger generations prioritize self-care, work–life balance, and well-being (Deshpande, 2020). Thus, we will see more consumer demands for content and products in this area.

You should also look out for combinatorial trends (Baig et al., 2023). *Combinatorial trends* in technology refer to the convergence or combination of multiple technologies or innovations that create new possibilities. The combination of advanced mobility, connectivity, and machine learning will unlock many new opportunities (Baig et al., 2023). In this chapter, we talked about web 3.0, IoT, AI, and more. When these technologies work together, we will see a surge of unprecedented creativity. For example, Dept and Hello Monday created a "Shoe Mirror" campaign, which combined AI technology and augmented reality. Here, the campaign used AI technology to analyze the outfits of people passing by vacant stores in city centers and recommend matching shoes for them. The augmented reality then seamlessly placed the shoes on people's digital feet, creating an interactive and personalized experience (Norris, 2023). By using combined technologies, marketers turned vacant stores in city centers into creative, interactive, revenue-generating initiatives. The impact of such convergence and innovation is poised to be multiplicative (Baig et al., 2023).

The field of social media marketing and business will be constantly evolving, which requires social media professionals to have passion, ambition, and ability to connect and adapt. It is also important for you to know what is unique about you and navigate through this evolving career with curiosity, persistence, integrity, and resilience (Cooper, 2022). Your journey as a social media marketing/communication practitioner will, at times, be challenging and uncertain. However, the opportunities and possibilities brought by social media are exciting and unforeseen. Your ability to grow personally and professionally through these opportunities and challenges will be worth the effort (Cooper et al. 2022). As the online environment moves toward increasing collaboration, it is important that you see your consumers as critical factors to your own success. It is essential to nurture your lifelong brand advocates. Be innovative, and embrace all opportunities brought by technology advancements. Now, let us examine how one brand enticed users to utilize their new technology.

Case Study: Samsung Refrigerdating

IoT provides utility with Internet connectivity and powerful data analytic capabilities to transform the way we work, live, and play. Samsung launched a series of smart "Family Hub" refrigerators that utilize IoT technology to make users' lives more integrated and efficient across multiple touchpoints. While smart refrigerators may have first been treated as a tablet stuck to a fridge door, the capability of this technology points out many opportunities and challenges in future media landscape.

The kitchen is often seen as a central space in a home where people get together most. The IoT "Family Hub" technology thus turns the family refrigerator into a converged digital dashboard. Family members can utilize the technology as a coordinating center to watch TV, display photos, leave notes, share recipes, calendars, or control smart home devices. It can also communicate with other smart devices, such as smart speakers and home automation systems, to create a connected home experience. Phone applications are synched with the systems so that users can change settings remotely. Voice control is also integrated, allowing users to interact with their smart refrigerator hands-free.

The refrigerator also uses AI to recommend recipes and meal plans based on user preferences (Tuohy, 2023). Its AI powered camera not only can notify when food is missing and needs to be restocked but also track in real-time to predict time frames for when items are expected to run low in the future. For example, even when a milk carton is ¾ full, the AI camera can tell users when they should plan to purchase milk again based on previous consumption patterns.

Users are also able to utilize the Family Hub as a social technology. Family can send messages to each other, vote on recipes, or even use Global Positioning System (GPS) tracking to see if another family member is already at the store. Integrating technologies across a family system prevents the duplication of tasks. It also automates many of the tedious chores at home, such as creating a shopping list or finding coupons for favorite items. More importantly, the smart refrigerator adds entertainment and social components in a basic household appliance.

Despite of the enormous potential of IoT technologies, such as the Samsung "Family Hub," it can be difficult to get users to see the value in an interconnected kitchen object. As mentioned previously in this chapter, 50% of customers cannot see the benefit of IoT technologies and thus, never connect devices (Purdy, 2023). In response, Samsung decided to enhance the "Family Hub" experience by creating a fun dating app that utilizes many of the integrated technologies to match users with others on the app.

Samsung (2023) describes "Refrigerdating" as a service that helps users find love based on the content of their refrigerator. The idea behind the app is that you can learn a lot about a person, including their preferences and socioeconomic status based on the contents of their fridge (Hollow, 2019). Smart refrigerator users can utilize this technology to view photos inside someone else's fridge to determine how compatible they may be in dating.

Choosing a mate based on pictures of food, but not pictures of the actual person may present a less superficial mechanism for matching, as the contents of a person's fridge could shed light on many other aspects of who we are. The site cautions users not to style their fridges before taking the pictures, because "cheating and relationships do not go together well." The technology also allows users to send personal messages to each other.

Here, you can see how Samsung uses IoT and AI technologies to create a social experience for users. Every person can utilize the technology differently from one another based on their individual preferences and goals. Maybe one user just likes the grocery list capability, while another family fully integrates the hub with other smart IoT devices in their home. When implementing IoT and AI technologies in your strategy, be sure to provide users the ability to customize options according to their own needs.

Today's users expect to have more options than ever before. However, if the structure of such one-stop smart technologies is frustrating or difficult to navigate, the multifunctional concept will lose its appeal with users. For many individuals, a simple, quick, and reliable interface structure remains a top priority. Providing users with the ability to choose which features they most want to use, and an interface that focuses on these choices, is still critical to success.

Discussion questions

1 What privacy and security concerns might you have when connecting to a "Family Hub" technology, like Samsung's smart refrigerator?
2 What are some advantages and disadvantages of a multifunctional application like "Family Hub"? What other IoT devices would you connect with to enhance efficiency in your daily life?
3 If you were going to integrate IoT technology and social media, how would you make IoT a more social and connected part of a user's life?

Summary

It may seem discouraging or risky to begin a career in a field as dynamic as social media marketing. However, this book attempts to provide the foundational tools for practitioners to apply to any digital landscape. What is most important is not how technologically savvy or advanced your marketing team proves to be. Instead, it is your ability to focus on fostering human relationships and connections. A 25-year meta-analysis demonstrates how the most successful health campaigns are those that incorporate theory into their design (King, 1999). The same is true for any campaign that is interested in influencing human behavior. Theoretical principles should guide every marketing decision that you make.

Part I of this book suggested that social media messaging decisions should be guided by human behavior change literature. The principles of diffusion, community and mobilization should be integrated into every content decision that you make. Find the appropriate balance between user participation and control over your messages based on your business goals. No campaign should begin without a strong audience analysis or end without a strong formative audience evaluation.

Part II further explained how and why people choose, disseminate and share media messages. It highlighted the importance of creating messages that consumers strongly identify with, as well as the importance of integrating these messages within a media structure that promotes interactivity. If the content of your message does not seem to be working in the ways in which you anticipated, this section offers some structural reasons why. The active within structures paradigm is a nuanced way to view social media users and will set you apart from other professionals in the field who are simply trying to disseminate their messages to sell a product.

Part III of this book offered tips for increasing business revenue and return on investment through social media marketing and business models. Not only did this section include emerging methods by which businesses are capitalizing on the changing industry, but also offered ways in which these strategies should change the approach to targeting consumers. While media messages traditionally target mass audiences, this section shows the importance of finding your or your product's niche – the smaller, the better. Communicating with individuals instead of large audiences will help transform customers into brand advocates for you and your product.

Part IV of this book applied the theoretical human behavior change principles to prosocial initiatives, such as health campaigns, civic engagement, communication for development, and entertainment–education interventions. Social media offers greater opportunity for equalizing power inequities. One of the most important lessons learned is that the strategy for promoting social change is no different from getting an individual to like your Instagram page or buy your product. Humans make decisions about their everyday lives in the same manner. A strong understanding of behavior change theories will help you persuade any consumer.

Part V of this book offered recommendations for the future of social media marketing and suggested that social media is unpredictable and constantly evolving. As businesses become more social in nature, users begin to view them as more human. The transition from a business to a prosocial brand is imperative for surviving in a world where increased transparency is an expectation from consumers.

While this book offers recommendations for future social media practices, it is not meant to serve as an exclusive reference. Perhaps the greatest responsibility of a social media practitioner is staying up-to-date with industry news. This field is exciting and offers many benefits, such as an outlet for creativity, flexible hours, and portable offices. Take advantage of the social media industry's largest advantage: the plethora of resources and mentors available.

Social media practitioners are drawn to social media because they love connecting with other individuals. This is the foundation of social media technology, and it should be the foundation of your goals, both professionally and personally. The line between public and private is becoming increasingly blurred. It is important that you take these concepts and apply to branding your social media sites. Remember, many of the suggestions offered in this book can easily be applied to your personal social media brand. Perhaps they can be used to persuade someone that you are the perfect candidate for the social media position of your dreams.

Key Takeaways

1 There are many changes emerging in the social media landscape, and it is your responsibility as a practitioner to stay connected to the industry.
2 Regardless of changes in the social media landscape, content and message decisions should be guided by human behavior change theories. The process by which humans make decisions will never change, and a strong understanding of foundational communication principles will prepare you for a lifetime career in the industry.
3 Social media marketers should integrate IoT and AI technologies into their strategy, aiming to increase customization, mobility, and consumer participation.
4 Today's Internet users are much more concerned about privacy and security issues, and this should be another focus of future business strategies.
5 Be innovative. Keep calm. And embrace all the opportunities and challenges of social media marketing and social behavior change.

References

Babic, B., Chen, D.L., Evgeniou, T. & Fayard, A.-L. (2020) A better way to onboard AI. *Harvard Business Review*. Available at https://hbr.org/2020/07/a-better-way-to-onboard-ai (accessed November 18, 2023).

Baig, A., Brown, J.S., Forrest, W.H.V.V., Hjartar, K. & Yee, L. (2023) Where is tech going in 2023? *Harvard Business Review*. Available at: https://hbr.org/2023/01/where-is-tech-going-in-2023 (accessed November 18, 2023).

Bauer, H.H., Barnes, S.J., Reichardt, T. & Neumann, M.M. (2005) Driving consumer acceptance of mobile marketing: a theoretical framework and empirical study. *Journal of Electronic Commerce Research*, 6(3), 181–192.

Campaigns of the World (2022) Heinz A.I. ketchup. Available at https://campaignsoftheworld.com/digital/heinz-a-i-ketchup/.

Cooper, R. (2022) *12 Attributes of Extraordinary Media Professionals*. London: Rowman & Littlefield.

Cooper, R., Mahoney, M.L. & Tang, T. (2022) Looking forward. In: L.M. Mahoney & T. Tang (eds) *Handbook of Media Management and Business*. London: Rowman & Littlefield.

Cormode, G. & Krishnamurthy, B. (2008) Key differences between Web 1.0 and 2.0. *First Monday*, 13(6). Available at http://firstmonday.org/ojs/index.php/fm/article/view/2125 (accessed November 18, 2023).

Davenport, T.H., Guha, A. & Grewal, D. (2021) How to design an AI marketing strategy. *Harvard Business Review*. Available at https://hbr.org/2021/07/how-to-design-an-ai-marketing-strategy (accessed November 18, 2023).

De Freitas, S. & Levene, M. (2003) Evaluating the development of wearable devices, personal data assistants and the use of other mobile devices in further and higher education institutions. *JISC Technology and Standards Watch Report*, (TSW030), 1–21.

Deshpande, S. (2020) 10 Consumer trends that will spark innovation in 2020. *Forbes*. Available at https://www.forbes.com/sites/saradeshpande/2020/01/16/10-consumer-trends-that-will-spark-innovation-in-2020/?sh=1ec304f11011 (accessed November 18, 2023).

Ellison, N.B., Vitak, J., Steinfield, C., Gray, R. & Lampe, C. (2011) Negotiating privacy concerns and social capital needs in a social media environment. In: S. Trepte & L. Reinecke (eds) *Privacy Online*, pp. 19–32. Berlin: Springer.

Entrepreneur (2023) How can marketers use ChatGPT? Here are the top 11 uses. Available at https://www.entrepreneur.com/science-technology/how-can-marketers-use-chatgpt-here-are-the-top-11-uses/445015 (accessed November 18, 2023).

Giustini, D. (2007) Web 3.0 and medicine. *BMJ*, 335(7633), 1273–1274.

Hendler, J. (2008) Web 3.0: chicken farms on the semantic web. *Computer*, 41(1), 106–108.

Hiezl, K., & Gyurácz-Németh, P. (2021) Service through personal encounters or technology: the preferences and privacy concerns of Generation Z. *EATSJ-Euro-Asia Tourism Studies Journal*, 1, 76–92.

Hobbs, R. (2010) *Digital and Media Literacy: A Plan of Action*. Geneva: UNAIDS. Available at http://www.knightcomm.org/wp-content/uploads/2010/12/Digital_and_Media_Literacy_A_Plan_of_Action.pdf (accessed November 18, 2023).

Hollow, M. (2019) Can your refrigerator improve your dating life? *The New York Times*. Available at https://www.nytimes.com/2019/03/12/well/family/can-your-refrigerator-improve-your-dating-life.html.

King, R. (1999) Sexual behavioural change for HIV: Where have theories taken us? Available at http://www.who.int/hiv/strategic/surveillance/en/unaids_99_27.pdf (accessed November 18, 2023).

Kulp, P. (2022) Heinz taps state-of-the-art AI to design its next ad campaign. *AdWeek*. Available at https://www.adweek.com/commerce/heinz-taps-ai-design-next-ad-campaign/ (accessed November 18, 2023).

Kundariya, H. (2021) How is the IoT changing social media marketing. Available at https://www.trickyenough.com/how-is-the-iot-changing-social-media-marketing/.

Livingstone, S. (2004) Media literacy and the challenge of new information and communication technologies. *The Communication Review*, 7(1), 3–14.

Manning, C. (2020) Artificial Intelligence definitions. *Stanford University*. Available at https://hai.stanford.edu/sites/default/files/2020-09/AI-Definitions-HAI.pdf (accessed November 18, 2023).

Markoff, J. (2006) Entrepreneurs see a web guided by common sense. *New York Times*. Available at http://www.nytimes.com/2006/11/12/business/12web.html?ex=1320987600&en=a54d6971614edc62&ei=5090&partner=rssuserland&emc=rss&pagewanted=all (accessed November 18, 2023).

McCarthy, J., Minsky, M.L., Rochester, N. & Shannon, C.E. (1955) A proposal for the Dartmouth summer research project on artificial intelligence. *AI Magazine*, 27(4), 12–12.

Norris, P. (2023) 18 Impressive examples of AI in marketing. *Social Media Strategies Summit*. Available at https://blog.socialmediastrategiessummit.com/10-examples-of-ai-in-marketing/ (accessed November 18, 2023).

Pearce, K. (2009) Media and mass communication theories. In: S.W. Littlejohn & K.A. Foss (eds) *Encyclopedia of Communication Theory*, pp. 623–627. Thousand Oaks, CA: Sage Publications.

Picard, R.W. & Liu, K.K. (2007) Relative subjective count and assessment of interruptive technologies applied to mobile monitoring of stress. *International Journal of Human-Computer Studies*, 65(4), 361–375.

Purdy, K. (2023) ars Technica. Available at https://arstechnica.com/gadgets/2023/01/half-of-smart-appliances-remain-disconnected-from-internet-makers-lament/ (accessed November 18, 2023).

Rose, K., Eldridge, S. & Chapin, L. (2015) The internet of things: an overview. *The Internet Society (ISOC)*, 80, 1–50.

Sachs, E. (2023) The benefits of ChatGPT (and how it's reshaping digital marketing). *LinkedIn*. Available at https://www.linkedin.com/pulse/benefits-chatgpt-how-its-reshaping-digital-marketing-eric-sachs/ (accessed November 18, 2023).

Samsung (2023) Refrigerdating. Available at https://www.refrigerdating.com/about.

Shafer, N. (2023) Augmenting Artificial intelligences in fiction: evolving from primordial Internet memes to cybergods of disruption. In: V. Geroimenko (ed) *Augmented Reality and Artificial Intelligence: The Fusion of Advanced Technologies*, pp. 73–90. Cham: Springer Nature Switzerland.

Shankar, V. & Balasubramanian, S. (2009) Mobile marketing: a synthesis and prognosis. *Journal of Interactive Marketing*, 23(2), 118–129.

Sottile, Z. (2022) What to know about Lensa? *CNN*. Available at https://www.cnn.com/style/article/lensa-ai-app-art-explainer-trnd/index.html (accessed November 18, 2023).

Steimer, S. (2019) August 2019 CMO survey: hiring, AI on the rise. American Marketing Association. Available at https://www.ama.org/marketing-news/august-2019-cmo-survey-hiring-ai-on-the-rise/ (accessed November 18, 2023).

Thakkar, B. (2023) A new era of IoT: the social IoT/social network of things. Available at https://understandingecommerce.com/a-new-era-of-iot-the-social-iot-social-network-of-things/ (accessed November 18, 2023).

Tuohy, J. (2023) Samsung's new $5,000 32-inch tablet comes with a fridge attached. Available at https://www.theverge.com/2023/5/25/23737374/Samsung-family-hub-smart-fridge-matter (accessed November 18, 2023).

VentureBeat (2019) The meditation unicorn: Calm raises $88 million at $1 billion valuation. Available at https://venturebeat.com/mobile/the-meditation-unicorn-calm-raises-88-million-at-1-billion-valuation/ (accessed November 18, 2023).

Watters, A. (2023) 30+ Artificial intelligence statistics. *CompTIA*. Available at https://connect.comptia.org/blog/artificial-intelligence-statistics-facts (accessed November 18, 2023).

Wilson, E. (2018) How Starbucks uses predictive analytics and your loyalty card data. Institute of Business Forecasting & Planning. Available at https://demand-planning.com/2018/05/29/how-starbucks-uses-predictive-analytics-and-your-loyalty-card-data/ (accessed November 18, 2023).

Wirtz, B., Schilke, O. & Ullrich, S. (2010) Strategic development of business models: implications of the Web 2.0 for creating value on the Internet. *Long Range Planning*, 43(2–3), 272–290.

Index

Note: Page numbers in *italics* refer to *figures*; those in **bold** to **tables**.

Strategic Social Media: From Marketing to Social Change, Second Edition. L. Meghan Mahoney and Tang Tang.
© 2024 John Wiley & Sons, Inc. Published 2024 by John Wiley & Sons, Inc.